The International Business Environment

The International Business Environment

Diversity and the global economy

Janet Morrison

palgrave

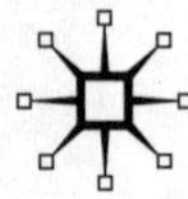

First published 2002 by
PALGRAVE
Houndmills, Basingstoke, Hampshire RG21 6XS and
175 Fifth Avenue, New York, N.Y. 10010
Companies and representatives throughout the world

PALGRAVE is the new global academic imprint of
St. Martin's Press LLC Scholarly and Reference Division and
Palgrave Publishers Ltd (formerly Macmillan Press Ltd).

ISBN 0–333–92144–5 hardcover
ISBN 0–333–92145–3 paperback

This book is printed on paper suitable for recycling and made from fully managed and sustained forest sources.

A catalogue record for this book is available from the British Library.

Library of Congress Cataloging-in-Publication Data

Morrison, Janet.
The international business environment : diversity and the global economy / Janet Morrison
p. cm.
Includes bibliographical references and index.
ISBN 0–333–92144–5 — ISBN 0–333–92145–3 (pbk.)
1. International economic relations. 2. International business enterprises. 3. International trade. 4. Globalization—Economic aspects. 5. Competition, International. I. Title.

HF1359 .M672 2002
337—dc21

2001058774

Editing and origination by
Aardvark Editorial, Mendham, Suffolk

Designed by The Company of Designers,
Basingstoke, Hampshire

10 9 8 7 6 5 4 3 2 1
11 10 09 08 07 06 05 04 03 02

Printed and bound in Great Britain by
the Bath Press, Bath

Contents

List of figures

List of tables

List of case studies

List of maps

Preface

This book is written as an introductory text for a wide range of business studies students, including those on undergraduate business studies courses and also postgraduate students new to the study of business and its relevant academic disciplines. It is not assumed that the reader has any prior knowledge of the subject. Readers who already have some acquaintance with this subject area should find that the international scope and up-to-date analysis provided will build substantially on their existing knowledge. The aim is to provide a clear explanation of the many aspects of the international environment in which business operates, which can serve as a foundation for more in-depth studies of the specialized areas of business activity such as marketing, human resource management and finance.

Any author who writes a book with a title as broad as this one embarks on a daunting task. The world of business has left no part of the globe untouched, and there is virtually no aspect of the environment which we can confidently say has *no* impact on business activities. Attempting to categorize and set out in a comprehensible order vast amounts of information has involved a continuous process of selection, both of topic headings and illustrative explanations. Readers will doubtless be able to point to numerous topics which I have neglected to include, or given insufficient attention. Given the impossibility of covering all relevant topics, I have selected those which seem to be either:

1. so basic as to be essential building blocks of knowledge, or
2. particularly relevant for the contemporary world in which we live.

As daunting as the selection of topics has been, even more challenging has been the task of presenting the material clearly and offering balanced comment, coupled with illuminating and interesting examples with which the reader can engage.

The business environment is permeated with differing values, country perspectives, industry perspectives, management perspectives, and many other variables. Attempting to do justice to all of them would simply swamp the text and lead to confusion, certainly on the part of the author! I have highlighted two themes – globalization and diversity – to provide an overarching perspective throughout the book. These themes, it seems to me, best represent the dynamic quality of the changing international environment. Developing these themes in the context of each chapter will, it is hoped, guide the reader through much disparate material.

I would like to thank Ian Morrison and Sarah Brown. Without their help and encouragement, this book would not have been written. I am also indebted to Palgrave's reviewers for their comments and suggestions. Finally, I would like to thank my employers, Sunderland University Business School, who allowed me a semester's sabbatical to devote to research. I hope that readers will find the time was well spent.

JANET MORRISON
Sunderland

Acknowledgements

The author and publishers wish to thank the following for permission to reproduce copyright material: MIT Press for Figure 1.4 from A. Chandler, *Strategy and Structure: Chapters in the History of American Industrial Enterprise* (1990); Financial Times for Figure 1.5 from J. Birkinshaw, 'The structures behind global companies' in *Mastering Management*, (suppl.) Part 10, Financial Times, 4 December 2000; Blackwell Publishers for Table 2.1 from D. Held, A. McGrew, D. Goldblatt and J. Perraton, *Global Transformations: Politics, Economics and Culture* (1999); Palgrave and Simon & Schuster for Figure 4.3 from M. Porter, *Competitive Strategy: Techniques for Analyzing Industries and Competitors* (1998); Pearson Education for Table 6.1 from P. Kotler, G. Armstrong, J. Saunders and V. Wong, *Principles of Marketing* (1999); Pearson Education for Table 8.2 from D. Keenan and S. Riches, *Business Law* (1998); Palgrave and Simon & Schuster for Figure 9.3 from M. Porter, *The Competitive Advantage of Nations* (1998); Palgrave for Minifile in Section 9.1.3. from M. Porter, H. Takeuchi and M. Sakakibara, *Can Japan Compete?* (2000); Harvard Business School Publishing for Figure 9.4 from L.T. Wells, *The Product Life Cycle and International Trade* (1972); Continuum for summary box in Section 10.2.1 from C. Freeman and L. Soete, *The Economics of Industrial Innovation* (1997); *Financial Times* for Case Studies 2.1, 2.2, 3.1, 3.2, 4.4, 5.3, 6.1, 10.4, 12.1 and 12.2. Every effort has been made to trace all the copyright-holders, but if any have been inadvertently overlooked the publishers will be pleased to make the necessary arrangements at the first opportunity.

List of acronyms

ACP	African, Caribbean and Pacific (countries)
AIDS/HIV	acquired immunodeficiency syndrome/ human immunodefciency virus
APEC	Asia-Pacific Economic Cooperation Group
ASEAN	Association of Southeast Asian Nations
BSE	bovine spongiform encephalopathy
CAD	computer-aided design
CISG	Convention on Contracts for the International Sale of Goods
DEFRA	Department for Environment, Food and Rural Affairs (UK)
ECB	European Central Bank
ECHR	European Convention on Human Rights
ECJ	European Court of Justice
EMU	European Monetary Fund
EPC	European Patent Convention
EPO	European Patent Office
ERM	exchange rate mechanism
EU	European Union
FDI	foreign direct investment
FSA	Financial Services Authority (UK)
GATT	General Agreement on Tariffs and Trade
GDP	gross domestic product
GM	genetically modified
GNP	gross national product
HIPCs	heavily indebted poor countries
HRM	human resource management
ICJ	International Court of Justice
ICT	information and communication technology
ILO	International Labour Organization
IMF	International Monetary Fund
IPO	initial public offering
ISO	International Organization for Standardization
IT	information technology
LBO	leveraged buy-out
M&A	merger and acquisition
MEA	multilateral environmental agreement
NAFTA	North American Free Trade Agreement
NATO	North Atlantic Treaty Organization
NGO	non-governmental organization
OECD	Organization for Economic Co-operation and Development

OPEC	Organization of Petroleum Exporting Countries
PCT	Patent Co-operation Treaty
PR	proportional representation
QMV	qualified majority voting
R&D	research and development
RPI	Retail Price Index
RTA	regional trade agreement
SME	small to medium-size enterprise
TNC	transnational corporation
TRIPS	Trade-related Aspects of Intellectual Trade Law
UK	United Kingdom
UN	United Nations
UNCITRAL	United Nations Commission on International Trade Law
UNIDROIT	United Nations International Institute for the Unification of Private International Law
US	United States
VERs	voluntary export restraints
WIPO	World Intellectual Property Organization
WTO	World Trade Organization

Maps

Africa and the Middle East

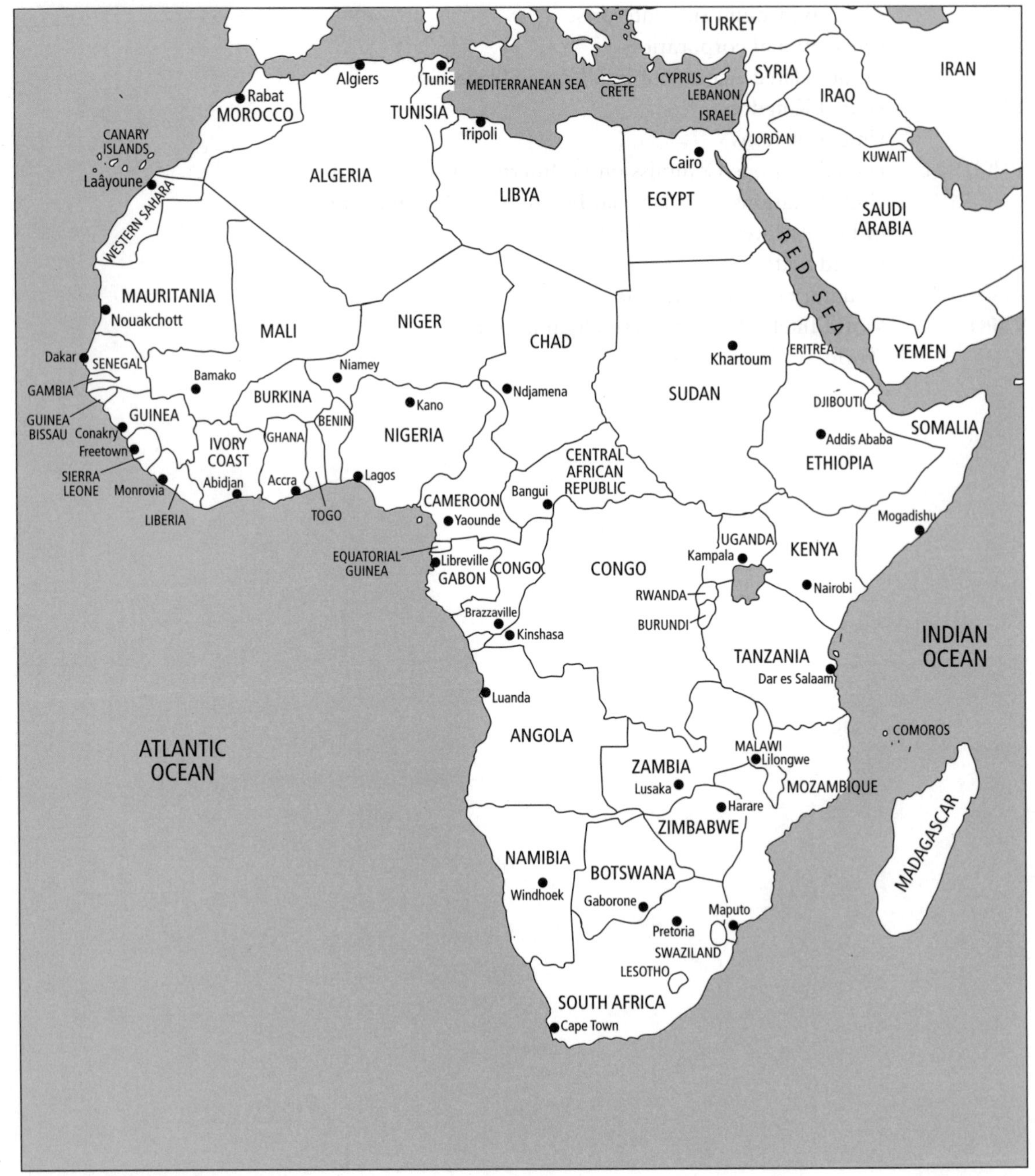

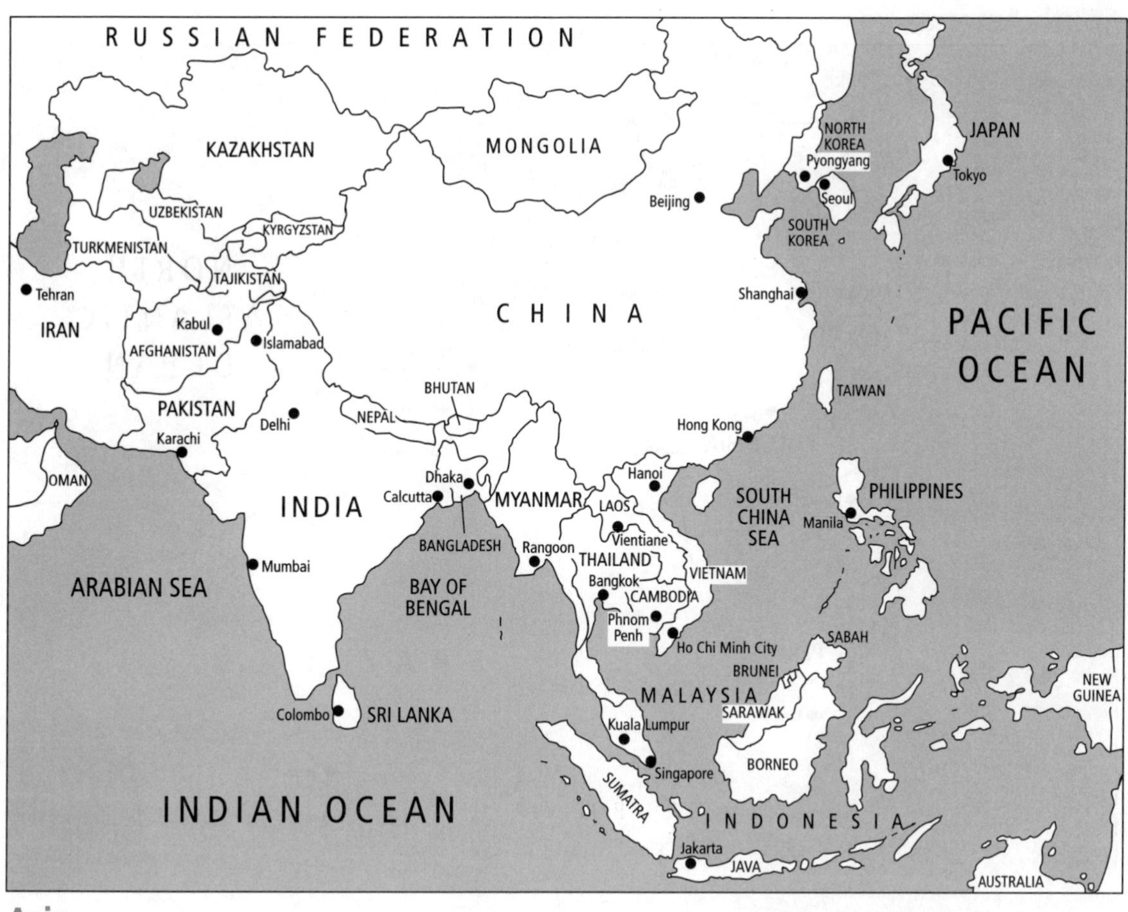

Asia

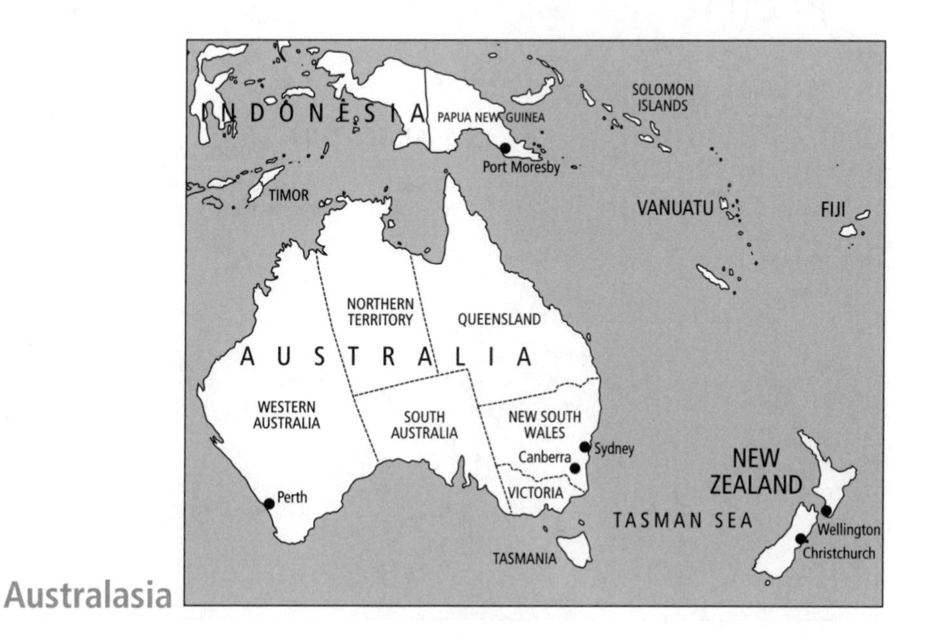

Australasia

South America

North America

Europe

ICELAND
NORTH ATLANTIC OCEAN
NORWAY
Oslo
SWEDEN
Stockholm
FINLAND
Helsinki
St. Petersburg
Tallinn
ESTONIA
RUSSIAN FEDERATION
Moscow
Riga
LATVIA
LITHUANIA
Vilnius
RUS. FED.
Minsk
BELARUS
REP. OF IRELAND
UNITED KINGDOM
London
DENMARK
Copenhagen
Amsterdam
NETHERLANDS
Brussels
BELGIUM
LUXEMBOURG
Berlin
GERMANY
POLAND
Warsaw
KAZAKHSTAN
Kiev
UKRAINE
Paris
FRANCE
Prague
CZECH REP.
SLOVAKIA
Vienna
Bratislava
Budapest
AUSTRIA
HUNGARY
MOLDOVA
Bern
SWITZERLAND
Ljubljana
SLOVENIA
Zagreb
CROATIA
ROMANIA
CASPIAN SEA
BOSNIA-HERZ.
Sarajevo
Belgrade
YUGOSLAVIA
Bucharest
BLACK SEA
GEORGIA
Tbilisi
Baku
AZERBAIJAN
ARMENIA
Yerevan
AZER.
PORTUGAL
Lisbon
Madrid
SPAIN
CORSICA
ITALY
Rome
MONTE-NEGRO
BULGARIA
Sofia
MACEDONIA
ALBANIA
Istanbul
Ankara
TURKEY
BALEARIC IS.
SARDINIA
GREECE
MEDITERRANEAN SEA
Athens
Rabat
Algiers
SICILY
Tunis
MOROCCO
TUNISIA
MALTA
CRETE
CYPRUS
SYRIA
IRAQ
Baghdad

Introduction

While the study of business activities from an academic point of view goes back many years, the notion of business studies as a coherent set of disciplines comprising whole degree courses is relatively new, having blossomed only in the last three decades. In that relatively short time, however, our views of how to approach business studies, both in the structured academic setting and in the world of business generally, have changed dramatically, in two major ways. First, it used to be customary to look on the business organization itself as taking centre stage, and to see the environment as being of less importance, simply 'background', and not directly relevant to the operations of business. This attitude has now given way to an approach which encompasses the business *in* its environment seen as an entirety, recognizing that there are no strict boundaries between the organization and its environment. The relationship is one of dynamic interaction: as social influences, for example, shape business activities, so businesses bring about changes in the society in which they operate. Indeed, our notion of the environment itself has broadened to encompass international forces. Second, the main focus of business studies has traditionally been national business life, bringing in the international dimension as an 'added-on' dimension only. This view, too, is no longer tenable. As business has become increasingly globalized, the distinction between home country and international environment has become blurred. The international dimension has moved from the periphery to the centre. For business managers, as for students of business, a recognition of the new centrality of the international presents a more complex and challenging environmental perspective, opening up broader horizons and presenting far greater opportunities in the wider global economy.

The perspective taken here is thoroughly international. While readers will find that core concepts and principles are explained in the context of the UK environment, equal attention is given to other geographic regions and to the interrelationships between regions and national economies. The major developed economies, including the US and Japan, as well as the transition economies of Central and Eastern Europe and Asia, are covered. Moreover, the growing integration of developing countries in the world economy, with their particular perspectives on international business, is also covered.

Much is now made of the opportunities, and risks, presented by the new economy, the high-tech world of global companies whose lifeblood is the internet, and who inhabit the borderless 'invisible continent'. But all companies, even virtual ones, still depend on business structures, employees and customers in the context of national environments, each with its own particular social and institutional make-up. This book takes a genuinely multidisciplinary approach, giving weight to all aspects of the business environment. These include: economic structures, social relations, cultural values, political institutions, technological development, global financial environment and the global competitive environment. The aim is to look at each sphere from the business point of view, and also to highlight the interactions between spheres in the international arena. Clearly, formal international links are an important consideration, but so too are growing informal relations between businesses, greatly enhanced by the growing use of the internet.

Given such a broad expanse of subject matter, this book can aspire only to give an introduction to each subject area. That said, the underlying premise is that an introduction to basic concepts, principles and frameworks which shape each subject area will be of primary help to the reader in gaining an understanding of the processes at work. Business examples and applications are integrated into the text, providing a balance between theory and practice. The reader will then be able to build on this foundation as specialist knowledge of other disciplines is assimilated. The book focuses on key themes which provide underpinning for the varied content of each chapter, enabling the reader to develop an overview of the forces driving the global economy.

Themes and plan of the book

Cutting through the complexity of the environment, we can discern a number of themes, which will recur in each of the chapters and form integrative links between the different aspects of the environment. These themes are:

- *Globalization*, or deepening global integration between businesses, governments and societies. The business environment has undergone rapid change in the last two decades, largely thanks to the advances of computing and information technology. These changes have impacted not just in the technological environment, but across the environmental spectrum, most particularly in the financial environment and competitive environment
- *Diversity* among national societies, groups, regions and organizations, which interact with forces of globalization. The tensions between global forces and local diversity impact on virtually every business, whether its managers are fully aware of the wider picture or not. Understanding the underlying currents helps considerably in determining appropriate business responses.

The chapters of the book are organized as follows. Chapter 1, *The internal environment of business*, provides an introduction to the business organization, outlining the main organizational structures and functions. It stresses the interactions between internal and external environments in an introduction to business strategy, which includes PEST and SWOT analyses.

Chapter 2, *The global economy and globalization processes*, introduces the theme of globalization, with an overview of globalization processes and their implications for business organizations and societies in which they operate.

Chapter 3, *The national economic environment*, examines the essential elements of a national economy, by which economies can be compared. For a business, this economic and financial profile is a key aspect of the business environment in any country.

Chapter 4, *Major economic systems*, looks at a variety of economic systems, focusing in particular on capitalist market economies and transitional economies in differing regions of the world. A theme will be the changing business environment emerging as national economic systems become more deeply integrated in global and regional economies.

Chapter 5, *The cultural environment: diversity and globalizaton*, focuses on the values, beliefs and behaviours that distinguish specific societies, and asks whether these are now giving way to the forces of cultural globalization. Underlying value systems influence organizations and business life generally in any society, and businesses are often at the forefront of culture change.

Chapter 6, *Society and business*, takes a broad view of social factors that impact on business: demographic issues; class divisions; ethnic, religious and other minorities; and gender issues. Also examined is the changing nature of work.

Chapter 7, *The changing political environment: national, regional and international forces*, seeks to highlight the ways in which political processes and systems provide a governmental structure for societies, which is essential to ordered decision-making and stability. Increasingly, interaction between governments and businesses across the globe demonstrates the need for businesses to grasp the differences in the exercise of political power in different societies.

Chapter 8, *The international legal environment of business: moving towards harmonization*, looks at the related area of legal and regulatory regimes, which impact directly on business. While every business appreciates the benefits of an efficient, predictable legal and judicial system, as the global economy extends to a greater variety of countries, businesses find themselves in an uncertain legal environment. This chapter attempts to demystify legal processes in national systems, while also looking at progress towards harmonizing laws across national boundaries.

Chapter 9, *World trade and the international competitive environment*, examines one of the more pronounced areas in which globalization can be said to be transforming the business environment. Increasing global trade has led to greater economic integration, regional groupings and greater international regulation.

Chapter 10, *Technology and innovation*, traces the ways in which technology and innovation emerge in different societies, and also how they become diffused, through technology transfer, to an ever-growing group of countries. Global companies have been key players in this process, but how is the pattern of technology development changing?

Chapter 11, *International financial markets*, again highlights an area in which globalization has moved apace, but also one in which there is concern over global financial stability and the widespread effects of financial crisis. Many international businesses have learnt the hard way about the interaction of global financial markets and the ramifications for business life in the societies most deeply affected.

Chapter 12, *Global change and challenges of the international environment*, brings together the themes, and highlights challenges for the future, which are bringing about changes in both the internal and external environment of businesses. Social responsibility of business, the natural environment and the information technology revolution are areas in which businesses face both opportunities and threats.

Features

The book is designed to present the content in a manner that is easily accessible, with a number of aids for the reader. While ideally one would begin with Chapter 1 and read each successive chapter in order, the book has been designed so that any chapter can be read alone, and the reader will be aided by suitable references to earlier relevant chapters given in brackets. The content of each chapter is divided into sections and subsections, which are outlined at the start of the chapter, and also appear in the Table of Contents. Each chapter also sets **Learning Objectives** at the beginning, to clarify the particular outcomes which the reader can expect from the chapter. **Conclusions** at the end of each chapter provide a concise list of important points by way of summary.

The list that follows outlines other aids that have been included:

- Key concepts, key terms, principles and organizations appear in **bold** letters when used for the first time They are defined in a **Glossary** at the end
- References are given in brackets in the text, for example (Smith, 1991). The **References** section at the end of the book is a list of all references in the main text. References within case studies are given at the end of each case study. For newspaper reports, the name of the paper and publication date are given in brackets in the text, as in (*Financial Times*, 6 November 1999)
- **Points to Remember** boxes appear throughout each chapter. These are not a substitute for reading the section, but should help to consolidate the main points
- Boxes labelled **'Minifile'** contain extended examples of particular points, to complement the main text

- Several short **Case Studies** are given in every chapter. These appear in boxes at appropriate points in the text. Each case study consists of a business application of an issue which arises in the international environment. They feature all types of business and all areas of the globe. Each case study has case questions at the end, which can be a basis of group discussion or a short assignment
- **Webalert** boxes appear throughout the text. These refer the reader to websites for additional information, which in turn often contain links to related sites. Every effort has been made to ensure that these addresses are accurate, but websites are constantly changing, and they do sometimes move house. The Webalert boxes will provide a starting point for further exploration of the topics. They offer a variety of sources, including public information services, governmental offices, non-governmental organizations and companies themselves. A word of caution, however. Every organization has its own perspective and values, which its website is designed to present to a wider public. While providing helpful information, its interpretation of that information is likely to reflect its own perspective, and may well downplay or leave out aspects of the organization which are less than flattering. A balanced picture is probably best obtained by checking out a number of sources. An unfortunate trend for the student is that many databases provided by public authorities and research bodies, while available on the web, are available only on payment of a subscription (sometimes considerable). These bodies do usually provide summary information freely, and universities may pay subscriptions, on behalf of their students, to acquire access to an entire database. (The data in this text derives entirely from freely available sources, at the time of access)
- Suggestions for **Further reading** are given at the end of each chapter. These include a variety of sources. Some are specialized textbooks on the subject for more in-depth study. Others are expositions by well-known authorities in the field, whose works are seen as 'landmark' books or articles. Others are compendiums of articles by a number of scholars, whose journal articles are often difficult to track down in isolation
- Besides the questions at the end of each case study, a number of **Review questions** are given at the end of each chapter. These are either for self-study or discussion, to check that you have grasped the main points and issues in the chapter
- Two **Assignments** are given after each set of review questions. These are broader in scope than the review questions. They require some independent research and considered critical analysis of the issues
- The book contains a number of **maps** for reference. Developing an understanding of the geographical location of nations and regions may

seem incidental, but is immensely useful in understanding the substantive issues discussed in the text.

The study of the international business environment has never been more interesting – or more challenging. While no one can purport to have all the answers, it is hoped that this book at least points readers on a sound path to understanding the ever-changing world of international business. The advice of Confucius, some 2,400 years ago, is still appropriate:

> Extend your learning and hold fast to your purpose; question closely and meditate on things at hand: there you will find the fullness of your humanity. (Leys, S. (tr.) 1997)

Chapter 1

The internal environment of business

Outline of chapter

LEARNING OBJECTIVES

1. To identify key elements of the internal and external aspects of the business environment and their dynamic interaction
2. To recognize different types of business ownership and different designs of business structure and their implications for how businesses are run
3. To appreciate the many dimensions of change in organizations, in the context of the changing international environment
4. To use simple strategic planning tools, including PEST and SWOT analysis

1.0 Introduction

Business takes place the world over, in a huge diversity of societies and between widely varying organizations. The business environment has become more complex, with expanding and deepening ties between societies and between the many organizations within those societies. Moreover, many large organizations now see themselves as truly global in scope, not rooted in any one society. The business environment may be visualized in terms of layers, beginning with the immediate internal environment within the organization, and moving outwards to the external environment surrounding the business and influencing its organization and operations (see Figure 1.1). The external environment includes an array of dimensions, including economic, political, legal and technological factors. While only a few decades ago these external aspects were seen as centring on the home country of the business, the environmental horizon of business has now widened to take in a host of international forces, which interact with national and local factors.

Tensions exist between an organization and the external forces that impact on it, from local through to international, and these tensions are reflected in its internal environment. This chapter sets the scene by focusing on the essential elements of the internal environment, beginning with the ways in which different types of organization are formed and structured. Business organization, processes and strategy change over time, responding to changing factors in both the internal and external environments. The chapter will cover a wide range of organizations. When we think of inter-

Figure 1.1 The business organization in its environment

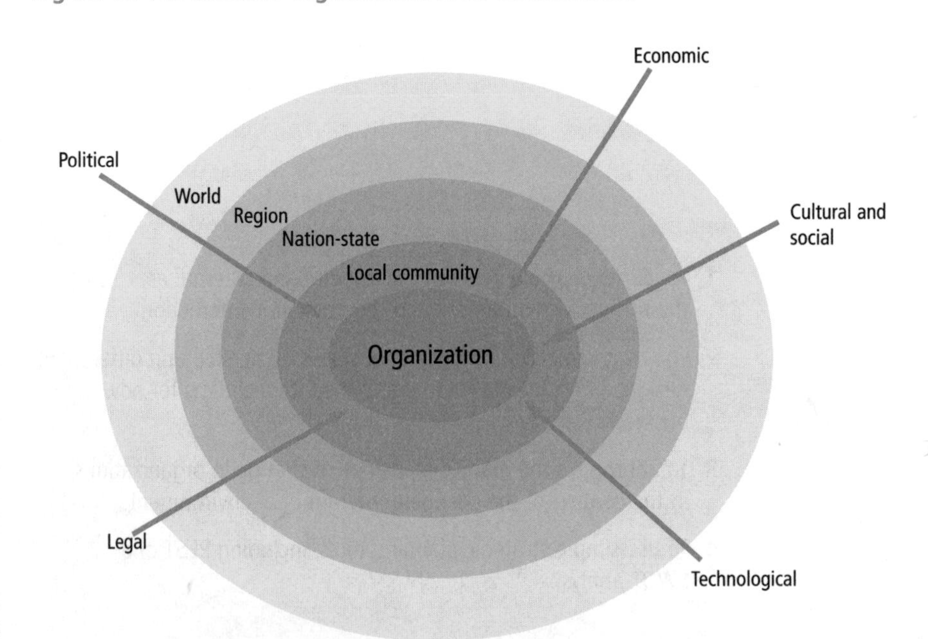

national business, we tend to think of large multinationals, but most of the world's businesses are very much smaller, and, increasingly, these smaller firms are becoming international in their outlook. A large American corporation such as IBM may seem to have very little in common with a family-run firm in Hong Kong. Yet both face challenges common to businesses over the centuries, such as how to achieve a smooth-running and efficient organization and how to satisfy the needs of customers. Their responses may be very different, but both will be addressing universal issues, each in its own way.

1.1 What is business?

Business refers to the vast array of economic activity, in which goods and services are supplied in exchange for some payment, usually money. It includes buying and selling, manufacturing products, extracting natural resources and farming. While the word covers business activities in general, as in the term 'the business community', it is also used in relation to individual businesses. Businesses generally aim to make a profit, but there are also numerous not-for-profit enterprises in every society, such as charities and educational bodies. Business has been around a long time. Ancient societies grew prosperous largely because of thriving business activity, extending to trade with other countries (Landes, 1998). The urge to do business also seems to be universal, taking place in all societies, even in communist societies which do not officially recognize private enterprise. When we look at the variety of products that are taken for granted in modern consumer societies, such as motorcars, convenience food, fashion and entertainment, all have arisen through business activities.

Typically, they begin in a small way, nurtured by a talented and enthusiastic founder, the entrepreneur, who commits his or her own funds as well as energy to the enterprise. The **entrepreneur** is:

> one who creates a new business in the face of risk and uncertainty for the purpose of achieving profit and growth by identifying opportunities and assembling the necessary resources to capitalize on them. (Zimmerer and Scarborough, 1998, p. 3)

While many fall by the wayside, some go on to develop into the large enterprises that we are familiar with today. McDonald's, the fast-food restaurant, for example, started life as a single hamburger outlet in the US, in 1955, and has grown into a global company with thousands of restaurants in 116 countries. Like other successful companies, it has evolved as an organization, becoming more complex as it has grown. A large proportion of its restaurants, mainly those in the US, are run as franchises, by which individual entrepreneurs own the business and operate it under an agreement with McDonald's.

International business refers to business activities that straddle two or more different countries. Businesses are increasingly looking beyond the bounds of their home country for new opportunities. A company may begin by selling its products or purchasing raw materials abroad, and go on to producing its products abroad. Or, as in the case of McDonald's, open restaurants abroad. Nowadays, thanks to advances in communication technology and transport, it is easier for companies to expand a variety of business activities across national borders. However, 'going global' adds considerably to the complexity of the organization (Bartlett and Ghoshal, 1998). The domestic business does not simply grow bigger, but international activities add a new dimension, which will be reflected in the organization of the company, and how it is run. When a company expands to the extent that a large portion of its business is outside its home country, it becomes a global business. (This will be discussed in Chapter 2). Its shareholders, too, may be scattered across the globe. McDonald's now derives over half its profits from outside the US, and indeed, its growth overseas is stronger than its growth at home.

WWW
WEBALERT

Websites on entrepreneurship:
http://entrepreneurship.mit.edu
http://www.entreworld.com
The UK Department of Trade and Industry has a business support site at
http://www.dti.gov.uk/support/index.htm
The UK Small Business Service is at
http://www.businessadviceonline.org

1.2 Classification of businesses

Businesses may be classified according to their form of ownership and also by size. The two variables are related, in that businesses of sole traders tend to be small, while company structures are more suited to large organizations. We look at each type of classification in turn.

1.2.1 Forms of business ownership

Three basic forms of ownership in most countries are: sole trader, partnership and limited company.

Sole trader

The simplest type of business is the **sole trader**, or self-employed person. For the sole trader, such as a small shopkeeper or small farmer, the business is highly personal, and responsibility for its success or failure rests on his or her shoulders. When the shopkeeper buys goods for the shop, or the farmer buys seed, the bill has to be paid by him or her personally. The sole trader typically owns the building and equipment used by the business. As the business is personal to its owner, it may end when the owner retires, unless there is another family member or purchaser to carry it on. If the business fails, the personal wealth of its owner can be used to cover the business's debts, and, in the worst scenario, the owner's resources could be wiped out, in order to pay the business debts. This risk is known as 'unlimited liability', and is one of the major drawbacks of being in business as a sole trader. Another is that, although family businesses may carry on indefinitely, there is limited scope for expansion, and family businesses usually remain small. Research suggests that 'the high degree of personal control limits the effective size of such businesses' (Whitley, 1995, p. 201). In Asian countries, the family business is a major form of business activity. Expanding family businesses often decide to convert the business into a limited company.

For individual entrepreneurs, the franchise provides a less risky route to starting a business. The **franchise** agreement allows a businessperson to trade under the name of an established brand, backed by an established organization (the 'franchisor'), while retaining ownership of the business. Under the agreement, the business owner ('franchisee') pays fees to the franchisor organization for the right to sell its products or services. The franchisee does not have the freedom over the business that an independent owner would have, but stands a greater chance of success due to the strength of the established business 'formula' of the brand. Besides McDonald's, Burger King and other fast-food chains, there are numerous other goods and services providers, such as car rental companies, which have grown through the use of franchising.

Partnership

The **partnership** as a form of business involves two or more people carrying on a business in common, with a view to profit (Morse, 1991). A partnership may be any type of business, but commonly has been adopted by professional people such as accountants and lawyers. The partnership is called a 'firm', although this term is now used generally to refer to a company, not just a partnership. The partnership as a form is midway between the sole trader and company. Partners share the firm's profits, and are all liable for its debts. While a limited partnership is possible, most partners, like the sole trader, have unlimited liability for the debts of the business. Therefore, a partnership relies heavily on personal trust between partners. The partnership is not a separate entity in the eyes of the law, but the partners can be sued (that is, face court proceedings) in the firm's name. To overcome the problems of unlimited liability that can arise when professional people are sued, firms take out considerable insurance cover.

'Partnership' is also used to describe a variety of relationships between two businesses, or between a government agency and a business. For example, a joint venture between two companies in different countries (discussed in Chapter 2) may be referred to as a partnership, the basis of which is co-operation to achieve a common goal. Partnerships in this broader sense may include a variety of both formal and informal alliances between organizations.

Company

The company is the preferred form for businesses when they grow beyond a size that can be managed personally by a sole trader. The **company**, also called a corporation, is a legal entity separate from the members who comprise it. Thus, the organization takes on a more impersonal character than the family business. The company is said to have 'perpetual succession', which means that it continues in existence, although its members may come and go over time (Morse, 1995, p. 5). As the company has a separate existence as a legal person, it involves greater dependence on formal documents. While there are several types of company, most companies are formed by registration, which is the filing of prescribed documents with the relevant government authority (Companies House in the UK, for example). In the US, companies register in one of the 50 states. When companies fail, they do not simply die, but must go through a legal procedure of 'winding up'.

From the point of view of a growing business, the advantage of converting into a company is that of attaining 'limited liability', which derives from the separate corporate status which the company enjoys. This means that the shareholder is liable only up to the amount of the face value of the shares acquired. Unlike the business owned personally by the sole trader, the company is legally owned by its shareholders, known as stockholders in many countries, including the US. A share in a company is a type of personal property, and the whole of a company's shares are its share capital, also known as **equity**.

Companies may be divided into private companies and public companies. Private companies are not allowed to offer shares to the public, whereas public companies do, although they need only offer a portion of their shares, such as 25 per cent. The private company is usually small, often with only a few shareholders who are family members. The public company is a much larger organization, and, when its shares are traded publicly on stock

WWW
WEBALERT

Companies House is at http://www.companieshouse.gov.uk
The Virgin Group is at http://www.Virgin.com

exchanges, it is likely to attract more public interest. Vodafone and Tesco are public companies, but there are some examples of high-profile, private companies, such as Virgin. In the UK a public company has 'plc' after its name, to distinguish it from private companies, which are simply 'limited'.

State-owned enterprises

State-owned enterprises differ from those owned by private individuals, in that they are owned and run, in effect, as limbs of government, often providing services for the public generally. They are often referred to as 'nationalized industries', such as Petroleos de Venezuela, the Venezuelan state-owned oil company. These enterprises are thus in the 'public sector', while 'private sector' refers to businesses owned by private citizens. State-controlled enterprises have played an important part in economic activity in many countries, and they vary in organization and business orientation. While they have had a reputation as sluggish and inefficient, a trend from the 1980s onwards has been for nationalized industries to be '**privatized**', that is, converted into public limited companies, offering a portion of shares to the public. In many cases, the state retains a significant proportion. These privatized companies have become fitter and more responsive to consumers than they were as nationalized industries, and also have branched out into

POINTS TO REMEMBER

Types of business ownership

- *Sole trader* – Business under the ownership and control of an individual, often extending to family members; depends on personal control, and becomes harder to manage as the business grows. Example: small craft shop
- *Partnership* – Two or more people in business together, sharing the profits; depends on trust between the partners. Example: professionals such as accountants or lawyers
- *Private limited company* – formation of a separate legal entity, the company, through registration and filing of documents (Memorandum of Association and Articles of Association in the UK); not allowed to offer shares to the public. Example: Virgin Atlantic
- *Public limited company (plc)* – Limited company which is registered as a plc and offers shares to the public. Example: Marks & Spencer plc
- *State-owned enterprise* – an entity owned and controlled by government, such as a nationalized industry; known as a public sector enterprise. Example: Petroleos de Venezuela, the state oil company of Venezuela. Privatization is the process of selling these enterprises to private investors, although the state often retains a large stake. Example: British Telecom

world markets. In Europe the telecommunications industry and utilities, such as gas, water and electricity, have been privatized in this way. (Privatization is examined in more detail in Chapter 3.) Global companies which still have significant stakes owned by the state include the car maker, Renault in France and the telecommunications company, Deutsche Telekom in Germany, in which the state is the largest shareholder.

1.2.2 Classification of businesses by size

The size of a business may be determined by a variety of criteria, including number of employees, turnover and market share (Buckley, 1999). However, these criteria are interpreted differently in different national and regional contexts, largely reflecting the size of the economy. While in some contexts 499 employees is used as the upper limit for a medium-size business, in many others, including the legal definition of a medium-size company under the UK Companies Act 1985, an upper limit of 249 is used. A commonly used classification based on the number of employees is:

- *Small:* 0–49 employees (also includes businesses run by a single individual with no employees)
- *Medium:* 50–249 employees
- *Large:* 250 or more employees.

However defined, **small to medium-size enterprises (SMEs)** provide an important source of employment and economic activity in all countries. They account for roughly 60–70 per cent of employment in OECD (Organization

Figure 1.2 Proportion of businesses, employment and turnover in small, medium and large firms in the UK, at the start of 1999

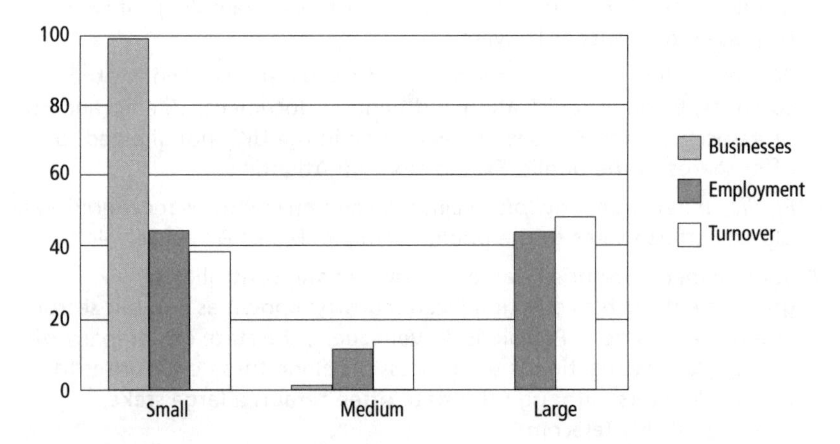

Source: DTI (2000) *Small and Medium Enterprise (SME) Statistics for the UK*, 1999 (Office for National Statistics).

for Economic Co-operation and Development) countries, and 30 per cent of world exports of manufactures (UNIDO, 2000). SMEs range from informal 'micro-enterprises' to firms working at the forefront of advanced technology. SMEs are associated with entrepreneurial activity, in that they are more flexible than large organizations, and are often able to specialize in 'niche' markets. Increasingly, these opportunities have become international in scope, facilitated by advances in information and communications technology (Buckley, 1999; Gankema et al., 2000).

Figure 1.2 gives a breakdown of the UK's 3.7 million enterprises in 1999. It shows that, following the classification above, less than 7,000 are large; 24,000 are medium; and the huge majority are small, accounting for over 99 per cent of all businesses. There are major differences, however, between industries. In the construction industry, nearly 84 per cent of employment is in SMEs, while in finance, the proportion is only 21 per cent (DTI, 2000). These figures are shown in Table 1.1.

Table 1.1 SME share of employment in the UK, by industry, start of 1999

	Total employment (000s)	SME percentage share
All industries	21,746	55.4
Agriculture, forestry, fishing	452	97.6
Mining and quarrying	83	30.8
Manufacturing	4,334	49.6
Electricity, gas and water supply	139	2.6
Construction	1,542	83.7
Wholesale, retail and repairs	4,416	52.1
Hotels and restaurants	1,598	55.6
Transport, storage and communication	1,538	39.8
Financial intermediation	1,043	21.1
Real estate, business activities	3,146	69.6
Education	255	83.8
Health and social work	2,107	41.7
Other social/personal services	1,111	76.7

Source: DTI (2000) *Small and Medium Enterprise (SME) Statistics for the UK*, 1999 (Office for National Statistics).

1.3 Business organization

An **organization** may be defined as 'two or more people who work together in a structured way to achieve a specific goal or set of goals' (Stoner and Freeman, 1992, p. 4). This broad definition encompasses many types of organization. It includes, for example, police forces, hospitals and schools, as well as the vast array of business enterprises that make up modern consumer society. A business organization aims to generate profits by producing products or delivering services that customers are willing to buy at prices they are willing to pay. Physical resources, including plant, machinery and offices must be organized, and functions such as finance, purchasing and marketing must be co-ordinated, to enable the entire enterprise to function smoothly as a unit.

While every organization wishes to make the most of its expertise and resources, there is no one type of organization which can be said to be an ideal model that suits all businesses. There is a large body of organization theory, which studies 'the structure, functioning and performance of organizations and the behaviour of groups and individuals within them' (Pugh, 1997, p. xii). **Structure** has been defined as 'the design of organization through which the enterprise is administered' (Chandler, 1990, p. 14). It includes both formal and informal lines of authority. Organizational structures can be divided into three broad categories. The first is organization based simply on function. The second is the divisional structure, based on products, brands or regions. Third, there is the organizational structure based on a matrix, the aim of which is to bring together the benefits of the other types. We look at each in turn.

1.3.1 The functional approach

The functional approach to organization starts from the premise that all business activities can be looked at in terms of functions. In a small business, the workers may well turn their hand to several different functions, while in larger organizations, there is a group of specialized workers for each function. Functions depend in part on the type of business. Product design and production, along with research and development, feature mainly in manufacturing firms, whereas all firms have need of finance, human resource management and marketing functions. The main functions, which appear in Figure 1.3, are:

- *Finance and accounting* – control over the revenues and outgoings of the business, aiming to balance the books and generate sufficient profits for the future health of the firm. This function is far more complex in large public companies than in SMEs.
- *Human resource management (HRM)* – formerly known as 'personnel management', HRM focuses on all aspects of the management of people

in the organization, including recruiting, training, and rewarding the workforce.

- *Marketing* – marketing focuses on satisfying the needs and expectations of customers. Marketing covers a range of related functions, including advertising, pricing and distribution of goods.
- *Product design* – product designers, mainly in manufacturing companies, are specialist engineers, who develop new products and improve existing products, from the beginnings of a single 'prototype', through to testing and revision of the design before large-scale production can begin.
- *Research and development (R&D)* – R&D is the scientific and technical research which underlies new products. Without an R&D focus, companies risk falling behind competitors in innovative products.
- *Production* – production focuses on the operational processes by which products are manufactured, such as assembly lines. Production increasingly relies on sophisticated machinery and computerized systems. Quality, safety and efficiency are major concerns of production engineers and managers.

The functional organizational approach is depicted in Figure 1.3. There is a risk in this type of organization that each functional department will become inward looking and lose sight of organizational goals. Within the formal structure, the functional specialists must be co-ordinated into a smooth-running whole. Central management and, in particular, its chief executive officer (CEO) is at the pinnacle of the organization. The CEO is therefore crucial in co-ordinating the departments. **Management** is the:

> process of planning, organizing, leading and controlling the work of organization members, and of using all available organizational resources to reach stated organizational goals. (Stoner and Freeman, 1992, p. 4)

Figure 1.3 Organization based on functional departments

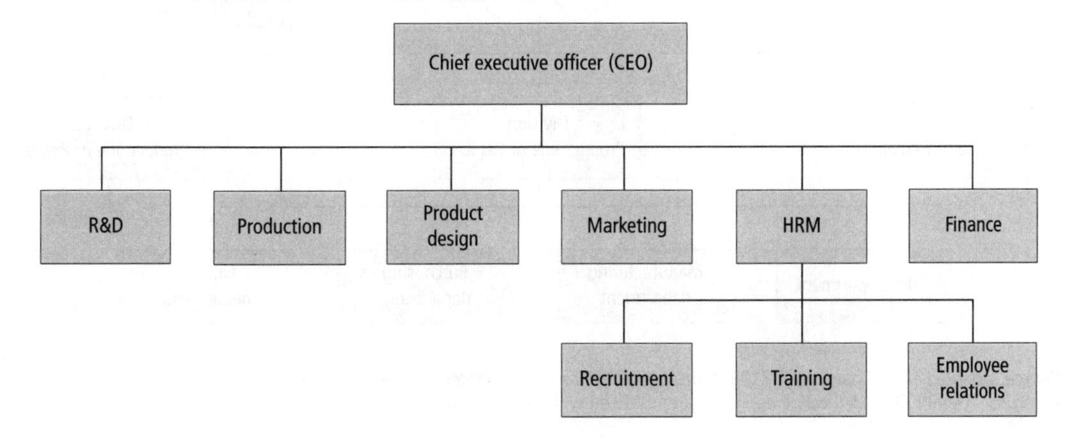

The larger the company, the more cumbersome this structure becomes. For large companies, which produce a number of products in different regions of the world, this structure has given way to the more decentralized divisional structure.

1.3.2 The divisional structure

When a company has grown to the extent that it has a number of successful products in different regions, it may structure the organization into business units or divisions, which may be based on product, brand, or geographical region (see Figure 1.4). Known as the **multidivisional structure**, this has been one of the major structural innovations of modern corporations, seeking to solve the problems of how to decentralize a large company, while still maintaining overall co-ordination of the parts. A full account of its development is given in Alfred Chandler's *Strategy and Structure* (1990). In it he recounts the experiences of General Motors and the American chemical corporation, Du Pont, which adopted the multidivisional structure in the early 1900s. The principle is that each division is headed by a division manager who has responsibility for managing the division as a profit centre in its own right. The division itself may be a separate company, known as a subsidiary company, whose major shareholder is the 'parent' company. The company's executives at head office concentrate on the broader corporate aims, leaving the divisions considerable independence. The head office will have centralized functional departments, such as finance, for the group as a whole. A divisional structure based on product divisions has been adopted by a number of global companies, including General Electric, British Telecom and

Figure 1.4 The multidivisional structure

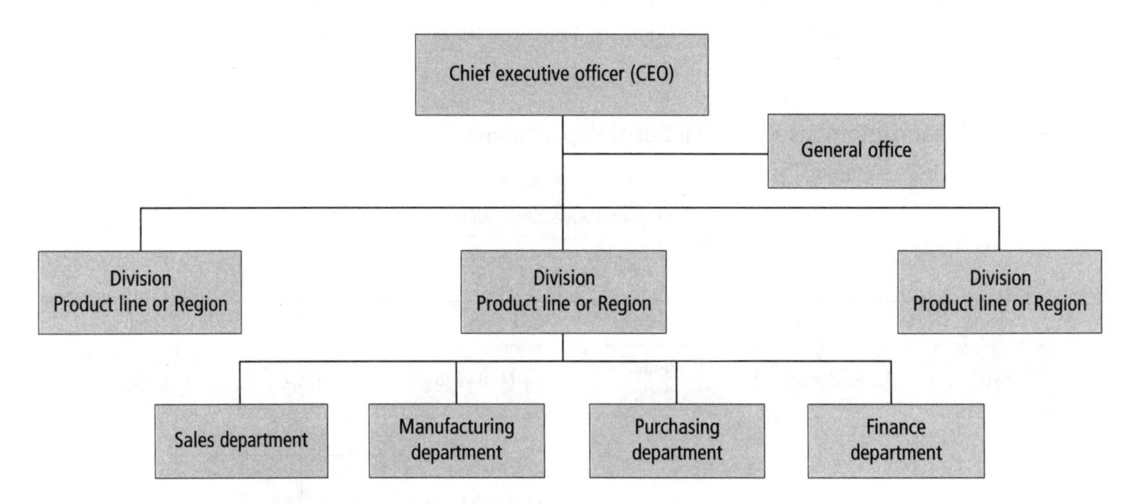

Source: Adapted from Chandler, A. (1990) *Strategy and Structure: Chapters in the History of the American Industrial Enterprise* (Cambridge, MA: MIT Press) p. 10 (reproduced with permission).

Ericsson. An advantage of this approach is the ability to co-ordinate activities to produce and market a particular line worldwide, but a drawback tends to be that its standardized approach overlooks differences in national markets (Birkinshaw, 2000).

The area division is a way of addressing different regional conditions. In this type of organization structure, country or region managers preside over area divisions, and are responsible for all the company's activities in that area. The area may be, for example, Asia Pacific, in which case the area manager has charge of operations in that area, including control over resources. A main advantage of the area division structure is that it is able to respond to regional needs. It also lends itself to decentralization, that is, the delegating of decision-making down to the divisions. Many global companies, including Nestlé and Unilever, have been organized in this way, although they have found that it is difficult to achieve economies of scale in development and production (Birkinshaw, 2000). They have tended to move towards global product divisions or a combination of geographical regions plus product divisions, as Unilever has done.

The **holding company** may also be said to be based on divisions, in that a parent company is the owner of a diverse array of subsidiary companies. However, unlike the multidivisional companies described above, the holding company exerts little control over the separate companies and provides few general functions for the group as a whole. The companies within the group operate, in effect, as independent organizations.

1.3.3 The matrix

The **matrix** is a way of structuring the organization to incorporate the benefits of other types of structure, such as the functional organization, product divisions and area divisions. It involves two lines of management, as indicated in Figure 1.5. The product manager must co-ordinate with the area manager for the launch of a new product in that region. In theory, this allows the company to respond to local trends, and also derive the benefits of globally co-ordinated product management. In practice, however, it is difficult to reconcile these different lines of authority, and the system can lead to deadlock in decision-making (Bartlett and Ghoshal, 1990). Thus, although the matrix theoretically should provide flexibility, it can lead to inefficiency. Some companies adopt a compromise, using product divisions, but adding country management where it is specifically needed, for example in developing countries such as China (Birkinshaw, 2000). In the early 1990s, the Swiss–Swedish electrical engineering company, ABB, put in place a matrix structure, but changed to a divisional structure based on products and technologies in 1998. In 2001, the company underwent a further restructuring, in which the divisions were replaced by four 'consumer segments', aimed at developing a greater customer orientation.

Figure 1.5 The global matrix

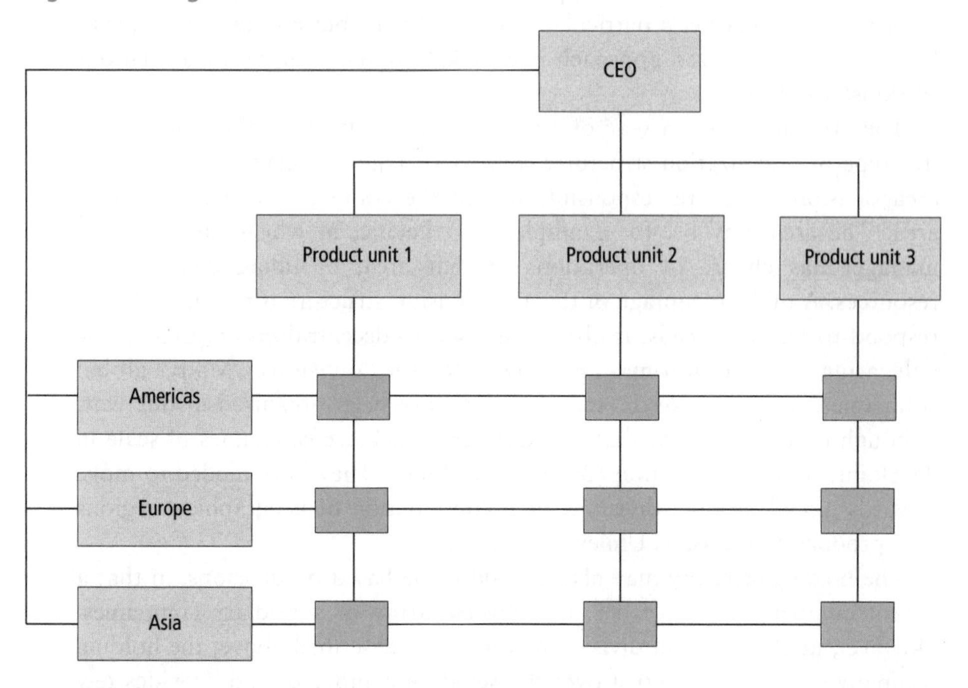

Source: Birkinshaw, J. 'The structures behind global companies', *Mastering Management*, (Suppl.) Part 10, Financial Times/Pitman, 4 December 2000, p. 4 (reproduced with permission).

1.4 Organizations and change: business strategy

No two organizations, even two with similar outward structures, will be run in exactly the same way. Differences in behaviour, values and overall atmosphere are part of a business's **organizational culture**, and are particularly evident in situations of turbulence and uncertainty. Some businesses become set in their ways, assuming that structures and processes which served well in the past will continue to do so into the future. In a competitive environment, they are likely to lose out to more efficient and innovative rivals. Forward-looking organizations look for ways to reform their structures and improve communications within the organization and with its customers. Change may be radical or it may be gradual, that is, introduced incrementally, step by step. If an organization has been 'drifting' for a number of years, then looming crisis may dictate that it needs a radical shake-up involving restructuring. Changes need not involve entire restructuring, but a redefinition of the aims of the company within the existing structures. It is easier to change structures than to change organizational culture, which represents ingrained ways of doing things. A takeover may be the catalyst of radical change in structure and processes. Or, if one division is underperforming, a merger with another

Case study 1.1 Restructuring at Procter & Gamble

Procter & Gamble (P&G), formed by William Procter and James Gamble in Cincinnati in 1837, is one of the oldest global companies. Its brands include Ivory soap, Crest toothpaste and Ariel detergent, along with many others. For much of its history, the company has been innovative in producing new consumer products and new marketing techniques, such as the soap opera. However, despite its record of reliable profit growth, by the 1990s P&G had become weighed down by bureaucratic hierarchy. According to Richard Tomkins, 'the company became formula-driven, risk-averse and inbred. Even the smallest decisions had to be referred to senior management. Individuality was frowned upon: employees learnt how to write memos, how to speak and how to think' (*Financial Times*, 12 June, 2000). Times became harder for the well-known brands, which were losing sales to copycat products and supermarket own brands. The big supermarket chains, such as Wal-Mart, grew more powerful, and were able to demand lower prices from manufacturers.

In a restructuring in 1990, P&G's chief executive closed 30 plants worldwide, cutting 13,000 jobs. This move brought down prices, but damaged employee morale. The need was for more innovative products, as Ivory soap had fallen behind Unilever's Dove moisturizing soap, and Crest toothpaste had been overtaken by Colgate's Total. In 1999, a new chief executive, Durk Jager, took radical measures to dismantle the company's multilayered bureaucracy. Aiming to recreate entrepreneurial spirit, he took power away from country-based divisions and created global product managers, with greater control over their budgets. But the change from country-based divisions to product divisions proved very expensive, and the costs did not translate immediately into greater sales. Further, the radical changes had a disorientating effect on employees. It has been estimated that of P&G's 200–300 top managers, only 20 per cent were left doing the same job they had done 18 months previously.

Arguably, Jager did what was necessary to drag the company into the twenty-first century, and the company's turnaround would have come over time. But shareholders expected a speedy recovery, which was not forthcoming. After only 18 months in office, in which three profit warnings had to be issued, he was forced to go.

Sources: Tomkins, R., 'Revenge of the Proctoids', *Financial Times*, 12 June 2000; 'Durk's dismissal', *Financial Times*, 12 June 2000; Jones, A., 'Consumed by the consumer', *Financial Times*, 23 May 2001.

Case questions

In what ways did Procter & Gamble's organizational culture and structure need to be changed?

Did Jager try to do too much too quickly, or was shock therapy necessary in the circumstances?

Procter & Gamble's website is at http://www.pg.com

division may be advisable. The timing of change and decisions as to whether it should be revolutionary or incremental are issues of strategy.

Strategy is often thought of simply as planning, but in fact it is much broader in scope. It encompasses not just physical changes such as shutting down a division, but also changes of corporate focus and attitudes on the part of the workforce. Chandler defined strategy as:

> the determination of the basic long-term goals and objectives of an enterprise, and the adoption of courses of action and the allocation of resources necessary for carrying out these goals. (Chandler, 1990, p. 13)

Chandler believed that structure follows strategy. His reasoning was that if a company sees new opportunities created by the changing environment, say by technological change, it alters its strategy, and then changes its structure accordingly. This approach views strategy as a 'top-down' process. However, in a rapidly changing environment, strategies may emerge as events unfold. Strategy is often a combination of 'deliberate' strategy, that which has been originally intended, and 'emergent' strategy, which has arisen from events not part of the intended strategy (Mintzberg, 2000). In this way, some large organizations, such as ICI, found that strategy emerged slowly, as changes in beliefs and structure became settled (Pettigrew, 1997). Case Study 1.2, on Honda's success in America, shows the importance of accident and good luck in shaping strategy.

Awareness of changes taking place in the environment and new opportunities is captured in the concept of **strategic thinking**, which can be defined as bringing together all the information available from those within the organization and converting that knowledge into a vision of the aims that the business should pursue. As Mintzberg explains:

> in the case of emergent strategy, because big strategies can grow from little ideas (initiatives), and in strange places, not to mention at unexpected times, almost anyone in the organization can prove to be a strategist. (2000, p. 26)

Experience suggests, therefore, that strategy is more diffuse and complex than the idea of planning suggests. The flexible organization with open communication, able to adapt its strategy to the changing environment, is more likely to spot and exploit new opportunities than the one with a rigid structure.

Case study 1.2 Honda and the US motorcycle market

It had been accepted that Honda's penetration of the US motorcycle market had been based on a deliberate strategy to target the bottom end of the US market, with the 50cc Supercub. However, research by Richard Pascale in 1984 revealed a very different story. He found from speaking to Honda's executives that they were confident that the Honda 50 was a brilliant design, but they had had difficulties in raising production capacity in Japan. When they went to the US in 1959, they set themselves a target of exporting just 6,000 machines per year for several years, leaving the actual timescale unspecified. They reckoned on 25 per cent of each of their four products: the 50cc Supercub, and the 125cc, 250cc and 305cc machines.

The dramatic success of the 50cc came about through 'accident, good luck and the Honda US executives' willingness to respond to events and learn from the market' (Barwise, 1997). They concentrated first on selling the larger bikes, as they thought they were more suitable for the US market, where everything was bigger and more luxurious. However, these machines started to break down, as they were being driven harder and longer than in Japan. The Honda executives themselves used the Honda 50s to ride around Los Angeles on errands. They attracted attention, including a call from a Sears buyer. While they were apprehensive that the small bikes would dent the macho image of their machines, they felt compelled to sell them when their bigger bikes were struggling. Surprisingly, the retailers buying the Honda 50 were not motorcycle dealers, but sporting goods stores.

Barwise concludes: 'Honda was able to turn its initial design advantage in Japan and its unplanned success in the US into world domination, which it still enjoys 30 years later' (Barwise, 1997, p. 565). Honda's success demonstrates that successful strategy may emerge, rather than be the result of deliberate planning.

Sources: Barwise, P. (1997) 'Strategic investment decisions and emergent strategy', *Mastering Management*, Part 15, Financial Times/Pitman, pp. 562–71; Pascale, R.T., 'Perspectives on strategy: the real story behind Honda's success', *California Management Review*, Spring 1984, pp. 47–72.

Case question

What do we learn about emergent strategy from Honda's success with the Honda 50 in the US?

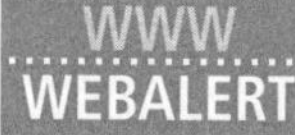

Honda is at http://www.hondamotorcycle.com/

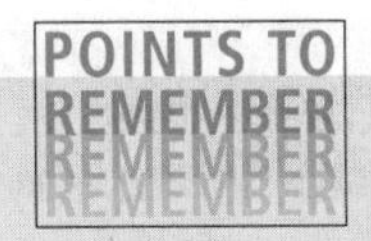

Varying approaches to strategy

The *planning approach* holds that:

1 Strategy formation should be a controlled, conscious, formalized process
2 Responsibility for the overall process rests with the chief executive in principle, although responsibility for its execution rests with staff planners in practice
3 Detailed strategic plans that result from this process are then implemented

The *emergent strategy approach* holds that:

1 Strategy is a combination of intended and unintended. Some intended strategy is not realized. The part that is realized is deliberate strategy
2 Much realized strategy emerges from events that were not part of the intended strategy. This is emergent strategy

Sources: Mintzberg, H. (2000) *The Rise and Fall of Strategy*, London, Pearson; Barwise, P. (1997) 'Strategic investment decisions and emergent strategy', *Mastering Management*, Financial Times/Pitman, pp. 562–71.

1.5 Hierarchies and networks

Whatever their structure, large companies, in order to manage their growing complexities, tend to become hierarchical. A **hierarchy** essentially differentiates people in terms of power in a vertical fashion. Those at the top are the chief decision-makers in the organization, whereas those at the bottom, who carry out the routine activities of the business, have little decision-making power. There may be many layers of management and supervision in between. Each worker in the hierarchy has a definite position, with lines of authority above and below, in a system known as **bureaucracy**. When we think of bureaucracies, we think of the benefits of efficiency, with each task fitting into an overall whole, as in an assembly line. But we also tend to think of bureaucracies as inflexible and dependent on procedural formalities. They function best in unchanging environments, but in the context of a rapidly changing competitive environment, companies are shifting away from the bureaucratic model in order to introduce more flexibility, more open communication and quicker responses to customer needs.

One of the obvious reforms of bureaucratic structures is to reduce the number of layers, or flatten the structure. The structure may be flattened by reducing layers in the middle if there are too many layers of middle management. Or the power to take decisions may be decentralized to lower levels, through empowerment, one of the major developments in HRM thinking. **Empowerment** holds that employees at all levels in the organization are 'responsible for their own actions, and should be given authority to make decisions about their work' (Peiperi, 1997). The rationale behind empowerment is that those at the lower levels have considerable knowledge of operational matters and are able to respond more quickly. Recent theory stresses that one of the organization's major assets is knowledge, which is dispersed throughout its structure. Managements therefore need to look for ways to allow this knowledge to be tapped and channelled into new products, for example. It is increasingly recognized that products are not the sole preserve of product engineers, but involve cross-functional co-operation. Empowerment also allows the formation of cross-functional links.

At the organizational level, empowerment ties in with the **network organization** (Jackson and Schuler, 2000). The network organization does not really represent a new type of structure, but a new way of looking at the lines of communication and informal links within the preceding structural frameworks. Networking is 'the informal overlay that cuts across whatever formal structure is chosen' (Birkinshaw, 2000, p. 4). Thus project teams may be drawn from different functional groups or different area divisions. It may thus speed up decision-making, which in any large organization tends to become sluggish and slow. Positional structure still exists, but project activities which cross structural boundaries bring the flexibility needed for dynamic processes (Fukuyama, 2000). The tools for networking are very much enhanced by the use of email communications, which can cut across divisional boundaries. A project team can thus be assembled from various locations across the globe. Network organizations are also more likely to develop links with other organizations, creating networks across organizational boundaries (Jackson and Schuler, 2000). It is often said that networks rely on 'social capital', that is, shared norms and a relationship of trust, rather than formal authority structures.

Hierarchies versus networks

- *Hierarchies* are based on formal rules and lines of authority in centralized bureaucratic structures. There is little delegation from the centre. This type of organization becomes inflexible, unable to respond to a changing environment
- The *network organization* relies on shared norms and values, rather than formal rules. Networks allow information to flow freely within the organization. Informal, self-directed groups of workers provide a more flexible means of co-ordination within the organization than formal hierarchies

1.6 Marketing orientation

While marketing is one of the functional areas highlighted above, companies in the last 25 years have come to give greater weight to marketing as a corporate goal, not simply confined to marketing departments. Some companies are 'product led', taking the approach that the aim of marketing is to promote the company's products. The marketing-oriented company, by contrast, takes the view that finding out what customers want and satisfying those needs is a primary aim of the company. The **marketing concept** may be defined as:

> the philosophy that an organisation should try to provide products that satisfy customers' needs through a co-ordinated set of activities that also allows the organisation to achieve its goals. (Dibb et al., 1997, p. 15)

The focus on customer satisfaction thus pervades the whole organization. Marketers need to work with production staff to determine product features and benefits desired by customers. Marketers are also needed to assess the volume to produce and the variety of the company's products needed. Co-ordination between marketing, finance and production is therefore essential. Moreover, with consumer tastes rapidly changing, it is clear that rapid response to markets dictates that product development must be compressed into the shortest possible time span. Most of Hewlett-Packard's revenues come from products that did not exist a year before (Ridderstråle, 2000). The transformation of Corning towards a marketing-oriented company can be seen in Case Study 1.3.

1.7 Corporate governance

Just as thinking has evolved on what the aims of a business should be and how it should best be structured, there has also been lively debate in the business world on the question of whom the business exists for. The question turns on issues of **corporate governance**, which are about who has ultimate control of the company and the mechanisms for exercising that control. Corporate governance differs from business to business, and will change as a business grows, largely because of the changes which take place in the way the business is financed. In a closely knit family firm, such as a Chinese family business, the business exists to swell the wealth of the family (Whitley, 1995). The entrepreneur who founds a business with his or her own personal funds both owns and runs the business. Amazon.com is an example (see Minifile).

When the enterprise grows and becomes a public company, outside investors gain greater influence as the proportion of shares they hold increases. However, companies differ considerably in their shareholder

Case study 1.3 Changes at Corning

To many people, Corning is synonymous with Pyrex ovenproof dishes. However, in the past five years, Corning has transformed itself from a consumer glassmaker to the world's largest producer of fibreoptic cables, which form the backbone of the internet and modern communications systems. The company, which has been in existence since the days of Thomas Edison, now accounts for over 40 per cent of the market in fibreoptic cables. Corning now has three operating segments: Telecommunications, Advanced Materials and Information Display.

The transformation has come about through changes in strategy and culture. Corning was thought of as a company proud of its technology and products. In the past, when it invented new types of glass, it then looked for buyers. Every product it sold had resulted from its own technology. In the 1960s, it developed a flat glass with no glare, but found no buyers until two decades later, when it found a market in computer screens. This scenario would not happen today. The company has now adopted a market-driven approach: 'identify a customer need, then design a product or service to fill it' (Deutsch, 2001). It has recognized that with the speed of technological change, it is often more efficient to acquire companies with relevant technology, in order to get a product to market as quickly as possible and increase manufacturing capacity.

Corning has thus sought acquisitions and partners to exploit many new products in the telecommunications market. Its net income from its fibreoptic and cable business increased 65 per cent in the third quarter of 2000, compared to the same period in 1999. In 2000 it spent $10 billion in acquiring companies that make the pump lasers which generate and transmit signals down fibreoptic highways. Beside its telecommunications businesses, Corning supplies key components for emissions control and reducing pollution.

Corning's growth is music to the ears of shareholders, who saw the share price quadruple in 2000, and maintain its value when other technology shares were stumbling. The ovenware business, sold nearly four years ago, is now just corporate history.

Sources: Deutsch, C., 'At Corning ideas now match markets', *The New York Times*, 7 January 2001; Corning, Inc., *Quarterly Report* (SEC form 10-Q), 24 October 2000.

Case questions

In what ways has the new strategy at Corning transformed the company?

What are the lessons for other businesses

WWW
WEBALERT

Corning's website is at http://www.corning.com

profile. In Continental European companies, it has been common for founders and family members to retain large shareholdings. Examples are the French car maker, PSA Peugeot-Citroën and the Italian car maker, Fiat. A controlling block of shareholders acts as a deterrent to takeover. In marked contrast, US and UK companies tend to have more fragmented patterns of share ownership, and the result has been a much more active takeover market. Most modern shareholders take no part in running the business. They buy shares as an investment only, to see their investments grow and reap annual dividends from the company's profits. Their timespan tends to be short term. As shareholding has spread throughout the population and large institutional investors, such as pension funds, have become prominent, shareholder value has become an important concern for corporate executives in their strategic planning.

Minifile

THE RISE OF AMAZON.COM

1994	Founder, Jeff Bezos, starts Amazon.com with $10,000; borrows $44,000
1995	Founder's father and mother invest $245,000
1995–96	Business 'angels' invest nearly $100,000
1996 (May)	Founder's family invest $20,000
1996 (June)	Two venture capital funds invest $8 million
1997	Initial public offering: three million shares offered to the public, raising $49.1 million

Amazon.com grew from a start-up online bookseller to one of the largest retailers on the Web in just four years. Its growth and the innovations it brought to online retailing were largely down to its charismatic founder, Jeff Bezos. In its first two years, Amazon.com was mainly kept in the Bezos family. This changed dramatically with the arrival on the scene of venture capitalists, companies which specialize in spotting 'rising stars', providing funds on a much larger scale, and taking them to the public offering stage.

Bezos's vision was that Amazon.com would be not just a bookseller, but at the centre of e-shopping. He linked up with several other companies to sell toys, sportswear, pet supplies and electrical goods. Still, the company made losses in 1999, as costs soared more rapidly than sales.

Sources: Brooker, K., 'Amazon vs. everybody', *Fortune*, 140, (9): 8 November 1999; Mayer, C., 'Developing the rules for corporate governance', *Mastering Management*, Part 6, Financial Times/Pitman, 6 November 2000.

In addition to accountability to shareholders, corporate governance has taken on broader implications, as managers have become more aware of the interrelationships between the internal and external environment of the company. This broader concept is that of stakeholders. A stakeholder may be anyone, or even the community generally, who has an interest in the company, directly or indirectly. Besides shareholders, it includes employees, trade unions, customers, suppliers, the investing public generally and the local community. Stakeholders can thus be very diverse, and there is scope for conflict between shareholder and stakeholder interests. For example, shutting down a factory may please shareholders, but harm employees and the local community. Reconciling the interests of shareholders and other stakeholders has thus become an important consideration for corporate strategy. Moreover, media interest helps to generate debate on stakeholder issues.

1.8 Tools for formulating business strategy

Business strategy must take into account both the external and internal environment of the organization. Two traditional tools, PEST analysis and SWOT analysis are given below. While both tend to oversimplify the processes, they do serve to highlight major issues.

1.8.1 PEST analysis

Analysis of the external environment may be expressed by the acronym **PEST**, standing for political, economic, sociocultural, and technological factors. Also known as environmental scanning, the PEST analysis is a useful tool for monitoring and evaluating forces which affect the organization over the long term. Research has shown that environmental scanning is linked to company performance (Thomas et al., 1993). Below are the headings, with a few questions that arise under each one:

- *Political–legal environment* – Is the existing government a stable one, and what is the strength of any opposition to it? What constraints has the government imposed on business, or is likely to impose in the future? In the European Union (EU), what forthcoming legislation, such as a new law on mergers, is likely to affect the business?
- *Economic environment* – Is the economy growing, or is there a recession looming? Are wages and consumer spending rising? Which sectors of the economy are growing and which sectors are not? Which regions of the country are experiencing the best growth? Is there high unemployment?
- *Sociocultural environment* – Is the society culturally diverse? What are the educational levels of the population generally? To what extent do women have educational opportunities and play an active part in business life? What is the pattern of family life – is there a large proportion of single-parent families, or are extended families the norm?
- *Technological environment* – What is the level of technology education and training which would influence the recruitment of skilled staff? Is technological innovation encouraged? What funding is available, from government and elsewhere, for technology development? How computer literate is the society generally?

Figure 1.6 PEST analysis in the international business environment

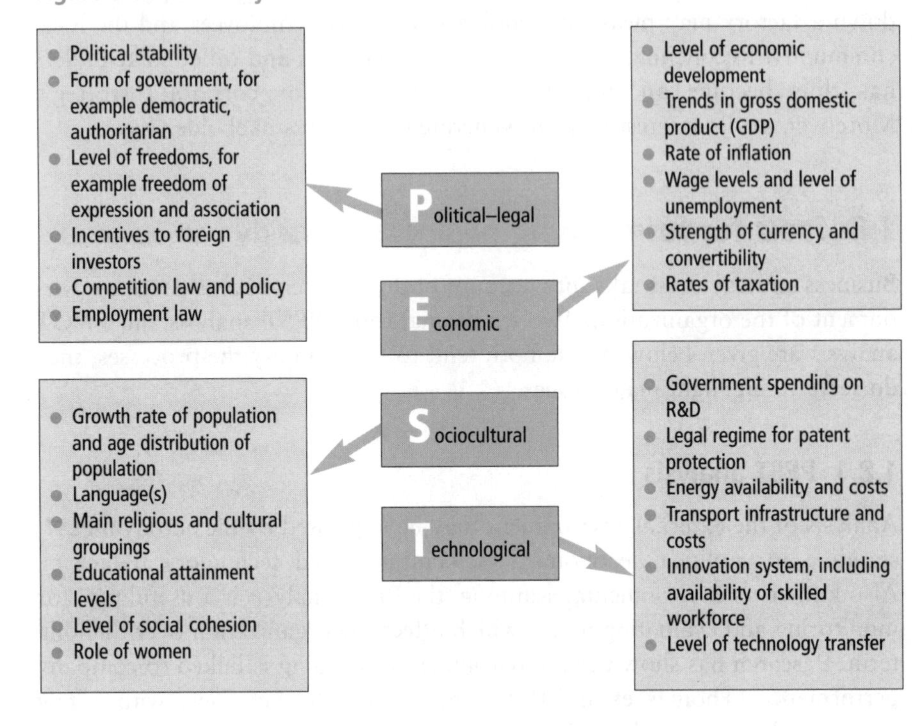

Answers to these and many other questions present an environmental profile of any society, which differentiates it from other societies, even those in the same geographic region. The PEST analysis is thus particularly useful for strategic managers in international businesses which operate in a number of different national environments. Figure 1.6 provides a summary of the key variables in the international environment.

The PEST analysis, while helpful as a tool, clearly does not cover all relevant aspects of the business environment. Legal factors are commonly grouped with political factors, as in the summary above. By expanding the acronym to LE PEST C, we can include legal factors as a separate heading, followed by ecological factors. Lastly, the competitive environment is added, to provide the basis of more comprehensive environmental scanning. These headings form the framework for the chapters of this book, with the addition of a separate chapter on the financial environment. The ecological environment is dealt with in Chapter 12.

Clearly, if a business is considering expanding in its home market, it will already have a good deal of knowledge about each of these aspects of the environment. On the other hand, if it is considering expanding to Vietnam, for example, it will probably know little. The more knowledge it acquires the better, in order to avoid making costly mistakes. When the firm has done its research on Vietnam, it must ask itself, why should this firm in particular do business there?

1.8.2 SWOT analysis

The **SWOT analysis** is a commonly used planning tool, which assesses the firm's strategic profile in terms of its strengths, weaknesses, opportunities and threats. Focusing on both internal and external environments, it serves to highlight a firm's distinctive competences, which will enable it to gain competitive advantage.

The SWOT analysis is usually expressed as a matrix: strengths and weaknesses in the top boxes relate to the company itself, while opportunities and threats, in the lower boxes, reflect relevant aspects of the external environment (Figure 1.7). Some of the key issues which are addressed in a SWOT analysis are:

External environment: opportunities and threats:

- What are the main factors in the societal environment (political–legal, economic, sociocultural and technological)?
- What is the market strength of competitors?
- What new products or services, including those of the firm and competitors, are in the pipeline?
- What is the level of consumer demand and can it be expected to remain stable?
- What is the likely threat of new entrants in the market for the firm's products?

Internal environment: strengths and weaknesses:

- Does the organization have a structure that helps it to achieve its objectives?
- Does it have clear marketing objectives and strategy?
- Does the organization use information technology (IT) effectively in all aspects of its activities?

Figure 1.7 SWOT analysis

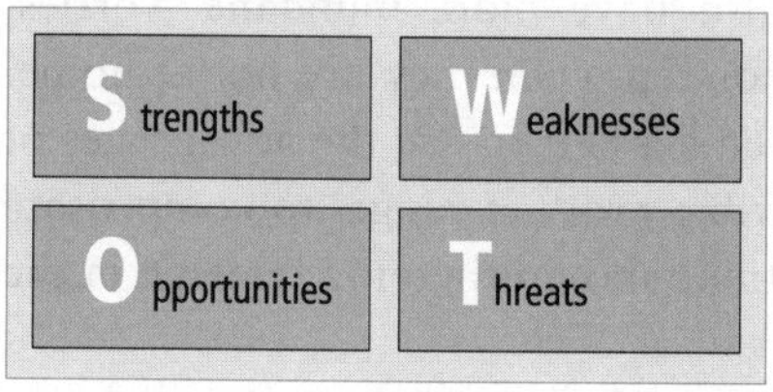

Strengths	Weaknesses
Opportunities	Threats

Figure 1.8 SWOT analysis for a business selling wine online

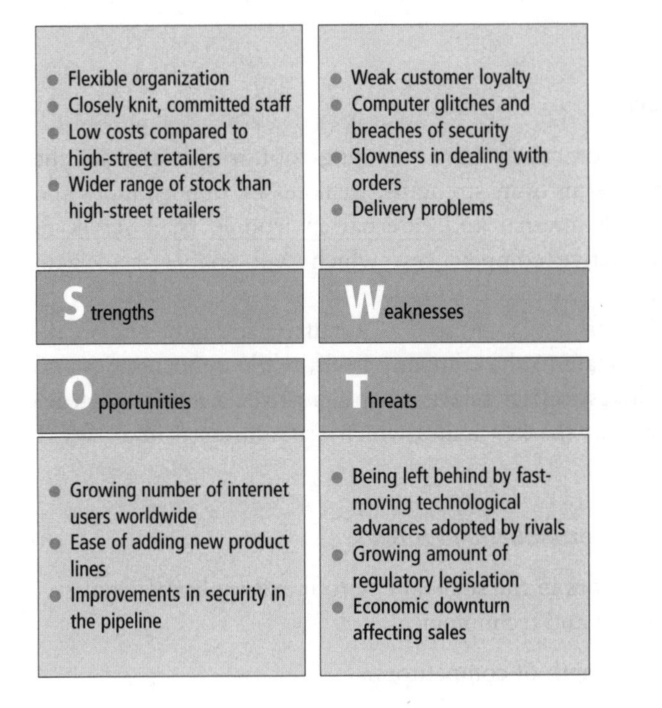

- Does its investment in R&D match or exceed that of competitors?
- Does the organization meet its financial objectives?
- To what extent does the firm have clear HRM objectives and strategies in areas such as employee motivation, staff turnover and provision of training?

Figure 1.8 sets out an example of a SWOT analysis for an online retailer (it runs no bricks-and-mortar outlets).

In the example of the online wine merchant, the SWOT analysis will be useful in formulating strategy, taking advantage of opportunities, such as growing markets from new internet users. It will also help to minimize the effects of threats or anticipated threats. The SWOT analysis shows that there are lingering doubts in the minds of many consumers about buying goods and services online, and many dotcom companies have struggled to build a customer base. It takes only one highly publicized security failure to damage consumer confidence. Consumers may also have more mundane worries, such as cases of wine being left on the doorstep when they are not at home. The online wine merchant must therefore endeavour to use the advantages of online selling, such as a greater, more flexible product range, to compensate for the perceived drawbacks. Strategic options should therefore emerge in the SWOT analysis.

The SWOT analysis can be carried out in planning teams or by groups of executives (Piercy and Giles, 1989), and their impressions can be quite different. It has been found that higher level managers tend to take a broad overview, seeing organizational factors as strengths, while lower level ones single out marketing and financial factors (Mintzberg, 2000, p. 276). This suggests that people's views are influenced by their own position in the business, and the SWOT exercise can serve to widen the perspectives of participants in the planning process.

While this chapter has focused on the internal environment of the organization, it has emerged that key aspects such as structure, processes, change and strategy are tied in with many aspects of the external environment, so that change becomes an interactive process. This is exemplified, for example, in the market-oriented company. The external environment, moreover, comprises a number of layers – some immediate, such as the local community and home-country government, but others more remote, such as regional and international forces. Interactions and tensions also arise between these layers of the external environment, and these tensions, too, are part of the international business environment. The following chapters will describe both the relevant forces and their spatial dimensions. For example, legal constraints may be imposed by local authorities, national governments, regional bodies (such as the EU) or international institutions (such as the World Trade Organization (WTO)). For a business, there are crucial differences between these different types of authority and their impact on commercial activities: they may overlap or even conflict with each other. Hence, understanding the processes at work globally will considerably enhance business decision-making.

1.9 Conclusions

1. Business covers a wide range of economic activity, including buying and selling goods, manufacturing products and providing services. International business refers to those activities between organizations in two or more countries.

2. Businesses may be sole traders, partnerships or companies. Typically, businesspeople set out as sole traders and convert the business to a limited company.

3. When they expand, businesses become more formally structured. Business organizations may be designed on a functional structure, a multidivisional structure or a matrix structure. No single structure can be said to suit all businesses.

4 Business strategy may evolve in many ways, emerging over time, rather than simply being the product of formal planning. Flexible organizations are more likely to be able to adapt strategy to the changing environment than rigid, or hierarchical organizations.

5 As consumer tastes change rapidly, a marketing orientation, in which the organization is oriented towards satisfying customer needs, has become important in the competitive environment.

6 While shareholder value is a key focus of company executives, companies have a broad range of other stakeholders, including employees, customers and the community at large. The task of corporate governance, therefore, can often be seen as one involving balancing many stakeholder interests.

7 Two common tools used in formulating strategy are the PEST and SWOT analyses. Although they oversimplify complex processes, they serve to focus on key elements of strategic planning.

Review questions

1. What are the advantages and disadvantages of being a sole trader?
2. What are the aspects of the limited company which distinguish it from other types of business ownership?
3. Why are SMEs important to the economy?
4. Explain the reasons behind the adoption of a multidivisional structure for large companies.
5. What is a matrix structure? Assess its advantages and drawbacks in practice for the large organization.
6. What is meant by 'emergent strategy', and how does it differ from a strategic planning approach?
7. Contrast the bureaucratic organization with the network organization. Why is networking now seen as preferable from the organizational point of view, as well as from the perspective of individual employees?
8. A customer orientation is now seen as essential, but what does this imply in terms of organizational structure?
9. How does corporate governance differ from the day-to-day management of a company?
10. Explain the shareholder and stakeholder perspectives on corporate governance.
11. What is the function of a PEST analysis?

Assignments

1. Assume you are the CEO of a large international company in the snack food industry which owns a number of different brands marketed in Europe, Asia and the Americas, with different brands appealing to different national tastes. Assess the advantages and disadvantages of different types of corporate structure for the company.
2. Construct a SWOT analysis for a small company that brews traditional ale.

Further reading

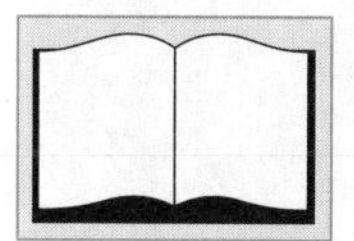

Brown, A. (1998) *Organisational Culture*, 2nd edn (London: Pitman)

Johnson, G. and Scholes, K. (1998) *Exploring Corporate Strategy*, 5th edn (London: Pearson)

Mintzberg, H. (2000) *The Rise and Fall of Strategic Planning* (London: Financial Times/ Prentice Hall)

Mullins, L. (1998) *Management and Organizational Behaviour* (London: Financial Times/ Prentice Hall)

Pugh, D.S. (ed.) (1995) *Organization Theory: Selected Readings*, 4th edn (London: Penguin)

Wheelen, T. and Hunger, J. (2000) *Strategic Management and Business Policy*, 7th edn (New Jersey: Addison Wesley)

Chapter

2

The global economy and globalization processes

Outline of chapter

1. To gain an overview of the processes of globalization
2. To appreciate the role played by transnational corporations in globalization processes
3. To understand the changes in organizations and their strategies in the global and local environments
4. To gain broad appreciation of the issues facing companies and societies generally in the changing global economy

2.0 Introduction

The second half of the twentieth century saw processes of globalization impacting on people's lives across the world: from cosmopolitan urban centres to rural outposts; from advanced industrial complexes to craft workshops. Increasing interconnectedness and interdependence between people, organizations and governments have been facilitated by improvements in technology, especially in the spheres of communication and transport. Yet, while all would agree that the global economy is a reality, the extent of its reach and the depth of its penetration into social and economic life present different configurations in different parts of the world.

This chapter takes a broad overview of the world economy. First, it aims to examine the forces of globalization in perspective; and, second, to assess changes that are taking place in the context of international business. Focus will inevitably fall on multinational corporations, which have been the driving force behind globalization. Their global strategies, centred on overseas production, have been key factors in the interrelationships we now see between economic, political, social, cultural and technological environments in the global economy. This overview will outline the broad contours of these relationships, to be followed by more specific analysis of these environmental dimensions in succeeding chapters.

2.1 Globalization

'Globalization' is not a single, all-encompassing process sweeping the globe. The term more accurately describes a number of processes by which products, people, companies, money and information are able to move freely and quickly around the world, unimpeded by national borders or other territorial limitations. The pace and impact of change may differ from one sphere of activity to another. The use of the term only began in the 1960s, and gained common currency in the 1980s (Waters, 1995). Globalization has brought about dramatic changes in the ways in which people live and work, opening up new opportunities but also creating new risks and uncertainties from forces which seem remote and unfathomable. A consumer in Europe may be affected by upheaval in the financial markets in Asia. A worker in an Asian factory may lose his or her job as a result of a decision taken in a company boardroom in Michigan. The worldwide repercussions of the Asian financial crisis of 1997 brought home to many the interconnectedness of financial markets, which has been one of the most spectacular examples of the effects of globalization. Interpretation of these trends, their impact on local communities and ultimate benefits or detriments are issues of extensive debate. Some commentators see the emergence of an era of the borderless global marketplace. This extreme view has been called '*hyperglobalization*' (Gray, 1998). While not subscribing to it himself, Gray summarizes this school of thought, which:

> envisions the global economy as inhabited by powerless nation-states and homeless corporations. As the powers of sovereign states wither, those of multinational corporations wax. As national cultures become little more than consumer preferences, so companies become ever more cosmopolitan in their corporate cultures. (Gray, 1998, p. 67)

In contrast to the hyperglobalization view, there is the less extreme '*transformational*' view, described by Held et al., as shown in Table 2.1. This view acknowledges globalization as a driving force reshaping modern societies, but takes a more tentative stance on its outcomes, which are transforming the economic, social and political environments in which we live. In this changing global order, shifting patterns are emerging in the functions and powers of companies and governments, and through the emergence of other important forces, such as regionalism. It is argued that, as we live in a constantly changing environment, outcomes are uncertain, and predictions of a world system are premature. This more cautious approach looks at globalization as a complex set of processes, often uneven, rather than a linear progression. It stresses that, while economic globalization has accelerated, local differences, often with deep social and cultural roots, have revealed underlying tensions in the international business environment. Its historical trajectory, shown in the last column of Table 2.1, may be characterized by both deepening integration *and* fragmentation. As the transformational view takes account of the underlying complexity of globalization processes, it has come to be widely recognized as a more valid approach than that of the hyperglobalization school of thought.

Table 2.1 Globalization: two schools of thought

	Hyperglobalists	**Transformationalists**
What's new?	A global age	Historically unprecedented levels of global interconnectedness
Dominant features	Global capitalism; global governance; global civil society	'Thick' (intensive and extensive) globalization
Power of national governments	Declining or eroding	Reconstituted, restructured
Conceptualization of globalization	As a reordering of the framework of human action	As a reordering of interregional relations and action at a distance
Historical trajectory	Global civilization	Indeterminate: global integration and fragmentation

Source: Adapted from Held, D., McGrew, A., Goldblatt, D. and Perraton, J. (1999) *Global Transformations: Politics, Economics and Culture* (Cambridge, Polity Press), p. 10.

WWW
WEBALERT

The International Monetary Fund (IMF) offers a number of issues briefs on its website. One of these, 'Globalization: Threat or opportunity?' is at
http://www.imf.org/external/np/exr/ib/2000/041200.htm

The website of the International Forum on Globalization is http://www.ifg.org

2.2 Internationalization versus globalization: the role of foreign direct investment

Economic globalization, in a sense, has been happening for centuries. International trade was economically important long before industrialization transformed production methods, and before modern technology transformed transport. Wealth generated by companies through international trade could be seen as contributing to the wealth of national economies of sovereign states (Hirst and Thompson, 1999). The growth of international trade relations, greatly enhanced by industrialization and improvements in transport in the late nineteenth century, has been described as a process of **internationalization** (Dicken, 1998). Production, companies, and industry were still essentially based in national economies. National economies were to a considerable degree autonomous, and economic policy issues, such as the imposition of tariffs, were matters for national governments to decide. Growth in world trade was a hallmark of internationalization in the period before 1914. The world before the First World War could be accurately described as a global market, reflecting flourishing international flows of goods, services, capital and people. However, the depth of economic integration has been described as 'shallow', characterized by arm's-length transactions between independent companies based in national economies (Dicken, 1998, p. 5). **Globalization**, by contrast, represents deeper integration, in that international interactions become qualitatively transformed from exchange transactions to long-term, multidimensional links.

At the heart of this deeper integration is **foreign direct investment (FDI)**. Companies may decide to invest in foreign firms in a number of ways. A foreign portfolio investment consists of buying shares (equity), usually under 10 per cent, in the foreign company as an investment only, with a view to relatively short-term gains. By contrast, the FDI investor aims to play a more direct role, with deeper involvement in the management of the company as a productive unit. That control can come through sufficient ownership of the foreign company's equity to give control (usually 30 per cent or more), or contractual, non-equity agreements that give control of the foreign affiliate company. These links, both equity and other alliances, affect both the *home* country (that of the investor) and the *host* country (that of the company invested in).

The growth in FDI has had a pervasive impact on international business. No longer could it be said that a company, its factories and the products it manufactures are necessarily the products of its home nation. Such is the geographical dispersal of production, that a 'German' car may actually be manufactured in South Carolina and a 'Japanese' car in the UK. If the majority of the parts that go into a car assembled at the Nissan plant in the UK are British, it would be logical to think of the car as British. Yet the company, and many of the companies supplying components, are Japanese. With the acquisition by Renault, the French car manufacturer, of a 36.8 per cent share in Nissan in 1999, control effectively passed to Renault, reducing the influence of Japanese managers in Nissan. While consumers might still think in terms of 'Japanese' cars or 'German' cars as having distinctive national characteristics, the concept of national origin of many complex products such as motor vehicles would seem to have ceased to contain any real meaning in the global economy (Reich, 1991).

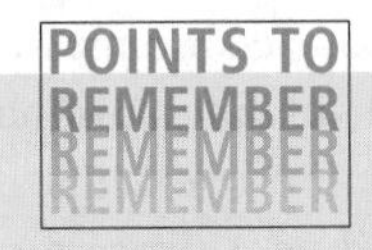

Internationalization versus globalization

- *Internationalization processes:* Extensions of economic activities across national borders, growing *quantitatively*
- *Globalization processes:* Both geographical extensions of economic activity (as in internationalization) and the *qualitatively* different functional integration of internationally dispersed activities

Source: Dicken, P. (1998) *Global Shift: Transforming the World Economy*, 3rd edn (London: Paul Chapman) p. 5.

2.3 Transnational or multinational corporations

While 'multinational' suggests a very large, multidivisional company, the **transnational corporation (TNC)**, has been defined as 'a firm which has the power to co-ordinate and control operations in more than one country, even if it does not own them' (Dicken, 1998, p. 177). This definition by Dicken emphasizes that scope, rather than sheer size, is critical. He highlights three characteristics of the TNC:

- its co-ordination and control of various stages of individual production chains within and between different countries

- its potential ability to take advantage of geographical differences in the distribution of factors of production (such as natural resources, capital, labour) and in state policies (such as taxes, trade barriers, subsidies, and so on)
- its potential geographical flexibility – an ability to switch and to re-switch its sources and operations between locations at an international level. (Dicken, 1998, p. 177)

The growth of TNCs has coincided with industrialization and expansion of trade from the early nineteenth century to the present. TNCs now control a third of world output and about two-thirds of world trade. TNCs vary considerably in size and organizational structure. Advances in information technology and communications have made it possible for small to medium enterprises (SMEs) to 'go global'. For example, in 1996, four-fifths of all Swedish TNCs were SMEs. Small and large firms alike have found that they must seek investment opportunities overseas in order to remain competitive. As a result, the number of TNCs has increased enormously: between the end of the 1960s and the end of the 1990s, the number of TNCs in the 15 most important developed countries had increased from 7,000 to 40,000 (United Nations, 1999a). This growth in the number of TNCs reflects the growth in FDI worldwide.

Most TNCs start life as national companies and expand through internationalizing their operations. They may have a range of motives for doing so, depending on the advantages they hope to gain and the requirements of their particular industry. Proximity to natural resources may be paramount for extraction industries such as mining and oil. For manufacturing industries, availability of abundant low-cost labour may be paramount. For many TNCs the decision to locate in a particular country is guided by the existence of local and regional markets. The particular location can thus become an 'export platform'. Indeed, TNCs may acquire local companies to speed up the process of entering new markets. The TNC which has fashioned a global corporate strategy may thus divide operations between locations, depending on the particular advantages of each. The economic, political and cultural environments also play important roles. Government incentives to overseas investors can enhance the attractiveness of a location. The attractions of Mexico, for example, stem from the availability of low-cost labour, proximity to the large American market and the incentives offered to foreign investors. From the perspective of the host country, on the other hand, FDI may bring mixed blessings, as the example of Brazil in Case Study 2.1 shows. It highlights the importance of governmental and institutional factors in both attracting FDI and promoting strong local companies, as well as the possible conflict between these sets of goals.

Case study 2.1 Brazil's soaring foreign investment: a mixed blessing

Brazil is one of the most attractive countries in the world for FDI, particularly for US and European companies; 405 of *Fortune* magazine's top 500 companies have subsidiaries in Brazil. As a result, the country attracted nearly $30 billion in direct foreign investment. While this would appear to be cause for celebration, a debate has emerged about 'denationalization' and the need to create multinationals of their own. In an important antitrust case in 2000, Brazil's competition authority sanctioned the merger of the country's two largest breweries, to create Ambev, making it the world's fifth largest drinks company. The companies' strongest argument for the merger was that, on their own, both would be liable to foreign takeover. The new company now hopes to launch its best-selling product on the world market. One of Ambev's co-presidents said: 'Companies that remain in one market are increasingly vulnerable ... With the merger we have the platform to become a Brazil-based multinational.'

Brazilian companies in several industries, including petrochemicals, banks and airlines, have sought help from the government to finance the creation of national champions. This position is supported across the political spectrum. Some industry experts claim that the bulk of the FDI has gone only into constructing assembly plants, rather than investment in research and development (R&D), or well-paid jobs in marketing or design. 'The fear is that FDI is only creating "plantation" industry in Brazil, while all the value-added parts of the business remain abroad,' said the former head of the National Development Bank, Antonio Barros de Castro.

The case in favour of government support for Brazilian multinationals is part of the broader project to boost exports. However, sceptics caution that Brazilian companies lobbying for government handouts find the export case a useful one, masking the fact there are other causes of the weak export performance, such as the high cost of financing, steep tax rates, expensive and poor quality transport. On the other hand, research on 85 of the biggest multinationals in Brazil found that in 1998 they invested US$1 billion on research and new technology. The debate highlights the double-edged sword of FDI for Brazil.

Source: Dyer, G., 'Brazil hunts for new national champions', *Financial Times*, 4 May 2000 (reprinted with permission).

Case questions

Why is Brazil attractive to foreign investors?

What are the pros and cons of FDI for Brazil?

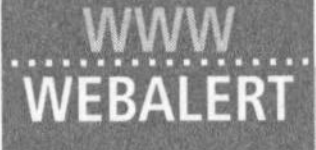

All aspects of FDI in Brazil may be found at
http://www.geoinvestor.com/countries/brazil/economic.htm

2.4 The growth of TNCs as drivers of the global economy

The growth of international trade and transnational manufacturing in the late nineteenth and early twentieth centuries is linked to the growth in TNCs in the major industrial countries of the period. The large UK investors focused on primary products, including mineral extraction and agricultural commodities, during the period before 1914, making the UK the largest holder of foreign capital assets (Dunning, 1993). The bulk of these investments were in developing countries, mainly those under British colonial rule.

Taking advantage of advances in technology, US, British and other European companies invested in overseas production in areas such as machinery, textiles, food, and chemicals. Many inventions, such as the steam engine, electric turbine, and railway locomotive, which originated in Britain, spread to Europe and the US. US companies industrialized later than their European counterparts, and were better placed to take advantage of technological innovation, making use of electrical power and the internal combustion engine to transform factory production processes. Consumer goods of consistent quality could thus be produced for vastly expanded markets, allowing companies to benefit from economies of scale. By the end of the nineteenth century, Ford cars and Singer sewing machines were becoming global brands.

The effects of changes in both manufacturing and transport brought about dramatic changes in society. In America, a bare eight per cent of workers were engaged in manufacturing in 1870, and only one in five lived in a city of 8,000 or more inhabitants. By 1910, the percentage engaged in manufacturing had risen to one third, and the percentage living in cities had risen to more than one half (Reich, 1991). The population of Chicago, the crossroads of East–West commercial activities, grew from 109,260 in 1860 to a staggering 2.2 million in 1910. The large American conglomerates, such as US

Table 2.2 The world's top five TNCs by foreign assets, 1997

Rank by foreign assets	Corporation	Country	Industry
1	General Electric	United States	Electronics
2	Ford Motor Company	United States	Automotive
3	Royal Dutch/Shell Group	Netherlands/United Kingdom	Petroleum
4	General Motors	United States	Automotive
5	Exxon Corporation	United States	Petroleum

Source: United Nations, *World Investment Report 1999* (Geneva: United Nations), p. 78.

Steel, American Telephone & Telegraph, General Electric, Standard Oil, Ford Motor Co. and General Motors, date from this era. These giant companies, whose names are still familiar, exemplify the dominance of American companies in the world economy during the first half of the twentieth century. A look at the league table (Table 2.2) of the five largest TNCs in terms of foreign assets in 1997 shows the extent of American dominance.

2.5 International business in the context of post-war shifts in international power

The period following the Second World War brought changes in both the world economy and world political structures, which went hand in hand. The war had brought severe disruption, and even devastation, to much of the industrialized world, with the exception of America, whose large corporations were thus in a position to expand their already dominant position in the world economy. The destruction was worst in Germany and Japan, where the industrial base and infrastructure had to be rebuilt from scratch. Post-war economic development in both countries has been termed an 'economic miracle'. Major factors (which are examined in detail in Chapter 4) were the ability to exploit technological advances in production and information and the strong role of government in the development processes. The success of corporate rebuilding in both countries provided 'models' of economic development which drew world attention, as well as emulation. Moreover, rapid internationalization of Japanese companies soon had an impact in key sectors such as the motor industry and electronics. Japanese companies targeted the American market, where their competitive strengths soon unsettled domestic producers. In 1960, Japan produced 165,000 automobiles; by 1991, the figure had risen to 13 million, a quarter of the world's output. In 1960, the US produced more than half the world's automobiles, but by 1991, its share had dropped to 18 per cent (Stutz and de Souza, 1998). In the space of less than three decades, the Japanese economy grew to become an economic superpower.

On the political front, the post-war world was dominated by the divide between the 'Western' countries (which included Japan) and the 'Eastern bloc' (which represented the Soviet Union and its satellite countries in Central and Eastern Europe). The East–West 'cold war' has been depicted as one between rival civilizations, the one representing democracy, liberal values and the market economy; the other representing authoritarianism, communist ideology and the state-planned economy. The cold war, with its ideological poles of freedom and authoritarianism, dominated international relations and also investment patterns as economic power blocs developed in both East and West.

The disintegration of the Soviet Union in the early 1990s marked the end of the cold war, creating newly independent states in the former Soviet territory and in the satellite countries of Central and Eastern Europe. These nations represent enormous cultural and social diversity, suppressed under authoritarianism, but allowed to flourish with independence. Referred to as **transition economies**, they have instituted market reforms and set about dismantling state-owned industries through privatization (these changes will be discussed in Chapter 4). At the same time they have designed new democratic political institutions. In the reinvigorated business climate, their new leaders have actively encouraged foreign investment. Foreign TNCs, for their part, have been attracted by cheap labour and prospects of expanding

Case study 2.2 Hugo Boss in the Ukraine

For the German fashion group, Hugo Boss, manufacturing in Kiev has been successful, largely thanks to the efforts of Dietmar Kung. Kung worked initially with two formerly state-owned textile factories which had been privatized by handing them over to their employees. When one of these went bankrupt, Kung managed to acquire it, helped by a deal with an Irish investment company, which took 35 per cent of the equity and, importantly, a promise of guaranteed orders from Hugo Boss. For Hugo Boss, the big attraction was cheap labour, with wages of about $50 (£31) a month, compared with a typical $1,000 in Germany. The factory presented a contrast between past and present, Soviet-style winter coats in clumsy shapes, manufactured alongside designer jackets for Hugo Boss. The Hugo Boss goods are made entirely out of imported fabrics and components.

The workers producing for Boss are specially trained and are paid bonuses for meeting quality standards. Kung says the hardest battle was changing the workers' mentality: 'They wanted to stay as a collective, with everybody treated the same and paid the same. I said: "No. Those who work better must be paid more."' With Hugo Boss buying 80–100 per cent of output, turnover has risen since the 1997 currency crisis to $3 million in 1998. The plant has invested in new equipment, including a computerized control room that will enable the plant to receive designs electronically from Hugo Boss in Germany and transfer them directly to cutting machines in Kiev. However, Kung sees a danger in too much dependency on Hugo Boss and would like it to develop its own brands.

The organization's structure is inefficient, as only 60 per cent of staff are directly involved in production (compared with 95 per cent in a similar factory in Germany). Changes will come only slowly, as agreement must be reached with the company's 650 employee-shareholders. However, small improvements are taking place all the time. Kung says: 'For the textile industry, countries such as Poland already count as developed. Ukraine is not easy, but it is the future for us.'

Source: Wagstyl, S. 'Rare seam of success in Ukraine's fabric', *Financial Times*, 28 December 1999 (reprinted with permission).

Case question

What are the advantages and drawbacks of Kiev as a location?

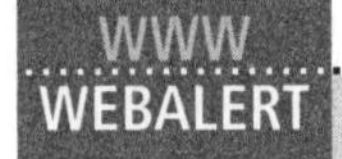

Websites on FDI in Ukraine:
http://www.oecd.org/sge/ccnm/pubs/gd/cdge2011/present.htm
http://www.westukraine.nte/e_index.htm

The website of Hugo Boss is http://www.hugoboss.com

markets covering an area of roughly 400 million inhabitants. The prospects of early European Union (EU) membership for the Czech Republic, Hungary, Poland, Slovenia and Estonia, with others to follow, served to enhance their appeal for foreign investors. In marked contrast to these success stories, the collapse of the Russian economy in the 1990s and the political disintegration of Yugoslavia into its separate national units represent the difficulties of transition. The decade following the end of the cold war, therefore, has revealed the complexities of the political, cultural and social environment, but it has also shown the extent of global integration, in which local and national interests are increasingly bound up with the forces of globalization. These forces are illustrated in Case Study 2.2, on FDI in the Ukraine.

2.6 Trends in globalization processes

The transformation from internationalization centred mainly around trade to globalization of production accelerated from the 1970s onwards. By far the most important player has been, and still is, the US. Yet, as the global economy has become more widely ramified, US companies have lost their former dominant position in outward FDI. US TNCs' share of global FDI stock dropped from nearly two-thirds in the early 1970s to one-third by 1990. Inward investment in the US, on the other hand, grew dramatically, from $13 billion in 1970 to $550.7 billion in 1994 (Stutz and de Souza, 1998). These figures represent an increase from 11 per cent of world totals in 1975 to 21 per cent by 1985. These inward investors were not just companies from Europe and Japan, but also from the newly industrialized economies of Southeast Asia, such as Korea's large industrial conglomerates, which have invested heavily in both Europe and the US.

It is generally true that the home countries of most outward investors are in the developed world, while developing countries are net recipients of foreign investment. Outward investment is dominated by relatively few TNCs: 100 control about one-fifth of global foreign assets. These corporate giants are overwhelmingly from the developed countries, nearly 90 per cent coming from the '**triad**' blocs (the US, EU countries and Japan). The US is the largest outward investor and also the largest recipient of inward investment. The 1990s saw a declining share of FDI flowing to developed countries and a

Figure 2.1 World inflows of FDI

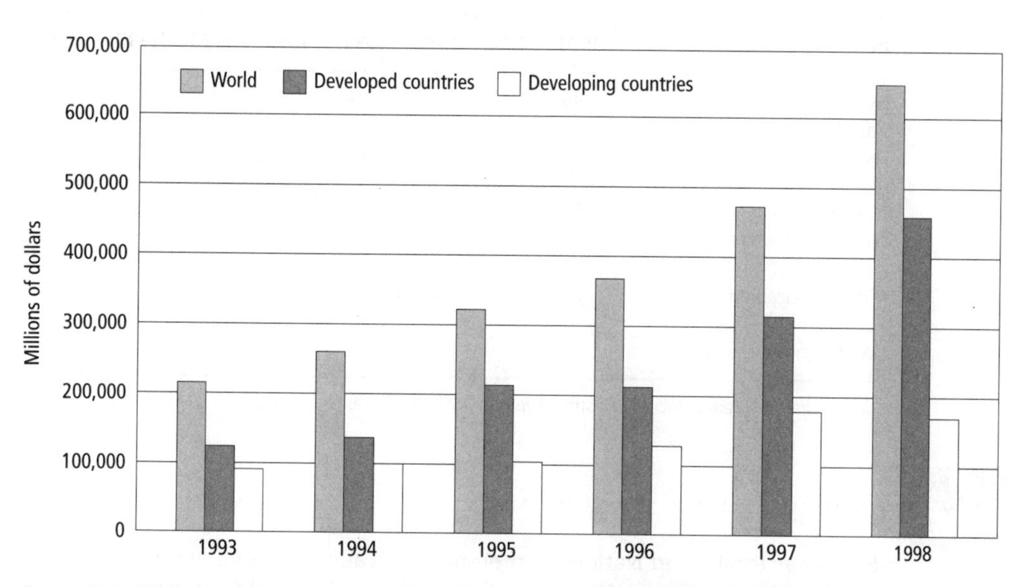

Source: United Nations, *World Investment Report 1999* (Geneva: United Nations).

corresponding growth in investment in developing countries, as can be seen in Figure 2.1. This trend was reversed in 1998, which registered a 39 per cent increase in inflows to developed countries (UN, 1999a, p. 11). The UK gained substantially in terms of both inward and outward investment, as is shown in Figure 2.2, although outflows have outstripped inflows in the 1990s. The share of FDI in developing countries reached a peak of 37 per cent in 1997, and declined to 28 per cent in 1998 (UN, 1999a, p. xx). Commenting on the

Figure 2.2 UK FDI: inflows and outflows

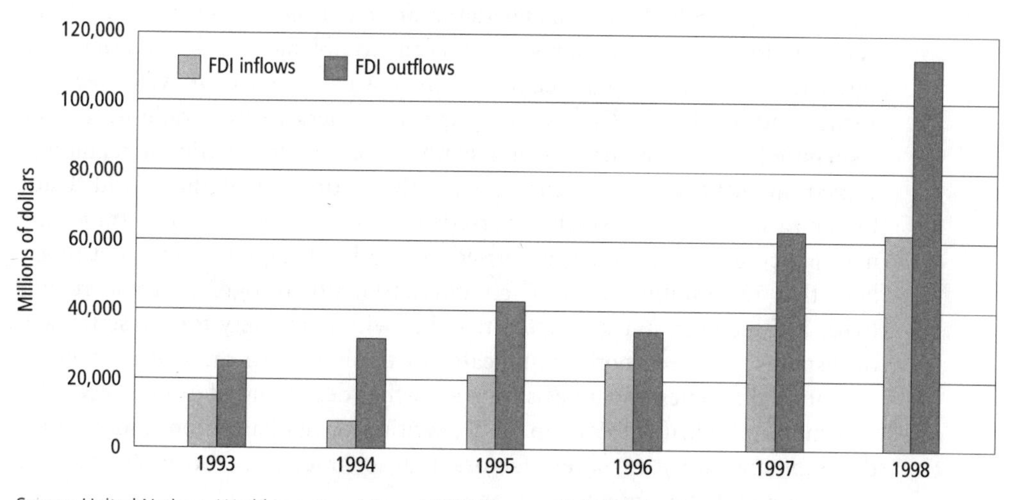

Source: United Nations, *World Investment Report 1999* (Geneva: United Nations).

Table 2.3 National regulatory changes, 1991–98

Item	1991	1992	1993	1994	1995	1996	1997	1998
Number of countries that introduced changes in their investment regime	35	43	57	49	64	65	76	60
Number of regulatory changes, of which:	82	79	102	110	112	114	151	145
More favourable to FDI	80	79	101	108	106	98	135	136
Less favourable to FDI	2	–	1	2	6	16	16	9

Source: United Nations, *World Investment Report 1999* (Geneva: United Nations) p. 115.

WWW
WEBALERT

Each year the United Nations Conference on Trade and Development (UNCTAD) publishes its World Investment Report. Highlights are available from its website at http://www.unctad.org/en/pub/pslwir99.htm

The International Chamber of Commerce's world business organization site is http://www.iccwbo.org/

changing nature of FDI, the *World Investment Report 1999* found that, 'increasingly ... TNCs are ... operating internationally through non-equity arrangements, including strategic partnerships', noting in particular a rise in information technology partnerships (UN, 1999a, p. xviii).

National governments in both developed and developing countries have made regulatory changes to attract investment, as Table 2.3 shows. Reducing regulatory controls, known as **liberalization**, has been accompanied by trade liberalization. These measures have been complemented by international agreements, the most significant of which was the General Agreement on Tariffs and Trade (GATT), whereby many barriers to free trade have been dismantled (although many still remain in place). International regulation gained an institutional dimension with the setting up of the World Trade Organization (WTO), which superseded GATT in 1994. World trade and national competitiveness are discussed in detail in Chapter 9. Suffice it to say here that the establishment of an internationally recognized trade regime (with 135 member states to date), together with machinery for the settlement of disputes, has been both an indicator of the impact of the global economy on national regimes and a basis for the further deepening of global networks.

Amin and Thrift (1994, pp. 2–5), writing on globalization and regional development, identify seven factors that characterize the widening and deepening global economy. They are:

1 Increasing centrality of financial structure, and degree of power exerted by financial structures over businesses and national economies.
2 Increasing importance of knowledge as a factor of production, whereby 'knowledge structure' is less and less tied to particular national or local business cultures.
3 Transnationalization of technology, coupled with an enormous increase in the rapidity of redundancy of given technologies.
4 Rise of global oligopolies, facilitated by accelerated technological change, the mobility of capital and advances in transport and communication.
5 Rise of transnational economic diplomacy and the globalization of state power, with 'plural authority' structures replacing traditional power structures.
6 Rise of global cultural flows and 'deterritorialized' signs, meanings and identities, while retaining cultural heterogeneity.
7 Rise of new global geographies, with emphasis on the local within global networks.

As Amin and Thrift point out, there are numerous strands within each of the above factors, and each is the focus of research and debate on the precise nature and scope of the globalization trends. Detailed analysis of each of these spheres will follow in later chapters of this book. Focus at present is on the seventh factor, the rise of new global geographies, which serves as a theme linking all seven factors.

TNCs are able to shift production from one location to another with unprecedented ease. To meet the challenges of the changing competitive environment, the TNC views its operations from a global perspective in which strategy formulators seek to take advantage of the benefits offered by each specific geographic location. Sourcing components from widely dispersed locations has become a trend in evolving global strategy. It is estimated that a quarter to a third of world trade is intra-firm trade, that is, between affiliated companies of the same parent, which trade with each other across national borders (Gray, 1998).

Global networks now function at numerous geographical levels, from local through to transnational. The rise of regional groupings, such as the EU and the North American Free Trade Agreement (NAFTA), has facilitated both regional trade and cross-border investment. **Regionalism**, which will be discussed in detail in Chapter 9, can be seen as a parallel trend to globalization in the global economy, linking neighbouring states, which often share historical and cultural links, as well as economic ties.

Globalization can hardly be said to have yet produced a borderless 'deterritorialized' world. It would be more accurate to say that globalization represents a 'redefinition of places', in which 'the local meets the global'

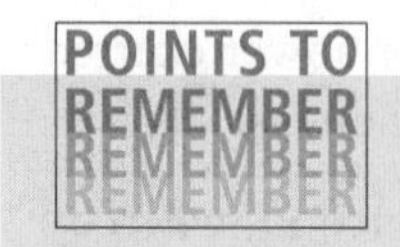

Trends in globalization processes

- Increasing geographic 'scanning' ability of large TNCs
- Increasing flows of FDI, encompassing a wider range of countries
- Liberalization of regulatory controls on FDI by governments, including privatization
- Growing international regulatory regimes, such as the WTO
- Growth in regionalism, through organizations such as the EU
- Interfirm networks, extending from local to global

(Amin and Thrift, 1994, p. 10). Global networks traverse national boundaries, reaching down to the local level. The result has been greater interconnectedness and interdependencies between the various levels – transnational, regional, national and local. Firms, often in partnership, have played the key roles in these new networks. The remaining sections of this chapter look at globalization from the point of view of the firm.

2.7 Globalization of the firm

The question of why firms seeking foreign expansion locate in particular places and not in others has given rise to location theories based on costs of production and the markets for the firm's products (Dicken and Lloyd, 1990). An influential early theorist, Alfred Weber, devised a location theory based on the least-cost approach. A company, he argued, would choose a location which offers the lowest transport and labour costs. Further, he argued that costs are reduced by **industrial agglomeration**, which is the concentration of several producers in a single location. Proximity of suppliers and customers is a crucial factor, which supports the clustering of industries in particular locations.

Perhaps the most comprehensive theoretical attempt to explain FDI is John Dunning's 'eclectic' paradigm. It is also called the '**OLI paradigm**', after the variables which, according to Dunning, affect a firm's decision to internationalize, namely advantages of ownership, location and internalization (Dunning, 1993, pp. 76–9). Under *ownership-specific advantages* we find property rights over assets, broadly defined and including both tangible and intangible resources: these include capital, technology, labour, natural resources, know-how, organizational and entrepreneurial skills. Second, the firm can consider *internalization advantages*. This element, derived from the theory of the firm developed by economists, looks to the reduction of transaction costs through hierarchical organization as an alternative to reliance on market forces. A firm may thus acquire control of the supply of raw materials or components, achieving vertical integration which reduces costs. Third, the firm looks to advantages offered by particular locations, or *location-specific advantages*. These include the cultural, political and social environment of the country: low labour costs, government incentives and the size and structure of markets.

The contribution of Dunning has been to offer a multidisciplinary theoretical framework highlighting the interrelatedness of the three variables. The decision to produce abroad depends on all three conditions being satisfied, but the configuration of the factors, and their relative importance to each other, will vary from one firm to another, and from situation to situation. The inbuilt flexibility of interpretation is one of the strong points of the framework as an analytical tool.

In relation to market-driven TNC investment, Peter Dicken envisages a sequential process, starting with the firm serving only the domestic market, and moving through stages to overseas production (Figure 2.3).

A company currently producing for its domestic market may see continued growth as dependent on entering overseas markets. Typically, it will export its products initially using the services of an agent and, depending on sales, seek a more long-term presence in the overseas market. As Dicken's model indicates, this expansion may take a variety of forms. The company may **license** a local manufacturer to produce the product, where intellectual property rights such as patents (for inventions) and trademarks (for brands) are involved. In this arrangement, the local company buys the right to use the

Figure 2.3 Sequential development of a transnational corporation

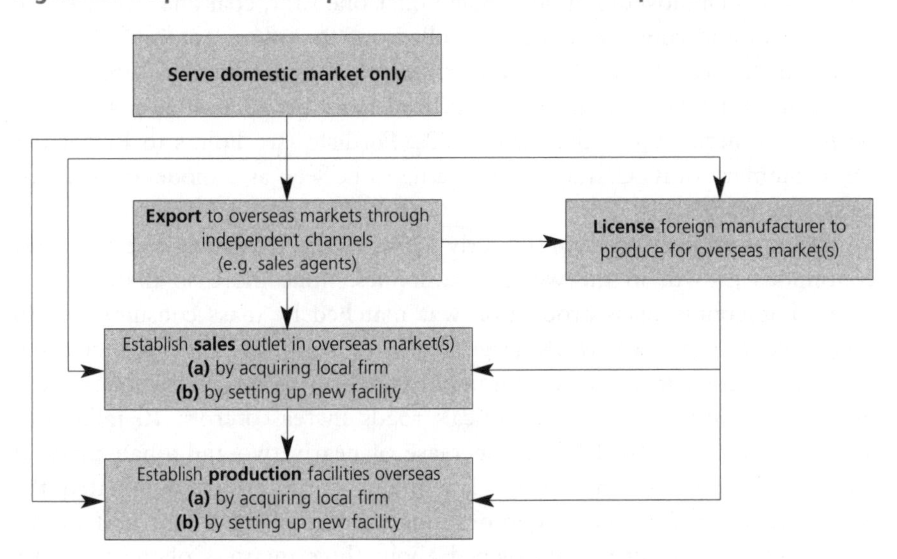

Source: Dicken, P. (1998) *Global Shift: Transforming the World Economy*, 3rd edition (London: Paul Chapman Publishing) p. 191.

trademark or process, and may gain expertise in the process. It is possible for a company seeking overseas expansion by this means to exert a good deal of control through careful drafting of the licensing agreement, and, importantly, through the build-up of trust between the parties.

The stage of setting up local production commonly involves a joint venture. The **joint venture** is an agreement with a local partner to produce or sell a product or service. The setting up of a new facility by a foreign firm, such as a new plant on a 'greenfield' site, is prohibited in some countries, and finding a local partner is a necessity, as in China. Even where not a legal requirement, the joint venture has become a popular option for foreign investors, as local firms' 'inside' knowledge of the business environment is invaluable. The joint venture may involve the formation of a new entity in which both partners acquire ownership. Typically, the local firm holds a 51 per cent stake and the foreign firm 49 per cent. Nonetheless, the industry expertise of the foreign partner gives it the upper hand in management control of the operation. A good deal of trust between the partners is required to make a success of the joint venture, especially given the likely cultural differences between the partners (Hoon-Halbauer, 1999).

2.8 Industrial production: the legacy of Fordism

The changing nature of industrial operations, largely as a result of technological advances, has had a profound impact on manufacturing industries in particular. As industrialization took hold, the factory became the basic unit of production from the late nineteenth century onwards. The growth of the factory probably reached its zenith with Henry Ford. In Ford's River Rouge plant, which employed 35,000 people under one roof, coal and iron went in at one end, and complete Ford cars rolled out the other. **'Fordism'**, as it has been called, encapsulates the characteristics of mass production. While at the lowest level it served to describe industrial mass production as practised in post-war America up to the early 1970s, Fordism (see Points to Remember for a summary of its characteristics) came to be seen as a model of this type of system generally.

The post-war period from the early 1950s to the 1970s was one of almost continuous growth in the world's economies, none more so than the US, where burgeoning mass production was matched by mass consumption. In this 'golden age', America's large factories supplied an ever-increasing demand for consumer goods – automobiles, television sets, refrigerators. The numbers of automobiles on America's roads increased from 10 million in 1949 to 24 million by 1957, an increase of nearly two-and-a-half times in only eight years (Reich, 1991). The major corporations dominated the economy: about 500 major corporations accounted for about half of the nation's industrial output and owned about three quarters of the country's industrial assets. General Motors alone accounted for three per cent of the

Essentials of Fordism

- Large factories where there was mass production based on assembly line processes, operated by semi-skilled workers
- Recognition of trade unions with industry-wide collective bargaining powers
- Standardized products designed for mass markets, with long runs
- Growth dependent on rising productivity based on economies of scale, and growing demand generated by rising wages
- Organization based on the large, multidivisional corporate structure, controlled from the centre
- Production systems based on internalization of processes where economies of scale are achievable
- Oligopolistic corporations controlling markets and leading to control of prices

gross national product in 1955, making it the world's largest manufacturing company. The expression, 'what is good for General Motors is good for the country', contained more than a grain of truth.

Then, in the 1970s, the boom faltered. A major factor was the fourfold increase in oil prices brought in by the Organization of Petroleum Exporting Countries (OPEC). But there were other factors too. Labour costs and wage settlements had been rising, as had costs of raw materials. Meanwhile, companies in other parts of the world were becoming more competitive, leading to demands for protectionism for US industries. The Bretton Woods international monetary system, designed in 1944 to keep national currencies in line with each other, disintegrated in 1971, when the US adopted a floating exchange rate. These events can be interpreted as simply part of the natural cycle of economic activity, which consists of long waves of boom followed by slump. On this interpretation, a slowdown was bound to follow the golden age. However, many commentators see deeper causes, largely stemming from the tendencies inherent in Fordism from the outset. Thus, explanations of the break-up of the Fordist system have become part of a larger debate on the development of modern capitalism in the context of globalization.

As a system producing high-volume, standardized products, Fordist production was inflexible and bureaucratic: the launch of a new product typically required several years' planning, entailing the complete alteration of production machinery. Bureaucratic hierarchies depended on detailed production manuals and job descriptions, leaving little scope for individual initiative, and also engendering boredom and minimal job satisfaction for those blue-collar workers doing monotonous, repetitive jobs. Labour relations with management were highly confrontational, based on a system of national collective bargaining. The success of the system depended on sustained consumer demand for the mass-produced goods it churned out. If consumer taste shifted to non-standard or customized products, or if consumer spending slumped, companies were left high and dry. Recession in the 1970s brought home the unpalatable truth that the large American companies had become uncompetitive globally.

Challenges from Japanese manufacturers, later to be joined by those from newly industrialized countries, highlighted what was called the crisis of Fordism and a engendered a rethinking of industrial organization.

2.9 Post-Fordist organizations

It is generally agreed that Fordism, in its industrial, economic and political embodiments, represented the end of an era, but there is less consensus about the new era unfolding. The terms 'postindustrial' and 'postmodern' have been used to describe the **post-Fordist** era. Some scholars take the view that what followed Fordism has been a transitional phase, rather than a radical break with the past (Amin and Thrift, 1994, p. 2). There is agreement on some aspects of the post-Fordist industrial landscape, focusing on the increasing importance of technological advance and the need for flexibility in response to markets.

The post-Fordist world is one in which diversity and specialization are replacing conformity and standardization. As a consequence, industries and

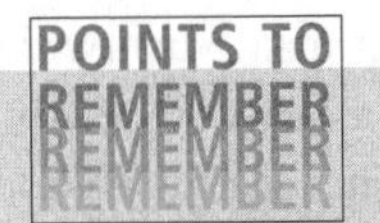

Post-Fordist industry

- The increasing importance of technology and information systems in the new industrial 'paradigm'
- Replacement of mass consumerism with recognition of a variety of consumer markets, in which choice, quality and product differentiation are paramount
- Decentralization of management structures
- Fragmentation of industrial complexes into smaller production units capable of flexible specialization
- Shifting geographical centres of industries, with more localized clusters of firms
- Organizational flexibility and decentralized management structures within the firm, recognizing the need for flexibility in the assigning and carrying out of tasks by management and workers

firms may vary considerably in their organizational structures and corporate cultures. For example, industrial relations are influenced by the particular social and cultural environment in which a firm is located. Confrontational labour relations can be counterproductive, and there are numerous ways to achieve a more consensual approach to employee relations, some involving direct worker participation and some involving the mediation of trade unions. The 'Californian' model of an unstructured workplace, with no unions, flexible contracts and strong corporate culture, suits Silicon Valley, but is not universally applicable. On the other hand, the Japanese model, which has been hugely successful, seems to present a hybrid of Fordist and post-Fordist characteristics.

The Japanese model has been called one of '**flexible mass production**' (Sabel, 1994, p. 122). The large Japanese manufacturing companies, such as Toyota, the leading car maker, allow for flexibility in production and organization within a hierarchical structure. While producing for mass markets, the system of centralized product development is nonetheless able to respond to changes in demand, making use of technology to reduce development time. New automated manufacturing equipment facilitates the rapid implementation of changes and variations in the product. This flexibility is reflected in a workforce trained to understand the entire process involved in the new technology, enabling workers to change tasks with ease and to operate just-in-time delivery systems. High levels of knowledge and training are also essential to the Japanese philosophy of quality control, which emphasizes worker involvement and contribution (summed up in the concept of ***kaizen***). A consensus-based system of worker participation is a long way from the confrontational labour relations of classical mass production.

A culture of co-operation, it has been argued, reflects a tendency towards collectivism in Japanese society generally, leaving open to question the transferability of these production systems into other cultural environments. Nonetheless, the Japanese model has been copied the world over, by Western companies as well as by Japanese companies in their foreign transplants. Its attractiveness lies in the successful combination of goals which had been seen as mutually incompatible: price competitiveness through scale economies, responsiveness to changes in demand, emphasis on quality and more harmonious labour–management relations. Writing in 1989, Sabel cited a dramatic case: at Freemont, California, Toyota and General Motors rebuilt an abandoned General Motors assembly plant, reorganized work according to Toyota's principles and rehired selected employees from the old facility – which had a history of bitter labour disputes – to operate the new one. The New United Motors Company became almost 50 per cent more efficient than the old General Motors plant on the same site, and also almost 50 per cent more efficient than comparable General Motors assembly plants which were modernized while Freemont was closed (Sabel, 1994, p. 137).

Minifile

KAIZEN

The medium-size company, AB Electronics in Cardiff, is one of many that have found dramatic increases in productivity as a result of *kaizen* training. The company, which makes car components such as wiper motors and heating controls, exports about half its annual output. Its managing director says: 'Despite the strength of sterling, we have been able to compete more effectively in global markets as a direct result of using *kaizen* principles'. The new approach involved dividing the workforce into multi-level teams, including staff from administration, production logistics and other departments. A team would be given a week to concentrate on a particular issue, for example, the wastefulness of the product-labelling process. This is known as the '*kaizen* blitz'. The team would then have authority to make changes, including buying new equipment. '*Kaizen* has changed our company culture,' said the managing director, 'and is directly responsible for reducing scrap, improving quality and improving health and safety'.

The operations manager of another company, Avon Automotive, which has successfully used *kaizen* techniques, highlights three potential problems:

1. The deepest pitfall is to bite off more than you can chew. Tackle small elements of the business relating to specific processes
2. Failure to sustain the changes made
3. The most fundamental problem is reluctance by senior managers to devolve responsibility. Avon Automotive's operations manager says that 'when staff know they can question everything and are allowed by senior managers to make changes, they build a tremendous enthusiasm for their work and a commitment to improvement'.

Source: Smith, D.S., '*Kaizen*: that's Japanese for helping Britain work better', *The Sunday Times*, 16 January 2000.

A leading book on *kaizen* is *The Kaizen Blitz: Accelerating Breakthroughs in Productivity and Performance*, by Laraia, A.C., Moody, P. and Hall, R. (John Wiley, 1999).

WWW
WEBALERT

See the Kaizen Institute's website at http://www.kaizen-institute.com/kzn.htm

The *kaizen* blitz was pioneered by the Association For Manufacturing Excellence, whose website is http://www.ame.org/

2.10 Organizational changes and TNCs

TNCs increasingly seek a greater variety of organizational forms for their international activities, which have accompanied the geographical dispersal of their operations. The proliferation of strategic alliances and other innovative types of co-operative alliance reflects the need for greater organizational flexibility in the complex international environment, as well as the perceived need to develop relational ties in the differing cultural environments of each location. Globalization and localization strategies are thus perceived as complementary, rather than contradictory.

Modern organizational forms for international companies have evolved in a number of ways. The firm may have multiple divisions which are subsidiary companies wholly owned by the parent company. Or, as is increasingly common, it may subcontract or 'outsource' products and services. The **subcontractor** is legally an independent firm, who supplies goods or services on the basis of market exchange. Subcontractors in the manufacturing industries often build up informal, relational links with customers over time, even formalized by cross-shareholdings (especially common in Japan), but remain legally independent. Contrast their position with that of the **subsidiary**, which is owned by a parent company. For the TNC, acquisition of a subsidiary is, as we have seen, a means of internalization, circumventing the risks of the open market. By contrast, restructuring in the auto industry at the end of the 1990s saw a shift towards **externalization**, whereby the auto companies look beyond existing suppliers, seeking competitive terms from other suppliers in global marketplaces, aided by use of the internet. A result has been the 'freeing' of suppliers, who themselves are free to seek customers independently. General Motors spun off its components subsidiary, Delphi Automotive Systems, in 1998. In just under a year Delphi had drummed up new non-General Motors business amounting to 60 per cent of its total business. Ford's components subsidiary, Visteon, is also seeking independence from its parent, forming its own alliances as a first step.

In the new era of post-Fordist industrial restructuring, the global corporation has effectively 'localized' its strategy. The corporate strategies of the multinationals rely on their ability to co-ordinate production in their various geographical centres, seeking the greatest efficiency in each. The availability of abundant cheap labour in some countries and regions, in Asia and Latin America for example, has given these locations favoured status, whereas economic development in less endowed parts of the world, such as Africa, has hardly progressed. The five most popular host countries in the developing world for FDI investment are China, Brazil, Mexico, Singapore and Indonesia. These countries accounted for 55 per cent of FDI flows to all developing countries in 1998 (UN, 1999a). FDI flows to the 48 least-developed countries, on the other hand, account for only 1.5 per cent of flows to developing countries generally, and only 0.5 per cent of world FDI flows. Globalization, then, has favoured some cities and regions, but not others. An example of this is the thriving software industry which has grown up in the unlikely setting of Bangalore in India. A consequence has been rivalry between regions at sub-national level to attract foreign investors.

2.11 Global and local markets

Improved transport and communications, and especially the rise in e-commerce, have brought the notion of a global marketplace closer to reality. However, the spread of global markets does not necessarily imply a growing uniformity in consumer tastes and the melting away of national markets. Theorists of globalization in its extreme form, as described earlier in this chapter, predicted the fading away of local differences and diminution of local autonomy. Yet, global corporate strategy has moved away from the production of a standard product for all markets. A major theme of this book is the continuing diversity which persists *within* the global economy. TNCs have become sensitive to locational differences of all kinds: cultural values, religious values, political sensitivities, legal constraints, levels of technological development and many other aspects of the business environment. The internet has made it possible for companies to acquire more information about local markets all over the globe. The ability to respond and adapt to local differences and changing tastes has become an imperative for the global company in the new competitive environment. Coca-Cola, the subject of Case Study 2.3, shows how the company's global strategy has evolved to accommodate local tastes and decentralized management.

2.12 Transnationality of the firm

Corporations, like individuals, are influenced by their own national environment and culture, but to what extent do they transform themselves into truly global companies as they grow? There is a school of thought which holds that corporations, as they become global, become 'denationalized' (Reich, 1991; Ohmae, 1995). However, there is considerable research to suggest that, in their structures and behaviour, companies reflect their national origins, and carry on doing so when they have become global enterprises (Dicken, 1998). Research by Pauly and Reich (1997) shows that national institutional and ideological frameworks form a 'permanent imprint' on multinationals based in the US, Germany, and Japan, the three home countries of 75 out of the world's top 100 multinationals. They conclude that there are enduring differences between companies of these different nationalities, which determine their internal governance, financial structures, R&D strategy, investment and other strategic decisions.

Since 1990, UNCTAD has compiled a 'transnationality index', composed of three ratios: foreign assets/total assets; foreign sales/total sales; and foreign employment/total employment. It has found that overall transnationality of the world's top 100 TNCs has grown from 51 per cent in 1990 to 55 per cent in 1997. The list of the top ten TNCs in terms of transnationality appears in Table 2.4. It is noticeable that no US or Japanese company appears in the list, an indication that companies originating in smaller domestic markets have

Case study 2.3 Putting the fizz back into Coca-Cola

Thirty years ago, Coca-Cola made one of the most memorable commercials in advertising history when it gathered a group of 200 people on a hilltop in Italy, each holding a bottle of Coke and singing: 'I'd like to buy the world a Coke'. In a sense, it was a defining moment for the notion of the global brand – the idea that the whole world could be united in its desire for a single product. The company even claims that Coke is the second most understood word on the planet after OK. The company took off as a global brand following the Second World War, when 64 bottling plants were built round the world to supply US troops wherever they were. A boom in global sales followed. But in the late 1990s, the company suffered a series of setbacks which, it now sees, reflected its not having moved with the changes in the world environment.

What went wrong? The company became overcentralized, insensitive, slow to react to consumer tastes. Decisions on local marketing, local communications and even which local charity to support were taken in Atlanta, the corporate HQ. It was slow to respond to contamination scares in Europe, and its image suffered as a result. There have been clashes with antitrust regulators in Europe and Chile, which also damaged the company's reputation, and its share price. Coca-Cola has now begun a radical rethinking of its organization and its strategy. Coca-Cola has decided to decentralize, to localize its strategy, starting with the laying off of 6,000 workers (21 per cent of the workforce) at its Atlanta headquarters in the US. The company aims to give much more power to local managers. They will be able to devise their own marketing strategies and choose the products from the Coke portfolio that are best suited to local tastes.

The new chairman, Douglas Daft, says:

> we do not do business in markets; we do business in societies... In our recent past, we succeeded because we understood and appealed to global commonalities. In our future, we'll succeed because we will also understand and appeal to local differences. The 21st century demands nothing less. (Daft, D., *Financial Times*, 27 March 2000)

The company is aiming to respond to the growing consumer demand for healthier drinks, such as energy drinks, water and juice. It estimates that in the future, China will become its biggest market.

Sources: Liu, B., 'Coca-Cola cuts 21% of workforce', *Financial Times*, 27 January 2000; Daft, D., 'Back to classic Coke,' *Financial Times*, 27 March 2000; Tomkins, R., 'Global chief thinks locally,' *Financial Times*, 1 August 2000; States, A. 'Message in a bottle,' *Financial Times Business*, 13 January 2001.

Case question

Why has a strong global brand such as Coke changed course?

Coca-Cola is at http://www.cocacola.com

Table 2.4 The world's top TNCs in terms of degree of transnationality, 1997

Transnationality Index	Foreign assets	Corporation	Country	Industry	Transnationality Index (%)
1	23	Seagram Co.	Canada	Beverages	97.6
2	14	Asea Brown Boveri (ABB)	Switzerland	Electrical equipment	95.7
3	52	Thomson Corp.	Canada	Printing and publishing	95.1
4	9	Nestlé SA	Switzerland	Food	93.2
5	18	Unilever N.V.	Netherlands	Food	92.4
6	82	Solvay SA	Belgium	Chemicals/ pharmaceuticals	92.3
7	75	Electrolux AB	Sweden	Electrical appliances	89.4
8	27	Philips Electronics N.V	Netherlands	Electronics	86.4
9	15	Bayer AG	Germany	Chemicals	82.7
10	20	Roche Holding AG	Switzerland	Pharmaceuticals	82.2

Source: United Nations, *World Investment Report 1999* (Geneva: United Nations) p. 83.

higher degrees of transnationality. While measurements such as these are limited as tools, they are indicative, along with results of other research, that the global company is still more myth than reality.

It might be expected that the trend towards localization should impact on the TNC, eventually weakening the home-base bias and strengthening local links. However, the depth of local embeddedness can vary enormously, depending on central management decision-making and the degree of local autonomy of foreign units. Bartlett and Ghoshal (1998) envisage four types of TNC organization:

1 *the multinational organizational model* – the large firm decentralizes its overseas operations, giving a high degree of autonomy to local units. While local responsiveness is achieved, fragmentation and lack of overall co-ordination are disadvantages.

2 *the international organization model* – there is more control by the centre over the overseas units in this model, and more co-ordination from the company's headquarters. This model is conducive to exploiting firm-

specific assets such as technology advances or market power, as exemplified by the large American companies.

3 *the classic global organizational model* – in this model the parent company exerts tight control over overseas units, allowing little scope for local decision-making. The Japanese plants established in the US in the 1970s and 80s are examples of this model.

4 *the complex global organizational model* – this fourth model is emerging through the development of integrated global networks. The other three models represent a choice: either local autonomy or central control. By contrast, this model, which takes into account the more recent forms of strategic alliances, seems to combine the twin goals of localization and central co-ordination.

If a production unit is allowed to choose its own suppliers among local firms, then this externalization will allow it to develop its own relational ties with other firms in the area. Hence, networks grow up over time, and the firm becomes enmeshed in the local social, cultural and political environment. The growth of these 'industrial districts' benefits local firms and the local host economy. However, it need not follow that greater strategic involvement of subsidiaries at the local level will translate into strategic roles in the organization overall. The organization is ultimately looking to achieve global strategic objectives, which are served by weighing up the advantages of specific locations. As the growth of FDI in the global economy has demonstrated, a company may favour one location for the time being, but abandon it and relocate tomorrow, as costs and markets dictate. Even the capital investment associated with building new manufacturing units does not guarantee long-term commitment. In 1993, Hoover closed its vacuum cleaner factory in Dijon in France with the loss of 600 jobs, and then created 400 new jobs at its Scottish plant, where new working practices and wage structures would result in reduction in costs by a quarter. The French government immediately protested at the apparent transfer of jobs from France to Scotland, but their protests were in vain.

2.13 The globalization debate

The overview of the processes of globalization outlined here show TNCs as the drivers of the global economy, with freedom to move among the world's states and regions at will. Whether globalization is seen as essentially beneficial, increasing overall well-being, or, at the other extreme, essentially unchecked power threatening well-being, depends considerably on one's point of view. The low-skilled worker who has just lost a job due to cheap foreign competition is likely to feel a victim of globalization; while shareholders and directors in a successful global company will extol its benefits, as will countries whose economies grow as a result of foreign investment. For the opponents of globalization the most worrying fact is that a company as a capitalist enterprise exists, first and foremost, to maximize its profits. While it does much that is good, such as providing employment, filling shops everywhere with high-quality goods and leading technological innovation which promotes well-being, it is also capable of much that is bad, such as damaging the environment, creating risks to human health and widening the gap between the world's haves and have-nots. As we have seen in this chapter, the benefits of globalization have not as yet trickled down to all the world's countries: on the contrary, economic growth has brought growing inequalities between nations.

One of the aspects of globalization that is particularly worrying to sceptics is that large commercial organizations are perceived as unaccountable to wider society. How to devise governance mechanisms that reconcile corporate interests with society's broader interests is one of the major challenges facing the large TNCs. (This challenge is discussed in Chapter 12.)

Companies are becoming increasingly sensitive to the environments in which they operate. No doubt, this stance partly reflects the perception that shareholder value is sensitive to human and environmental issues. In a world of instant communication, corporate disasters make news the world over. Global economic integration has transformed societies, but the process has revealed a multiplicity of divergent interests, values and goals, not simply between countries but between groups and regions within societies. Understanding the changing dynamics of these interactions is a key to business success in the globalized environment.

2.14 Conclusions

1. Through processes of globalization, products, people, companies, money and information move freely across national borders. While international trade has been thriving for centuries, the deeper economic integration which defines globalization has taken off only since the end of the Second World War.

2. Facilitated, above all, by technological advances in communications and transport, globalization has brought about growing interconnectedness between people, organizations and governments in global networks.

3. The driving force behind the new global economy has been the TNCs, whose global strategies have rested primarily on FDI, which has played a transformative role, particularly evident in emerging economies around the world.

4 Globalization of production has brought about a renewed focus on the local within the global enterprise. TNCs, seeking location-specific advantages, while naturally drawn to cheap labour, increasingly recognize the significance of wider implications of local diversity in cultural, political, social and technological environments.

5 'Fordist' mass production systems of the 1950s and 60s, producing standardized products for mass consumer markets, have given way to a variety of organizational changes, involving greater decentralization and localization. An aim of newer, 'flexible specialization' models is to be able to respond quickly and efficiently to the demands of changing markets.

6 Geographical dispersal of functions within the global company, combined with more flexible organizational structures, have led to a growth in strategic alliances between firms, local and global, blurring organizational boundaries.

7 The undoubted power of TNCs has been highlighted by the geographical scanning ability. The globalization debate has focused on questions of accountability of TNCs, highlighting the multiplicity of interests and values that make up the international environment.

Review questions

???

1. How is globalization distinguishable from internationalization?
2. What are the leading schools of thought on the extent and depth of globalization?
3. What are the chief features of the transnational organization?
4. What is FDI? Give three of the reasons for FDI on the part of companies.
5. How have the post-war shifts in international power led to (a) growing FDI; and (b) changing patterns of FDI?
6. What is the role of national liberalization policies in attracting FDI?
7. What are the elements of Dunning's eclectic paradigm of FDI?
8. What were the advantages and drawbacks of Fordist production systems?
9. How do localization strategies fit into global strategies for the global company?
10. What are the broad contours of the controversy over the direction of globalization?

Assignments

1. Examine the major globalization processes at work in today's world economy, and assess their impact on the international business environment.
2. Assess the extent to which transnational corporations' FDI strategies have generated rethinking of organizational links across national borders, including greater localization within a global strategy.

Further reading

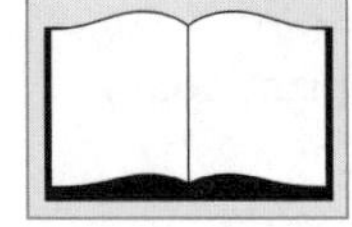

Dicken, P. (1998) *Global Shift: Transforming the World Economy*, 3rd edn (London: Paul Chapman)

Giddens, A. (2000) *Runaway World: How Globalization is Reshaping our Lives* (Andover: Routledge)

Held, D., McGrew, A., Goldblatt, D., and Perraton, J. (1999) *Global Transformations: Politics, Economics and Culture* (Cambridge: Polity Press)

Hirst, P. and Thompson, G. (1999) *Globalization in Question*, 2nd edn (Cambridge: Polity Press)

Reich, R. (1991) *The Work of Nations: Preparing Ourselves for 21st Century Capitalism* (London: Simon & Schuster)

Zysman, J. (1996) 'The myth of a "global" economy: enduring national foundations and emerging regional realities', *New Political Economy*, **1**(2): 157–84

Chapter 3

The national economic environment

Outline of chapter

LEARNING OBJECTIVES

1. To define and apply the major concepts used to analyse the macroeconomic environment
2. To appreciate the aims and role of national economic policies
3. To understand the ways in which changes in national economies affect business planning and operations

3.0 Introduction

The economic activity of every nation-state makes up its national economy. There is considerable diversity among national economies. This is in large part due to the fact that the world's nearly 200 nation-states differ widely in size, geography, population, climate and natural resources. These differences have direct effects on the types and intensity of economic activity that are viable. For example, trade is traditionally more likely to prosper in a coastal state than in a landlocked one. States rich in natural resources, such as minerals and oil, have developed national economies built round these rich natural endowments, whereas, as was seen in the last chapter, labour-intensive manufacturing industries have gravitated to states with large populations offering abundant labour. No country has unlimited resources. In each, the national economy represents the processes which determine how to allocate scarce resources so as to satisfy the needs and wants of those within its territory. The ways in which national economies exploit their differing natural endowments are influenced by a host of factors, including historical forces and the social and cultural norms of their peoples. This diversity will be explored in the next chapter, while this chapter will introduce the concepts by which all national economies may be analysed and compared with each other.

There are numerous economic 'players' in every society, including businesses, consumers and governments. Each has particular interests, often conflicting with other groups. Consumers would like lower prices, but, as employees, they also desire higher wages. Balancing the interests between groups in the economy is a complex process, in which government plays a key role, both directly and indirectly. Governments both take in and spend large sums of money, and they also act indirectly through policy formation, which is an important element in the nation's economic environment. National economic forces and government responses affect businesses in their planning in both the short and long term. Moreover, businesses are themselves major players in shaping the economic environment. Therefore, this chapter will explore the dynamic interactions which take place within the economy, highlighting the interests of groups in society and the importance of government policies and activities for business.

3.1 The macroeconomic environment: flows of economic resources

Economists study both the overall activity in the national economy and the economic activity which takes place between businesses and consumers. **Macroeconomics** is the study of national economies, while **microeconomics** refers to the study of economic activity at the level of individuals and firms. The two areas of economic study are related. A country's macroeconomic environment consists of its national output, employment levels and consumer prices generally. However, these data are compiled by aggregating data from individuals and firms, so that microeconomic analysis feeds into macroeconomic analysis and policy-making. As an example, microeconomic analysis may focus on motor vehicles in particular, including the market and prices, and this information forms part of the macroeconomic picture of total employment and prices in the economy as a whole.

Flows of economic resources in the economy can be depicted as a model based on circular flows. While this type of model is greatly oversimplified, it does serve to show the interaction between the main groups, businesses and consumers, as can be seen in Figure 3.1. Businesses provide employment and wages to households, while consumers spend earned income on goods and services. At the same time, both businesses and individuals pay taxes to government, which are used to fund public spending and social security. By increasing or decreasing public spending or by altering the tax regime, it is therefore possible for government to influence spending by firms and consumers. For example, public spending on government projects will provide firms with more orders and greater need for workers. These workers, in turn, will purchase consumer goods. Therefore, the 'injection' of government funds will have had a general effect on the economy, referred to by economists as a 'multiplier' effect, because of its ripple effects across the economy. It should also be noticed that effects of international flows are

Figure 3.1 Circular flows of income in the economy

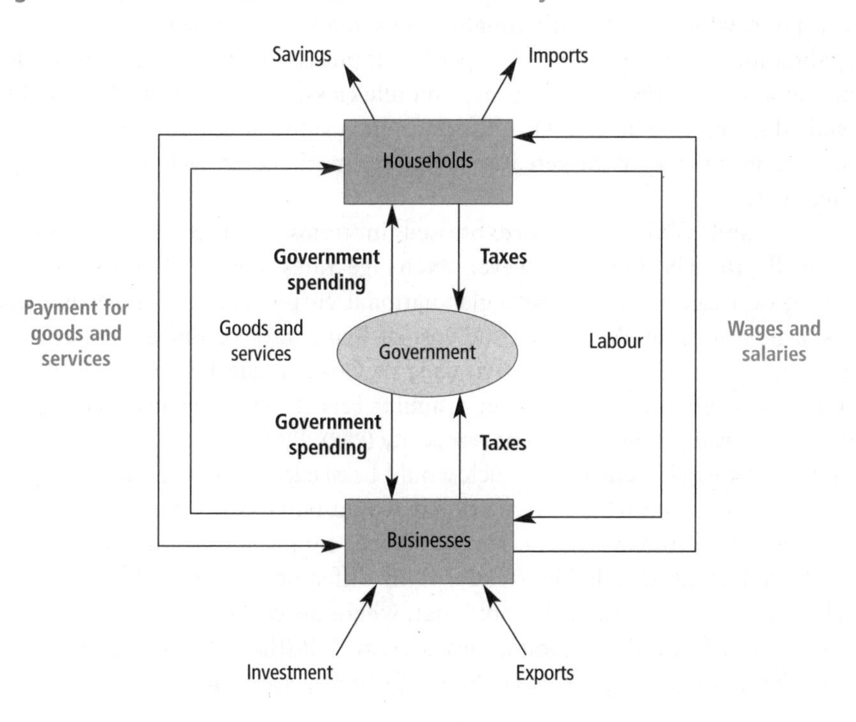

taken into account in Figure 3.1. Consumers buy imported products, which is depicted as a 'leakage' from the circular flow. Similarly, when firms export products, the income that arises is an injection, as is overseas investment.

3.2 Gross domestic product and gross national product

The economy of a nation-state is capable of being measured in a number of ways. One of these is **gross national product (GNP)**. GNP represents the total income from all the final products and services produced by a national economy, including income that national residents earn from overseas investments, in a given year. It is the broadest measure of a nation's economic activity. It includes **gross domestic product (GDP)**, which represents the value of the total economic activity produced within a country in a single year, including both domestic and foreign producers. GDP and GNP vary enormously from one country to another, in part reflecting the size of a country's population. A country with a large population will have a large GDP. For comparisons, GDP or GNP per head (per capita) is often used. A large country such as the US (with a population of nearly 275 million) has a large GNP, $7,921.3 billion, with a GNP per head of $29,340 (see Table 3.1). By contrast, India (population, 980 million) has a GNP of $421.3 billion, and a GNP per capita of only $430. GNP per head represents an average figure. It does not take account of the distribution of wealth within the country. Some countries may have extremes of wealth between the rich and poor, while others with roughly the same GNP per head may be more egalitarian. India has a low GNP per head, but is nonetheless seen as a huge potential market because of its large middle class, made up of well-to-do and well-educated consumers. This information is valuable for companies whose marketing strategy is targeted at emerging markets, as well as for foreign investors.

GDP and GNP must be expressed in terms of a common currency, normally the US dollar. However, exchange rates vary: the dollar may be strong or weak against a particular national currency, and this needs to be taken into account. Moreover, the cost of living varies from one country to another. The dollar may buy two cans of Coke in the US, but five French francs may buy only one Coke in a similar French outlet. Hence, economists use the measure of **purchasing power parity (PPP)**. PPP estimates the number of units of the foreign currency which would be needed to buy goods or services equivalent to those which the US dollar would buy in the US. The advantage of using PPP estimates to measure GNP per capita is that they more accurately reflect relative living standards in different countries. In the list of selected countries in Table 3.1 note that, where the cost of living is *lower* than it is in the US, GNP per capita, measured at PPP (the last column), is higher than the figure in the previous column. Examples are Chile, China and India.

Where the cost of living is *higher* than in the US, the figure in the last column is lower than in the previous column. This group of countries includes France, Germany and Japan.

Table 3.1 Size of the economy in selected countries

Economy	GNP, 1998 ($billions)	GNP per capita (dollars)	GNP per capita, measured at PPP (dollars)
Argentina	324.1	8,970	10,200
Brazil	758.0	4,570	6,160
Chile	71.3	4,810	12,890
China	928.9	750	3,220
France	1,466.2	24,940	22,320
Germany	2,122.7	25,850	20,810
Greece	122.9	11,650	13,010
India	421.3	430	1,700
Indonesia	138.5	680	2,790
Japan	4,089.9	32,380	23,180
Korea, Rep.	369.9	7,970	12,270
Malaysia	79.8	3,600	6,990
Mexico	380.9	3,970	8,190
Netherlands	388.7	24,760	21,620
Poland	150.8	3,900	6,740
Sierra Leone	0.7	140	390
South Africa	119.0	2,880	6,990
Spain	553.7	14,080	16,060
United Kingdom	1,263.8	21,400	20,640
United States	7,921.3	29,340	29,340

Source: World Bank (2000) *World Development Report 1999/2000* (Oxford: Oxford University Press) Table 1, p. 230.

Up-to-date economic development indicators are published by the World Bank at http://www.worldbank.org/data/wdi2000/worldview.htm

3.3 Industrial structure

Economic activity may be divided into sectors. All economies change over time, and looking at trends in the performance in different sectors provides useful indicators, especially relevant to the economy's need for specific types of employment. The sectors of the national economy are:

- *Primary sector* – refers to agriculture and the extraction of natural resources, such as oil and minerals
- *Secondary sector* – refers to manufacturing industry, producing industrial products, and also processing primary commodities, such as food. Much of the food we eat is, in effect, industrially produced
- *Tertiary sector* – refers to the service industries, including banking and finance, information technology, tourism.

Historically, the major change that has taken place in terms of economic development has been **industrialization**, marking the transition from a mainly agricultural economy to an industrial one. This pattern of structural change can be shown by looking at the industrialized nations of Western Europe and the US. As industrialization progressed, the numbers employed in agriculture dwindled. These countries now have very small percentages of their populations engaged in agriculture, under 5 per cent. Similarly, extractive industries, such as mining, have also declined. Coal mining, once the dominant industry in areas of England and Wales, has now all but disappeared. Manufacturing, usually looked on as the backbone of an industrial economy, has declined in importance, while there has been a surge in the service industries. As Table 3.2 indicates, services now account for more than two-thirds of GDP in the US and UK. Much manufacturing has been transformed by high-tech operations, which require fewer workers, while low-tech, labour-intensive industries have often relocated in developing countries, for their location-specific advantages, as shown in the last chapter.

Looking at recent trends, growth has been linked particularly with computing and information technology (IT). In these high-tech areas, the US has played a dominant role, which, throughout the 1990s, enabled it to achieve sustained economic growth and low unemployment, as well as low

Table 3.2 Structure of output for the United Kingdom and United States, 1998

	GDP ($millions)	Agriculture	Industry (total)	Manufacturing Industry	Services
United Kingdom	1,357,429	2 (2)	31 (43)	21 (27)	67 (55)
United States	8,210,600	2 (3)	27 (33)	18 (22)	71 (64)

Notes
1. Columns 2–5 represent value added as per cent of GDP.
2. Percentages for 1980 given in brackets.

Source: World Bank (2000) *World Development Report 1999/2000* (Oxford: Oxford University Press) Table 12, p. 252.

inflation. However, economic conditions and competitive forces, both domestic and international, present a dynamic, changing scene, in which there can be no guarantees of indefinite prosperity. The signs of a slowdown in the US economy were apparent by the end of 2000, prompted, it was generally felt, by overinvestment in new technology industries. At the same time, growth in service-sector jobs has been driven in large measure by greater demand for data-processing and telecommunications services, such as call centres. Many of these jobs are now relocating in developing countries. It is estimated that up to 5 per cent of all service-sector jobs in industrialized countries could potentially relocate in developing countries (ILO, 2001a).

3.4 Inflation and unemployment

Inflation and unemployment are linked phenomena which affect all economies, varying in their severity and persistence between countries and regions. They directly affect businesses in terms of costs of raw materials, wages, prices of finished products and availability of labour. National policy-makers naturally seek to maintain price stability and low levels of unemployment. However, growing interdependence among economies limits their room for manoeuvre, while at the same time making national economies vulnerable to external forces.

3.4.1 Inflation

Inflation can be defined as the continuing general rise in prices in the economy. Its effect is to make the country's currency worth less. The opposite phenomenon is 'deflation', or falling prices, which is much less common. (Japan is the most notable example in the 1990s, where deflation accompanied economic recession.) The rate of inflation is expressed as a percentage rise or fall in prices with reference to a specific starting point in time. These rises and falls are tracked in the consumer price index for every country, usually making allowances for seasonal adjustments, such as seasonal variations in food prices. In the UK the Retail Price Index (RPI) represents a basket of products and services purchased by the average consumer, and is calculated on a monthly basis. In the UK, the cost of housing is included in the index, whereas in other European countries it is excluded. An alternative index, the RPIX, which excludes mortgage payments, gives a rate known as the 'underlying rate of inflation'. Comparing inflation rates between countries can be somewhat imprecise because of the different ways of measuring inflation. The European Central Bank (ECB) (discussed further below) has devised a Harmonized Index of Consumer Prices (HICP) for comparing inflation in the member states of the euro-zone.

Economists point to a number of causes of inflation. 'Demand-pull' and 'cost-push' arguments are two of the most commonly advanced causes. The demand-pull explanation holds that excess demand in the economy, which may be the result of cheap borrowing or tax cuts, encourages producers to raise prices, and these then lead to rises in wage demands as workers strive to maintain their standard of living. The cost-push argument holds that excessive costs drive up prices. As a significant element of costs is accounted for by wages, this theory becomes linked with the demand-pull argument. Rising wage costs tend to be passed on to consumers in the form of higher prices, thus creating what is known as the 'wage-price inflationary spiral'. This point is illustrated in Case Study 3.1 on Ireland.

The damaging effects of high inflation can be widely ramified. A country's domestic producers will find their goods less competitive in global markets, and foreign investors may turn to countries where inflation is lower. High

POINTS TO REMEMBER

Inflation and unemployment

Inflation – continuing rise in prices, which in turn is likely to cause wage inflation, as workers strive to maintain standard of living

- It is expressed as an annual percentage rise in prices
- Increasing costs (such as the price of energy) and increasing demand in the economy are two related causes

Unemployment – measure of the section of the population willing to work, but unable to find employment

- It is expressed as a percentage of the total available labour force
- Unemployment may rise if shifts in the industrial structure leave some workers without the skills needed for the jobs available
- Other factors affecting unemployment are high wages and weak demand in the economy

inflation tends to force up interest rates, to enable investors to achieve a real return on their investments. However, high interest rates may adversely affect growth rates, by reducing domestic demand. The importance of energy costs as a driver of inflation was highlighted in the oil price shocks of the 1970s, which quadrupled the price of oil. Resultant increases in energy and transport costs affected all industrial sectors and sent inflation soaring in developed economies. To bring down inflation, governments can resort to imposing controls on prices or wages, but these measures can be damaging. In particular, they can lead to rising unemployment, as employers cut back on costs. In an environment of relatively low inflation, monetary policy, which will be discussed below, is therefore designed to prevent inflationary pressures arising.

3.4.2 Unemployment

Full employment, contrary to what it implies, is used by economists to refer to a country's natural rate of unemployment which exists in all societies. What we commonly refer to as **unemployment** reflects the percentage of people in the workforce who are willing to work but are without jobs. The internationally agreed definition was devised by the International Labour Organization (ILO) and is known as 'ILO unemployment'. It consists of people who:

- are without a job, want a job, have actively sought work in the last four weeks and are available to start work in the next two weeks, or
- are out of work, have found a job and are waiting to start it in the next two weeks.

During the years following the Great Depression of 1929, unemployment was very high, as was inflation. Along with inflation, unemployment again rose in the period following the oil price shocks of the 1970s. While levels of unemployment have come down in most industrialized countries, they have been high in the countries of Central and Eastern Europe which are making the transition to market economies (see Chapter 4).

Unemployment may be 'structural', meaning that jobs have been lost due to changing technology or industries relocating in other regions or other countries. Or it may be 'frictional', which refers to the usual turnover in the labour force that happens, for example, when people are out of work looking for new jobs. Long-term unemployment is a cause of concern to governments: social security payments will rise, or, in countries which lack extensive state benefit schemes, the burden of individual hardship may fall on families. Moreover, social and political unrest can be triggered by problems associated with high unemployment. It should be borne in mind that overall rates of unemployment tell only part of the story. Almost all countries experience regional disparities in unemployment, differing rates between age groups and differing rates between men and women. Governments therefore target policies to attract businesses to particular geographical areas and to raise the skill levels of the workforce. In Britain, the more prosperous region of London and the southeast contrasts with the northern regions, where levels of unemployment are higher, creating the phenomenon known as the 'north–south divide'. Italy is another example of the north–south divide, between the prosperous north and poor south, although inflows of foreign investment into the south have helped to balance this picture.

Economic growth, inflation and unemployment are related, although among economists there are differing interpretations of the relationship. All countries wish to see sustained growth and a low level of unemployment. The risk is that when there is full employment, this will exert inflationary pressure. On the other hand, if there is high unemployment, growth may slow. These points are illustrated in Case Study 3.1.

3.5 Balance of payments

Balance of payments refers to credit and debit transactions between a country's residents (including companies) and those of other countries. Transactions are divided into the current account and capital account. The **current account** is made up of trade in goods (the merchandise trade account), services (the services account), and profits and interest earned from overseas assets. The **capital account** relates to transactions involving the sale and purchase of assets, such as investment in shares. If a country has a current account deficit, this means that it imports more goods and services than it exports. If it has a current account surplus, it exports more than it imports. Governments grow concerned if there is a current account deficit, and in particular, a trade deficit, as it suggests that the country's companies are uncompetitive. In the 1980s and 90s, the US ran current account deficits with Japan. From the mid-1980s the UK, paradoxically, improved its competitiveness in terms of attracting foreign investment, while its trade balance suffered, as shown in Figure 3.2.

The balance of payments reflects demand both at home and abroad. It also reflects exchange rates (discussed in Chapter 11) and the relative costs of domestic production. Governments can exert influence by varying the exchange rate, raising interest rates (to slow down growth), or by imposing tariff barriers such as import duties and quotas. Raising interest rates will decrease demand, and possibly deter future investment. The world's main trading countries are now linked in regional and multilateral trade groupings which, as will be discussed later, have brought down trade barriers, so that governments are no longer able simply to restrict imports. Nor would they be advised to do so, because of the risk of retaliation by trading partners. In globally integrated production networks and markets, government objectives

Figure 3.2 UK trade with countries inside and outside the EU

(a) UK exports of goods

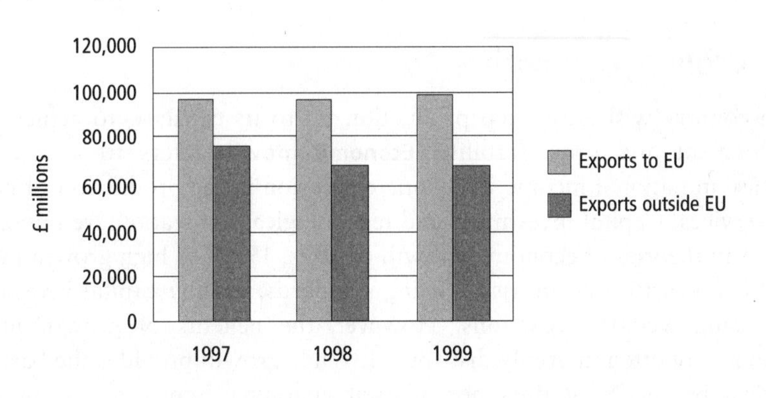

(b) UK imports of goods

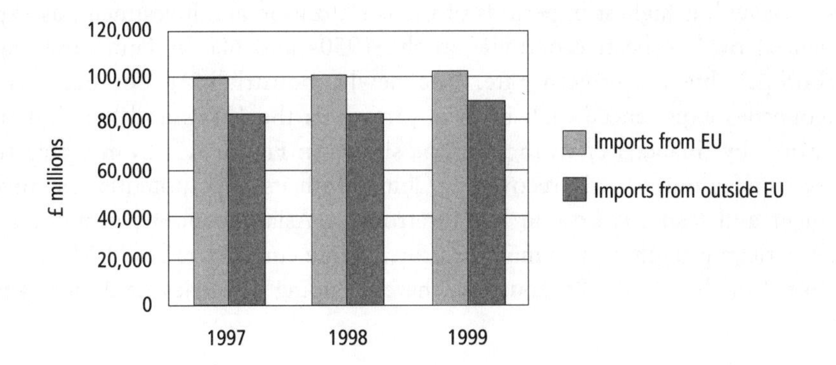

(c) UK balance of trade in goods

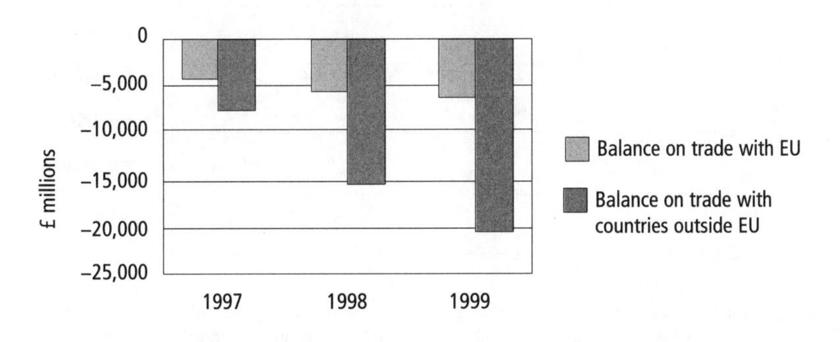

Source: Office for National Statistics (2000) *UK Trade* (London: ONS).

and the means of achieving them have therefore become complex calculations, involving a number of internal and external considerations.

3.6 Economic growth

Each country wishes to keep production up to its capacity, to achieve full employment and price stability. **Economic growth** refers to a country's increase in national income, reflecting expansion in the production of goods and services. Capital investment and technological innovation are important factors in theories of economic growth (Coates, 1999). A high growth rate in GDP is taken to indicate rising living standards, healthy capital investment and rising welfare provisions. However, the benefits of growth in the economy are often unevenly distributed. While growth provides the basis for national prosperity, it does not in itself guarantee improvements in well-being for the whole of society, especially in countries where there is rapid population growth, weak institutions or wide inequalities of income and opportunities between groups.

Growth is highest in periods of industrialization and investment, as experienced by European economies in the 1950s and 60s. Ireland now enjoys Europe's highest growth rate. The newly industrializing Southeast Asian countries experienced high rates of growth in the 1980s and 90s, but were struck by financial crisis in 1997, as shown in Figure 3.3, from which their economies only slowly recovered. China, with its huge potential for investment and trade, is now at the forefront of Asian economic growth. Latin American growth rates remain healthy, despite currency crises in Mexico and Brazil in the 1990s. By contrast, the developing countries of Africa, which

Figure 3.3 Trends in world GDP growth

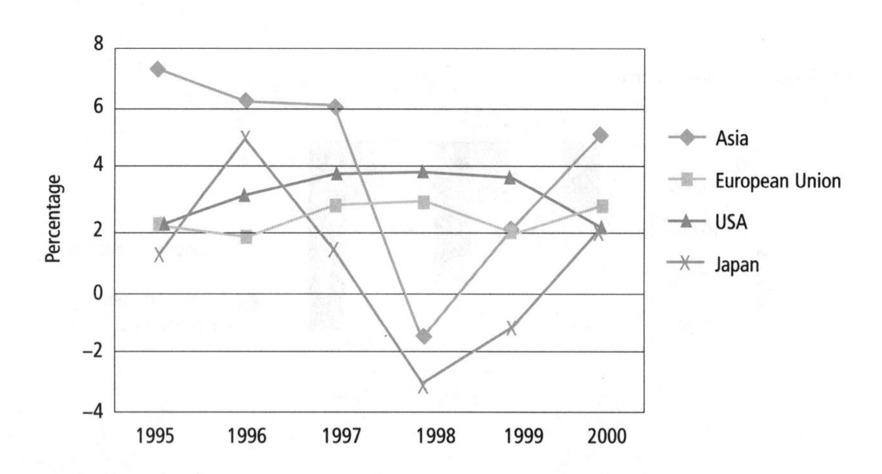

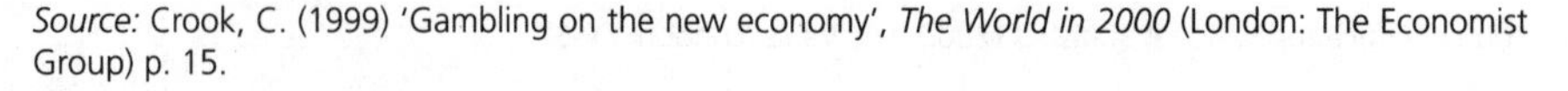
Source: Crook, C. (1999) 'Gambling on the new economy', *The World in 2000* (London: The Economist Group) p. 15.

still rely on primary commodities, remain generally poor. These countries seek foreign investors, but they have suffered from political and social instability, and have had little success in diversifying their economies. Progress on these fronts will be crucial to their prospects for economic growth.

Case study 3.1 Ireland's fast-growing economy

In the early 1990s, Ireland was suffering from an unemployment rate of over 14 per cent, and the government's main worry was creating jobs. From 1994 onwards Ireland has been enjoying an investment boom which has transformed its economy. Overseas investors, and US companies in particular, have been attracted by Ireland's low tax regime and pool of skilled workers for high-tech enterprises. Ireland has attracted a third of all US electronics investment in Europe. In 1999, the cost of Irish production workers was estimated by the US Bureau of Labor Statistics to be half that of Germany and two-thirds of the European average. By 2000, unemployment was down to 4.1 per cent, and the government, confronted with a shortage of skilled labour, was looking for ways of increasing the numbers of technology and computer science graduates.

The economy has grown at a rate of 8 per cent a year for the past six years, which is about three times the growth rate of other nations in the European Union (EU). The government is enjoying a current budget surplus equivalent to 4.3 per cent of GDP. However, inflation, running at about 6 per cent, is considerably higher than European levels and is fuelling wage rises. Measures such as an increase in exchange and interest rates are commonly used to bring down inflation. However, as Ireland is in the euro-zone, these rates are determined by the ECB in Frankfurt. Fiscal policy in the euro-zone is still left to member states, and the Irish government might be expected to pursue a tighter fiscal policy. But instead, it has continued to pursue expansionary policies, despite critics' concern that the economy is overheating. The Budget of 2000 contained plans both to reduce taxes and increase public spending. The public spending will go towards improving the public infrastructure, which has showed signs of strain during the economic boom. The reduction in taxes, it is hoped, will lure people back into the workforce, to ease labour shortages.

Should the Irish just sit back and enjoy the economic boom, or are there clouds on the horizon? The European Commission has expressed concern that Ireland's economic policies contradict the Commission's guidelines. Irish competitiveness was enhanced by the low value of the euro in the first 22 months of the common currency's existence. An appreciation of the currency, combined with continuing wage inflation, could pose problems for Irish competitiveness. Further, a slowdown in the US could be damaging, given the economy's dependence on inflows of foreign investment from US multinationals.

Sources: Brown, J.M., 'Prosperity brings new challenges', *Financial Times*, 3 October 2000; Norman, P. and Brown, J.M., 'Irish handling of economy irks Brussels', *Financial Times*, 24 January 2001.

Case question

What worries have accompanied Ireland's exceptional economic growth and what are the effects of European monetary policy on Ireland?

3.7 The business cycle

All countries experience fluctuations in their economies, enjoying periods of prosperity followed by periods of downturn. Long cycles, or waves, can be distinguished from the pattern of shorter term fluctuations, often referred to as the **business cycle**. The nature and causes of cycles have generated intense debate and differing viewpoints among economists (Maddison, 1991). Long-wave analysis rests on theories of capitalist development and innovation (discussed in Chapter 10). We focus here on the shorter term fluctuations of the business cycle. The cycle can be divided into phases of prosperity, recession, depression and recovery:

- *Prosperity* – the expansive phase, in which total income is high and unemployment is low. Optimism pervades the economy, and consumers are inclined to spend
- *Recession* – the phase of economic downturn, when confidence is waning and unemployment is rising, as consumers and businesses spend less. In this period governments can take a number of measures, such as lightening the tax burden or reducing interest rates, to stimulate the economy
- *Depression* – the phase when recession deepens to a near total lack of confidence in the economy, with high unemployment and weak consumer spending. Through policy adjustments, governments may be able to prevent recession from deteriorating into depression
- *Recovery* – the phase of upturn from recession or depression, in which confidence is returning, unemployment is declining and consumers resume spending. Recovery, however, may be a false dawn if prosperity, which may seem just round the corner, does not materialize.

The worst depression of the twentieth century, the Great Depression of 1929, affected most countries of the world, lasting up to three years in countries worst affected. Governments now take a stronger regulatory role than they did before the Second World War, and major bank failures, which were an aspect of the Great Depression, are now less likely (Maddison, 1991). Governments use monetary and fiscal policy to ward off the extremes of 'boom and bust' which are associated with the most severe swings of the business cycle. An interest rate cut is quicker to take effect than a reduction in taxes, but tax reductions provide a more direct boost to consumer spending. In the US in 2001, the reduction in interest rates was accompanied by an announcement by the newly elected President George W. Bush, of backdated tax cuts. It should be noted that as national economies have become interdependent, economic downturn in one country, especially the US, is likely to have widespread repercussions in the world economy. Regional economic integration has intensified this interdependence and left governments with less room to manoeuvre. Regional integration has been most advanced in the EU, where national policies have become intertwined with EU policies, as will be seen in the next section.

WWW WEBALERT

Statistics for the EU, covering a wide range of data, can be found at the Eurostat site, which is http://www.europa.eu.int/comm/eurostat/

UK economic data, including the latest economic indicators, are at the Treasury's website, http://www.hm-treasury.gov.uk

3.8 The role of government in the economy

Governments seek policies which ensure economic growth, low inflation and low unemployment, but there is divergence of opinion on the extent to which they should intervene, or, alternatively, allow market forces to prevail. The role of government varies considerably between different types of economic system, which will be discussed in greater detail in Chapter 4. For present purposes, looking at economic systems in general, it is safe to say that most governments are now tending towards more market-oriented policies, with targeted intervention to maintain stability. **Fiscal policy** refers to the budgetary policies for balancing spending with taxation, while **monetary policy** refers to policies for determining the amount of money in supply, rates of interest and exchange rates.

Economic thinking has come a long way since the classical economist, Adam Smith, spoke of the 'invisible hand' of the market guiding the economic system, in *The Wealth of Nations* (Smith [1776] 1950). Governments and central banks now exert control through monetary and fiscal policies, but economists have long been divided on issues of economic policy. John Maynard Keynes, founder of the 'Keynesian' school, as it came to be known, was the major economic theorist to argue against pure market forces. He argued for 'demand management' through fiscal policy, such as cutting taxes or increasing public spending, to achieve full employment. His major work, *The General Theory of Employment, Interest and Money* (Keynes, 1936), dates from the inter-war period, when, in the wake of the Depression, unemployment was a major problem. The other important school of thought is the 'monetarist' school, whose leading authority is Milton Friedman. Monetarists advocate the use of monetary policy to limit the supply of money. This philosophy dominated the government of former Prime Minister Margaret Thatcher in the UK, where it held the ascendancy during the 1970s and 80s, when inflation was a major problem. Economic thinking and research are constantly evolving between these two schools of thought, and this is reflected in more recent government policy, which looks both at inflation targets and the need for reducing unemployment. We look first at the institutional framework for the formulation of policies.

3.8.1 Institutional framework of economic policy

In most countries, governments are required to submit a national budget annually, setting out plans for public expenditure and the raising of money, which must be approved by the legislature. The Treasury is the government department responsible for overseeing spending policy and making budget recommendations to the government. The government minister responsible for delivering the budget in the UK is the Chancellor of the Exchequer, a powerful position in government. Numerous groups and interests look for favourable treatment in the budget, and chancellors, like finance ministers in all governments, are also subject to political pressures, such as the inevitable pressure to bring in tax cuts just before general elections. However, in most countries, while fiscal policy rests with governments, monetary policy has generally become the preserve of the central bank. The **central bank** is at the pinnacle of the country's financial system. It is responsible for issuing the country's notes and coins, and implementing the government's monetary policy by, for example, setting interest rates. It is also the banker to the government and the lender-of-last-resort. Most central banks are institutionally independent of government, to avoid undue political influence. In the US the central bank is the powerful and respected Federal Reserve. Its chairman through the 1990s, Alan Greenspan, is revered as having been largely responsible for America's sustained economic boom.

In the UK, while the Bank of England is a limb of government, an independent Monetary Policy Committee of the Bank is established to advise the government on a regular basis, in order to ensure that policies are seen to be free of short-term political influence. In Germany, the Bundesbank gained a reputation as a strong, independent institution. As will be seen, an implication of European Monetary Union is that the ECB has now taken on many of the powers of national central banks in the EU states that are in the eurozone. At international level, the International Monetary Fund (IMF), which

WWW
WEBALERT

The website of the European Central Bank is
http://www.ecb.int/

Other central banks are:

UK:	http://www.bankofengland.co.uk/
France:	http://www.banque-france.fr/
Germany:	http://www.bundesbank.de/
Ireland:	http://www.centralbank.ie/
Spain:	http://www.bde.es/
Italy:	http://www.bancaditalia.it/

will be discussed in Chapter 11, supervises international exchange rate stability, and also has considerably expanded its role into areas of economic policy once thought to be purely 'domestic' national policy. The institutional framework of economic policy has thus become more complex as globalization has impacted on national economies.

3.8.2 Fiscal policy

Government spending accounts for about 40 per cent of GDP. This public expenditure covers social security, health, education, defence, infrastructure and many other headings. Governments must raise large sums of money in order to fund public spending. In terms of circular flow analysis, if the government reduces taxation or increases public spending, then there will be increased demand for goods and services in the economy. Conversely, if taxation is increased or public spending reduced, demand contracts, having a detrimental effect on businesses and possibly leading to a rise in unemployment. The fiscal framework in the UK is based on five central principles: transparency, stability, responsibility, fairness (including that between generations) and efficiency. Two fiscal rules exemplify these principles. The first is the 'golden rule', which holds that the government will borrow each year only to invest, and not to fund current spending. The second, the 'sustainable investment' rule, stipulates that the public sector net debt will be held at a 'stable and prudent' level (HM Treasury, 2000).

Public spending is funded in the main from direct and indirect taxation, social security contributions and borrowing. Income tax and corporation tax are types of direct taxation, while VAT and petrol duty are indirect taxes. The balance between direct and indirect taxation varies between countries. In Britain, the government derives more revenue from indirect than direct taxes, whereas in many other EU countries, the reverse is true. Income tax, in contrast to indirect taxes, is a progressive tax, which means that the tax burden rises in accordance with income. For businesses, tax considerations can be crucial when considering future investment. Tax concessions to corporate taxpayers or to start-up companies, for example, can encourage investment. In a survey of foreign pharmaceutical companies investing in Ireland, the low rate of corporation tax, as shown in Figure 3.4, was found to be the most important motive (Bourke, 2000). Governments are aware that, while a favourable tax regime helps to attract investors, 'footloose' investment may be lost to another country which offers a more favourable tax regime. Governments can thus use fiscal policies for particular objectives, such as to foster enterprise and innovation. An example is the R&D tax credit introduced in the UK in the 2000 Budget. On the other hand, across-the-board measures, such as a reduction in the rate of income tax, can ignite inflationary pressures.

Governments enjoy a budget surplus when they receive more in revenue than they spend. It is common, however, for governments to be in deficit,

Figure 3.4 Corporation tax rates in selected countries

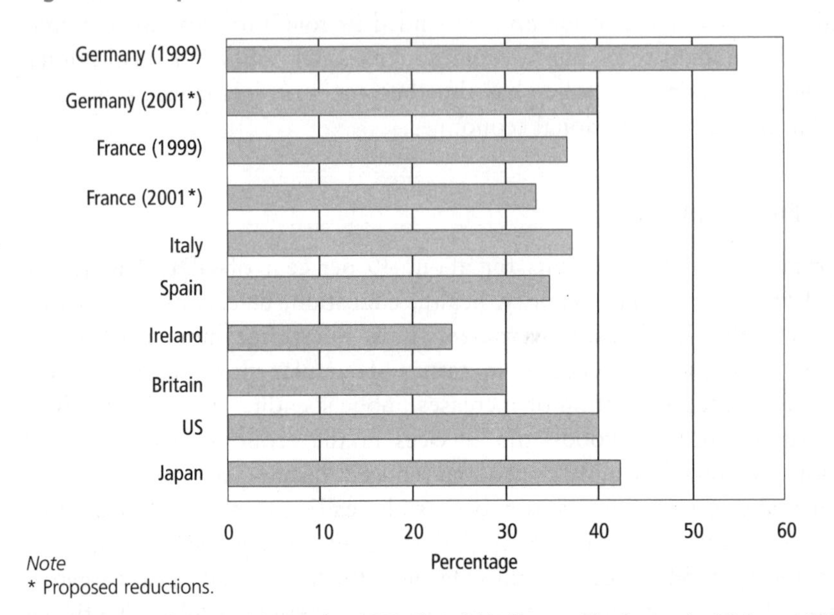

Note
* Proposed reductions.

Sources: Financial Times, 29 September 2000; Financial indicators, *The Economist*, 26 August 2000.

spending more than they receive in revenue. The fiscal difficulties experienced by governments are highlighted in Case Study 3.2 on China, which faces mounting demands for public spending, while struggling to increase tax revenues. In the UK the **public sector borrowing requirement** (PSBR) represents the deficit which exists to the extent that public spending exceeds receipts. The debt that accumulates over the years is known as the **national debt.** National debt, expressed as a percentage of GDP, can grow to large proportions, causing mounting problems for government finances, and in extreme cases even the payment of interest becomes problematic. The convergence criteria for entering the EU's EMU, or Maastricht criteria, specify that the government deficit (PSBR) should be below 3 per cent of GDP, and national debt should not exceed 60 per cent of GDP. UK national debt as a proportion of GDP declined for most of the post-war period, but rose again in the 1990s, peaking at 44 per cent in 1996–97. Since then, it has fallen to about 37 per cent of GDP. In 2000, the UK had a budget surplus of £17 billion (nearly 2 per cent of GDP). Thus, on both deficit and debt criteria, the UK falls within the Maastricht criteria.

3.8.3 Monetary policy

Monetary policy governs the quantity of money in circulation, the rate of interest and the exchange rate. It is important to remember that changes in one country have implications in other countries, particularly its neighbours

Case study 3.2 Fiscal strain in Beijing

China's national debt in 1998 was 20.5 per cent of GDP, not necessarily a cause for alarm, but almost five times the level of five years before. In most Western countries budget revenues typically total 40 per cent of GDP, but, in China, these amounted to only 12.4 per cent in 1998. Its precarious position has been likened to Russia. What is more, China's banks, with bad debts totalling 25 per cent of their assets, are in need of recapitalization. For the government to make good the losses would bring the burden of state debt up to 50 per cent of GDP. While the government may be reluctant to do so, its thoughts must be focused on the situation in the two years following World Trade Organization (WTO) entry, when foreign banks will be able to offer services directly to Chinese companies, in competition with Chinese banks, for the first time.

Apart from sickly banks, China faces two other fiscal demands. The first is welfare spending. China is embarking on the daunting task of constructing a welfare system, initially for the 300 million urban inhabitants, to be extended to 900 million rural dwellers. The numbers of unemployed, estimated at 16–18 million in the cities and 100 million in the countryside, are likely to increase further after WTO entry, as domestic businesses struggle to compete. The second fiscal demand stems from the drive by the government to develop the vast, but impoverished, west of the country. This will require huge infrastructure investment. Logically the government is turning to foreign investors to ease the funding burden on the state. Reform of the tax system and capital markets will be needed. At present, local authorities gain revenue through numerous fees, which the central government would like to replace with official taxes. Such a measure, it estimates, would double the level of tax revenues. Economists recommend the creation of a liquid bond market, governed by supply and demand, along the lines of Western bond markets. At present, interest rates on bonds are determined by the central bank, the People's Bank of China. The government may find it difficult to give away control of capital markets, but may find it has little alternative, if it is to avoid budgetary crisis.

Source: Kynge, J., 'China's fraught fiscal future', *Financial Times*, 11 January 2000 (reprinted with permission).

Case question

How does the financial system in China impact on foreign businesses, and how is this likely to change in future?

and its trading partners. Money supply, interest rates and exchange rates are interrelated. For example, a reduction in interest rates designed to boost the economy will usually have an effect of reducing the value of the currency, as the foreign exchange dealers shift funds out of the country. If money supply is increased, exchange rates tend to fall.

Governments must decide whether to set 'targets' for each of these variables. 'Money supply' denotes the availability of liquid assets in the economy. However, it can be defined in a number of ways. It can refer to just notes and coins ('narrow money'), or it can also include less liquid assets, such as bank accounts ('broad money'). In the UK, the Bank of England monitors money supply under the various definitions. But, given the widespread use of credit, instead of notes and coins, for consumer and business spending, attempts to control money supply can be somewhat ineffective.

In the UK, the government sets an inflation target, leaving the Bank of England's Monetary Policy Committee (MPC) to set interest rates in order to meet the target. The Labour government which came into office in 1997 set a target of 2.5 per cent for the annual increase in the RPI excluding mortgage interest payments (RPIX). RPIX inflation remained below the target from April 1999, averaging 2.25 per cent. Falling import prices are partly responsible, contributing to competitive pressure on domestic producers and retailers. Inflation remained low in 1999 despite a doubling in the price of oil. However, services inflation presented a different picture, rising from 4.25 per cent to 5.5 per cent in 1999, reflecting growing demand and less competitive pressure in services. Household spending grew 4 per cent in 1999, driven by rising real incomes and falling unemployment. Interest rates fell from 7.5 per cent in mid-1998 to 5 per cent in summer 1999. From September 1999, the MPC raised interest rates by one percentage point, in a move aimed at slowing down household consumption. The strength of sterling contributed to keeping down the prices of goods, along with the depreciation of the euro. In the euro-zone, by contrast, goods inflation was pushed up by the euro's weakness.

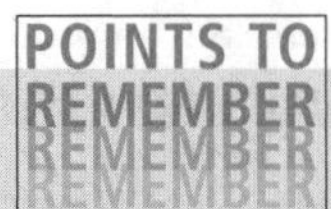

How monetary and fiscal policies are formed

- *Monetary policy framework* – institutional framework governed by the central bank, which is responsible for monitoring and regulating money supply, exchange rate and interest rates. For euro-zone states, the European Central Bank now controls monetary policy
- *Fiscal policy framework* – government authorities, chiefly the ministry of finance, which monitor and formulate policies for government spending and the raising of revenues, including taxation. Where governments are democratically elected, fiscal proposals must be presented in an annual budget and approved by the country's legislature

3.9 European Monetary Union (EMU)

For the member states of the EU, growing economic integration has brought about a diminishing of national economic autonomy. One of the pillars of the EU is the **European Monetary Union** (EMU), which now comprises 12 of the

15 member states of the EU. Proposals for EMU were agreed under the Maastricht Treaty of 1992, to commence in 1999. The ECB was established, to oversee monetary policy for all members of EMU, and in particular to set interest rates centrally. A common currency, the euro, was introduced on 1 January, 1999. Coins and notes are due to be introduced in 2002. Each government must meet the 'Maastricht criteria' on convergence (see Minifile).

Of the EU's 15 member states, 11 joined the euro-zone at the outset. They are Belgium, Germany, France, Ireland, Italy, Luxembourg, the Netherlands, Austria, Portugal, Spain and Finland. Greece was admitted in 2001. The Danish people voted against membership in a referendum in September 2000, the result of which was 53.1 per cent voting 'no' and 46.9 per cent voting 'yes' to the euro. The Danish vote sounded a note of caution to the British government, whose own plan for a referendum was set back. As in Denmark, the issue of the common currency has divided public opinion in Britain. Those in favour point to the convenience of the single currency, especially for businesses which regularly transact business in a number of European member states. They note also the fact that some large companies either in Britain already, or thinking of investing, are likely to migrate to the euro-zone. Those against joining the euro point to the strength of sterling outside the euro-zone, and the erosion of national sovereignty which it would entail. Nonetheless, the euro is spearheading greater economic integration across the EU, as transnational corporations with pan-European supply chains, such as the motor companies Nissan and Toyota, are now requiring suppliers to deal in euros, even in the UK and other states not in the euro-zone.

Minifile

MAASTRICHT CONVERGENCE CRITERIA

The convergence criteria, which are listed below, provide five 'tests' for EU countries wishing to join the euro-zone. However, they were not intended to be applied rigidly, and initial applicant countries were given considerable leeway in the interpretation of these requirements. Notwithstanding, the governor of the ECB announced in 2000 that, in his view, Britain would not be able to sidestep the two-year requirement of ERM membership (the fifth criterion) (*Financial Times*, 24 November, 2000).

1. *Sustainability of public finances:* government deficit (PSBR) should not exceed 3 per cent of GDP
2. *Public debt under control:* the ratio of national debt to GDP should not exceed 60 per cent, unless the ratio is sufficiently diminishing and approaching the value 'at a satisfactory pace'
3. *Price stability:* inflation should not exceed that of the three best-performing countries by more than 1.5 per cent
4. *Interest rate stability:* long-term interest rates should not exceed the three best-performing countries by more than 2 per cent
5. *Exchange rate stability:* countries should observe 'normal' fluctuation margins within the ERM margins for two years, without devaluing against the currency of any other member state

Source: Economic and Monetary Union, *Financial Times*, 23 March 1998.

The Labour government, re-elected in June 2001, is committed to joining the euro-zone, but stresses that the timing of Britain's entry will need to be carefully planned. The Chancellor, Gordon Brown, is concerned that the ECB needs to become more open and accountable. He has set out five further tests, in addition to the formal convergence criteria, which must be satisfied before Britain can join the single currency. Unlike the formal criteria, which are quantitative, the tests are matters of judgement. They are:

- Is there sustainable convergence between Britain's economic structures and those of the euro-zone?
- Is there flexibility within the euro-zone decision-making structures to cope with economic change?
- What is the impact of EMU on long-term investment prospects in the UK?
- What is the impact of EMU on the UK's financial services industry?
- What is the impact of EMU on the UK's growth and employment?

A major concern of the Chancellor is that entry into the euro-zone would inevitably require a lowering of interest and exchange rates to euro-zone levels, which could set off inflation and cause economic instability. Clearly, much depends on entering at the right exchange rate. When the government is confident that the five tests have been satisfied, the issue will be put to the electorate in a referendum.

The euro has not as yet led to convergence among the 11 original member states. Growth rates and inflation differ significantly. Fiscal policy, for the time being, remains a preserve of national governments, which are able to vary the tax burden on individuals and corporations in line with national goals. Governments in member states have set themselves a heavy agenda of structural reforms, to reduce taxation and public expenditure and deregulate

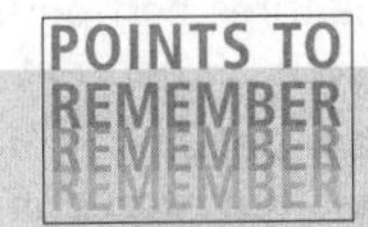

European Monetary Union (EMU)

- The Treaty of European Union, which dates from 1992, laid the groundwork for the EMU, by authorizing the creation of the ECB
- In 1998, governments of the 11 original members of the EMU, known as the 'euro-zone', appointed a president and board to govern the ECB
- In 1999, there began the fixing of exchange rates of the currencies of member states to the European currency, the euro
- From 2001, Greece, having fulfilled the convergence criteria, was admitted to the euro-zone
- Euro banknotes to be put into circulation 1 January 2002

product and labour markets. Programmes to reduce the tax burden in Germany and France are under way, as Figure 3.4 indicated. The German government aims to reduce the top rate of corporation tax from 55 per cent to 40 per cent. Reducing the corporate tax burden is arguably desirable in its own right, as part of a programme of business incentives. It may also be seen in the wider context of EU convergence, reflecting the influence of growing cross-border economic activity in the euro-zone.

The major disappointment in the euro's first two years has been its dramatic slump in value. Launched at a value of US$1.17, it slumped to $0.84, losing a third of its value in its first 22 months. In September 2000, the ECB and other central banks co-ordinated a rescue operation, aimed to stop the downward spiral. Observers felt that the euro's weakness stemmed largely from the strength of the US economy, and that a slowdown in the US would prompt a recovery of the euro, luring investors to Europe. Structural reforms in euro-zone economies, mentioned above, should aid the process, but progress is likely to be uneven so long as these still remain in the hands of the 11 national governments. Although the European Commission has aspired to achieve a co-ordination of economic policies within member states, not simply those in the euro-zone, as yet, economic goals and policies still diverge among the member states. As has been seen, national economies throughout Europe are shaped by elected governments, reflecting divergent social and cultural values, which influence economic activities. As a result, societies have evolved differing economic systems, which are further evolving in the context of regionalization and globalization, as will be explored in Chapter 4.

3.10 Conclusions

1. The macroeconomic environment can be depicted in terms of flows of resources, income, production and expenditure.

2. GNP and GDP are used to measure the size of national economies.

3. Economic activity may be divided into primary, secondary and tertiary sectors. The world's industrialized nations have seen a relative decline in manufacturing industries and an upsurge in service industries, especially those in the high-tech sector.

4. Controlling inflation and unemployment are major concerns of modern governments, in order to achieve sustained growth in the economy.

5. Balance of payments calculations are used to assess a country's trade with other countries. A trade deficit indicates that it imports more than it exports.

6	While the fluctuations of the business cycle affect all economies, governments use monetary and fiscal policies to avoid the damaging effects of severe swings.
7	Public spending and taxation are matters of governments' fiscal policy. Reducing taxation or increasing public spending are seen as ways of stimulating the economy.
8	Monetary policy usually rests with central banks. Altering interest and exchange rates are seen as tools for controlling inflation. Within the EMU (the euro-zone), interest and exchange rates are determined by the ECB, while fiscal policies are still determined by national authorities.
9	Regional and global economic integration limits the room for manoeuvre once enjoyed by national governments over economic policies.

Review questions

???

1. In what ways is the circular flow diagram useful to show overall economic activity in the national economy?
2. How are GDP and GNP per capita used to compare countries, and what are their limitations?
3. Describe the three sectors of the modern industrial economy. Which is growing the most rapidly and why?
4. Define inflation and explain what its damaging effects can be on a national economy.
5. What are the dimensions of unemployment which impact on different business locations and what government policies can be used to deal with sectoral or regional unemployment?
6. Why is the balance of payments important to policy-makers and why are governments concerned if there is a current account deficit?
7. What factors cause economic growth and which countries at present show the strongest rates of growth?
8. Describe the stages of the business cycle. How do they impact on business activities?
9. In what ways do governments control monetary policy and how has their room for manoeuvre become more limited with economic integration?
10. What are the implications of EMU? Is EMU bringing about convergence between member states?

Assignments

1 Looking at the key indicators of the macroeconomic environment, what policy instruments are available to national decision-makers and to what extent are they now limited by factors beyond their borders?

2 From the business point of view, assess the pros and cons of joining the euro-zone.

Further reading

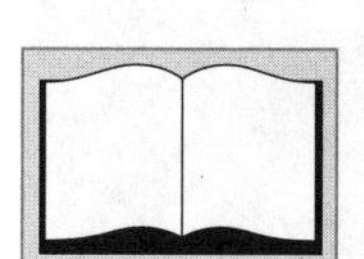

Dunning, J. (ed.) (1997) *Governments, Globalization and International Business* (Oxford: Oxford University Press)

Eijffinger, S. and deHaan, J. (2000) *European Monetary and Fiscal Policy* (Oxford: Oxford University Press)

Maddison, A. (1991) *Dynamic Forces in Capitalist Development* (Oxford: Oxford University Press)

Parkin, M., Powell, M. and Matthews, K. (1997) *Economics*, 3rd edn (Harlow: Addison Wesley)

Chapter

4 Major economic systems

Outline of chapter

1. To identify the distinguishing features of different economic systems and how they impact on business structures and activities
2. To appreciate the defining principles of capitalism, as exemplified in major Western economies
3. To distinguish between different models of capitalist market economy and how they are evolving in the global environment
4. To assess the strength and content of regionalization and economic integration in the context of national economic pathways

4.0 Introduction

Each nation must come to terms with how to allocate scarce resources to satisfy the needs of those within its territory. This is the chief function of its economic system. Economic systems vary from society to society. The values and attitudes that a society attaches to activities of production, such as work and wealth accumulation, are key to its economic system, as are the values that it holds about how wealth should be distributed. While there are recognized factors of production, made up of capital, labour and land, there are numerous ways in which their ownership and use may be organized. They range from total state ownership and control at one extreme to free-market capitalism at the other extreme. In practice, most systems fall somewhere between these two. However, there are major differences in economic systems from society to society, which impact on business organization and operations. Moreover, economic systems are not static, but are influenced by changes in the national, regional and international environment.

An observable trend across all continents has been the shift towards more open markets and away from state ownership and control. This trend has brought greater opportunities for the expansion of business enterprises into wider markets globally. On the other hand, governmental regulation of enterprise has proliferated, adding to the complexity of business activities. The aim of this chapter will be to examine the main types of economic system, both in their 'ideal' forms and how they function in practice in major nation-states. We will look at how national economies fit into broad categories, adapting systems in national environments. Trends in both developed and transitional economies will be highlighted, as business organizations play key roles in the changing environment. Finally, we assess the impact of globalization and regionalization on the business environment.

4.1 Overview of world economic systems

The world's major economic systems are usually classified in rather a broad-brush manner as capitalism on the one hand and socialism on the other. This polarized view of economies probably fitted reality most accurately during the cold war period, when economic systems were seen in the context of dominant ideologies – complete world pictures of societal structures and human values. The socialist states were the state-planned, collectivist economies, while the capitalist states were free-market economies. With the crumbling of the Soviet Union and market reforms taking place in the other major socialist power, China, this dualistic view has given way to a much more fragmented and diverse spectrum of contrasting economic systems. There are now hardly any avowedly socialist states left, and even they, notably North Korea and Cuba, have made tentative steps to open up their economies. On the other hand, while all systems now seem to be some hue of capitalism, there are significant differences between them, and the inclusion of social welfare elements indicate how capitalism as a model has evolved since its early days.

4.2 Capitalism: elements of the market economy

The force behind nineteenth-century industrialization in Europe and the US was capitalism. **Capitalism** rests on the principle that a **market economy**, in which ownership of production is in private hands, is preferable to a state-run economy, in which ownership and control of the means of production reside in the state. The underlying assumption of capitalism is that, through each individual's pursuit of self-interested economic activity, society as a whole benefits. This guiding principle is associated with capitalism in its purest form, or laissez-faire capitalism. The main examples of the laissez-faire model are Britain and the US, the countries in which capitalism as an economic system took shape (featured in the first two Minifiles in this chapter). It comprises three key elements: freedom of enterprise, competitive markets and private property.

Minifile

THE UNITED STATES ECONOMY

GDP for 1999 (billions)	$9,190.4
GDP per head	$33,900
GDP rate of growth 1998–99	4.1%
Unemployment in 1999	4.2%

Key points:

1 World's strongest economy, and foremost example of free-market capitalism

2 Consistently impressive growth rates in the 1990s attributable to corporate restructuring, flexible working and innovations in information technology (IT)

3 Dominant global position in IT and international finance

4 Social problems, such as persistent poverty and the provision of medical care for the poor and elderly, are continuing difficult issues for government

Sources: OECD, *OECD in Figures 2000*; ILO, *World Employment Report 2001.*

WWW WEBALERT

Up-to-date US economic data is available from the Economic Statistics Briefing Room of the White House, at http://www.whitehouse.gov/fsbe/esbr.html

The US Gateway to Government, providing links to all government departments, is at http://www.whitehouse.gov/WH/html/handbook.html

4.2.1 Freedom of enterprise

Freedom of enterprise is the right of all individuals in a society to pursue their own choice of business activity, in the place they wish to pursue it. Freedom of enterprise flourishes in an open society, in which individuals are free to compete in the marketplace and accumulate private wealth. Freedom of enterprise, however, is not an absolute concept. In practice, there are many limitations and constraints on the setting up of business and the way in which it operates. It is easier to get started in some countries than in others. Figure 4.1 shows that the US, UK and Australia have business environments more favourable to start-ups than other countries. Japan has the least favourable conditions, being characterized by bureaucratic regulation which acts as a barrier to entry for both domestic and overseas firms. Governments play a balancing role between encouraging free enterprise and stifling it by over-regulation. Individual entrepreneurs are much less likely to flourish in an environment hemmed in by hundreds of bureaucratic regulations governing location and planning permissions, building requirements and employment regulations – all of which are referred to as 'red tape'. At the same time, transparent and fair regimes of business regulation are part of a system of free enterprise. A stable and impartial legal framework is an important pre-requisite for free enterprise to flourish. If connections with government officials or the payment of bribes are necessary to carry on business, corruption sets in, inhibiting the operation of a free market. As was seen in the last chapter, authorities can facilitate business development in numerous ways, through incentives, 'enterprise zones' and advantageous tax regimes.

Figure 4.1 Cost of forming a private limited liability company, 1999

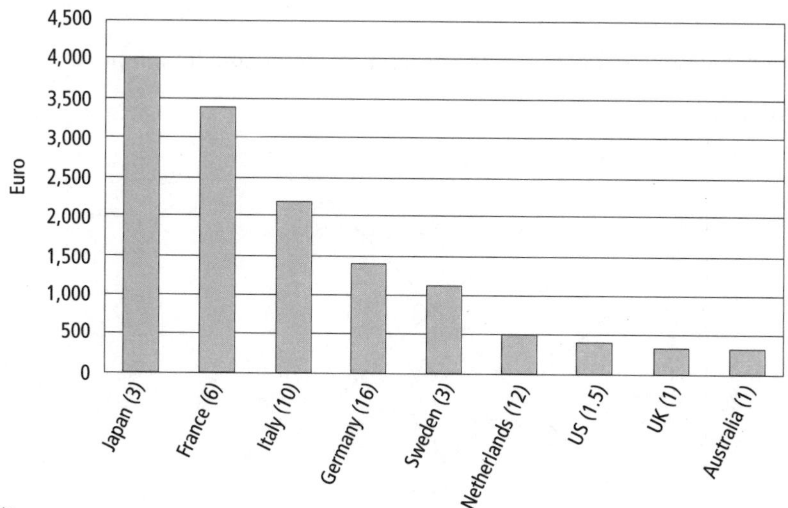

Note
1. Number of weeks given in brackets after each country.

Source: Union of Industrial and Employers' Confederations of Europe (UNICE), in *Financial Times*, 23 March 2000.

Other constraints on freedom of enterprise arise from the perceived need for regulation in the social, economic and natural environment. A factory may emit pollutants which ruin the agricultural crops in the adjacent field, or even in the neighbouring country. Factory processes which are unsafe or employ child labourers may be economically efficient, but harmful to health and unethical. Human rights and protection of the natural environment have now become major concerns for both governments and businesses. The legal and ethical environment of business in most countries now curtails these practices.

4.2.2 Competitive markets: supply and demand

The essence of the market economy is competition, whereby businesses compete against each other in offering goods and services to the public. Entrepreneurs in a marketplace are competing for the consumer's money, through supply and demand.

Demand arises from the consumer, and market demand represents the sum total of the demands of all the individual consumers. **Supply** originates with producers, and market supply represents the total availability of the good in the market in a particular period, from all producers. Demand in this context means demand that is backed up by the ability to pay, under specific economic conditions, or 'effective demand'. It should therefore be distinguished from needs and wants of consumers. A consumer may wish to have a luxury holiday, or feels the need for one, but this wish will not be turned into demand unless matched by an ability to pay. Demand theory holds that if demand for the product is greater than supply, the price will rise, and producers may be encouraged to produce more. If supply exceeds demand, the price will fall and producers will respond by producing less of the product.

Figure 4.2 Supply and demand: the determination of equilibrium price

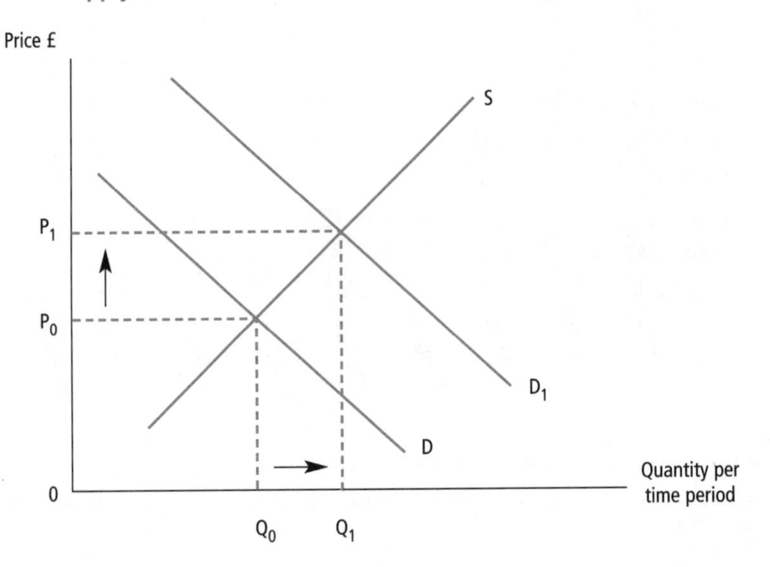

The relationship between supply and demand determines the price of a good. The 'equilibrium price' is that which is obtained when demand and supply are equally matched. In Figure 4.2, this is the point at which demand and supply curves intersect. When the price is above the equilibrium price, supply is greater than demand and therefore must fall. If the price is below the equilibrium price, demand is greater than supply and the price will rise. Thus, the system adjusts to the wants of consumers. Figure 4.2 shows an increase in demand for a product from D to D_1, with supplies remaining constant. This increase, which could be caused by a number of factors, such as a change in consumer tastes favouring the product, will cause the price to rise, as the product is perceived to be in short supply. Producers will respond to the opportunity to sell more of the good, and new producers are likely to enter the market, thus increasing supply. A new equilibrium price, P_1 is reached, reflecting the new levels of both supply and demand at Q_1.

Producers at any given time are encouraged to allocate resources to producing the products in demand, as these will have higher prices and yield greater profit. As has been seen in previous chapters, the producers who are quicker to respond with new products to meet shifts in consumer tastes are more likely to profit than slower rivals.

Also important in markets is the cost of production, as the producers with higher costs and higher prices will be undercut by more efficient producers. The producer's profit depends on the difference between the selling price of the goods and the cost of their production.

For business planning, it is important to be able to assess the level of demand for a product and the effect of price on the consumer's decision whether to purchase it. The responsiveness of one variable to another is known as **elasticity**. 'Price elasticity' refers to the effect of price changes on the quantity demanded by consumers. The concept of price elasticity can be expressed as a formula:

$$E = \frac{\text{\% change in quantity demanded}}{\text{\% change in price}}$$

If the percentage change in quantity is greater than the percentage change in price, then demand is relatively *elastic*, that is, sensitive to price changes. In this case, the price elasticity is greater than one. However, if the percentage change in quantity demanded is less than the percentage change in price, demand is relatively *inelastic*, implying that it is not very sensitive to price changes. In this case, the value of price elasticity is less than one. Clearly, goods such as necessities will have a low value of elasticity, in that a household will be compelled to buy, whatever the price. On the other hand, for goods which are seen as luxuries, such as package holidays, an increase in price can sharply affect demand.

Demand is also influenced by changes in consumers' income, as an increase or decrease in income will affect the consumer's decision to purchase. This concept is known as 'income elasticity', expressed as the formula:

$$\text{Income elasticity} = \frac{\%\ \text{change in quantity demanded}}{\%\ \text{change in income}}$$

Goods may be classified as normal, superior or inferior, depending on consumer perceptions. For normal goods, such as household electrical appliances, an increase in income will lead to an increase in demand. For goods perceived as inferior, such as low-cost or low-quality food products,

Case study 4.1 Demand for mobile phones

Despite predictions that the market was saturated, mobile phone sales continued to rise in 2000. Nokia, the world's largest handset manufacturer, sold 128 million handsets in 2000, out of an estimated total world market of 405 million, up 45 per cent on 1999. Far from disappointing but, such had been the explosive growth of the mobile phone market, these figures were less than the predicted 135 million Nokia expected to sell, and world demand of at least 420 million. As a consequence, Nokia's share price suffered an 18 per cent drop.

In the UK in 2000, mobile phones stood out as a success story amidst general gloom over manufacturing output. From 1996–99, household spending on mobile phones, including line rental and vouchers, increased fivefold. The biggest increases were in the poorest households. While 80 per cent of the richest households have mobiles, ownership among the lowest 10 per cent more than doubled in 1999. Sixty per cent of the entire population had mobiles by 1999. This would seem to leave few besides babies, toddlers and the very elderly. Where is stable demand growth to come from?

Replacements for existing handsets already represent 40–50 per cent of Nokia's global sales. However, the replacement market is highly vulnerable to wider economic conditions, such as recession. It is hoped that improvements in technology and changing handset fashions will encourage growing numbers to upgrade their handsets. In the past, technological innovation has always rescued the industry, particularly in the mid-1990s, when the arrival of higher quality digital handsets rejuvenated the flagging analogue market. Mobiles using the high-speed General Packet Radio Switching (GPRS) system suffered delays in production in 2000. With the third-generation handsets just round the corner, many customers may delay replacements a while longer.

The possible health risk of handsets and masts is a factor which could influence consumer attitudes towards mobile phones. Although research is inconclusive, the British government has recommended that parents limit the time children are allowed to use mobiles and operators are reducing the amount of marketing aimed at younger customers. However, one trend which has spread is text messaging, which took five years before it gained rapidly in popularity, especially among younger users.

Sources: Roberts, D., 'Wake-up call for mobile investors', *Financial Times*, 11 January 2001; Smith, D., 'UK goes upwardly mobile', *Sunday Times*, 10 December 2000.

Case question

What are the factors which influence current and future demand for mobile phones?

demand may decline as income increases, and consumers turn to better quality, more expensive products. Consumer expectations and tastes change over time and vary from country to country. Calculating the elasticities of demand can help organizations in decision-making about particular markets, but it should be remembered that they hold for particular sets of conditions, which may change.

Minifile

THE BRITISH ECONOMY

GDP for 1999 (billions)	$1,324.4
GDP per head	$23,300
GDP rate of growth, 1998–99	1.7%
Unemployment in 1999	6.0%

Key points:

1. Labour government under Prime Minister Tony Blair, elected in 1997 and re-elected in 2001, has pursued a 'third way' agenda between market capitalism and social justice
2. Sustained economic growth, mainly in service sector
3. Health and education are main areas of government and public attention, with problems of quality and exclusion of most concern
4. Persistence of north–south divide, contrasting depressed northern areas with booming southeast
5. Welfare-to-work policy to encourage the unemployed back to work
6. Plans to join the euro-zone, but no timetable

Sources: OECD, *OECD in Figures 2000*; ILO, *World Employment Report 2001*.

4.2.3 Private property

The third of the elements of capitalism is private ownership of property. Property includes capital, goods and the property that exists in a person's labour. Private ownership is linked to incentives in capitalism: the system aims to assure citizens that they personally will be the beneficiaries of their property and labour. On the other hand, wealth accumulation within capitalist systems has tended to concentrate in the hands of the few, producing a wide gap between rich and poor. The extreme inequalities of income distribution, which are inherent in the capitalist model, have led to government intervention to protect the weakest in society through a host of social welfare measures, such as income support and housing benefit. In the US and UK, these measures have been seen as a 'safety net', whereas in other countries, as will be discussed later in this chapter, they have taken on a much stronger role.

An area of private property which is growing in economic significance, is intellectual property. **Intellectual property** refers to the 'products' of human ingenuity. They include patents for new products or processes; copyright for written, musical and artistic works (which includes computer software); and trademarks for a company's logos. In common with other types of property, the inventor of a new product wishes to exploit it for gain and to be assured that others will not steal the idea and set up in business producing an identical product. Patents also protect new technology. As capturing technological advances is crucial to competitive advantage, the monopoly granted by a patent may be worth a great deal of money in global markets. Internet technology, along with its many benefits, has made life much easier for infringers, while firms are finding it difficult to protect their intellectual property, especially across national borders (see Chapters 8 and 10).

4.3 Market structures

Economists analyse markets in terms of their degree of competition. At one end of the spectrum lies the ideal 'perfect competition', and at the opposite extreme exists monopoly. Under perfect competition, there are many buyers and sellers, none of whom is able to influence the price to a greater extent than the others. Players can come and go freely, as there are no barriers to entry or exit. In a monopoly, by contrast, there is only one player, and no competition at all, leaving the monopolist in a position to determine price and quantity. In reality, perfect competition hardly exists and markets experience degrees of competition along the continuum from one extreme to the other. The emergence of monopolies and oligopolies has accompanied capitalist development and some of these concentrations of economic power are of global proportions. These forms of economic concentration are often created by mergers of already powerful companies. They are generally viewed as damaging to consumer interests. As *The Economist* pointed out in its survey of the twentieth century, economic concentration presents a paradox of capitalism: the encouragement of individual enterprise is the incentive of capitalism, but business, if it grows too big, destroys incentives (*The Economist*, 11 September 1999). Governments have thus evolved systems of regulation and competition policy.

4.3.1 Porter's five-forces model of industry structure

Michael Porter devised a model to explain the forces that determine the competitive intensity of an industry and thereby the profit potential for companies within the industry. He defines an industry as 'the group of firms producing products that are close substitutes for each other' (Porter, 1998a, p. 5). The five competitive forces are depicted in Figure 4.3. The stronger these forces, the greater threat they pose, and the more constrained a company is in its ability to raise prices and increase profits in the short term. However, in the long term, a company may respond to strong competitive forces with strategies designed to alter the strength of particular forces to its advantage. As Porter says:

> The goal of competitive strategy for a business unit in an industry is to find a position in the industry where the company can best defend itself against these

Figure 4.3 Porter's five-forces model: forces driving industry competition

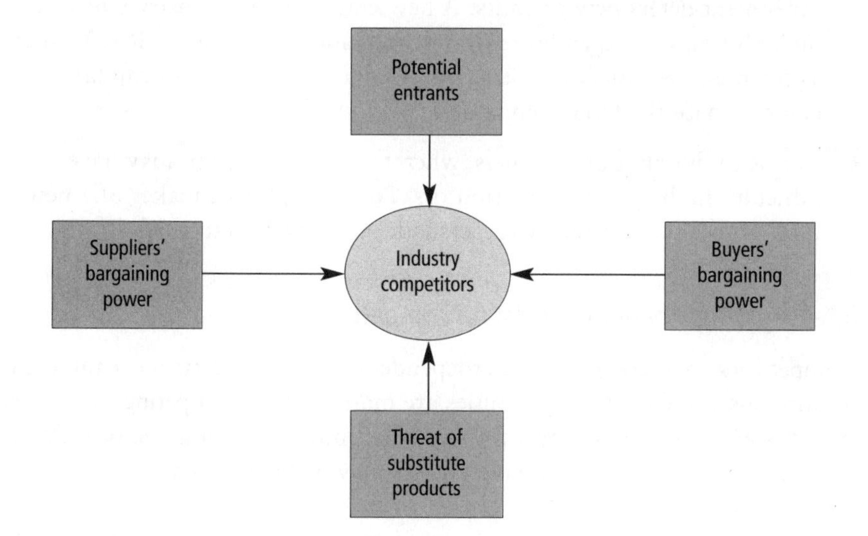

Source: Adapted from Porter, M. (1998a) *Competitive Strategy: Techniques for Analyzing Industries and Competitors* (New York: Free Press) p. 4 (reprinted with permission).

> competitive forces or can influence them in its favor ... The key for developing strategy is to delve below the surface and analyse the sources of each. (Porter, 1998a, p. 4)

We look at each of the five forces in turn.

Potential entrants

New entrants offer an industry greater capacity and greater competition for market share, thus posing a threat to existing competitors. The extent of this threat depends on barriers to entry. If barriers are high, then the threat of new entrants is low. Sources of barriers to entry include:

- Economies of scale, whereby unit costs decline as the volume produced increases. New entrants may thus have to enter on a large scale or not at all. If they enter on a small scale, they face cost disadvantage.
- Product differentiation, which may be based on building brand identification over time, entailing substantial expenditure on advertising. New entrants, for example, in the soap powder market, which is dominated by a few strong brands (such as Ariel and Persil) are faced by the huge potential costs of advertising and promotions to gain market share.

- Capital requirements, whereby the necessity to make a huge capital investment deters new entrants. A new entrant in an industry which relies on high levels of expenditure on research and development (R&D), such as the pharmaceutical industry, will need a huge amount of capital to compete with the large companies.
- Access to distribution channels, whereby the new entrant may have difficulty finding willing distributors. For example, the maker of a new food product may struggle to persuade supermarkets to stock it.

Intensity of rivalry among existing competitors

Competitors in markets are interdependent. Prices, advertising campaigns, promotions and customer warranties are monitored by competing firms, who then respond. The intensity of rivalry depends on several factors (Porter, 1998a, pp. 17–23). The following factors may be highlighted:

- Numerous or equally balanced competitors – where firms are numerous, companies tend not to keep a close eye on competitors' moves, but where they are more equally balanced, each tracks others' moves with a view to countering competitors' strategies.
- Rate of industry growth – where an industry is growing rapidly, there is plenty of opportunity for firms to expand. Where an industry is growing slowly, on the other hand, competition centres on gaining market share.
- Product or service characteristics – if a product is so basic as to be essentially the same, regardless of supplier, then it resembles a commodity, and the buyer's choice depends on price and services, where intense competition results.
- Level of fixed costs – where there are high fixed costs, there is pressure for companies to fill capacity, cutting prices in order at least to cover fixed costs. An example is the airline industry. Scheduled flights may fly at less than their capacity of passengers, and airline companies offer discounted fares through various outlets.
- High exit barriers – these are the 'economic, strategic, and emotional factors' that keep a company in an industry (Porter, 1998a, p. 20). It may have invested in particular assets, for example, which would be difficult to sell or convert to other uses. Managers are inclined to carry on business so long as they are not making huge losses.

Pressure from substitute products

A substitute product is one that performs the same function as the industry's product. Substitute products may appear to be different – tea and coffee, for example, are quite different, but serve the same function. Substitutes in effect place a ceiling on the prices that companies in the industry can charge. If the price of coffee rises steeply, consumers will be likely to switch to tea.

Bargaining power of buyers

Important buyer groups can be powerful in forcing down prices or bargaining for higher quality or better terms. They may be in a position to play off one producer against another. The buyers who are in the strongest positions are those who (1) purchase a large proportion of the seller's output; or (2) can change to alternative suppliers with ease, as the product is a standard one.

Bargaining power of suppliers

Key suppliers can threaten to raise prices or reduce quality. A supplier is in a powerful position if (1) the supply industry is dominated by a few powerful companies (such as the petrol industry); or (2) there are few available substitutes for its product (again, such as petrol).

4.3.2 Monopoly and oligopoly

Economic concentration in its extreme form is found in the monopoly. A **monopoly** exists if a single firm is the sole supplier in a market, and new entrants are precluded. Such a situation may exist even in a market economy, where there is 'imperfect' competition. Some industries, such as public utilities, have been seen as natural monopolies, largely because of the scale economies to be gained, and are defended on the grounds that they are in the public interest. However, monopolies seldom operate in the consumer's interest. The monopolist is in a position to control supply and determine price, with no fear of being undercut by rivals or losing customers to producers offering an improved product. The monopolist may be inefficient as a producer, but has little incentive to streamline procedures or staffing levels. The monopolist thus faces no competitive pressure to offer the consumer a better product or a better deal. The pure monopoly is now becoming rare, as state-owned industries are being dismantled in most countries. More common are the industries dominated by a few powerful players.

An **oligopoly** exists when a few large producers dominate a market. The oligopolistic market is characterized by a lack of price competition, as firms are reluctant to increase or reduce prices for fear of sacrificing market share. These markets are also noted for large amounts of advertising and brands, which constitute non-price competition. The growth in transnational corporations (TNCs), along with trends towards industry consolidation, has produced numerous oligopolistic industries. They include oil, motor vehicles and soap powder, to name just a few. Some markets are dominated by just two producers. This market structure is known as 'duopoly'. Prices and sales in an oligopolistic market are heavily influenced by the interplay between producers. To understand their strategies, economists often use 'game theory', which, as in ordinary everyday games, looks at the ways players seek to maximize their own positions in given situations (Parkin et al., 1997). As in ordinary games, too, there is the temptation to cheat. One common way is by collusion, which may be a price-fixing agreement or a carve-up of markets. When firms engage in such agreements systematically, a **cartel** is said to exist. The cartel is generally assumed to be anti-competitive and against the interests of the consumer.

WWW WEBALERT

Resources on competition policy are available on the internet

For the UK, see http://www.dti.gov.uk/cacp/cp/default.htm
This site provides links for UK, EU and international policy

The Competition Commission is at
http://www.competition-commission.gov.uk/

The Competition Act 1998 is available at
http://www.hmso.gov.uk/acts/acts1998/19980041.htm

For EU competition policy, see the European Commission website at
http://www.europa.eu.int/comm/competition

4.3.3 Competition policy

Most countries have enacted legislation to curtail monopolists (known as **antitrust law** in America) and anti-competitive practices such as price-fixing agreements through cartels or informal groups of companies, aimed at controlling the market. The Organization for Economic Co-operation and Development (OECD) sees 'hard core cartels' as a 'major public policy problem' for developing as well as developed countries, costing economies worldwide billions of dollars (*Financial Times*, 6 June 2000).

Competition law provides for notification and approval of mergers and takeovers. The UK has had legal mechanisms for the regulation of monopolies and restrictive trade practices since 1948, when the Monopolies and Mergers Commission was set up. With the Competition Act of 1998, this area of the law is now being harmonized with European Union (EU) law, and a new Competition Commission has been set up. Under the new law, 'abuse of a dominant position' in the UK constitutes an infringement, in keeping with Article 82 of the Treaty of Amsterdam (which came into force in 1999). Agreements which 'prevent, restrict, or distort' competition also constitute infringement (in accordance with Article 81 of the Treaty of Amsterdam), unless the agreement can be brought within one of the exemptions, the criteria generally being the potential benefit to consumers.

US antitrust law goes back even further, to the Sherman Act 1890, but cartels, holding companies, and trusts, which had by then grown powerful, were not easily tamed. Moreover, the US courts have tended to tread lightly on big business (Kovacic and Shapiro, 2000). The US has more global companies by far than any other country, and size is seen as an advantage in global competition. Still, there are examples where the federal authorities have brought high-profile antitrust cases, such as that against Microsoft. The case, featured in Case Study 4.2, highlights the ambivalence of Americans to

Case study 4.2 Microsoft takes on the antitrust authorities

Microsoft was founded in 1975 by college dropout, Bill Gates, at the age of 20. At 44, and worth an estimated $85 billion, he stepped down as chairman and chief executive officer. But when his successor at the helm took over, the company's fate seemed to be hanging in the balance. Antitrust actions against Microsoft's software empire, specifically for its 'tie-in' sales of applications and operating systems, began in 1990 and continued throughout the 1990s. In the 'browser wars' with its bitter rival, Netscape Communications, Microsoft inserted contract clauses to prevent manufacturers of computers and internet services companies from distributing Netscape's browser software. Microsoft was alleged to have violated a court order issued in 1995. In 1997, The US Justice Department and 20 US states brought an action against the company for anti-competitive practices designed to maintain a monopoly in its Windows operating systems and to extend that monopoly to internet browsing software, by forcing manufacturers of personal computers to install its internet browser, Explorer, as a condition of installing Windows.

In 1998, Judge Thomas Penfield Jackson found against Microsoft, and it looked possible that the court would order a 'structural' remedy involving the break-up of the company. However, Microsoft was successful in its appeal against a break-up in 2001, and it seemed that the tide was turning back in its favour. The appeal court remained of the view that the company had used anti-competitive means to maintain its monopoly, through the integration of the two products, Windows and its browser software, but it seemed likely that the remedy awarded would be a less radical 'conduct' remedy, such as requiring Microsoft to offer versions of Windows with and without new applications. A more conciliatory atmosphere stems partly from the shift of administrations in the White House, from the tougher line of the Democratic Clinton administration, to the less strict antitrust policies of the Republican Bush administration, which took office in 2001. Whatever the court orders, Microsoft's relations with the regulators are likely to be in the spotlight for years to come.

Sources: Wolffe, R. and Kehoe, L. 'Operating error', *Financial Times*, 5 April 2000; Alexander, G., 'Trust busters fail to tame the Microsoft beast', *Sunday Times*, 30 April 2000; Wolffe, R., 'Twin options suit Justice Department', *Financial Times*, 29 April 2000; Wolffe, R., 'Microsoft tries to update legal history', *Financial Times*, 20 July 2001; Brinkley, J., 'Microsoft cites AT&T to fight breakup', *New York Times*, 15 May 2000.

Case question

In what ways are consumers, including business consumers, getting a bad deal as a result of Microsoft's monopoly and how would greater competition benefit consumers?

big business: Bill Gates is the epitome of the American dream on the one hand, but represents corporate might against the individual on the other.

The EU Commission has become increasingly influential in its role in regulating competition, and is perceived as taking a harder line on large mergers than American authorities. For example, a proposed merger between General Electric (GE) and Honeywell in 2001 was cleared by US federal authorities, but rejected by the EU Commission, as it was felt that GE would gain an unfair advantage in the aircraft engine and avionics industries.

The OECD, known as the rich countries' 'club', now has 29 members. Its website is divided into a number of themes and provides a great deal of data and analysis. It is at http://www.oecd.org

Public utilities such as water, electricity supply, gas, postal services and telecommunications have long enjoyed monopoly status as nationalized industries in many countries. The process of transferring them from state ownership to private sector companies is privatization. From the 1980s onwards, privatization of these state monopolies has been a continuing trend. In the UK the process began in the 1980s. Ownership is transferred to a company, which then offers shares to the public. Typically, the state retains a large share, such as a 40 per cent stake or more. However, privatizations do not open the door directly to competition, as the new companies have customarily enjoyed privileged status in the early phase of their existence. In the UK, privatizations in the 1980s were accompanied by the establishment of independent regulatory, or 'watchdog', bodies to oversee the interests of consumers. Only in the 1990s were markets opening up, and competition starting to bite, offering consumer choice and product differentiation. Deregulation of both gas and electricity in the EU was hastened by an EU Directive requiring member states to open up 30 per cent of gas and electricity supply by late 2000 (see Table 4.1).

Privatizations of telecommunications have created new global players, such as British Telecom (BT) and Deutsche Telekom, which are themselves acquiring other telecommunications services through further privatizations. In this way, Deutsche Telekom has acquired considerable stakes in Central and Eastern Europe. These acquisitions are a logical response to the loss of the domestic monopoly, but, in addition, a major force at work is the need to maximize shareholder value, which is paramount for corporations in market economies.

Table 4.1 Opening of the electricity market in the European Union, 1996–99

Country	Percentage opened to competition
Austria	30
Belgium	35
Denmark	90
Finland	100
France	30
Germany	30
Greece	30
Italy	30
Ireland	30
Luxembourg	–
Netherlands	33
Portugal	30
Spain	45
Sweden	100
UK	100
EU total	65

Source: Financial Times, 6 June 2000.

Laissez-faire capitalist model

- Entrepreneurial, individualistic culture
- Limited government intervention in markets
- Little state ownership
- Social legislation as a safety net
- Emphasis on shareholder value in corporate governance

4.4 Social market capitalism

The concept of the welfare state dates from the aftermath of the Depression of 1929, when Western governments introduced systems of social security, unemployment benefit and other programmes now taken for granted. To many, mainly those on the political right, these measures are seen as an essential social safety net in the market economy, while to those more to the left, social justice is seen as a goal in itself. The **social market model** gives a social justice dimension to the capitalist model. Often called the 'mixed economy', its main features are state ownership in key sectors and extensive social welfare programmes which reduce the inequalities inherent in the pure capitalist model. State ownership and private ownership exist side by side. Major concerns such as heavy industry, banks, oil companies and airlines may be state-owned. Seen as national champions, they are naturally protected from takeover bids, and, should they fall on hard times, can be helped out by the state.

Minifile

THE FRENCH ECONOMY

GDP 1999 (billions)	$1,326.0
GDP per head	$21,900
GDP rate of growth 1998–99	2.4%
Unemployment in 1999	12%

Key points:

1 French capitalism as a model characterized by the strong, centralized state
2 Liberalization and diminishing role of the state in the 1990s, in letting the market lead, as evidenced in privatizations and international expansion of French firms
3 Tradition of extensive welfare state provisions and government subsidies
4 The introduction of the 35-hour week, accompanied by state subsidies to firms, is bringing about greater flexibility in employment, but has been opposed by the trade unions

Sources: OECD, *OECD in Figures 2000*; ILO, *World Employment Report 2001.*

The social market model has evolved differently in the diverse societies in which it has been adopted. In Sweden the emphasis is on an extensive welfare state to reduce social inequalities (Pontusson, 1997). France and Germany (see Minifiles) also have extensive social welfare policies, but they differ in the role played by the state in economic life. In France, the centralized state has created a more 'statist' model, while the German model is more 'corporatist', based on co-operation between the state, business and labour (Vitols, 2000). In Germany, '**co-determination**' is the principle by which workers are legally entitled to a say in company management. Germany is a more decentralized state than France. As such, it contrasts with the laissez-faire model of the US and the statist model in France (Streeck, 1997). Many tiers of government in Germany, however, have tended to create complex regulatory regimes for businesses to navigate through.

Minifile

THE GERMAN ECONOMY

GDP 1999 (billions)	$1,934.0
GDP per head	$23,600
GDP rate of growth 1998–99	1.3%
Unemployment 1999	8.7%

Key points:

1. High cost of reunification of East and West and high costs of social welfare programmes have created huge government deficits
2. Deregulation in former state monopolies of telecommunication and electricity
3. Dominance of the private company, but growth occurring in entrepreneurial activity and corporate restructuring in large companies
4. Government policies to reform corporate taxation and reduce state subsidies
5. Unemployment in the former East German region running at 19%, and wages 15% lower than in the West, creating some disillusionment

Sources: OECD, *OECD in Figures 2000*; ILO, *World Employment Report 2001*.

In both France and Germany, deregulation and growing market orientation, often referred to as liberalization measures, have in recent years pushed back state regulation and introduced greater competitiveness (Vitols, 2000). In the process, French and German companies have become more active in overseas investment. The acquisition by Renault (40 per cent owned by the French government) of a 36.8 per cent stake in Nissan is an example, as are the acquisitions of water suppliers in many parts of the world by French utilities companies. Germany has had to overcome the problems of rebuilding former East Germany after reunification, where unemployment and the need to modernize outdated industries have presented major challenges. From the business perspective, corporate restructuring represents a shift towards shareholder value as a priority, and a growing market for corporate control through takeovers and mergers.

POINTS TO REMEMBER

The social market model of capitalism

- Significant state involvement in economy
- Bureaucratic regulation of business
- Extensive social welfare programmes
- Corporate governance based on social priorities, rather than shareholder value
- Closed system of corporate control and little takeover market

4.5 Asian capitalism

Economic activities in any country are embedded in the social and cultural experiences of its people. Industrialization and economic development in the nations of East and Southeast Asia are often grouped together as representing a distinctive model of Asian capitalism. Their development can be seen in three phases: first, Japan; second, the Asian 'tiger' economies; and lastly, China. In looking at their capitalist development, their similarities and differences become apparent.

4.5.1 Japan

Japan, like Germany, faced the task of rebuilding its industries after the Second World War. The state provided economic guidance, and hence Japan is looked on as the 'developmental state' model (Johnson, 1982). The use of 'industrial policy', rather than outright state ownership, has been a chief feature of its economic development, relying on co-operation between the three centres of power – the bureaucracy, politicians and big businesses (see Minifile on Japan). Business in Japan has traditionally been organized around groups of companies, or ***keiretsu***, linked by cross-shareholdings and informal networks with suppliers and customers. The *keiretsu*, usually centred around a main bank, have served as a source of generous loans, but also have provided a bulwark against hostile takeovers and a deterrent to market entry by outsiders. The reliance on interlocking corporate structures as a source of economic dynamism has given rise to the notion of 'alliance capitalism' as a category to cover the range of economic systems in which interfirm relations, rather than free-market exchange, predominate (Gerlach, 1991).

The Japanese view of the company stands out against its Western counterparts. The company is seen as a family and as a focus of loyalty, rather than simply as a source of income. This outlook is often depicted as the Confucian work ethic, in which collective values and consensus, rather than individualism and self-interest, are the driving force. The guarantee of a

Minifile

THE JAPANESE ECONOMY

GDP for 1999 (billions)	$3,104.7
GDP per head	$24,500
GDP rate of growth 1998–99	1.4%
Unemployment in 2000	4.9%

Key points:

1. State guidance and industrial policy led Japan's post-war economic 'miracle'
2. Collapse of the 'bubble' economy in 1990 left intractable problems of weak, debt-burdened banks, in need of restructuring
3. Closely knit *keiretsu* groups, which were the engine of economic growth, are now fragmenting in the face of market forces
4. Companies have been slow to restructure and reduce capacity, necessary if competitiveness is to be restored

Sources: OECD, *OECD in Figures 2000*; ILO, *World Employment Report 2001*.

job-for-life has been taken for granted by Japanese workers, a fact that has impeded efforts to restructure in the era of global competition. Case Study 4.3 illustrates the ways in which restructuring and cost-cutting were imposed by new French management from outside. From a position of economic powerhouse in the 1980s, the Japanese economy descended into stagnation in the 1990s. While the immediate cause was a collapse of the banking and financial system, the longer term causes lay with the failure of the system to adapt to global competition. Reluctance by the government to recognize the scale of the financial woes and reluctance by companies to downsize and restructure, even when making losses, have hampered recovery.

Case study 4.3 Turnaround for Nissan

In the 12 months after Renault, the French car maker, acquired a controlling stake (36.8 per cent) in Nissan, French-led management achieved a remarkable turnaround for the company. In 1998, Nissan had debts of ¥2,000 billion (£13 billion) and was on the verge of collapse. The instigator of change was the aptly nicknamed Carlos Ghosn, 'Le Cost Killer', who took over as chief operating officer (now chief executive officer). The difficulties faced by Nissan were those of the traditional Japanese manufacturer: powerful managers in lifelong appointments, huge staffs and a tangle of connected *keiretsu* companies in supply and distribution relationships. Ghosn's revival plan tackled the problems head-on. Five factories would be closed, 21,000 jobs lost and the *keiretsu* suppliers would be halved. The brand was in need of restoration, and new products would be launched. Targets were to return to profitability by the end of 2000 and to reduce the debt by 50 per cent. To the surprise of many, Ghosn more than achieved both targets. Such radical reforms had been impossible to achieve within the traditional Japanese company structure and culture. In particular, the dismantling of the *keiretsu* ties had an immediate effect on the bottom line. Nissan offered its suppliers a deal: if they did not become competitive, the company would go elsewhere. If they did, it would help them.

While the UK remained outside the eurozone, the future of Sunderland's Nissan plant, however, looked in doubt. The next generation Micra seemed likely to go to the Renault factory in Flins, France. The British government stepped in with an aid package of £40 million to the Sunderland plant, to entice Nissan to opt for the UK. Shortly after the package was approved by the European Commission in 2001, Nissan decided in Sunderland's favour, confirming a £200 million investment, and lifting Sunderland's output from 330,000 to 500,000 vehicles a year. A note of caution was sounded, however, for the Sunderland factory's local component suppliers, who face even stiffer competition to do business with Nissan.

Sources: Ibison, D., 'A blueprint for revival', *Financial Times*, 6 November 2000; Burt, T. and Hargreaves, D., 'Brussels approves aid for Nissan plant', *Financial Times*, 18 January 2001.

Case question

What were the problems faced by the new French management at Nissan and what has been the key to the successful turnaround of the company?

4.5.2 Later industrializing economies of Asia

Japan served as an example to other Asian 'late industrializers'. The East Asian countries of South Korea, Singapore, Taiwan and Hong Kong (now part of the People's Republic of China) became known as the 'Asian Tigers', whose economies took off in the 1980s. They were followed by other Asian countries, the Philippines, Thailand, Indonesia, Malaysia. Last to join has been China, whose command economy has been much slower to welcome market reforms. In this section we identify key elements of Asian economic systems, assessing those features which have contributed to economic growth. The Asian economic 'miracle', as it was called, came to an abrupt halt in July 1997, with a series of financial crises (discussed in detail in Chapter 11).

The original tiger economies are all of Chinese cultural heritage, and the notion of the Confucian ethic underpinning their societies is perhaps the strongest feature they have in common. The Confucian priority given to the family and filial duty has provided a culture based on diligence and loyalty to the firm. The traditional Chinese family business has played a dominant part in economic development in all of these societies. Even so, the state has also played an important role. Taiwan, with its strong export-oriented economy, has had state-owned industries in key sectors, which account for one-third of its gross domestic product (GDP), but is currently embarked on a privatization programme.

The city-state of Singapore has also adopted an approach of state intervention, but has refrained from state ownership, instead welcoming foreign direct investors. The city-state can claim 5,000 international companies within its borders. Singaporeans have tolerated a high degree of state interference in business, but are reluctant to complain, as the government has provided a well-managed economy and prosperity. This is the basis of the 'social contract' between Singapore's government and its three million inhabitants. Following the Asian financial crises of 1997, they submitted to austerity measures, which reduced salaries; at the same time, families and firms shoulder many welfare burdens which are provided routinely by the state in most Western societies. A report in 1998 found that public spending on social welfare programmes amounts to just over 5 per cent of GDP in Singapore and Hong Kong, 10 per cent in South Korea and Taiwan and about 15 per cent in Japan. By contrast, the figure is 25 per cent or more in Europe (London School of Economics, 1998).

South Korea's economic development owes its impetus to the large family-owned conglomerates, or *chaebol*, which expanded aggressively overseas during the 1980s. While these groups, including Daewoo, Hyundai and LG, are often compared with Japanese *keiretsu*, there are some basic differences. The *chaebol* are family owned and controlled, not equity-based, as in Japan. Whereas the *keiretsu* is often based on a main bank, finance in Korea is provided by preferential bank loans, effectively guaranteed by the state. It emerged in the late 1990s that *chaebols*' overseas expansion had rested on unsound lending practices, in a web of implicit guarantees between the state, the banks and the business community. These relationships form the basis of what is called 'crony capitalism', in which personal connections carry more weight than objective business considerations. The build-up of bad loans was especially acute in the case of Daewoo, which has had to be broken up into its separate businesses. South Korea has received International Monetary Fund (IMF) loans to help rebuild its economy, but, at the same time, the IMF imposed conditions for restructuring and opening markets which the nation has been slow to implement. (These are further discussed in Chapter 11.) Until recently, South Korea has had no links with the communist regime across the border in North Korea. Contacts are now cautiously being made, which could lead to an opening up of the North Korean economy (see Minifile).

Minifile

THE TWO KOREAS

Since the end of the Korean War in 1953, the line that has divided North and South Korea has represented two different worlds: the impoverished, isolationist and heavily militarized communist state to the north and the prosperous, democratic, tiger economy to the south. The economic disparity between them is much greater than between East and West Germany before reunification. The south's living standards are ten times higher than those in the north, where famine and malnutrition have been major problems. The disparity in life expectancy is more than 20 years: 72.4 years in the south, and 51 years in the north. South Korea has a population of 46.4 million and a GDP per capita of $13,280 (adjusted for purchasing power). North Korea's population of 22 million has a GDP per capita estimated at less than $900 per person (adjusted). Executives of South Korean conglomerates Samsung and LG are planning to invest in production of consumer electronics in the north, but poor infra-structure, unreliable power supplies and a patchy transport network are major obstacles.

There had been almost no communication between the two Koreas until a historic meeting between the two leaders in the spring of 2000. The two signed a wide-ranging communiqué, aiming to achieve economic co-operation initially, and eventually reunification. However, there is a long way to go, and, looking at the German experience, the government of Kim Dae Jung of South Korea, in particular, has cause to be cautious. The cost of rebuilding infrastructure and transport will largely fall on the south. While South Korean companies are keen to invest north of the border, they seek improvement in the laws to protect foreign investment and intellectual property. The South Korean population is cautious about reunification, supporting it in principle, but fearful of the increase in taxes that might be needed to bail out their northern brethren.

Sources: Struck, D., 'High hopes mark talks between two Koreas', *Washington Post*, 14 June 2000; 'Kimraderie, at last', *The Economist*, 17 June 2000; Burton, J., 'South Korea faces up to huge financial cost of modernising the North', *Financial Times*, 16 June 2000.

Political instability is a major factor in the late industrializing states of Malaysia and Indonesia, where ethnic divisions are a source of social and political unrest. Both have traditions of authoritarian leadership, bolstered by military establishments. Both have relied on foreign direct investment as a driving force for economic growth. The Chinese have a strong economic presence in Indonesia: although they make up only 4 per cent of the population, they control more than 70 per cent of listed companies (Beeson, 2000). The toppling of President Suharto, in 1998, brought to an end a 32-year reign, which saw impressive economic growth (averaging 4.6 per cent annually from 1965 onwards) and much improved infrastructure, education and economic prosperity for Indonesians. President Suharto was known as the 'Father of Development', but was also at the centre of a family business empire noted for its corruption. The overthrow of the Suharto regime left a void, and, although there is optimism that the new democratic system will bring the stability needed for economic growth, the future looks uncertain.

4.5.3 An Asian model of capitalism?

We now summarize and assess the extent to which the economic systems of Japan and Southeast Asia's newly industrialized countries present a new Asian model of capitalism. These economies present features in common, but also divergences. All are mixed economies, combining market forces with state guidance. They differ considerably, however, in their perception of the role of the state, varying from a regulatory role, as in Japan, to a more interventionist role, as in Korea. While the Confucian ethic is often said to underpin the Asian model, this generalization, too, conceals a good deal of cultural diversity. Some countries are predominantly Muslim, while in the countries which do have a Confucian cultural heritage, Confucian values have evolved over time. The family firm as a focus of loyalty is much more prevalent in Taiwan and Korea than in Japan, where the company 'as community' has taken the place of the family. It has been suggested that the strongest thread running through Asian capitalism is its embeddedness in social and cultural experience which emphasizes the collectivity rather than the individual. However, as global economic integration deepens, these economic systems are undertaking liberal reforms and opening markets. Stable democratic governments and greater transparency in regulatory regimes are seen as the way forward to stability and sustainable growth for Asian economies.

Lastly, China, the largest Asian country, is also undertaking market reforms, but still within the framework of the one-party state bequeathed by

The Asian model of capitalism

- Strong state intervention
- Bureaucratic regulation of business
- Corporate culture based on the company as family
- Groups of companies, both formal and informal, which act as barriers to new entrants and takeovers
- Weak welfare state provisions

the communist revolution. Before looking at the evolving Chinese economic system, we identify the main elements of the planned economy.

4.6 The planned economy

The **planned economy**, also known as the 'command economy', is based on total ownership and control by the state of the means of production. The economy is based on collectivism rather than individualism and private enterprise. Production is governed by state plan rather than by supply and demand, and prices are set by the state. The aim is achieving targets rather than satisfying consumers' wants. Overproduction, inefficiencies and inflexibility are recurring problems in this type of system, which goes some way to explaining why these systems in their pure form have not been successful in the long term. While their designers maintained a vision of socialism as the ideal society, in which all would be equal, the reality has been stark inequalities under communist-party domination of the state. The two leading examples of communist states have been the Soviet Union and China.

4.6.1 The Soviet Union

The Soviet Union (USSR, or Union of Soviet Socialist Republics) dates from 1918, with the overthrow of the Russian Czar by the Russian revolutionaries, led by Lenin. Their Marxist-Leninist ideology imbued the economic development of the Soviet Union for 74 years. The first five-year plan dates from 1928, when agriculture was collectivized. The Soviet Union expanded, putting in place satellite regimes in Eastern and Central Europe, supported by Russian military might. While state planning brought industrialization and economic growth, its emphasis was on heavy industries, which were inefficient and highly pollutant, while it neglected consumer goods. The Soviet system simply could not keep pace with modern industries in market-based economies. Numerous liberalizing reforms were attempted, to restructure and introduce flexibility, but all failed in the end. *Perestroika* (literally, reconstruction), 1987–89, introduced some freedom of contract between enterprises and some latitude for enterprises to decide what to produce, but these modest reforms were too little, too late. The breakaway of the satellite states started in 1989, and collapse of the Soviet Union itself finally came in 1991. With the dismantling of communism, these independent states now have both democratic constitutions and transitional market economies in place.

4.6.2 From state plan to market: the example of China

While China is an ancient civilization, the current state of China (its full name is the People's Republic of China) dates only from the communist revolution of 1949. Communist rule has changed substantially since then, as its ideological underpinning has evolved. The Maoism of the early years (based on the teachings of Mao Zedong) was in the vein of orthodox Marxism-Leninism. The period from 1958 to 1979 proved to be disastrous for China's people, millions of whom died from famine. Liberal economic reforms began only in 1979, under the leadership of Deng Xiaoping. Thereafter, China's economy grew dramatically, achieving 10 per cent average growth rates for the next two decades. The prosperity of its people has also grown, although there are wide variations between the rural standard of living and that enjoyed by the new urban dwellers.

China's leadership seems committed to economic reforms, and is keen to open up the country to market forces. An indication is the $46 billion in foreign direct investment (FDI) that flowed into the country in 1998, mainly through joint ventures with partners from Western economies. Its admission to the World Trade Organization (WTO) will further open up its economy. Yet there are doubts casting shadows over China's economic and political direction. China's growth slowed in 1999 to 7 per cent. This rate of growth is still healthy compared to its Asian neighbours, but experts suggest that major restructuring is needed, so that sustainable growth can be achieved. Starting from zero in 1979, China's economy is now about 40 per cent privately owned and the percentage is continuously rising. (China amended its constitution in 1999 to allow for the private ownership of property.) A worrying aspect of China's economic development has been its unevenness: the prosperous coastal areas contrast markedly with the vast, less-developed inland area. In common with the old Soviet Union, China is dependent on coal; its state-owned heavy industries are inefficient and damaging to the environment. Restructuring is clearly needed, but there are risks of rising unemployment as inefficient factories are closed. It is estimated that as many as 20 million workers in the state-owned enterprises are surplus to requirements. Further, the World Bank estimates that there may be as many as 100–200 million surplus workers in rural areas. Attracting foreign investment throughout China will play a crucial part in providing new employment.

By contrast, Central and Eastern Europe presents a group of transition economies in which economic and political transformations are proceeding hand in hand.

4.7 Transition economies in Central and Eastern Europe

The Soviet bloc started to break up in 1989. East Germany was united with West Germany in 1990. In the early 1990s, the states of Hungary, Poland, Czechoslovakia, Romania and Bulgaria became independent states. Further fragmentation resulted in the creation of separate Czech and Slovak Republics, as well as the separate Balkan republics of Croatia, Bosnia and the Yugoslav Federation. The Soviet Union itself broke up into 15 separate

Table 4.2 Economic profile of candidate countries for EU membership (1999 estimates)

Country	Population (millions)	GDP per capita (in US$)	GDP growth rate %	Unemployment %
Czech Republic	10.30	5,189	–0.2	9.4
Hungary	10.10	4,853	4.5	7.0
Poland	38.70	3,987	4.1	13.0
Slovenia	2.00	10,020	4.9	7.4
Slovak Republic	5.40	3,650	1.9	19.02
Estonia	1.40	3,564	–1.1	12.3
Lithuania	3.70	2,880	–4.2	14.1
Latvia	2.40	2,582	0.1	14.4

Source: European Bank for Reconstruction and Development (EBRD) (2000) *Transition Report 2000* (London: EBRD).

republics. The three Baltic republics – Estonia, Latvia and Lithuania – went their own way. Russia, which had been the largest of the Soviet republics, adopted a new constitution in 1993, but its economic and political transition has been less successful than that in the more peripheral parts of the Soviet empire. It is important to remember that the former Soviet republics had experienced the socialist planned economy since 1928, whereas the states of Central Europe and the Baltic states were 'sovietized' only in 1948, and thus had recent memories of real independence and a market economy (Bradshaw, 1996). These states were therefore better placed to make the transition to market economies. Economic profiles of these more successful states, now on the threshold of EU membership, are provided in Table 4.2.

4.7.1 The process of transition

'Transition' implies the shift from one economic system to another, while 'reform' is a milder form of change, implying altering aspects of an existing system (Bradshaw, 1996). Reforms, such as limited privatization, had taken place to varying degrees throughout the Soviet empire in the 1980s, but they had not been sufficient to turn round these declining economies. The legacies of communism left the newly created states with a host of problems which could not be wiped out overnight. All had weak economies which had been dependent on the Soviet Union. Their state-owned enterprises largely comprised out-of-date, inefficient heavy industries which polluted the environment. Like the Soviet Union, they produced insufficient consumer goods. The planned economy had fixed both prices and wages, leaving little scope for individual incentive. In Poland, the agriculture sector, which had been highly productive and a source of exports before the Second World War, deteriorated so badly under communism that shortages led to food riots in the early 1970s.

The conversion of a planned economy into a market economy can be carried out by 'shock therapy' or a gradualist approach. Shock therapy aims to set up market institutions in as short a time as possible, while gradualism involves dismantling communism over a longer period of time. Shock therapy was the preferred approach in Poland, whereas Hungary adopted the more gradualist approach. Both countries had had recent experience of market economies. It is arguable that a combined approach could be the most effective: initial shock therapy, instituting irreversible institutional changes, followed by gradualist measures, such as piecemeal privatizations, to spread out the pain of laying off workers (Bradshaw, 1996). By contrast, shock therapy in Russia in 1992 was less successful, reflecting deep historical and cultural factors that have worked against a smooth transition.

Whatever the pace of transition, four interrelated processes may be identified as keys to its success (Bradshaw, 1996). These are stabilization, liberalization, internationalization, and privatization. We look at each in turn.

Stabilization

Inflation has been a major problem in Central and Eastern European economies. The lack of consumer goods available during communist rule had resulted in a build-up of personal savings. When consumer goods became freely available, a boom in spending led to price rises, fuelling inflation. Controlling inflation required wage restraint and keeping the money supply under control. This was easier said than done, as demands on the state came from several directions at once: the unemployed, who were casualties of the new market forces; pensioners, whose savings had been wiped out; agricultural workers who had grown dependent on subsidies. The Polish, Hungarian and Czech economies all declined in the early transitional period from 1989 to 1992, but, since then, their economies have recovered and unemployment and inflation have both gone down.

Liberalization

In the planned economy, wages and prices are determined by government. When state control was removed and prices were freed, the result was a price shock for consumers who were accustomed to paying prices for commodities which were less than world market levels. Price liberalization thus contributed to inflationary pressures. In the long term, there should be no place in a market economy for inefficient, uncompetitive, state-run enterprises. However, in the shorter term, political pressures compelled governments to subsidize them, largely to keep unemployment under control. Liberalization was perceived as a threat to industrial and agricultural workers in particular. In Poland, for example, the movement to overthrow Soviet rule was led by the Solidarity trade union, supported by the Polish Catholic Church, both of which are still powerful, and both of which are sceptical about liberal reform policies. Solidarity has been a key political player in coalition governments since the first free post-communist elections in 1991.

Internationalization

Crucial to the transition economies is their opening up to trade and investment. As privatization proceeds, the state withdraws from its direct role in trade, and takes on more of a regulatory role, as befits a market economy. The industries in post-communist states were largely uncompetitive, and there has been political pressure to maintain a protectionist policy. Some feared that liberalization would open markets to a flood of imports, leading to a balance of payments crisis. As the 1990s progressed, however, liberalization has brought economic benefits. Trade and flows of FDI have grown, indicating the potential of these emerging markets and the perception that they have become politically stable. More than 70 per cent of the imports into the Czech Republic, Poland and Hungary now come from EU member states, while more than 60 per cent of their exports go to EU states. This economic integration is the strongest driving force behind their prospects of gaining membership of the EU.

Privatization

Privatization encompasses the conversion of state enterprises to privately owned and operated companies, and also the fostering of new start-up enterprises. Small-to-medium-size businesses were some of the earliest and easiest to privatize, as they could be taken over by their managers and workers. Medium and large-scale enterprises have been more difficult to privatize. They could be sold to their own managers, but those in the strongest position were the former communists, and public opinion was hostile to the thought that these individuals would be chief beneficiaries of privatization. Sales to foreign buyers also risked hostile public opinion. Case Study 4.4 gives a Polish example of the benefits of bringing in foreign investors. The 'leveraged' buy-out (LBO) by workers (financed by government loan) was a favoured method. The large-scale enterprises have been the most difficult, and politically sensitive, to privatize. Two methods have been to sell them or allow them to be taken over by joint ventures, bringing in a foreign investor, usually one based in a Western European country.

Case study 4.4 Winiary Soups in Poland

'We had a dream of our factory after privatization and that dream has been fulfilled', says Karol Madrowski, Managing Director at food manufacturers Winiary. His dreams have been realized courtesy of Nestlé, which paid around $60 million for a 45 per cent stake in Poland's best-known brand producer in 1997. The Swiss company promised to invest a further $30 million and Madrowski's plant, in Kalisz, western Poland, has enjoyed a transformation. By way of an example, he points to a flower bed planted where the coal tip had been. 'We don't need the coal any more as our new energy installation is gas fired and employs 3 where once we needed 39 people', he says. Now employees sit watching computers put the right mix of ingredients into Winiary's dehydrated soups and puddings. Once the same people in the same place had dragged the same ingredients around by hand. Product quality and hygiene labs have been brought onto the shop floor to bring home to the employees how important these factors are. The red and yellow branding has been modernized so that products are instantly recognizable on shop shelves. And the walls of the plant have been repainted in the same colours to reinforce identification with the product.

Consumers and employees alike are encouraged to come up with new ideas for products and recipes to encourage brand loyalty, a concept alien to the plant's old masters, the central planners. The three-year investment programme has consumed $50 million, which is more than Nestlé originally promised it would spend on modernising the plant. This is also more than the $40 million Nestlé's rival, CPC Amino (owned by Bestfoods, now part of Unilever), has spent. 'Poles eat 300 instant soup servings a year', says Nestlé's commercial manager. Nestlé has been surprised at the size of the market given that instant soups came late to Poland. They were first brought to the market by CPC under their Knorr brand in April 1996. Sales have since grown exponentially, reflecting a society which is working harder and leaving itself less time for meals.

Pre-1995, Winiary had begun to lose market share to CPC and, without privatization, the company would have begun to slide downhill fast. The Nestlé investment has brought spending on new equipment and technology, as well as reorganization of the company and development of its distribution and marketing functions. It has invested in people, including MBA-style management training as well as courses in Switzerland, backed by language training.

Source: Bobinski, C., 'There's an ally in my soup', *Financial Times*, 27 October 1998 (reprinted with permission).

Case question

What are the strengths, weaknesses, opportunities and threats relating to Winiary? Construct a SWOT analysis to illustrate them

4.7.2 Prospects for the transition economies of Central and Eastern Europe

Wide discrepancies exist among the post-Soviet states. The Central European states have made the greatest progress towards market economies, having started earlier than the former Soviet republics. The states of Poland, the Czech Republic, Hungary, Slovenia and Slovakia had more recent experience of the market economy and private ownership. They also had relatively homogeneous societies, without major cultural, linguistic and religious rifts, ensuring a more stable basis for their new democratic institutions. Ethnic and religious divisions in the former Soviet republics and in the former Yugoslavia have hampered economic transition. Major problems in all the transition economies have been inflation, unemployment and the urgent need to modernize industries and infrastructure. Privatization and the opening of markets to competition have brought greater integration with Western European economies. Membership in the EU is seen as the ultimate milestone achievement for all these transition economies, although some are closer to that goal than others. The benefits of economic integration are now recognized by all; only the timing and terms of EU accession are subject to negotiation.

POINTS TO REMEMBER

Transitional economies of Central and Eastern Europe

- Privatization of former state-owned enterprises
- Setting up of new legal and regulatory framework
- Progress in overcoming problems of unemployment and inflation
- Fragile democratic institutions
- Increasing integration with Western European economic structures

4.8 Globalization and regionalization

Starting with the capitalist model of a market economy, we have seen a number of different interpretations evolve in different contexts. Globalization is bringing about greater integration between economies, but this is not to say that there is a clear picture emerging of a 'global model' of capitalism. Diversity has been especially obvious in two areas: (a) the involvement of the state in the economy; and (b) corporate ownership and control. State guidance of business is more active in some economies than in others. Corporate governance is more market-oriented towards shareholder value in the Anglo-American models than in either the Asian or the social market models of Europe. However, there is also considerable divergence within each region, as national development paths within any region can differ considerably, despite sociocultural similarities between countries.

Nonetheless, regionalization has been taking place throughout the world. It has generated growing economic links and co-operation within a geographic region, both on the part of businesses and governments. Countries within an identifiable geographic area may have shared historical experiences, such as the need for Western European countries to rebuild after the Second World War. The end of the cold war, dominated as it was by the two power blocs, has seen the emergence of regional co-operation and integration. The trend is more advanced in some regions than in others: the EU is much more advanced than either the North American Free Trade Agreement (NAFTA) or the ASEAN Free Trade Area.

The EU is the most deeply integrated region. The extent to which it provides the basis of a definable regional capitalism is much debated. As has been seen, liberalization of the social market model is proceeding, with more opening of markets and greater labour flexibility. However, these developments must be seen in the context of globalization. There is not as yet a consensus on the philosophy of the new European capitalism. For governments, the twin needs to attract transnational capital and compete in globalizing markets are uppermost. On the other hand, many perceive an erosion of social protection and problems of growing inequalities, while others object to the giving up of monetary sovereignty. There remain national identities and interests, complicated by enlargement, which will entail new European institutional arrangements (see Chapter 7). Moreover, at the corporate level, there is divergence on issues of corporate governance. The potential for conflict between shareholder interests and those of broader stakeholder groups adds to the complexities facing businesses with pan-European operations.

4.9 Conclusions

1. Economic systems range from the planned economy to capitalism, reflecting society's values regarding production and the accumulation of wealth.

2. Capitalism rests on three essential principles: free enterprise, competition and private property. While the US and UK have historically come closest to the laissez-faire model, state intervention and welfare state measures have become a feature of modern capitalist systems generally.

3. Economic concentration in the form of monopolies and cartels creates imperfect competition, and most states have antitrust and anti-competitive practices legislation for their control.

4. Social market capitalism, as exemplified by France and Germany, has relied on greater state ownership and more extensive social welfare programmes. The current trend in these systems, however, is towards liberalization of markets.

5 Asian capitalist models, including Japan, have also relied on strong state guidance. The Asian model, however, is underpinned with Confucian values of the strong family and the company itself as family.

6 The planned economy as a system is giving way to market forces, as exemplified by China, where privatization and foreign investment are rapidly transforming the economy.

7 Post-communist transitional economies of Central and Eastern Europe, while they have struggled to overcome the problems of restructuring outdated industries, have become increasingly integrated into the advanced Western economies.

8 The impact of globalization on economic systems can be seen in the trend towards liberalization of markets. At the same time, regionalization, most advanced in the EU, is gathering pace in the increasingly globalized environment.

Review questions

1. What are the distinguishing characteristics of capitalism as an economic system?
2. Why are monopoly and oligopoly considered to be 'market imperfections'?
3. What is 'competition policy' and what role does it play in market economies?
4. Which countries are considered strongholds of the social market model of capitalism and how are their economies evolving at present?
5. What are the specific strengths of the Asian model of capitalism? In the case of Japan, how did these strengths seem to translate into weaknesses in the 1990s?
6. What are the elements of the transition process towards a market economy in (a) China; and (b) the transition economies of Central and Eastern Europe?
7. What are the links between globalization and economic regionalization?

Assignments

1. To what extent has the evolution of the capitalist market economy displayed divergence along regional lines?
2. Examining the transition economies, assess the progress to date towards market liberalization in the context of the business environment and offer

an appraisal of the opportunities and threats posed by the economic environment for would-be foreign investors.

Further reading

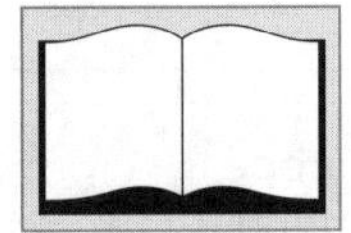

Coates, D. (1999) *Models of Capitalism* (Cambridge: Polity Press)

Cook, M. and Farquharson, C. (1998) *Business Economics* (London: Pitman)

Landes, D. (1998) *The Wealth and Poverty of Nations* (London: W.W. Norton)

Mattli, W. (1999) *The Logic of Regional Integration: Europe and Beyond* (Cambridge: Cambridge University Press)

Schnitzer, M. (2000) *Comparative Economic Systems*, 8th edn (Cincinnati: South-Western)

Chapter

The cultural environment: diversity and globalization

Outline of chapter

LEARNING OBJECTIVES

1 To identify the dimensions of culture in society which impact on international business activities
2 To understand the origins of cultural diversity based on national and other collective cultural identities
3 To assess the importance of cultural values and expressions in the modern global environment
4 To appreciate the role of organizational culture in international enterprises

5.0 Introduction

The process of globalization has brought people from different parts of the globe and from different cultural backgrounds into routine contact with each other and each other's cultures. But does greater interaction imply that people are drawing closer together and becoming more like each other? An international businessperson will argue on the basis of personal experience that negotiating a business deal in Morocco is very different from negotiating a similar deal in Japan or Germany. In each case, achieving a successful outcome, in both the initial agreement and the long-term business relationship, will depend on sensitivity to language differences, value systems and norms of behaviour between themselves and their hosts. In short, being attuned to cultural differences can directly affect the success or failure of the project.

This chapter has two broad aims. The first is to gain an understanding of the many dimensions of culture, and their importance in how business is transacted between people across the globe. The second aim is to examine the impact of globalization in the dynamic cultural environment. While there is abundant evidence, such as the explosive growth of internet use, which points to an emerging global culture, there is also considerable evidence that local cultural identities are not withering away, as some expected, but are adapting and persisting in the new global environment. Therefore, we examine the interacting cultural dynamic between the global and the local. For international business, grasping this dynamic interaction is the key to 'riding the waves of culture' (Trompenaars, 1994). We begin by defining culture, looking at the dimensions of culture in society and the make-up of specific cultural identities among the world's peoples.

5.1 What is culture and how is it relevant to business?

Culture has been defined in many different ways, reflecting the variety of cultural phenomena that can be observed. Language, religious ritual and art are just a few examples of cultural symbols whose shared meanings form the unique fingerprint of a particular society. Culture can be broadly defined as 'a learned, shared, compelling, interrelated set of symbols whose meanings provide a set of orientations for members of a society' (Terpstra and David, 1991, p. 6). Inevitably, we all view and interpret the world around us through a cultural 'filter' to some degree. **Ethnocentrism** denotes the inflexible approach of relating to the world only in terms of our own culture, while **polycentrism** is the approach of attempting to overcome our own cultural assumptions and develop an openness and understanding of other cultures. Successful international business relationships depend in large measure on developing a polycentric approach in situations where cross-cultural issues arise, such as joint ventures.

Culture includes the system of values and beliefs shared by the group, and also norms of behaviour expected of group members. Values relate primarily to notions of good and evil, right and wrong. Values also include notions of the individual in relation to the group. An important distinguishing characteristic of particular Western value systems, for example, is the intrinsic value accorded to the individual. Where individualism is highly valued, the society's institutional and governance structures will seek to guarantee individual freedoms. The growth of democracy in countries with strong individualist cultures is no coincidence, but an outcome of value systems. By contrast, societies which place greater value on the collectivity, such as the family or the kinship group, are likely to develop institutional structures which are more paternalistic, that is, dominated by a father figure. These societies are likely to value group loyalty more highly than individual freedoms.

What is culture?

Culture is a learned, shared, interrelated set of symbols which unite and identify members of a society

Aspects of culture:

- Values and beliefs, including moral and religious beliefs
- Communication, including spoken and written language, and also body language
- Norms of behaviour, for example, associated with eating and drinking, dress
- Customs
- Art, music, dance, sport

Norms relate to patterns and standards of behaviour. They shape what is considered normal and abnormal behaviour within a society. Norms include the role of the family, the upbringing of children, the role of women and the respect accorded to age. Norms often reflect values, and, like values, can derive from religious beliefs and take on religious significance in many societies. Norms may also reflect customs which distinguish societies one from another. Manner of dress, food and the etiquette associated with eating and drinking are also obvious distinguishing features of a culture. For businesspeople in a foreign environment, an understanding of local culture is needed not just in the context of doing business, but in general social relations with hosts. Indeed, in Asian cultures, doing business is not confined merely to working hours, but blends into social occasions such as meals together. It is here that bonds of trust are built and where sensitivity to cultural values and norms can be critical.

Case study 5.1 Globalization and localization of McDonald's

The Big Mac is perhaps the foremost symbol of the globalization of fast food, universal, but distinctively American. The Big Mac was invented in 1958, and for the next three decades McDonald's restaurants were concentrated in America. In 1985, only 22 per cent of the company's 8,900 restaurants were outside America. By 1995, this had leapt to 38 per cent. A major breakthrough was the establishment of its restaurants in Russia, which has been so successful that it inspired a book, *To Russia with Fries* (Cohon, 1997), penned by the founder of the McDonald's Russian operation. McDonald's now has 28,700 restaurants in 120 countries. In 2000, it added about 1,500 new establishments outside America, compared to only 175 in its home territory. The company has prided itself on adaptations of its products in response to cultural diversity, for example the 'Maharaja Mac' in India, which is made of mutton, as Hindus consider cows sacred and do not eat beef. In the US in 1990, McDonald's announced that its fries were henceforth to be made from 100 per cent vegetable oil, thus attracting the custom of American Hindus. However, it emerged in 2001, that all along the fries have been flavoured with beef extract. News soon reached India, sparking off vandalism against targeted restaurants, although the company maintains that the fries sold in India are, in fact, vegetarian. In the US, lawsuits have been initiated against McDonald's by Hindus, for misleading its American customers.

The world's love of the Big Mac has been on the wane in the past few years, as sales have flagged. New branded products, such as the McPizza, have failed to catch on and food scares such as the BSE (bovine spongiform encephalopathy) crisis added to the slump in sales. In 2001 the company's shares were trading at 40 per cent below their 1999 value. In a change of strategy, the company has embarked on something of a spending spree, buying up stakes in other players in the food industry. These have included Chipotle Mexican Grill, Donatos Pizza, Aroma coffee bars and, most recently, the UK niche market sandwich shops, Pret A Manger. On the face of it, Pret A Manger looks an odd purchase for McDonald's. Pret has 104 shops in the UK and one in New York. It prides itself on fresh, high-quality sandwiches, made with chemical-free ingredients, and served in a modern, sophisticated environment – a long way from Ronald McDonald. McDonald's maintains that the purchase of Pret fits perfectly with the group's strategy of buying into different eating-out experiences. It is expected that Pret will continue to be controlled by local managers. Some of Pret's customers seem more doubtful, however, seeing the move as a sellout to the McDonald's global machine.

Sources: Rushe, D., 'Can the Big Mac take sushi and sandwiches to the States?' *Sunday Times*, 4 February 2001; Watkins, M., 'Pret A Manger sees business as usual', *Financial Times*, 1 February 2001; Goodstein, L., 'For Hindus and vegetarians, surprise in McDonald's fries', *New York Times*, 20 May 2001.

Case question

How has McDonald's changed its global strategy in response to the changing environment?

WWW WEBALERT

McDonald's website is at http://www.mcdonalds.com
Pret A Manger's website is at http://www.pret.com

Values and norms of behaviour are learned in the social context – we are not born with them. For this reason they are not fixed and static, but are capable of change. Societies may evolve over time, and individuals may change when they move to a new environment. Organizations, too, may change as they expand internationally. One of the themes of this chapter is the extent to which growth in interactions between cultures, and the growth of international markets and global brands such as McDonald's and Nike, leads to a global or 'cosmopolitan' culture. Spreading Western cultural symbols, such as Levi jeans, Western pop music and fast food, are often grouped together as signs of the globalization of culture. However, they have not supplanted local cultural preferences. The Big Mac and Coca-Cola epitomize the uniform standard product for all markets. But in fact, McDonald's has long been sensitive to differing local tastes, offering the teriyaki burger in Japan for example, although relying on their core brands as the mainstay of the business. Waning enthusiasm for hamburgers in their mature markets, however, has given impetus to a change of strategy, as Case Study 5.1 shows. Coca-Cola, too, has revised its global strategy in order to promote different brands for different markets. Similarly, entertainment and media industries, including music and film, present a mixed picture: the emergence of several global companies, but also much local output designed for local tastes.

5.2 National cultures

Research has shown that people have acquired their basic value systems by the age of ten (Hofstede, 1994). It is during these formative years that national culture exerts its strongest influence, through family and early schooling. **Nations** are distinguishable from each other by language, religion, ethnic or racial identity and, above all, by a shared cultural history. Together, these distinguishing characteristics blend into a **national culture.** National culture influences family life, education, organizational culture and economic and political structures. The sense of belonging to a nation is one of the most important focal points of cultural identity. In the course of time, myth mixes with historical events in the collective memory, and the associated symbols serve as powerful emotive links between present and past, and even future.

The **nation-state** combines the concepts of cultural bonds created by the nation with the territorial and organizational structures of the state. However, the world's peoples comprise many more nations than states, and hence most states contain multiple cultural and national identities. Historically, nations have sought self-determination for their own people, through nationalist movements. Thus new nation-states often represent the culmination of national aspirations and mobilization of nationalist movements to attain independence from existing ruling regimes in which they feel their interests are not properly represented. Largely as a result of the break-up of colonial empires, the number of nation-states has grown dramatically since the end of the Second World War. However, many of these states have proved to be ill-fitting administrative containers for the multiple social and ethnic groups within their borders.

Growing cultural awareness has also brought the tensions between national self-awareness and existing state institutions into the international limelight. We will look at two contrasting examples of nationhood and cultural identity: first, Japan, an old state with a homogeneous culture, and second, the new states of Eastern Europe, where heterogeneous cultures present challenges for nation-building as well as for constructing new institutions of state.

Elements of national culture

- Common language, or dialect
- Shared religious and moral values
- National symbols and rituals, such as flags, national festivals, particular places and monuments
- Shared history
- Patterns of family life and family values
- Roles of males and females
- Attitudes to education
- Relationship between the individual and group, including the work organization and the state
- Ways of resolving conflicts
- Geographic homeland

Japan has been described as an 'ethnic state' (Smith, 1991, p. 105) in that it is one of the few countries that approach the ideal of the one-to-one fit between nation and state. The cultural unity stems partly from the Japanese language, which is unique to Japan, and from the religion of Shinto, also exclusively Japanese, which reinforces national cohesion. A strong sense of national identity, coupled with group loyalty, was a major factor in Japan's impressive record of post-war reconstruction and economic development. Japan served as the first example that modern capitalism need not rest on accepted Western values of individualism, but can be built on an Asian value system. In the 1990s, however, as was seen in the last chapter, Japan's cultural strengths seem to have turned into weaknesses, inhibiting its businesses' ability to adapt to the changing global environment. Significantly, Nissan's regained competitiveness under Renault's control has been the outcome of restructuring imposed from outside traditional Japanese structures and values.

The nations of Central and Eastern Europe, by contrast, present a much less clear-cut picture. The boundaries of the modern states of Europe have not been constant, but have been drawn to reflect the winners' and losers' positions in numerous wars and political battles fought out over territorial claims. Similarly, the rise and subsequent disintegration of empires have left their mark across the cultural landscape. The Soviet Union suppressed dozens of nationalities within an all-embracing communist ideology. With its break-up, the peoples of Eastern Europe have rediscovered and asserted their national identity and cultural heritage. Cultural factors have played a part in the development paths of the independent nation-states which have emerged since the fall of the Berlin Wall in 1989. Poland, Hungary and the Czech Republic have built on a sense of community, with a single dominant language and constitutional safeguards for minority groups. By contrast, in Yugoslavia, a Balkan state, multiple nationalities which had been unified under authoritarian rule fragmented in the new state. The central governmental authority of the new Yugoslav federal state, in which the Serbs are the dominant group, was unable to maintain its legitimacy in the eyes of the different ethnic and religious groups. Croats, Bosnians, Slovenians and Macedonians have broken away to form separate states as homelands. The province of Kosovo, predominantly Muslim, which had been semi-self-governing within Yugoslavia, sought independence from the predominantly Orthodox Serbian establishment. Following the war in Kosovo in 1998, Kosovo's administration was taken over by United Nations (UN) and North Atlantic Treaty Organization (NATO) authorities. The destructive forces of ethnic hostility in the Balkans illustrate the power of historical cultural forces in the modern world. The examples of Japan and Yugoslavia present dramatic contrasts: in the first, the sense of nationhood unified people in a sense of social purpose; in the second, it led to ethnic conflict which destabilized society.

Just at the time that new national cultural identities are emerging in the former communist states, European integration is seeking to mould a new European sense of identity. Is European economic, social and political integration bringing about a sense of unified 'Europeanness' among the various populations of the member states? Europe as a whole lacks the shared sense of culture, history, ethnicity and language that identify nations as enduring entities. As we have seen, a person may have multiple cultural identities. A Hispanic American, for example, has a 'dual' identity, but both have relatively long histories and shared cultures. A European identity is more like a social construct, which would re uire 'mental re-programming', to use Hofstede's phrase (1994, p. 4). In his view, such reprogramming is not possible, given the wide national cultural differences between European nations, and their deep historical roots. Nonetheless, Europeans may feel national identity *plus* European identity, as has been found in the

Eurobarometer surveys of public opinion conducted on behalf of the European Commission. Respondents are invited to place themselves in one of four categories in terms of identity: nationality alone; nationality and European; European and nationality; and European only. Forty-six per cent felt themselves to be 'nationality plus European' (Eurobarometer, 1998). The majority, however, identified themselves by their nationality only. This suggests that perceptions of European cultural identity have proceeded more slowly than economic and political integration.

5.3 Languages

Language is the basic means of communication between people, which facilitates social interaction and fosters a system of shared values and norms. Language is much more than the vocabulary and grammar that make up written and spoken expression. The researchers, Hall and Hall (1960), distinguish between 'low-context' and 'high-context' cultures. In a **low-context culture**, communication is clear and direct; speakers come straight to the point and say exactly what they mean. America is a good example of a low-context culture. In a **high-context culture**, much goes unsaid; depending on the relationship between the speakers, each is able to interpret body language and 'read between the lines'. In this type of culture, ambiguity is the norm

Table 5.1 The world's top ten languages (1999)

Rank	Language	Population (in millions)
1	Chinese, Mandarin	885
2	Spanish	332
3	English	322
4	Bengali	189
5	Hindi	182
6	Portuguese	170
7	Russian	170
8	Japanese	125
9	German, Standard	98
10	Chinese, Wu	77

Note
1. Figures refer to first-language speakers in all countries.

Source: Summer Institute of Linguistics (2000) *Ethnologue*, at www.sil.org/ethnologue/.

and directness is avoided. Asian cultures fall into this type. For Americans, meeting people from high-context cultures can seem frustrating, as they are unsure where they stand, while their Asian counterparts are unsettled by their directness of approach, which may come across as insincerity.

In terms of numbers, the linguistic family of Chinese is spoken by the largest numbers of people, amounting to about 20 per cent of the world's population. Only about 5.4 per cent of the world's population have English as their native language, and they have been slightly overtaken in numbers by native Spanish speakers, as shown in Table 5.1.

The importance of English as a global language extends far beyond the number of native speakers. English is the commonest language for the global media and the internet, and the commonest second language. It was estimated in 1999 that 80 per cent of all websites are in English (United Nations, 1999b), and 80 per cent of the film industry's output globally is in English (Rose, 1999). Among the many people who travel internationally, English is a recognized means of communication, often when neither of the parties speaks English as a first language. These globetrotters include not only business-people and diplomats, but tourists, sportspeople, academics and students. The English language in these contexts is an intercultural means of communicating. By the same token, while Hindi is the official language of India, English as an associate national language facilitates communication between the many non-Hindi-speaking groups. India is one of the world's most multilingual countries, with 14 major languages and many more minor ones. English is spoken by about 50 per cent of India's population. Moreover, in the booming information technology (IT) industry, the predominance of the English language is proving a location advantage.

WWW
WEBALERT

For foreign language and culture specific resources on the web, look at this website:
http://www.itp.berkeley.edu/~thorne/HumanResources.html

For minority languages, the following website contains hundreds of links:
http://www.smo.uhi.ac.uk/saoghal/mion-chanain/Failte_en.html

In most countries, one or more dominant languages exist alongside minority languages, which may be concentrated in specific geographical regions. Canada has two official languages, English and French, and the minority French speakers have a history of separatist activism. Switzerland, by contrast, has four official languages (German, French, Italian and Romansh) which co-exist in harmony.

Linguistic diversity within a state may arise in several different ways. First, a minority language may represent a native culture, such as the Indian nations which inhabited North and South America before the arrival of

European settlers. The US, Australia and South Africa are all settler societies, where tensions erupted between the new arrivals and existing native cultures. These tensions are still observable today, as evidenced by the second-class citizen status of which native Americans complain.

Second, colonizing states introduced their own language into their colonies, using language as a tool of conquest. Thus, the language of Brazil is Portuguese, the language of the imperial power. The Western imperial powers of the sixteenth to the nineteenth centuries included the English, French, Dutch, Spanish and Portuguese. All left their national languages in their colonies, where the colonial language became that of the elites, as well as that of government and administration. The many indigenous peoples spoke native languages, but struggled to maintain their cultures in the tide of colonialism. Today, most of Latin America is Spanish-speaking, and Spanish companies have seen language as an advantage in their American expansion, as Case Study 5.2 demonstrates. Large parts of Africa are French-speaking. African countries, such as Zaire and Nigeria, have a cultural heritage of tribal loyalties, fostered by many different languages. Depending on the context, the use of English can overcome the problems of intercultural communication. However, choice of language is a matter of cultural sensitivity, and outsiders risk offending their hosts if they make the wrong choice in the circumstances.

Third, immigration can create linguistic diversity. Immigrants are faced with the difficulties of assimilation in a new culture, or maintaining a separate identity. Where immigrants are concentrated geographically, they may form a **subculture** in which they speak their home language. An example of the effects of immigration can be seen in the increase in numbers of Hispanic people in America. Hispanics, who are people of Latin American origin whose first language is Spanish, now make up 12 per cent of the US population, a proportion that grew 60 per cent during the 1990s (Therrien and Ramirez, 2000).

The strength of language as a cultural force is shown by the policies of national governments. Almost all specify an official language of the state and control the use of other languages. Authorities seek to exert these controls in the school system, as well as in the national press and other media. Deliberate policies to foster the national language may serve two purposes: they can stifle splintering effects caused by the use of minority languages, and they can help to push back what is seen as the tide of English. Minority groups that promote a strong separate identity can be a destabilizing factor within societies. In both France and Spain, for example, promotion by the Basque people of their own cultural identity, coupled with demands for autonomy, are a persistent feature. On the Spanish side of the border, these demands are only partially accommodated in Spain's system of 'autonomous regions', and militant Basques have often resorted to violence. The island of Corsica is part of France, but its separate identity and language (a dialect of Italian), coupled with cultural and historical links with Italy, have made it a thorn in the side

Case study 5.2 Spanish firms' success in Latin America

In the last 25 years, Spanish firms have become major investors in Latin American economies, successfully exploiting the fact that, as a result of Spain's colonial conquests, Spanish is the unifying language of more than 20 countries. While they welcome the investment, they cannot resist comparisons with the Spanish imperialism of old. Spanish companies, including some still partially owned by the state, now own Chile's largest telephone company, power company and waterworks. In addition, Spanish banks control roughly 40 per cent of the Chilean market. According to Humberto Illanies, the head of the union at Banco Santiago (also taken over by a Spanish group), 'Every time I turn on the lights, make a phone call, cash a cheque, or drink a glass of water, I'm putting money into pockets in Madrid ... It's as if we're a colony again, paying taxes to the Spanish crown' (Faiola, 2000).

The Spanish viewpoint is that Spain's new vibrant economy is seeking to build cultural bonds, not just economic might. Having endured four decades of the dictatorship of General Franco, post-Franco Spain has successfully made the transition to a democracy and open market economy. Spain now sees its model of transition as a guide for its former colonies, who are themselves now entering an era of reform, privatizing government-run enterprises and opening up their economies. Spanish companies now look outwards, to new partners in Europe (it joined the European Union (EU) in 1986, and is in the euro-zone) and to Latin America.

The general manager of Telefonica CTC in Chile, says, 'We have a shared language, but each nation is extremely different in Latin America. The Spanish are sensitive to that, while at the same time capitalizing on the similarities in our cultures to smooth the way in business deals' (Faiola, 2000).

The resurgence of the Spanish-speaking world is also evident north of the Rio Grande, where, in addition to the growing presence of Hispanics in the US, Spanish cultural influences have enjoyed a resounding impact on tastes in music, film, food and dance. This influence has extended beyond Spanish-speaking areas, to what is considered to be 'mainstream' American. The trend will not go unnoticed by company strategists in Spain. There is an ironic contrast between images of new Spanish national pride abroad and the separatist groups at home, such as Basques and Catalans, for whom old attachments remain strong.

Sources: Faiola, A., 'Spanish firms revive Latin America conquest', *Washington Post*, 14 February 2000; Cebrián, J.L., 'Spain's new world', The World in 2000 (*The Economist*, 1999); 'The conquistadors return', leader in The World in 2000 (*The Economist*, 1999).

Case question

From the perspectives of host societies, what are the pros and cons of Spanish expansionism in Latin America?

of French governments. The Corsicans have a long history of separatist violence, which has discouraged potential investors. In 2001, the French national assembly passed a new law designed to devolve limited powers to a Corsican assembly in areas such as the environment, tourism and culture. It includes provision for the teaching of Corsican in schools, and has caused controversy among those who support a strong central administration and the supremacy of the French language (Graham, 2001).

5.4 Religions

The system of values and beliefs that characterize a culture may be embodied in a particular religion. Research has identified over 15,000 distinct religions and religious movements among the world's population (Barrett, 1997). They range from simple folk religions to highly refined systems of beliefs, with set rituals, organized worship, sacred texts and a hierarchy of religious leaders. The major religions in terms of numbers of followers, Christianity and Islam, fall into this latter category. All religions call on their followers to believe in supernatural forces which affect their lives, and to follow prescribed moral rules. Religion may exercise considerable secular and political, as well as religious, power, and can form a major unifying force in society. Religious divides, both within and between states, can also be a source of friction.

In principle, most of the world's states adhere to the right of religious freedom, allowing multiple religions to worship freely. But in practice, there are exceptions, where the practice of particular religions is prohibited by state authorities. States may have a dominant or even an official religion, although most modern states follow the principle of separation of church and state. Religious affiliation may coincide with a sense of nationhood, as in Poland, where being a Pole and being Roman Catholic are integrally linked in the nation's sense of identity. The Church in Poland is still a potent force, but the government stepped back from a national Church in its new constitution in 1997, and opted instead for an expression of the importance of the Church in national life. In countries where religion is a major element of the cultural environment, sensitivity to local religious beliefs and practices is particularly important in building business relations.

The world's two major religions are Christianity and Islam (whose adherents are called Muslims). Both are 'monotheistic', that is, believing in one God, in contrast to a polytheistic religion such as Hinduism, in which there is a panoply of gods. Christianity and Islam are both 'proselytizing' religions, which means that they deliberately aim to expand numbers and convert new followers. Since 1970, numbers of Muslims have grown much more rapidly than numbers of Christians, as Table 5.2a shows. Numbers of Christians have grown at a rate roughly in keeping with the world population growth (60 per cent), whereas numbers of Muslims have grown at a rate far outstripping world population growth (104.6 per cent). Africa and Asia, which have the largest Muslim populations, are now also home to more Christians than the traditional centres of Europe (Table 5.2b).

Table 5.2a Growth of major world religions

Year	1900	1970	1997
Christians	558.1 (34.5%)	1,245.9 (33.7%)	1,995 (33.9%)
Muslims	200.1 (12.4%)	564.2 (15.3%)	1,154.3 (19.6%)
Hindus	203 (12.5%)	477 (12.8%)	806.9 (13.7%)
Buddhists	127.2 (7.8%)	237.3 (6.4%)	328.2 (5.6%)
Jews	12.3 (0.8%)	13.6 (0.4%)	14.2 (0.2%)
Non-religious	2.9 (0.2%)	556.2 (15.0%)	886.1 (15.0%)

Note
1. Numbers in millions, followed by percentage of the world's population (in brackets) underneath.

Table 5.2b Christianity – growth in membership by continent

Year	1900	1970	1997
Africa	8.8	118.7	309.6
Asia	20.1	90	299.2
Europe	368.8	493.7	526.6
Latin America and Caribbean	60	268.4	450.5
Northern America	59.6	173.3	207.4
Oceania	4.3	15	19.5

Note
1. Numbers in millions.

Source: Adapted from Barrett, David B. (1997) 'Annual statistical table on global mission: 1997', *International Bulletin of Missionary Research*, **21**(1): 24–5.

5.4.1 Christianity

Nearly 34 per cent of the world's population identifies with Christianity (see Table 5.2a). Through missionary activity, Christianity has spread from Europe and America to all parts of the globe. While all Christians believe in the divinity of Jesus Christ and regard the Bible as sacred, differences of interpretation have emerged, to cause theological splits among Christians. The first of Christianity's major splits occurred in the eleventh century between the Orthodox Church and the Roman Catholic Church. Roman Catholics are now by far the more numerous, comprising over half of Christians. But followers of the Orthodox rites are still very influential in many countries, such as Greece and Russia. The second major split in the Christian world occurred in the sixteenth century, when the Protestant Churches separated from Rome. Protestants went on to establish themselves throughout Europe and America, through different denominations, such as Methodists and Baptists. Protestantism is associated with the principle that individual salvation is achievable independently of the institutional Church. The position of the Pope and the sainthood are anathema to Protestants, and have been the root cause of many religious conflicts, some with long and bitter histories. Strong religious allegiance, therefore, while it has a personal and private dimension, also has social and political implications. Social associations and political parties in many countries are commonly based on religious affiliations and these form an essential dimension of the business environment. If there is an established religion in a location, a business must take account of its wider ramifications, while in locations where there are multiple religions, a business, as a good corporate citizen, should not discriminate, as in, for example, employment conditions. See Points to Remember box (section 5.4.3) for a list of the many ways in which religion impacts on business life.

5.4.2 Islam

Muslims number over a billion globally, spread among many different countries, ranging from the Middle East and Africa to areas now part of Russia, and extending as far as China and Malaysia in East Asia. They make up a majority of the population in over 30 countries and large minorities in others. Founded by the prophet Mohammed in the seventh century, **Islam** unites its followers through shared faith, shared ritual in everyday life and belief in the words of the Koran, the sacred book. For the Muslim, religious ritual is part of everyday life, not confined to worship on a particular day of the week. While codes of conduct form part of the values of all religions, Islam is particularly endowed with formal prescriptive guidance in all aspects of life, including social relations, social behaviour, rules for the consumption of food and drink and the role and appearance of women in society.

An enterprise culture is fostered in Muslim societies, and economic development is promoted. However, it is forbidden to earn a profit based on the exploitation of others. Interest payments are seen as sinful, and therefore the common forms of financing used in Western countries violate Muslim law. Muslim banking has developed systems complying with Muslim law, and Western businesses are able to make financial arrangements which accommodate both sides. These arrangements show the adaptability of Muslim institutions to modern business conditions. Similarly, state courts have grown up in Muslim countries, where traditionally there were only religious courts. State courts can apply both religious law and also Western-style commercial law, signifying an accommodation with Western legal forms. The issue of westernization divides Muslims. 'Westernization' refers to a society's adoption of Western culture and values, and is associated with processes of modernization, while 'Islamic fundamentalism' refers to the maintenance of the supremacy of Islam in all aspects of society. Westernization has not been universally welcomed by Muslims, many of whom see their religious values being undermined in the process.

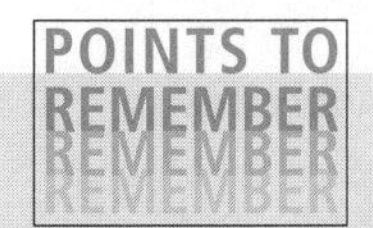

Countries home to the major world religions

- *Predominantly Roman Catholic countries* – Italy, France, Spain, Poland, Mexico (and other central American countries), Brazil (and other South American countries), the Philippines
- *Predominantly Protestant countries* – the UK, Germany, the Netherlands, Scandinavian countries (Norway, Sweden, Denmark, Finland), the US, Australia, South Africa
- *Predominantly Eastern Orthodox countries* – Greece, Russia, Romania
- *Predominantly Muslim countries* – Albania, Saudi Arabia, Egypt, Algeria, Tunisia, Morocco, Syria, Libya, Pakistan, Iran, Iraq, Indonesia
- *Predominantly Hindu countries* – India, Nepal

Oil-rich Iran experienced rapid modernization and industrialization under the Shah, who came to power in 1959. The Shah was a supporter of cultural westernization, and had close ties with the US, which had a strategic interest in Iran's oil wealth. But not all Iranians benefited from the country's oil boom: the agricultural sector and non-oil-related industry suffered, and the numbers of urban poor increased. The disaffected were successfully mobilized by the fundamentalist religious leader, Ayatollah Khomeini, who had lived in exile for most of the Shah's tenure. The Shah's regime was overthrown in 1979, and an Islamic regime of religious government took control. The Islamic revolution in Iran was the first in which a popular movement united by religious fundamentalism has overthrown an existing government. Iran's current government is cautiously embracing liberal economic reforms.

The process of modernization has brought urbanization, widespread literacy and education, greater communication with other cultures and also more exposure to the global media. Fundamentalists argue that Western materialism and liberal ethical values are adversely influencing young people especially, and in particular the urban young, who form the fastest growing section of Muslim societies. Women, too, have felt the conflict between

Western and fundamentalist values. Westernization has brought women more opportunities for education and greater mobility than would be possible in the restrictive regime of traditional Muslim societies. The requirement for women to cover their hair and wear long clothing has also been relaxed in some Muslim societies. The tension which is evident between fundamentalism and westernization in Muslim societies impacts on the business environment. New, younger leaders in a number of Arab states – Morocco, Jordan, Syria and the United Arab Emirates – are gradually introducing social and economic reforms and also welcoming foreign investors.

WWW WEBALERT

For information on the world's major religions, look at these websites:
http://www.islam.org/
http://www1.christianity.net/
http://www.buddhanet.net
http://www.hinduism-today.com/
http://judaism.com/

Also interesting is a site on comparative religions:
http://www.comparativereligion.com/

5.4.3 Asian religions

Asia has been a rich source of some of the world's oldest religions. Hinduism, Buddhism and Confucianism, among many others, originated in Asia and still have millions of followers.

Hinduism

Unlike either Christianity or Islam, **Hinduism** is polytheistic, its believers worshipping many different gods through many different rituals. The sheer diversity of Hinduism is a major feature, despite the fact that geographically Hindus are mostly concentrated in the Indian subcontinent. Hindus make up 80 per cent of the population of India. Hinduism is an ancient religion, older than all other major world religions. Its followers do not revere a single founder, nor do they follow one sacred scripture. In keeping with its ancient origins, Hinduism resembles folk religion, associated with rural communities and accessible to illiterate as well as literate followers. An important social and economic aspect of Hinduism is the **caste system** of rigid social stratification. This system, while officially abolished in the modern state, is still a force in Indian society, as is Hinduism itself. India's government has been led since 1998 by the Hindu nationalist party, the Bharatiya Janata Party (BJP), which is based on an alliance of smaller Hindu groups. The party has faced the challenges of bringing in liberal economic reforms while keeping the support of its traditional Hindu constituent groups.

Buddhism

Buddhism also originated in India, where it has some five million followers. Buddhism has also been an important religious influence in China and Japan. A feature of the Buddhist heritage in all these countries has been its assimilation with other religions: in Indian temples, Buddhism and Hinduism mingle; in Japan, Buddhist temples and Shinto shrines rub shoulders. Buddhism does not recognize the many gods of Hinduism, nor does it subscribe to the caste system. The Buddha's teachings form the basis of the religion. They centre on the 'eight-fold-path' whereby the individual goes through a series of rebirths before reaching *nirvana*. As the Buddha's teachings were never written down, Buddhism split into a number of different schools. The two major ones are the Hinayana, which subscribes to a more ascetic lifestyle, and is followed mainly in Sri Lanka, Thailand and Burma; and the Mahayana, which is less austere, and is followed in China and Japan. From this latter school arose Ch'an Buddhism, or Zen Buddhism, which became a quite distinctive sect, highly influential in the cultures of both China and Japan. Zen's attraction has been its simplicity and directness, with its emphasis on meditation and rejection of dogmatic teaching. Some large Japanese companies send new employees for Zen training.

POINTS TO REMEMBER

How religion impacts on business life

Religious beliefs and practices may have direct (and indirect) influence on many aspects of business life, including:

- Particular foods that are forbidden (for example beef for Hindus)
- Ban, or restrictions, on consumption of alcoholic drink
- Religious festivals, during which work may be forbidden or curtailed (for example Ramadan for Muslims)
- Requirements for daily prayers
- Weekly day of religious observance (for example Saturday for the Jewish faith)
- Clothing requirements (such as long clothing for women in Muslim societies)
- Requirement for women and men to be segregated in the work environment (Muslim societies)
- Restrictions on media, for example newspapers, magazines, television, deemed to conflict with established religion
- Restrictions on business hours and trading hours, for example the ban on Sunday shopping in some countries
- Religious law (for example in Muslim countries)

Confucianism

Confucianism is often considered the foundation stone of Asian values. Founded in the fifth century BC by the Chinese philosopher, Confucius, Confucianism is more a set of moral precepts than a religion. Simon Leys, the modern translator of the *Analects of Confucius*, describes it as 'an affirmation of humanist ethics ... the spiritual cornerstone of the most populous and oldest living civilization on earth' (Leys, 1997, p. xvii). At the heart of Confucianism is the family and 'filial piety', the paramount value of family loyalty. The countries with a strong Confucian heritage – China, Korea and Japan – have in common the prevalence of family-based social organization. In China, Confucianism was rejected by the communist revolution of 1949, but the recent opening up of China has led to a renewed interest in Confucius. Symposiums on Chinese cultural history in 1982 and 1986 were the first attempts to rediscover Confucian culture, as a prelude to blending the strengths of traditional Confucianism with the aims of modernization (Rozman, 1991). In this regard, the example of Japan stands out, for its success in adapting a Confucian cultural heritage to the needs of modernization.

WWW
WEBALERT

For websites on Asian business and culture, look at:
http://www.apmforum.com/default.htm (the site of the Asia Pacific Management Forum, which contains a wealth of information and links)
http://english.china.com/cdc/en/
http://www.japanecho.com/

5.5 Western values and Asian values: the debate

The sociologist Max Weber devised the theory that the 'Protestant work ethic', an ethic of individual endeavour, contributed to the rise of an enterprise culture and accompanying economic development in countries where Protestantism was dominant, such as England and Germany in the nineteenth century (Weber, 1930). He saw a connection between hard work, frugality and wealth creation. Protestants worked hard, not simply to gain pleasure from material well-being, but out of a sense of religious duty which rejected worldly pleasure as a goal in itself. Frugality dictated that gains should be invested wisely, enabling enterprises to prosper in the long term. This outlook on economic activity, known as the 'spirit of capitalism', fostered economic development. Moreover, Protestantism emphasized the individual's direct relationship with God, in contrast to the Catholic Church, for which the intercession of intermediaries was crucial. The value system based on individualism formed a logical foundation for individual freedoms in society generally, entailing both economic and political freedoms. These freedoms are the basis of the Western value systems that underlie the market economy in its 'pure' model, as outlined in Chapter 4. However, as was also pointed out, market economies are emerging in a variety of cultural environments which do not fit the traditional liberal Western pattern. The most striking example is the success of Asian economic development.

Asian nations differ greatly in their religious and cultural backgrounds, so there is no one system which one can point to as representing 'Asian values'. Nonetheless, the term is frequently used in a comparative context, to highlight contrasts with Western values. The closest approximation to a common thread running through Asian value systems is Confucianism. The **Confucian ethic** is usually depicted as a set of values in which loyalty, hierarchy and obedience to superiors are paramount, and the individual is subordinate to the group. Chris Patten, the last Governor of Hong Kong before it ceased to be a British colony and reverted to Chinese sovereignty in 1997, cites three issues which lie at the heart of the Asian versus Western debate: they are 'social order, the family and education' (Patten, 1998). As he points out, however, while the family as a unit is stronger in Asian countries, the traditional picture of family life is changing, especially as women are increasingly going out to work. Greater mobility, urbanization and a sense of insecurity in a changing environment are impacting on Asian societies, in much the same ways as in other parts of the world. Lee Kwan Yew, the former Prime Minister of Singapore, who is credited with orchestrating Singapore's remarkable economic growth – 8.5 per cent per annum between 1966 and 1990 – has long upheld the uniqueness of Asian values. However, he recognizes that, as the Asian economies mature, change is taking place, saying in an interview with the *Financial Times*:

> There will be significant modification of our original culture, but I do not see it being totally transformed. It is not possible. You can take a Chinese family and put it in the US and in two generations they may be completely Americanized, but you can't do that when you've got a large group influencing each other and sustaining the basic values they share. (10 October 2000)

5.6 Multicultural societies

Almost all modern societies are home to more than one ethnic or racial group. Ethnic groups may be indigenous, such as the Indian tribes of North and South America who existed long before the European settlers arrived, or they may be migrants to the country. It is an unfortunate fact that ethnic, racial and religious conflicts occur in virtually every modern society. When they reach widespread proportions, beyond the powers of authorities to control, the instability which results can hugely disrupt all types of economic activity, including agriculture, manufacturing industries, commerce and tourism.

Table 5.3 Population of Great Britain, by ethnic group and age, 1998–99

	Under 16	16–34	35–64	65+	All ages (=100%) (millions)
White	20	26	38	16	53.1
Black					
Black Caribbean	23	29	38	9	0.5
Black African	32	37	29	2	0.4
Other black	43	37	18	–	0.1
All black groups	29	33	33	6	0.9
Indian	24	32	38	7	0.9
Pakistani/Bangladeshi					
Pakistani	35	36	25	3	0.6
Bangladeshi	43	32	22	3	0.2
All Pakistani/ Bangladeshi	37	35	24	3	1.0
Other groups					
Chinese	15	40	39	6	0.2
None of the above	43	30	24	2	0.8
All other groups	38	32	38	3	1.0
All ethnic groups	21	26	38	15	56.8

Source: Office for National Statistics (2000) *Social Trends 30* (London: Stationery Office) Table 1.8, p. 25.

There are three broad approaches to ethnic minorities which are discernible within societies. The first approach is that of **assimilation**, in which the minority adapts to the values and norms of the majority. The UK adopted this approach in the 1950s and 60s, welcoming immigrants from former colonies in the Indian subcontinent, Africa and the Caribbean. These groups form the bulk of Britain's ethnic minorities today, which are 6.6 per cent of the total population (Table 5.3). More restrictive immigration laws from the 1970s onwards have greatly restricted the flow of immigrants. Britain, like most Western economies, sees immigration policy as a way of filling skills shortages, as in the health service and IT. Also taking the assimilationist approach to minorities, France has had a more liberal immigration policy, offering citizens of French colonies in the Caribbean and Africa a right to reside in France.

A second approach is that of the **melting pot**, in which waves of immigrants create a blend of many cultural values. The US is usually cited as the archetypal melting-pot society. When we look more closely, however, the national 'mainstream' culture which emerged reflected the nineteenth- and early twentieth-century European immigrants, while black and native Americans suffered discrimination. It is against this historical backdrop that modern patterns of cultural pluralism have evolved in the US, superseding the melting-pot model (Rex, 1996). The newer immigrants, such as Hispanic Americans, have tended to retain their cultural identities and close ties with their home countries, much facilitated by modern transport and advanced telecommunications, in contrast to immigrants of previous generations. Some 21 million Mexicans live and work in the US, mainly in the states bordering on Mexico and the southern sun belt. Their remittances to families at home amount to $7 billion a year and are Mexico's third largest source of foreign exchange, following oil and tourism.

The third model is that of **cultural pluralism**. In this model, numerous subcultures are recognized, but alongside a national identity which acts as a unifying bond. The UK government has recognized this approach in its White Paper on the integration of refugees, by saying: 'Britain has become and benefited from being a multi-cultural society. Inclusion in our society does not mean that a refugee is required to assimilate' (Home Office, 1999). Recent British policy has been somewhere in the middle between assimilation and cultural pluralism, recognizing cultural diversity as an aspect of modern society (Statham, 1999; Rex, 1996). The US has evolved from a melting-pot type of culture to a more culturally pluralistic one in recent years, as minority

Models of multicultural societies

- *Assimilation* – immigrants leave their home cultures behind, and adopt the culture and language of their new society. Citizenship in the new country is easily available. Examples: France, and the UK in the 1950s and 60s
- *Melting pot* – society evolves its own identity and culture, based on a mixture of the different cultures of which it is composed. Examples: 'settler' societies such as the US and Australia
- *Cultural pluralism* – immigrants form social subcultures which remain distinct. Examples: Germany, and to some extent the US, however, citizenship is more easily obtained in the US than in Germany

ethnic groups, both indigenous and immigrant, have been keen to assert a 'distinct but equal' status (Giddens, 1997, p. 236). The distinguished commentator, Sheldon Wolin, has observed that this policy can lead to a 'limited sort of inclusion' (Wolin, 1993, p. 479). Cultural pluralism can lead to social tension, especially in societies where there are economic inequalities between groups, as well as geographic separation. In Indonesia, authoritarian rule maintained an uneasy unity and social order which disintegrated on the fall of the Suharto regime in 1998. The instability which has ensued has deterred foreign investors and added to the problems of economic recovery following the Asian financial crisis of 1997.

WWW
WEBALERT

Internet resources on race relations and refugees include:
The Commission for Racial Equality at http://www.cre.gov.uk
The Refugee Council at http://www.refugeecouncil.org.uk
The Institute of Race Relations at http://www.irr.org.uk/
And a site on ethnic studies at
http://www.incore.ulst.ac.uk/cds/countries/index.html
This site provides a guide, plus links, to resources on conflict and ethnicity in regions across the world

5.7 Culture theories

Differences in national values and attitudes have been the subject of considerable research. Geert Hofstede has developed a theory of culture which holds that cultural and sociological differences between nations can be categorized and quantified, allowing us to compare national cultures. Hofstede's research was carried out among IBM employees in 50 countries. An obvious weakness of the research is its reliance solely on IBM employees, who are a special group in themselves and not necessarily representative of the countries in which they live. However, his research does yield interesting comparisons and contrasts between national cultures and has served as a benchmark for culture theories. Hofstede distinguishes four cultural dimensions, to which he later added a fifth, as variables. He uses these dimensions to compare value systems at various levels: in the family, at school, in the workplace, in the state and in ways of thinking generally. These cultural dimensions are now explained in more detail.

- *Power distance*, or the extent to which members of a society accept a hierarchical or unequal power structure. In large power distance countries, people consider themselves to be inherently unequal, and there is more dependence by subordinates on bosses. The boss is likely to be autocratic or paternalistic in these countries, in a type of management which subordinates may respond to positively, or negatively. In small power distance countries people tend to see themselves more as equals. When they occupy subordinate and superior roles in organizations, these situations are just that, roles, not reflecting inherent differences. Organizations in these countries tend to be flatter, with a more consultative style of management. Asian, Latin American and African countries tend to have large power distance, while Northern Europe has relatively small power distance.

- *Uncertainty avoidance*, or how members of a society cope with the uncertainties of everyday life. High levels of stress and anxiety denote high uncertainty avoidance countries. These cultures tend to be more expressive and emotional than those of low uncertainty avoidance countries. The latter have lower anxiety levels, but their easy-going exterior may indicate simply greater control of anxiety, not its non-existence. High uncertainty avoidance countries are in Latin American, Latin European and Mediterranean countries, along with Japan and South Korea. Ranking relatively low are other Asian countries and other European countries.
- *Individualism*, or the extent to which individuals perceive themselves as independent and autonomous beings. At the opposite pole is collectivism, in which people see themselves as integrated into 'ingroups'. High individualism scores occurred mainly in the English-speaking countries, while low individualism was prevalent in Latin American and Asian countries. Hofstede remarks that management techniques and training packages, which almost all originate in the individualist countries, are based on cultural assumptions which are out of tune with the more collectivist cultures (Hofstede, 1994).
- *Masculinity*, or the extent to which a society is inclined towards aggressive and materialistic behaviour. This dimension tends to present stereotyped gender roles. Hofstede associates masculinity with assertiveness, toughness and an emphasis on money and material things. At the opposite extreme is femininity, which denotes sensitivity, caring and an emphasis on quality of life. Conflict and competition predominate in more masculine environments, whereas negotiation and compromise predominate in more feminine environments. According to Hofstede's results, the most masculine countries are Japan and Austria, while the most feminine are Sweden, Norway, the Netherlands and Denmark.
- *Long-term versus short-term orientation*, or people's time perspectives in their daily lives. This dimension Hofstede added as a result of work by another researcher, Michael Harris Bond, who found different time orientations between Western and Eastern ways of thinking. Short-term orientation stresses satisfying needs 'here-and-now', and is more

Table 5.4 Ranks of selected countries on four dimensions of national culture

	Power distance rank	Individualism rank	Masculinity rank	Uncertainty avoidance rank
Group 1 (high power distance plus low individualism)				
Brazil	14	26–7	27	21–2
Indonesia	8–9	47–8	30–1	41–2
Malaysia	1	36	25–6	46
Mexico	5–6	32	6	18
Group 2 (low power distance plus high individualism)				
Finland	46	17	47	31–2
Germany	42–4	15	9–10	29
Netherlands	40	4–5	51	35
Sweden	47–8	10–11	53	49–50
UK	42–4	3	9–10	47–8
USA	38	1	15	43
Group 3 (varying patterns)				
France	15–16	10–11	35–6	10–15
Greece	27–8	30	18–19	1
Japan	33	22–3	1	7

Note
1. Rank: 1 = highest; 53 = lowest.

Source: Hofstede, G. (1994) *Cultures and Organizations* (London: HarperCollins) various tables.

characteristic of Western cultures, whereas long-term orientation stresses virtuous living through thrift and persistence, and is prevalent in Eastern cultures (Hofstede, 1996).

Hofstede was able to group countries together in clusters, and also to make correlations between the different dimensions. Some of these are shown in Table 5.4. For countries in Group 1, high power distance combines with low individualism, suggesting that where people depend on ingroups, they also depend on power figures. Conversely, in cultures where people are less dependent on ingroups, shown in Group 2, they are also less dependent on powerful leaders. There are some anomalies, however. France seems to have high individualism, but also medium power distance. Japan seems to be roughly in the middle in both power distance and individualism. Japanese companies are usually depicted as collectivist ingroups, akin to a family relationship. This apparent contradiction in the research could reflect the nature of his survey sample, which focused on employees of a large American multinational company.

More recent research by Fons Trompenaars also used the individualism/collectivism continuum as a key dimension. Trompenaars' research involved giving questionnaires to over 15,000 managers in 28 countries (Trompenaars, 1994). He identified five relationship orientations:

- *Universalism versus particularism* Cultures with high universalism place more weight on formal rules, whereas more particularistic cultures value relationships more than formal rules or agreements. Trompenaars found that Western countries, such as the UK, Australia and USA, tend to rate highly in universalism, whereas China rated highly in particularism.
- *Individualism versus collectivism* This relationship mirrors one of Hofstede's four dimensions, but the findings were somewhat different. Trompenaars found Japan to be much further towards the collectivist extreme. On the other hand, Mexico and the Czech Republic, which Hofstede had found to be more collectivist, now tend to individualism. This finding could be explained by the later date of the research data, reflecting the progress of market economies in both regions: the impact of the North American Free Trade Agreement (NAFTA) in the case of Mexico, and the post-communist transition to a market economy in the case of the Czech Republic.
- *Neutral versus emotional* In a neutral culture, people are less inclined to show their feelings, whereas in an emotional culture, people are more open in showing emotion and expressing their views. In the findings, Japan has the most neutral culture, and Mexico the most emotional.
- *Specific versus diffuse* In a specific culture, there is a clear separation between work and private life. In diffuse cultures, 'the whole person is involved in a business relationship', not merely the contracting role (Trompenaars, 1994, p. 9). Doing business in these cultures, therefore, involves building relationships, not simply focusing on the business deal in isolation. The US, Australia and the UK are examples of specific cultures, while China is an example of a diffuse culture.
- *Achievement versus ascription* In an achievement culture, people derive status from their accomplishments and records. In an ascription culture,

status is what matters, which could relate to birth, family, gender or age. The US and UK are achievement cultures, whereas China and other Asian cultures are ascription cultures.

The research of Hofstede and Trompenaars shed new light on the diversity among national cultures, dispelling the assumption that there is 'one best way' of managing and organizing people. International companies had assumed the universal application of management theories, but, in truth, many of their applications, such as pay-by-performance or management-by-objectives, were products of Anglo-Saxon culture and unsuitable for other cultures with different values and norms. Just as standardized products do not suit all markets, organizations cannot be standardized, but must adapt to local social and cultural profiles.

Cultural dimensions in Hofstede and Trompenaars

Hofstede's five cultural dimensions:

- Power distance
- Uncertainty avoidance
- Individualism versus collectivism
- Masculinity versus femininity
- Long-term versus short-term orientation

Trompenaars' five relationship orientations:

- Universalism versus particularism
- Individualism versus collectivism
- Neutral versus emotional
- Specific versus diffuse
- Achievement versus ascription

5.8 Organizational culture

Organizational culture or 'corporate culture', like national culture, focuses on values, norms and behavioural patterns shared by the group, in this case, the organization. Elements of organizational culture can be found in the Points to Remember box below. The organization, however, unlike the nation, is an artificial creation, and a corporate culture is one that is deliberately fostered among employees, who may have come to the company from a variety of different cultural backgrounds. As we saw in Chapter 2, companies tend to reflect the national culture of their home country, despite globalization of their operations. Swiss multinationals, such as the food giant Nestlé, are among the most transnational, whereas American and Japanese companies are among the least transnational. Switzerland is highly multicultural, with a mixture of national cultures, including German, French and Italian. Its organizations are thus well attuned to appreciating cultural differences in overseas subsidiaries. American or Japanese companies, on the other hand, are from countries of a dominant national culture and a single language. Boardrooms of both American and Japanese companies are dominated by home nationals, in contrast to Nestlé, whose board resembles a miniature UN.

POINTS TO REMEMBER

Organizational or corporate culture

Characteristics of organizational culture include:

- Common language and shared terminology
- Norms of behaviour, such as relations between management and employees
- Preferences for formal or informal means of communication within the company and with associated companies
- Dominant values of the organization, such as high product quality and customer orientation
- Degree of empowerment of employees throughout the organization
- Systems of rules that specify dos and don'ts of employee behaviour

Some multinational corporations see a strong corporate culture as a way of unifying the diverse national cultures represented by employees. Others evolve different organizational cultures in different locations, in effect incorporating multiculturalism within the company. The need to manage cultural diversity may arise through a number of routes: the acquisition of a foreign subsidiary; a merger with another company; or a joint venture. In joint ventures, in particular, the need for co-operation and trust between partners is the key to long-term success. Case Study 5.3 is an example of how one foreign investor solved the communication difficulties in China and provided a foundation of basic training for the Chinese workforce, from which it can now develop in the Chinese cultural environment with mainly Chinese management. As the case study points out, trust only grows over time and the Italian company had to develop a more long-term perspective than would be common in Western companies.

Case study 5.3 Italian business in China

Iveco, the truck subsidiary of Fiat, based in Nanjing, is the largest Italian investor in China. The company, which has been in China since the 1970s – before the start of liberalization – attributes its success to Sino–Italian cultural exchange. Iveco selected 400 Chinese engineers and other workers and trained them in Italy, where they learned Italian and gained on-site experience in Italian factories in the 1980s. Neither the Chinese nor the Italians spoke much English, so Italian was the obvious language to use. The Iveco representative in China, Donati, explains: 'We have tried to give the Chinese the possibility to understand our industrial culture and the opportunity to live our social life.' Importantly, there was $7 million in Italian government aid for the technical training of Chinese people on the exchange programme. In 1986, he arranged for 32 Italians to come to Nanjing to teach basic Italian to 370 local mechanics and other staff.

Iveco's extensive training programme stands in contrast to standard practice at many other foreign manufacturing ventures in China. Often, overseas management pays lip service to the importance of training, language teaching and cultural exchange. As a result, many Sino–foreign joint venture partners spend years bickering, jostling for power and misunderstanding each others' intentions.

Iveco's strategy also differs from that of Piaggio, another Fiat subsidiary, which makes mopeds. Piaggio did not go in for the training and exchange programme. It employed 15 expensive expatriates in a 450-person plant in Guangdong.

The Iveco project in Nanjing, which is a 50–50 partnership with its Chinese partner, was four years in the planning. Some foreign investors may feel that this is a long wait. But Donati says: 'Nobody can do business here with a short-term strategy. You have to have a long-term strategy'. When asked 'How long?' he replied emphatically, 'Thirty years'. The message for international companies is to adapt our know-how to the local conditions. Iveco continues to develop new production facilities in China. Meanwhile, the number of Italians in Nanjing is shrinking, down to 8, in a workforce of 3,000. The reason is that the company is developing local managers.

Source: Harding, J. 'The Italian job in China town', *Financial Times*, 2 February 1999 (reprinted with permission).

Case question

How would you describe Iveco's strategy in Nanjing and explain its advantages and drawbacks?

The global merger, between countries of different national cultures, is an illustration of the difficulties that can arise when strong national cultures clash. The merger in 1998 of the two automotive giants, Daimler-Benz of Germany and Chrysler of the US, highlighted the difficulties of merging Chrysler's lean, flexible and open style with the more structured, bureaucratic

Case study 5.4 A clash of corporate cultures at DaimlerChrysler

The merger of Chrysler Corp. of the US and Daimler-Benz AG of Germany in 1998 created DaimlerChrysler AG, the world's third largest manufacturer of motor vehicles. The aim expressed at the time was to blend their two very different corporate cultures into a new 'super culture' which drew from both sides: Chrysler had a reputation as a lean and flexible company, leading the way in cost effectiveness, whereas Daimler was more structured and bureaucratic. In reality, the deal was a takeover of Chrysler by Daimler, rather than a merger of equals.

The differences of culture became apparent almost immediately and turned out to be more difficult to overcome than had been anticipated:

- The official language became English, but the Americans found, not surprisingly, that their German colleagues were more comfortable in German, and often used German in private conversations, which they found unsettling. They also found that, without German, they could not integrate well at the social level.
- German managers were formal in their manner and dress, always wearing ties, and addressing colleagues by title and surname, while Americans were accustomed to dressing more casually and addressing each other by first names.
- The American managers found the office environment very different in Stuttgart. Although the summers could be hot, there was no air conditioning, which they took for granted at home. Offices and hallways were a 'smokers' paradise', which shocked the Americans, who were accustomed to a smoke-free environment. Photos of topless models, common in the German workplace, would amount to a sexual harassment issue in America. Americans found they were always expected to use the company canteen, which even served beer after five o-clock, for those who were working late.

In the end, the incompatibility of management styles was recognized and German culture came to dominate. The key figures in the Chrysler management team had departed within 12 months, leaving Chrysler struggling to deal with a new management team (headed by a German former Mercedes executive) at a time when the competitive environment was particularly difficult. Under the chairmanship of Jürgen Schrempp, Daimler now views Chrysler as a stand-alone division, focusing wholly on the US market. Chrysler, meanwhile, has struggled to replace ageing models and risks losing out in its traditionally strong markets of light trucks and vans. Insiders attribute many of Chrysler's troubles to the failure of the Germans to understand Chrysler culture.

Sources: 'DaimlerChrysler union challenges two cultures', *Detroit News*, 14 September 1998; 'Culture clash when car makers merge', *Detroit News*, 14 May 1998; 'Lessons from a casualty of the culture wars', *Business Week*, 29 November 1999; Burt, T., 'Colliding with Chrysler', *Financial Times*, 10 October 2000.

Case questions

How would you describe the culture clash at DaimlerChrysler?
To what extent has it been resolved successfully?

and stiffer style of Daimler-Benz (see Case Study 5.4). The two companies found huge differences in ways of working, decision-making, the conduct of meetings and the exchange of information. Blending the culture of different locations into a distinctive corporate culture, in which any of the company's employees feel at home in any of the company's locations, can strengthen a sense of corporate identity, but poses considerable challenges for international managers.

5.9 Culture change

Hofstede and Trompenaars both found wide variations in national cultures among the nations studied. Studies such as these risk giving an impression that national cultures are static. However, individuals, organizations and even whole societies do change over time. Industrialization as a global phenomenon has impacted on the social and cultural environments of societies as they pursue economic development. Patterns of economic development differ and so too do cultural adaptations to the changes taking place. Capitalist development is linked with individualist values, which, while reflecting the growth of capitalism in Europe, are no longer seen as valid for all the world's peoples.

The growth of Asian capitalism in Confucian cultures, which are generally more collectivist than individualist, has demonstrated how cautious we should be in making assumptions about cultural predispositions. Nonetheless, growing material well-being and prosperity, the benefits of education, new career opportunities and urbanization are some aspects of the changing environment that bring shifts in cultural values in all countries, although their impact differs from society to society. For most societies, impetus for cultural change comes about through external forces, such as foreign investors who bring in new organizational forms and technological advances derived from more advanced Western economies. Global companies may take an ethnocentric approach, attempting to replicate their own national culture in each foreign location, but, increasingly, as Case Study 5.3 shows, companies have found that managing cultural diversity through adaptation to local environments is more fruitful. In this way, change comes about gradually and impacts on *both* the local and the parent organizations.

5.10 Cultural globalization: myth or reality?

It has been argued by some notable commentators, such as Kenichi Ohmae, that economic globalization is leading to **cultural globalization**, which can be defined as movement towards a borderless world, in which cultural differences are fading in real significance (Ohmae, 1995). Ohmae points to the facts that some multinational corporations wield more power than governments and consumer markets are now globalized, rather than locally or nationally circumscribed. While Ohmae's views are persuasively argued, they risk oversimplifying a complex global picture. Cultural flows consist mainly of consumer products and entertainment. Both are now dominated by multinational companies from the developed world, but, despite the globalization of their organizations and strategies, international tastes still show considerable diversity.

5.10.1 Role of the media in cultural globalization

The volume of information now available and the ease of instant access from any part of the globe are defining characteristics of the information age, distinguishing our world from that of all previous generations. International cultural flows have reached unprecedented levels and their reach potentially extends to all societies, from the richest to the poorest. However, their reach is uneven, as shown in Table 5.5. Whereas in developed societies, television, radio and telephone ownership have reached saturation levels, there are many parts of the world to which their reach still hardly extends.

Table 5.5 Growth in television ownership

	1970	1980	1990	1997
World	81	127	206	240
Africa	4.6	18	41	60
America*	209	328	404	429
Asia	20	40	153	190
Europe	205	324	385	446
Oceania	188	300	378	427
Latin America and Caribbean	57	98	162	205
Southern Asia	0.9	6.4	29	54
Developed countries	263	424	492	548
Developing countries	9.9	27	124	157
Least-developed countries	0.5	3.5	13	23

Notes
1. Number of television sets per 1,000 inhabitants.
2. * includes the whole of the Americas.

Source: UNESCO, *1999 Statistical Yearbook* (Paris: Bernan Press) Table IV, S.3.

Broadcasts, films, commercial advertising, books, magazines and myriad internet resources offer larger amounts of cultural products than ever before available. They also familiarize consumers the world over with symbols and products which are increasingly seen as transnational, superseding the cultural bounds of nations. These cultural flows are dominated by large communications organizations, whose cultural reach and power is historically unparalleled. Media and telecommunications which were once under public ownership are now increasingly privatized and deregulated. Global media companies, such as Sony, Time-Warner, Disney or Bertelsmann, have dominated cultural output largely through capturing the latest technology. The takeover in 2000 of the media company Time-Warner by AOL, the internet company, is indicative of the perceived advantages of media mergers linking cultural content with the internet. Many see these developments, along with the predominance of English in the media, as signs of cultural globalization. On the other hand, despite Hollywood films and CNN, there persists a remarkable diversity of cultural output, reflecting differing national tastes and languages.

In film, television, and music, large media companies increasingly tailor entertainment output for local tastes and in local languages. In Asia and Latin America, where consumer markets are growing rapidly, audiences prefer local content over American popular culture (Rose, 1999). Media giants such as Sony have altered their strategies from the 1970s, when most of their output was American popular culture. Now, their growth area is international output, exemplified by Hindi-language and Mandarin-language programming for satellite television, which reaches huge audiences (Rose, 1999). While imports, especially American films and television series, have global reach, local and regional broadcasters and producers find eager markets for local and 'alternative' broadcasting. Similarly, marketing research organizations monitoring use of the internet now find that, as technology advances, websites are becoming more internationalized, offering multiple languages rather than English only (see Minifile on multilingual websites). Mass cultural consumption driven by global media does not seem to have swept away demand for local and national cultural products. This trend is particularly apparent in developing countries, as media penetration approaches the levels of developed countries.

A further point which should be made in connection with cultural globalization is that cultural values and norms run deep and change only slowly. A person in Asia, for example, may listen to Western pop music, wear Levi jeans and drink Coca-Cola, but not subscribe to the value system they represent. Indeed, in many countries with strong cultural identities, high-profile American companies may attract hostility and accusations of cultural imperialism, prompting a kind of backlash consisting of positive moves towards reasserting local values and symbols.

Minifile

MULTILINGUAL WEBSITES

English dominates the internet. Estimates are that 75–80 per cent of websites are in English, although only about 5.4 per cent of the world's population are native speakers of English. But, as international internet access grows, English looks set to lose its dominance. Increasingly, companies are making information available in multiple languages and conducting e-business in the consumer's own language. According to research, growth in Web usage and e-commerce in Europe and Asia will outstrip that of the US by between two and five times over the next few years. Global companies are now recognizing that cross-border commerce requires a new cross-cultural Web strategy. Language is an important element. Consumers are more likely to buy products and services online if they can use their own language. Sony sells its laptops to consumers through websites in 14 languages. The development of translation software, to respond quickly to queries in each language, was key to multilingual e-commerce. Also, however, prices need to be in local currency, dates must be expressed in the local format and weights and measures should be in the local system. Web designers need to be sensitive to colour and style preferences in different countries. Bright colours may be considered cheerful in one country, but have negative connotations in another. As white signifies death in China, it should be avoided, unless your business is funeral services.

Therefore, for a global company, Web strategy goes well beyond simple translation into a local language. Even for French companies, because of different dialects, a generic French site will not succeed in Haiti or Mozambique (Woods, 2000). As the internet reaches more and more consumers, local companies, which have a full grasp of the cultural issues and local language, are well placed to exploit their inherent advantages in local markets.

Sources: Woods, L., 'Clique here', *Corporate Legal Times*, **10**(98), January 2000; Perkin, J., 'Multilingual websites widen the way to a new online world', *Financial Times*, 7 February 2001.

5.10.2 Global culture and national culture

Smith contrasts national with global culture:

> Unlike national cultures, a global culture is essentially memoryless. Where a 'nation' can be constructed so as to draw upon and revive latent popular experiences and needs, a 'global culture' answers to no living needs, no identity-in-the-making. It has to be put together, artificially, out of the many existing folk and national identities into which humanity has been so long divided. (1990, p. 180)

Smith argues that global culture is more transitory and ephemeral, in comparison with the depth of shared history of national cultures. Symbols of Western consumer culture are certainly widely accessible and highly visible, but it is a huge leap to conclude that they therefore represent universal values. Wherever these products are sold in the world, their significance is differently interpreted according to the national culture of that particular market.

Marketing specialists are quick to point out that it is impossible to design a standard global marketing campaign guaranteeing success for a product in all markets. Although advanced media and communications technology bring people closer together in a spatial sense, this is a long way from the cultural shift which would be required to create a 'global village'.

5.11 Conclusions

1. Culture refers to a society's whole range of values and norms, which have developed through a shared history and experiences over a period of time. These cultural phenomena, which include language, religion and ethnicity, give a group of people a distinctive cultural identity.

2. The nation as a group of people is the dominant source of collective cultural identity. The growth in the number of nation-states since the Second World War reflects both the break-up of colonial empires and the pressures for national self-determination.

3. Most states are multicultural. While institutional design can accommodate minority identities, including religious and linguistic minorities, cultural conflict is a possibility, particularly in younger states whose institutions are not yet fully established.

4. Businesses are often ethnocentric in outlook, but in the international environment, a polycentric approach will make it easier for them to adapt to the different cultural environments of foreign operations.

5. The processes of industrialization and modernization have impacted on cultural values and social organization in all parts of the world, but their impact has varied from society to society. While Western individualistic values are traditionally linked to the development of capitalism, economic development in Asian countries has demonstrated the enterprise potential of Confucian value systems.

6. Research by Hofstede and Trompenaars, focusing on cultural dimensions as variables, while tending to present static pictures of national cultures, has provided useful tools for cross-cultural analysis, in terms of both organizational and societal cultural profiles.

7. Organizations, while they may develop their own specific values and behaviour, are also highly influenced by the national culture of their home country.

8. Cultures, both national and organizational, evolve over time, but changes are likely to take place only gradually, reflecting the deep-seated nature of cultural 'programming'.

9 The impetus behind cultural globalization has depended largely on the globalization of the media and the cultural symbols it represents. However, despite growing global economic integration, national cultural diversity shows little sign of fading into a uniform global culture.

Review questions

1 What are the main elements of culture?

2 What is meant by 'ethnocentrism'?

3 Explain the essential aspects of national culture. Why are strong national cultures often considered to be those of homogeneous societies?

4 What are the differences between a 'high-context' and 'low-context' language? Why do these differences matter in business negotiations?

5 In what ways are greater liberalization and westernization taking place in some Muslim countries?

6 What has been the impact of Confucianism on firms in Asia, including their structures and ways of doing business?

7 Explain three approaches to multiculturalism in society. How do these different approaches affect business relations?

8 What are the essential cultural dimensions described by Hofstede in his research?

9 How do the rankings of national culture produced by Hofstede shed light on international management practices in different locations?

10 List the main elements of organizational culture. Why is 'culture clash' a common problem in mergers between large companies?

11 Describe the role of the media in cultural globalization. Why are media companies now expanding local production in local languages?

Assignments

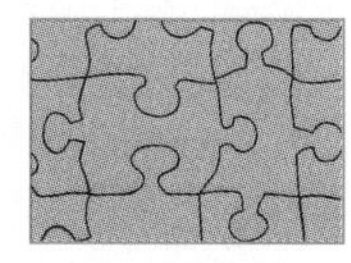

1 It is sometimes said that local diversity will inevitably fade away under the tidal wave of cultural globalization. Examine the evidence which supports this view and also the evidence which contradicts it.

2 For a global company from a Western economy contemplating a joint venture with a foreign partner in a newly industrializing Asian economy, what are the cultural difficulties likely to be encountered and what are your recommendations to enable the joint venture to succeed?

Further reading

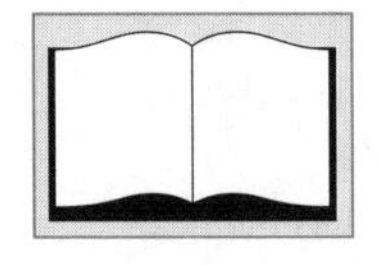

Bartlett, C. and Ghoshal, S. (1998) *Managing Across Borders: A Transnational Solution*, 2nd edn (London: Random House)

Held, D. (ed.) (2000) *A Globalizing World: Culture, Economics, Politics* (Andover: Routledge)

Hickson, D.J. and Pugh, D.S. (1995) *Management Worldwide* (London: Penguin)

Hofstede, G. (1994) *Cultures and Organizations: Software of the Mind* (London: HarperCollins)

Patten, C. (1998) *East and West* (Basingstoke: Macmillan – now Palgrave)

Schneider, S. and Barsoux, J.L. (1997) *Managing Across Cultures* (London: Prentice Hall)

Usunier, J.-C. (2000) *Marketing Across Cultures*, 3rd edn (London: Financial Times/Prentice Hall)

Chapter 6

Society and business

Outline of chapter

LEARNING OBJECTIVES

1. To identify the social groupings and interactions that make up societies
2. To understand the social changes taking place in industrial, developing and transitional economies and their impact on business activities
3. To appreciate how social stratification systems in diverse societies affect the international business environment
4. To assess the importance of social change in a variety of contexts relating to business, including the changing nature of work in the information technology (IT) age, gender and family issues

6.0 Introduction

Social interaction and social relations are among the most basic of human activities. Every society has distinctive characteristics in terms of population and way of life, some of the greatest distinctions being between industrialized and developing societies. Within societies there may be numerous cross-cutting ties: religion, gender, age, race or ethnic grouping. At the personal level, family and workplace ties are also important strands in each person's web of social interactions. Social groupings vary greatly in their sense of identity, internal cohesion, cultures and structures. Virtually every social grouping, from the broadest level of a whole society down to a small organization such as the family, is stratified in one or more ways. Social and economic status, such as class divisions within societies, affect occupation, lifestyle and education, for virtually all the world's people. Differences in the social environment from country to country, therefore, have a direct effect on international business operations and, in particular, on business practices and consumer markets.

Globalization in the spheres of technology and communication has immensely broadened the possibilities for social interaction between people

Social groupings

In any society, each person's attitudes and behaviour are formed in numerous social contexts. The first group of factors we have little control over, whereas those in the second group are mainly matters of choice

1 *Social groupings derived from natural circumstances (primary groups):*
   - National society
   - Subnational grouping, such as immigrant community
   - Race
   - Religion
   - Gender
   - Class or other status system (such as caste)
   - Age
   - Family
2 *Social groupings based on individual choice (secondary groups):*
   - Occupation
   - Workplace organization
   - Trade union
   - Other voluntary associations, such as sport and leisure clubs, political parties, interest groups

around the world. However, globalization, as we saw in the last chapter, has not as yet resulted in cultural homogenization. People are increasingly interconnected, but how do these changes affect societies and social relations? The main aim of this chapter is to delve into the nature of societies and other social groups, looking at the ways in which they interact in the international business environment. In a sense, this aim is focused on a 'moving target', as people and organizations proactively engage in changing and moulding the social environment, as well as responding to changes. The second aim, therefore, is to understand the interactive dynamic between the individual and society, in the context of global economic forces.

6.1 Types of society: the development of modern industrial societies

A **society** may be defined broadly as 'a system of interrelationships which connects individuals together' (Giddens, 1997, p. 18). The word 'society' is used in many contexts. First, it is often used to refer to the national society of the modern nation-state. However, as we saw in Chapter 5, while shared culture is the lifeblood of nations, the modern state is seldom a homogeneous society reflecting a single national identity. Most are home to numerous subcultures representing ethnic and linguistic diversity. These subnational groups, both indigenous and immigrant, may have considerable cohesion, especially if they are clustered in geographical areas where they continue to speak their own language. Issues relating to the social integration of these groups will be examined later in this chapter.

A second use of the term 'society' is to designate types of society on the basis of their means of subsistence. We frequently use the terms 'industrial society' and 'capitalist society' to refer to economies based on industrialized mass production, the type of society that most of us are familiar with. Industrialization refers to the shift from human and animal power to machine production, in which energy was derived from inanimate sources, such as water power, steam and the internal combustion engine. The Industrial Revolution, which started in the second half of the eighteenth century, brought about the dramatic social transformation of existing societies, beginning in Britain and spreading to other countries in Europe and America. Traditional societies, based primarily on agriculture, gradually evolved into industrial societies, whose economies were dominated by production and exchange of mass-produced goods.

The transition to an **industrial society** can also be described as a shift from traditional to 'modern' society. Ties to the land loosened as people left the rural way of life for work in the new factories in cities. Major social changes brought about by industrialization, which are all discussed later in this chapter, included urbanization, changes in the nature of work and changes in family life. These changes can be observed today in transitional economies

Case study 6.1 B&Q in China

B&Q, a subsidiary of the Kingfisher group, is the largest do-it-yourself (DIY) operator in Europe. Having run stores in Taiwan since 1996, it ventured into the mainland China market by opening a warehouse store in Shanghai in 1999. The store is a joint venture with a local concern, Home-Dec Building Materials. B&Q has a 30 per cent holding, but has full operational control over the store. B&Q's timing of its entry into the Chinese market was good. Until the mid-1990s, most urban Chinese lived in accommodation rented to them from their work units and had little incentive to decorate their homes. But the Chinese government is now promoting home ownership and a big decorating and furnishing market has developed.

B&Q has had to discover when it must adapt to the local market, and when it must insist on doing things differently. The aim of the two expatriate managers was to replicate as far as possible B&Q's UK store format: displays were erected by a team of store-fitters and engineers from the UK. Shanghai customers appreciate the clean, well-lit store.

Practical difficulties hamper the development of China's fledgling DIY market. Even though a five-day working week became standard in 1994, many Shanghainese commute long distances to work. Holidays are limited, often to 10 days a year. Shanghai is China's most densely populated city and space is at a premium: few people have a spare room or garage that could serve as a workshop for DIY.

The housing market in China is radically different from that in the UK. New properties in China are empty shells, with no flooring, no plaster on the walls or ceiling and no kitchen or bathroom units. To make such a place habitable goes well beyond the scope of ordinary DIY. Such cultural and practical differences translate into a markedly different sales profile from that of the UK. It is not so much a DIY market as a 'buy-it-yourself-and-get-a-team-of-workmen-to-do-the-work-for-you' market. Typical customers are young couples who are about to marry or have just bought a flat. They are often accompanied by the person who will carry out the decoration work. Many customers are unaccustomed to buying products in a supermarket. They expect a sales assistant to accompany them while shopping, lift goods down from the shelf and carry them to the checkout.

Human resources management (HRM) is often hard for foreign companies in China. B&Q Shanghai has the same personnel policies as in the UK. The company encourages informality: all employees wear the same uniform – a pale grey or blue T-shirt and an orange apron with the B&Q logo. They also refer to each other by their first names. This is a radical departure in hierarchy-conscious China. Local staff welcome the atmosphere. The local assistant store manager describes it as 'very open, much more diplomatic than in state-owned enterprises'. The attitude of local employees is helped by the prospect of rapid promotion and career development as B&Q expands in China. However, taking B&Q from one Chinese city to another may be as difficult as moving from one European country to another, as there are significant regional differences in labour markets, logistics, customer expectations and local government bureaucracy.

Source: Gamble, J., 'Assembling an empire with no instructions', *Financial Times*, 13 December 2000 (reprinted with permission).

Case question

How is B&Q benefiting from the social changes taking place in China?

such as China, where large numbers of rural dwellers are moving to the cities, looking for opportunities in the fast-growing economy. Case Study 6.1 reveals some of these changes. Developing countries are still predominantly agricultural, and the least developed, those in Africa, are only slowly becoming industrialized.

6.2 Stratification in societies

Throughout history, all societies have exhibited social and economic inequalities to a greater or lesser degree. 'Social stratification' refers to this hierarchy of groups into which people in a society are classified. This classification may be rigidly institutionalized, as in caste systems; or it may allow for upward mobility, as in a capitalist class society. We look first at the more rigid systems of stratification and then at classes in industrial societies.

6.2.1 Rigid social stratification

Rigid social systems were once the norm in most societies. Under feudalism, a person's position in life was determined by birth, fitting into a hierarchical and inflexible social order. Under slavery, which existed in the Americas from the sixteenth century, human be ngs were owned and controlled by other people, effectively treated as chattels which were bought and sold. Colonial administrations also used forced labour in various parts of the world, in construction work and mining, for example. Slavery as an institution and the slave trade were made illegal in most of the world in the nineteenth century. However, pockets of slavery have persisted, and new forms of forced labour are emerging in the modern global economy, aided by an alarming rise in the trafficking in human beings (ILO, 2001b). Forced labour in its modern incarnation can be broadly defined as work exacted by threats or coercion, restrictions on freedom of movement, with no pay or very little pay. It occurs in a variety of situations, including sweatshops, public works, domestic service and commonly arises from bondage through indebtedness (often to traffickers). Vulnerable groups include women, children, migrants and ethnic minorities. While these new forms of exploitation are for shorter periods, rather than for a lifetime, they share the essential characteristics of older forms of slavery, such as control over labour and lack of freedom. National authorities in almost all countries are now seeking to eliminate all forms of coercive labour, supported by a growing body of international law on human rights (ILO, 2001b).

A caste system is a rigid system of social stratification in which a person is born into a particular position which determines his or her place in society. India is perhaps the best-known example of a caste system based on religious beliefs. In Hinduism, a person is born into a caste and has no prospect of escape in the present lifetime. While the caste system was officially abolished in 1949, it is still very much a force in Indian society, especially rural society. The link between low caste and poverty in Indian society is thus perpetuated. Despite social inequalities based on caste however, India's growing economy has provided educational and employment opportunities which cut across caste boundaries in growth areas such as computing and IT.

Stratification in societies

- *Slavery* – extreme form of servitude, in which people are treated as forced labour and traded. While slavery and the slave trade have been abolished, new forms of forced labour and trafficking in human beings have emerged in many countries
- *Caste* – status in society is determined by birth. The caste system is associated with the Indian subcontinent
- *Class* – status dependent on economic position. Class societies are associated with capitalist development, allowing for upward mobility from lower to higher status

6.2.2 Social class

The dynamic of capitalist society is class-based conflict. Unlike systems of slavery and caste, a class system is not determined by birth, although the class of our parents does play a part in our educational and career prospects. A **class** may be defined as a grouping of individuals based on its economic strength in society, or, putting it in more theoretical terms, its position in relation to the means of production. Class differences rest essentially on economic inequalities, rather than any inherent characteristics of individuals. Social class is one of the key factors used by marketers in understanding consumer behaviour. There are a number of socio-economic classification systems in use by government statistical offices and market research organizations. Table 6.1 sets out a typical scheme applied to the UK, with percentages of the population in each class. While this classification is based mainly on occupation, it should be remembered that a number of other factors help to determine social class, including income, education and wealth.

In all class systems the upper class are the owners and controllers of economic resources. They may be self-made entrepreneurs who have accumulated wealth, or they may be senior managers in large corporations. The middle class comprises numerous professional and white-collar workers, in salaried posts. They may also be self-employed, small businesspeople. A distinction is made between upper middle class, which includes managerial and professional people, and lower middle class, which includes people such as administrators and other office staff, nurses and teachers. The working class is made up of manual and blue-collar workers. Again, the upper

Table 6.1 UK socioeconomic classification scheme

Class name	Social status	Occupation of head of household	Percentage of population
A	Upper middle	Higher managerial, administrative or professional	3
B	Middle	Intermediate managerial, administrative or professional	14
C1	Lower middle	Supervisors or clerical, junior managerial, administrative or professional	27
C2	Skilled working	Skilled manual workers	25
D	Working	Semi-skilled and unskilled manual workers	19
E	Those at the lowest levels	State pensioners or widows, casual or lower-grade workers	12

Source: Kotler, P., Armstrong, G., Saunders, J. and Wong, V. (1999) *Principles of Marketing*, 2nd edn (London: Prentice Hall) p. 233 (reproduced with permission).

working class made up of skilled workers, is often distinguished from the lower working class of unskilled workers.

Class structures differ in different societies. The 'diamond' pattern of UK society shown in Table 6.1 (relatively few at the top and bottom, with a bulge in the middle) is typical of many developed societies. But for many other societies, such as those in Latin America and Africa, the class structure is more of a pyramid, with a wealthy elite at the pinnacle and a large population of poor people at the base. Concentration of wealth in land ownership is one of the factors that perpetuates extreme inequalities in these countries. In the poorer countries whose economies are dominated by agriculture, the peasantry, who work on the land, form the largest class. Agriculture, including both farmers and labourers, is also economically and politically significant in many industrialized economies, as food is an important strategic resource.

6.2.3 Changes in capitalist society

All societies experience change, which may be gradual changes or radical transformation during particularly turbulent periods in their history. Some changes that have shaped modern capitalist societies are set out below.

- *The structure of corporate power:* The large corporation of today differs from the nineteenth-century company in which ownership and control resided in the owner-entrepreneur. Ownership is now dispersed among a wide group of shareholders, many of them large financial institutions. Moreover, managers and corporate boards of directors must now be responsive to a variety of stakeholder interests, in addition to those of the company's shareholders. Corporate power has thus become more diffuse and complex than in the days of the owner-manager.

- *The changing nature of white-collar work:* With the decline in manufacturing industries and the increase in the service sector, many more people now work in non-manual, white-collar jobs than in blue-collar jobs. However, many of these jobs are low-level clerical and administrative jobs, requiring little skill. The mechanization, or deskilling, of office work is largely responsible. Work which once involved individual responsibility has become routinized and repetitive; little individual initiative is involved and career prospects are few. This type of work may be hardly more skilled than manual labour used to be, but we probably still look on such jobs as middle class, rather than working class. Jobs that are subject to deskilling are likely to give way to automation, as workers are replaced by IT systems. These routine clerical jobs, such as work in call centres, are predominantly carried out by women (see Case Study 6.3 on call centres). Job security and job satisfaction are low and career prospects are poor (Stanworth, 2000). Moreover, many of these jobs are shifting to low-cost locations such as the Caribbean, India and Malaysia (ILO, 2001a).
- *Social mobility and the new middle class:* The growing middle class is associated with the growth of modern consumer society generally. Manual workers in industrial societies are now likely to be relatively far more affluent than their predecessors, and to enjoy the fruits of consumer society, such as home ownership. Many manual jobs have themselves changed with the introduction of computer technology, requiring a level of skill much higher than that needed for manual jobs of old. In their styles of life, these workers more closely resemble middle-class than working-class groups. They are likely to wear the same types of casual clothes in their leisure, enjoy the same types of entertainment, and drive similar cars. While football was once thought of as a working-class game, it has become absorbed into consumer society (see Case Study 6.2). Similarly, the foreign package holiday has now become almost universally accessible, while the traditional seaside holiday camps, with their working-class image, have struggled to compete.

The tastes and purchasing decisions of this new middle class are now increasingly being refined by market research analysis, providing information for marketing strategists in consumer goods and services. Marketing uses the concept of **segmentation** to break down consumer markets. Along with social class, segmentation can be based on geographic region, demographic factors

Case study 6.2 The new consumption of football

For many years, football as a spectator attraction has had a notorious reputation for poor treatment of the supporters who are its paying customers. The 1990s have seen the transformation of professional football, from the game watched mainly by working-class men standing on terraces to a global business supported by the affluent middle classes. The Premier League has seen the greatest changes. All-seater stadiums have replaced terraces, altering forever the spectator environment. Increases in ticket prices have followed, squeezing out many traditional fans. Key to the new era of football finance have been lucrative television and other media contracts, which facilitate the consumption of football worldwide, accompanied by new global marketing strategies for clubs, which increasingly see themselves as brands. Manchester United has been the most successful club in terms of global branding, with an estimated 20 million supporters worldwide. Media ties have developed further into new football club/media joint ventures, in which media companies own up to 50% of the shares. Manchester United captain, Roy Keane, has lamented that these days football spectators, nibbling their prawn sandwiches, have little idea what is going on out on the pitch. Where has the traditional fan gone?

Anthony King has researched 'the lads' who support Manchester United and the culture of fandom. Not surprisingly, he found fans unhappy with the transformation of the club, saying:

> it threatens the very foundations on which the success of United has been built: United should be careful, they have effectively cut off the local young supporters who cannot get tickets for games now. I remember catching the 255 bus to Old Trafford as a kid and the bus was packed with the lads the same age who knew they could play in the match. That same bus is empty nowadays. (King, p. 337)

Still, for the fans, football is central to their identities. For those who can still afford it, love of the team compels them to attend, even though they do not approve of the club's commercial strategy and heap disdain on the new fans who wear replica shirts. Football, unlike other consumer products, is one which can usually count on the fact that the customer is highly unlikely to switch brands.

Sources: King, A. (1997), 'The lads: masculinity and the new consumption of football', *Sociology*, **31**(2): 329–46; Harverson, P., 'Man Utd holding out to pick the strongest sponsorship team, *Financial Times*, 14 January 2000. Harding, J., 'Televised battle for Premier League soccer', *Financial Times*, 3 April 2000.

Case question

How has the new consumption of football reflected changes in the socioeconomic environment?

(age, gender and family structure), education and lifestyle (Kotler et al., 1999). Geographic region may have a strong cultural bond linking residents, which cuts across class divisions. Similarly, gender and age segmentation reflects prevalent social groupings and social interactions, also cutting across lines of social class.

6.3 Changing populations

The world's population stands at just over 6 billion people. Asia is the most populous continent, with 3.6 billion people. The populations of the developing countries, encompassing Asia (excluding Japan and Russia), Latin America and Africa, account for three out of every four people (UN Population Division, 1999). These populations are also experiencing the most rapid growth – over 95 per cent of the world's population growth is accounted for by developing countries. This trend is a cause for concern in that the bulk of the world's population growth into the first quarter of the twenty-first century will occur in the countries which are already struggling to provide sufficient food and improve the quality of life for their inhabitants.

Populations are not static, but constantly changing. They change naturally over time and across space. **Demographic change** refers to these population changes. They include births, deaths and migration. The difference between births and deaths produces a natural increase (or decrease) in population. Natural increase, or the excess of births over deaths, is the most common way in which populations grow, but migration is also an important factor. Migration may be within the same country, as in rural to urban migration, or international movement of people. These phenomena can have long-term effects on societies, both on the places people have left and those to which they migrate. Immigration may play a significant part in population growth over time, as the children of immigrants themselves add to the population. Demographic changes, while they take place at a slow pace, can have profound long-term effects on societies.

6.3.1 Ageing societies and implications for business

In industrialized countries, low birth rates, coupled with a growing proportion of elderly people, are creating a looming demographic crisis in the twenty-first century. Figure 6.1a shows that in the developed world the proportion of children is projected to decline from 18 per cent in 1998 to 14 per cent in 2050, while the proportion of older people will rise from 20 per cent in 1998 to 35 per cent by 2050. In the populations of the developing world, the pattern is similar, as shown in Figure 6.1b, but any demographic crisis lies much further into the future.

The United Nations' (UN) Population Division has published a report on replacement migration, detailing the extent of possible labour shortages which could threaten economic growth, unless immigrants are admitted to make up the shortfall in workers. The report estimates that even a massive influx of immigrants would have only limited impact on the declining and ageing populations in Europe and Japan (UN Population Division, 2000). By 2025, it is estimated that nearly one-third of the population of Europe will be pensioners. In the case of Germany, for example, to maintain the current proportion between the working population and over-65s would require an

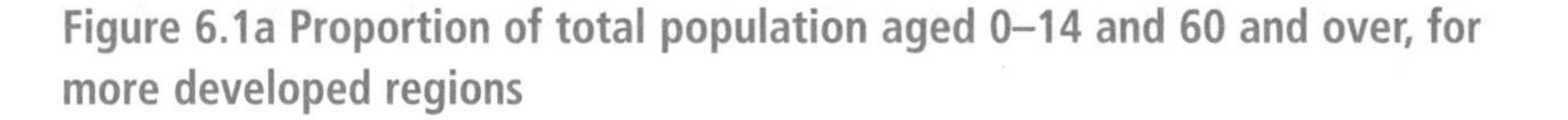

Figure 6.1a Proportion of total population aged 0–14 and 60 and over, for more developed regions

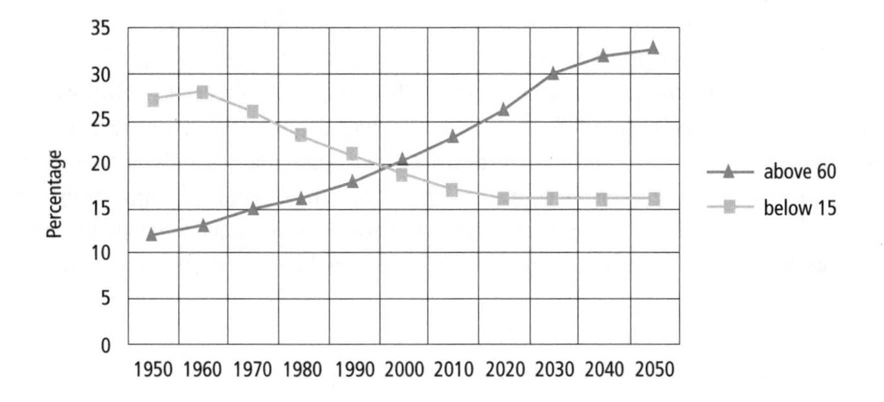

Figure 6.1b Proportion of total population aged 0–14 and 60 and over, for less developed regions

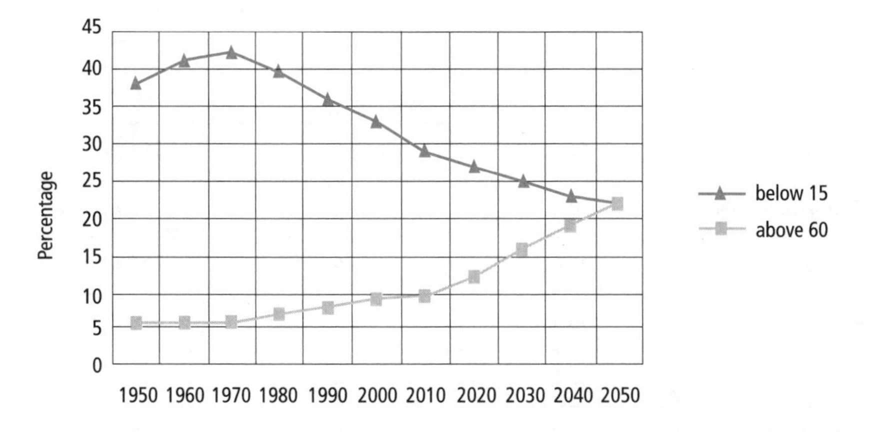

Source: UN Population Division (1998) *World Population Prospects: The 1998 Revision*.

average influx of 3.4 million migrants per year, more than ten times the number of immigrants entering Germany between 1993 and 1998. An alternative would be to raise the retirement age to 77. In reality, the trend, as shown in Table 6.2, has been towards earlier retirement, despite longer life expectancy. While the legal retirement age in most European countries is 65, the average, actual retirement age for men is 61 and for women 58 (OECD, 1998). The UN concludes that for the industrialized countries:

> Keeping retirement and health-care systems for older persons solvent in the face of declining and ageing populations, for example, constitutes a new situation that

poses serious challenges for Governments and civil society. (UN Population Division, 2000, p. 94)

There are long-term implications of these trends for business. Many businesses have seen opportunities for targeting older consumers, who have leisure time and money to spend. Saga Holidays specializes in holidays for over-50s and has expanded into other services such as insurance. Firms specializing in retirement flats, nursing homes, pharmaceuticals and health-care products will experience market growth. Large food manufacturers in the US have found an eager market for products such as fruit juices and snacks which are fortified to give health benefits beyond their normal nutri-

Table 6.2 Percentages of men aged 55–64 at work

	Percentage in work 1971	Percentage in work 1995	Percentage decrease 1971–95
Australia	84.4	60.9	–23.5
Canada	83.3	58.9	–24.4
Finland	73.2	46.0	–27.2
France	74.6	41.5	–33.0
Germany (western)	78.5	57.8	–20.7
Ireland	91.0	63.9	–27.1
Italy	59.3	44.1	–15.2
Japan	87.1	84.4	–2.3
Netherlands	80.6	42.3	–38.3
Norway	83.3	72.3	–11.1
Portugal	81.7	60.7	–21.0
Spain	84.6	54.9	–29.6
Sweden	84.7	70.4	–14.3
United Kingdom	88.4	62.4	–26.0
United States	82.1	66.0	–16.1

Source: OECD (1998) 'The Retirement Decision in OECD Countries', OECD Ageing Working Paper AWP 1.4, in the series *Maintaining Prosperity In An Ageing Society: the OECD Study on the Policy Implications of Ageing.*

tional value. Called 'nutraceuticals', these products, with names such as 'Wisdom' and 'Karma', are fortified with herbs such as ginkgo biloba and other supplements. This market nearly doubled from 1997, when it amounted to $2.68 billion, to 2000, when it had grown to $4.7 billion (Barnes and Winter, 2001).

Paying for pensions and medical care for the elderly is a potential problem if pensions and health insurance schemes prove to be inadequately funded. France, Germany and Italy have had generous state pension arrangements, but are now seeking pension reforms to control spiralling public expenditure on pensions. According to one estimate, pension payments in Germany could rise to as much as 18.5 per cent of gross domestic product (GDP) by 2035 (Hargreaves, 1999). In Britain, by contrast, where public provision is much less, the government only pays about 4 per cent of GDP in pensions, which is set to rise to just 5 per cent by 2030. Occupational and private pensions, which are commoner in the UK, face potential shortfalls, as retirees live longer and falling stock markets have eroded the values of pension funds and other investments. Present-day workers must therefore come to terms with the need to pay a greater proportion of their earnings into pensions than their parents had to pay.

Declining birth rates mean that businesses in key sectors may face a shortage of skilled labour which could affect production. European governments have begun to relax the rules of entry for immigrants with specialized skills. There are also steps which governments and companies can take to keep workers active longer. A UK government report in 2000 recommended the following:

- the introduction of age discrimination legislation (also covered in an EU anti-discrimination directive, Council Directive 2000/78/EC)
- raising from 50 to 55 the age at which early retirement schemes can be taken
- 'gradual' retirement arrangements with companies, to allow workers to continue working flexibly. (Cabinet Office, 2000)

6.3.2 International migration

The urge to move to 'greener pastures' is not a recent phenomenon. People have been on the move throughout history. Movements which result in a permanent change of residence are referred to as **migration**, and they are a normal aspect of most societies (de Haan, 1999). People move for a variety of reasons. Studies of the causes of migration divide these reasons into 'push' and 'pull' factors, and researchers often find that both sets of factors are relevant. Some 'push' factors are escape from poverty, natural disasters or religious persecution. Often, when these factors are involved, people move en masse across borders. 'Pull' factors include the prospect, real or imagined, of a better job and greater economic opportunities.

The most important historic examples of population outflow have been the movements of European settlers to the new worlds of the Americas and Australia. From about the sixteenth century, people emigrated in search of more space, economic riches, a better life and also, simply, adventure. The exodus of Europeans, mainly to the Americas, in the nineteenth century created the world's largest international population flow, amounting to a million arrivals a year in the years leading up to the First World War. Push and pull factors both played a part. In the early phase, people left the densely populated areas of Northern Europe to seek more space and a better living in America, but later immigrants came from the poor areas of Southern and Eastern Europe.

6.3.3 Recent patterns of migration

In the post-war period, migration has involved both push and pull factors, economic migrants as well as refugees. Globalization has seen the rise of an international labour market and greater mobility of workers. International migration has been mainly from developing countries to developed ones, chiefly in North America and the industrial areas of Europe. This flow of labour reflects the gulf between richer and poorer economies, as well as the rapid rates of population increase in the developing countries. Post-war economic development in France and Germany depended in large measure on immigrant labour. In Germany, many of these immigrants came as 'guest-workers', on short-term contracts. However, millions of these workers, a large proportion of whom were Turkish, stayed on and have become settled, although, as foreigners, they have not become assimilated into German society.

Migration impacts on both the sending and receiving countries. Highly skilled workers, such as scientists, doctors and engineers, come to industrialized regions from developing countries, forming a 'brain drain' which deprives their home countries of their skills, but provides broader individual opportunities for self-betterment. These workers are welcomed by industrialized societies, to fill gaps in their own workforces. On the other hand, poor, unskilled migrants, often without legal documentation, enter a country and find work in jobs that local people are reluctant to take (for example in agriculture). These people pose a number of issues for both government and society in recipient countries. Employment, housing, healthcare and education are some of the main areas where they have particular needs, often complicated by language difficulties. In the post-war period, Western governments have tightened immigration controls at borders, while at the same time recognizing an obligation under the UN Convention on Refugees (1951) to accept genuine refugees and asylum-seekers. However, the definition of refugee is interpreted differently in different states, some more broadly than others. The migrant who has little hope of entering as a refugee is thus tempted to use clandestine means, possibly relying on organized traffickers. Therefore governments have had to address the problems of controlling the growth of trafficking in humans, as well as the problems of individual asylum-seekers.

Within the European Union (EU), only EU citizens enjoy free movement; non-citizens are subject to different legal regimes in member states. Enlargement of the EU, bringing in the poorer states of Central and Eastern Europe, raises the issue of future immigration from low-wage economies. This prospect has pushed the immigration issue up the political agenda at both national and EU levels. Germany and Austria, in particular, would be likely destinations of new Eastern European migrants. In the 1990s, growing numbers of refugees from conflicts in Africa and the former Yugoslavia have entered EU countries. In Britain, the official numbers leapt from 4,000 to over 70,000 in 1999 (Home Office, 2000). Stricter laws on asylum-seekers came into force in 2000, in the Asylum and Immigration Act. The Act aims, above all, to streamline and speed up the processing of asylum-seekers, and also to impose penalties on traffickers. EU authorities now recognize that harmonization of the law is needed among its member states, in order to prevent a developing scenario of migrants 'shopping around' between countries.

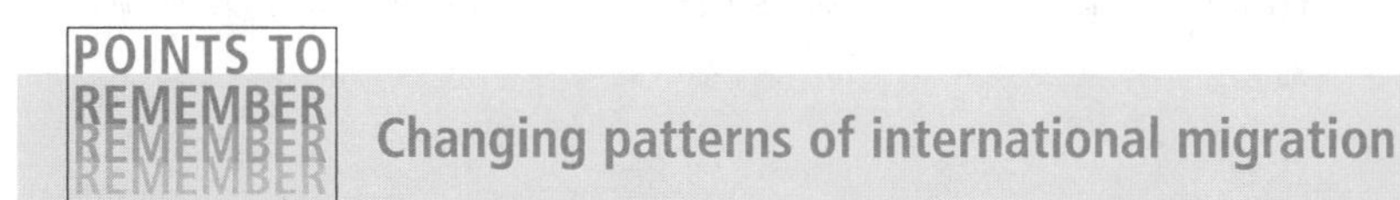

Changing patterns of international migration

- Historically, waves of immigrants from Europe to the new world have relieved population pressures in their homelands and have been openly welcomed in their destinations
- While the post-war modern state system presents considerable formal barriers to immigrants, most developed economies have benefited from immigrants' contribution to their economies
- Migration of people between continents has grown with the globalization of labour markets, most of the movement being from developing to developed economies
- Many of these newer migrants see themselves as following employment opportunities, part of a more mobile international labour pattern, in contrast to immigrants of earlier generations

6.4 Urbanism

Migration from rural areas to cities was commonplace long before industrialization. People were 'on the move' not just for economic motives, but for social and cultural reasons as well. The process by which a growing proportion of the population shifts to the cities is termed **urbanization**. At the start of

Table 6.3 Distribution of the world's population in urban and rural areas

	Population in 2000 (billions)	Population in 2030 (billions)	Annual average percentage growth 1950–2000	Annual average percentage growth 2000–30
Urban population				
World	2.85	4.89	2.67	1.80
More developed regions	0.90	1.01	1.41	0.37
Less developed regions	1.94	3.88	3.71	2.31
Rural population				
World	3.21	3.22	1.19	0.01
More developed regions	0.28	0.20	–.50	–1.19
Less developed regions	2.93	3.02	1.47	0.11

Source: United Nations Population Division (1999) *World Urbanization Prospects: The 1999 Revision.*

the twenty-first century approximately half the world's people live in urban areas. This proportion represents a rise from just over a third in 1975. By 2025, it is set to rise to two-thirds (World Bank, 2000a).

Urbanization is generally associated with economic development. Western countries, first to experience urbanization, are now about three-quarters urban, whereas developing countries, just 40 per cent urban in 2000, are expected to become 56 per cent urban by 2030 (UN Population Division, 1999). Most of the global population increase expected during 2000–30 will be concentrated in urban areas. The current rise in urbanization is now taking place mainly in developing countries, as shown in Table 6.3. However, the pattern of urbanization, and its social and economic effects, have differed between the industrialized Western economies and the developing economies. We look first at urbanization in Western economies.

6.4.1 Urbanization in Western economies

The technological developments of the Industrial Revolution provided the impetus for urbanization. These developments comprised three main elements:

1. The revolution in agriculture, which allowed farmers to produce more food with fewer workers

2 The transition to factory production systems, which attracted workers from the countryside

3 The transport revolution, which dramatically reduced the cost and increased the speed of transport of goods from one location to another, facilitating the distribution of food and other goods to an expanding urban population.

Urbanization accompanying economic development has followed a distinctive pattern, particularly observable in the US. With industrialization, firms were able to obtain scale economies by concentrating production in cities. The decision of a large firm to locate in a particular city can have a profound impact. For example, Detroit, the home of the motor industry in the US, attracted numerous firms connected with supplies to the major manufacturers. This is an example of industrial agglomeration, discussed in Section 2.7. Workers were attracted to the area, creating a healthy labour market. Detroit's heyday coincided with that of the mass production systems of Fordism, as we saw in Chapter 2. But with the shift to more flexible production in a global economy, firms looked carefully at advantages of a range of locations. High costs of labour and materials and scarcity of land were some of the factors that caused them to look to new locations. Factories closed down as companies looked for greenfield sites elsewhere, often abroad. The transition from the standardized Fordist economy to the flexible, information economy brought with it a more mobile workforce and changing industrial geography.

The landscapes of many American cities reflect the shifting centres of economic activity. As the major cities of the industrial north grew, the more affluent moved to the surrounding area, the suburbs. This process of 'suburbanization' peaked in the 1950s and 60s. The congestion, pollution, lack of space and high crime rates in the cities were all factors. A continuing problem of the inner cities has been urban decay, marked by run-down property, poor living standards and high crime rates. Meanwhile, some smaller towns and cities are booming. Those that are booming are often in areas where the new businesses in the information economy have taken hold, again attracting those with capital, technological expertise and innovative talents.

There are numerous internet resources on urbanization and the problems of cities throughout the world

The World Bank has an Urban Development website, with links on all issues connected with urbanization, including the environment, transport and regional issues. It is at http://worldbank.org/html/fpd/urban/map.html

The Urban Institute's website concentrates on American issues. It is at http://www.urban.org

In the UK, too, suburbanization resulted in a decline in the inner cities, although not as extreme as in the US. The northern industrial cities declined as manufacturing industries either closed down or moved, leaving behind problems of unemployment and declining infrastructure. On the other hand, new industries have sprung up in smaller towns and cities. Cambridge, for example, has become a centre for technology companies. Regeneration of inner cities has been part of government policy, aimed at improving housing and amenities. An important aspect of this policy has been to tackle the problems of road congestion and pollution caused by long commuter journeys from the suburbs, by attracting people back to urban centres. Much urban development, however, such as the high-rise office blocks and luxury apartments of the Docklands development in London, risks alienating poorer local residents and highlighting social divisions, rather than building a sense of community.

6.4.2 Urbanization in the developing world

The developing countries are now experiencing the fastest rates of urbanization, but, while urbanization has brought prosperity for the few, it has brought misery for masses of migrants to the cities. The growth is taking

Table 6.4 The world's ten largest cities

	Population in 2000 (millions)	Population in 2015 (millions)	Annual average percentage growth 1975–2000	Annual average percentage growth 2000–15
Tokyo (Japan)	26.4	26.4	1.2	0.0
Mexico City (Mexico)	18.1	19.2	1.9	0.4
Bombay (India)	18.1	26.1	3.9	2.4
São Paulo (Brazil)	17.8	20.4	2.3	0.9
New York (US)	16.6	17.4	0.2	0.3
Lagos (Nigeria)	13.4	23.2	5.6	3.7
Los Angeles (US)	13.1	14.1	1.5	0.5
Shanghai (China)	12.9	14.6	0.5	0.8
Calcutta (India)	12.9	17.3	2.0	1.9
Buenos Aires (Argentina)	12.6	14.1	1.3	0.7

Source: United Nations Population Division (1999) *World Urbanization Prospects: 1999 Revision.*

place with little planning and a haphazard infrastructure (Linden, 1996). In 1950, only three cities in developing countries were among the top ten in the world. As Table 6.4 shows, their positions are now reversed and only three are in developed countries. Tokyo is the largest urban agglomeration, but its population is not expected to grow further. By 2015, it will be joined by other megacities of over 20 million inhabitants, which are expected to be Mumbai (the Hindi name for Bombay), Lagos, Dhaka (Bangladesh) and São Paulo. Growth rates in Mexico City and São Paolo are slowing, while secondary cities in developing countries are growing more rapidly, creating even greater pressures on the limited infrastructure, although these cities do not receive the same international attention as the megacities (Linden, 1996).

Cities in the developing world struggle to cope with the pressures of huge and growing populations. Traffic congestion, pollution, sanitation and inadequate housing are endemic problems. Slum areas, with their proliferation of shanty dwellings, are particularly vulnerable to disease and natural disasters. According to a World Bank report, numbers in slum and squatter settlements will double in 25 years, and the average age of slum dwellers is decreasing (World Bank, 1999). The urban landscape in the developing world, therefore, exhibits a stark juxtaposition between modern high-rise centres, symbolic of new economic wealth, and the slum areas inhabited by the poorest inhabitants.

6.5 Labour relations

Relations between management and workers vary considerably, depending on both the internal environment of the organization and the wider social and cultural environment. Workers traditionally organize themselves into **trade unions** in order to achieve higher wages, better working conditions and greater security of employment. Workers in almost every country have organizations of this type, although countries vary in their approaches to organized labour. In some countries, trade unions have limited recognition and limited rights of collective negotiation. The right to strike, which is the workers' concerted withdrawal of labour, is the most potent weapon possessed by unions. A prolonged or widespread strike can take a heavy toll, in both economic losses and relations between employers and employees. Virtually all countries legally control strikes in a number of ways: membership balloting requirements for the call of a strike; cooling-off periods; and the prohibition of strikes in key public sectors. While the strike is used as a bargaining tool to obtain better employment terms, the strike as a barometer of social tension can also have a much broader significance. The high-profile walk-out can be directed not just against the employer, but against the political regime. Hence, the strike has been used to gain political voice in a number of countries. The Solidarity trade union in Poland, by orchestrating mass strikes in the shipyards, took the lead in the defeat of the communist regime. The union's political party grouping has governed Poland through most of the 1990s. Ironically, perhaps, the Gdansk shipyards, the birthplace of Solidarity, have now closed, victims of the harsh realities of global competition.

In industrialized countries, the growth in trade unionism took place in mass-production factories such as those in the motor industry. As well as in manufacturing, trade unions in Britain have also been strong in coal mining and shipyards. The decline in these latter sectors, together with the general decline in manufacturing jobs, has brought a steady decrease in trade union membership from the 1970s onwards. Union membership has declined from 13.3 million workers in 1979 to 7.1 million in 2000, comprising about 30 per cent of the workforce. A factor in this decline has also been a tightening of the law on strikes, which meant, for example, that a union's funds could be sequestered or frozen, in the event of unofficial strikes. The unions have fought back with recruitment campaigns, aimed at a wider variety of workers.

Only about 19 per cent of Britain's workers in the private sector are union members, while the percentage in the public sector is over 60 per cent. Union penetration is lower in the US, where less than 10 per cent of private sector workers are union members. Britain's largest union, UNISON, which represents professional, technical and administrative workers in the public sector, has 1.4 million members, 72 per cent of them women. UNISON, by adapting to the new employment structures, has moved away from the traditional trade union model built on a male-dominated, solidly working-class environment of manual work, to reflect the more diverse and flexible workforce in service and administrative employment. Still, in the private sector, two-thirds of workplaces have no union presence, and one-third of workplaces have no formal structures for representing employee interests. By contrast, in Germany, 'workers' councils' give employees a formal role in company decision-making, which extends to operational measures, such as the hiring and firing of employees. The system of workers' councils has been criticized as inflexible, inhibiting the ability of companies to compete.

WWW
WEBALERT

Internet resources on trade unions offer insights into their activities and policy positions on a range of issues. Some are listed below:

For the UK perspective see the Trade Union Congress website at http://www.tuc.org.uk

The International Confederation of Free Trade Unions has features on unions and the industrial environment throughout the world. It is at http://www2.icftu.org/

UNISON's website is at http://www.unison.org.uk/home/index.htm

For the American perspective, the American trade union federation, AFL-CIO has a site at http://www.aflcio/org/home.htm

However, attempts to reform the law on workers' councils have met resistance, as they are embedded in Germany's 'consensus' capitalism. The EU Directive on worker consultation, requiring companies to consult workers over large-scale redundancies, corporate restructuring and other strategic issues, was initially opposed by the British government, and accepted only with provisos that it is phased in over seven years and does not apply to companies with fewer than 50 employees.

6.6 Gender and work

Men enjoy greater status and wealth than women in virtually every society. Gender inequality has been accepted over many generations as somehow dictated by nature, reinforced by the stereotyped picture of the father as sole breadwinner and the mother as homemaker. This picture has persisted even though women now make up nearly half the workforce outside the home, as shown in Figure 6.2. Nonetheless, women still bear the major burden of bringing up children. Historically, women have lagged behind men in educational opportunities, career opportunities, pay and citizenship rights. Women achieved the right to vote and stand for public office in most Western societies in the last century, but only in the last 25 years of the twentieth century have they achieved legal rights to equal pay with men for equivalent work. In practice, however, while women's pay has improved in relation to that of men, they still fall behind in both pay and opportunities.

In the UK in 1999, women's weekly earnings were 74 per cent of men's earnings, compared with 54 per cent in 1970 (ONS, 2000b). This increase in wages largely reflects the impact of legislation, including the UK Equal Pay and Sex Discrimination Acts, as well as European Community law. Under

Figure 6.2 Women in the workforce

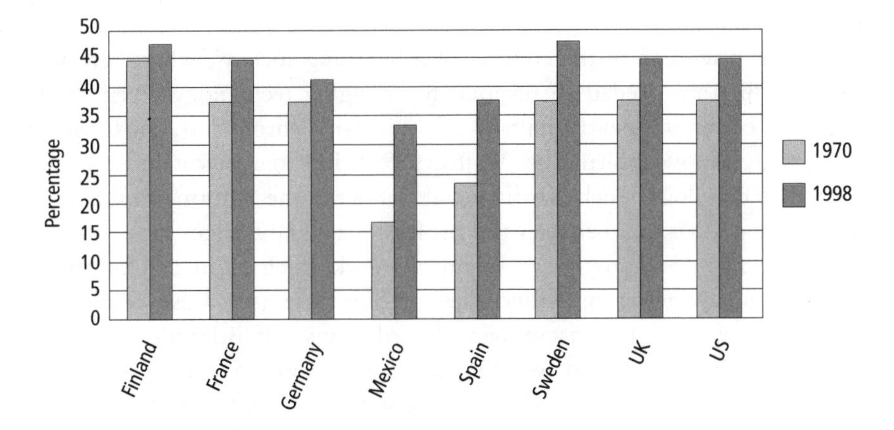

Source: World Bank (2000) *World Development Indicators 2000*, Table 1.3.

Table 6.5 Composition (by percentage) of weekly pay of UK employees: by gender and type of work, April, 1998

	Overtime	Profit related	Payment by results	Shift premia	Average gross weekly earnings (£)
Males					
Manual	14.1	1.1	3.7	3.4	327
Non-manual	2.8	1.0	3.7	0.6	505
Females					
Manual	6.8	0.9	2.9	2.8	210
Non-manual	1.8	1.8	1.6	0.8	329
All employees	5.4	1.0	3.1	1.4	383

Source: Office for National Statistics (2000) *Social Trends 30* (London: Stationery Office) Table 5.10, p. 87.

these laws, the employee is entitled to equal pay for work of equal value. Of EU countries, the UK has the highest percentage of women working part time. Here, approximately four out of every five part-time jobs are filled by women (ONS, 2000c). Only in the 1990s, as a result of EU initiatives, have part-time workers gained employment rights, such as pension rights and employment protection rights, on a par with full-time employees. Part-time work is currently 25 per cent of the labour force, and is predicted to rise to 31 per cent by 2006. The rise in part-time work, along with other types of non-standard work, such as teleworking from home, are aspects of a growing flexibility in the definition of 'work' in response to global competitive pressures.

Work is now seen in the context of a 'learning society', where retraining and reskilling are needed to respond to changing technology. Even though women account for nearly half of all university enrolments, most women workers are in low-skilled jobs (Walby, 1999). In some sectors most affected by new technology, such as financial services, the information age has brought new divisions between the professional 'knowledge' jobs, occupied mainly by men, and low-grade technical work, such as in call centres, in which women and ethnic minorities predominate (see Case Study 6.3). Women are very scarce in company boardrooms. Of Britain's largest 100 companies (the FTSE 100), women account for only 5 per cent of board directors. Nearly half of the FTSE 100 companies had no women on their boards at all in 1999 (*Financial Times*, 7 November 2000).

Case study 6.3 Call centres – the new assembly lines

'Thank you for calling. One of our customer service advisers will be with you shortly', says the friendly voice at one of Britain's call centres, an industry that is expanding by 40 per cent a year. It is estimated that two workers in every hundred are now working in call centres and three-quarters of these are women. Telesales have been around for a long time, but the boom in call centres only began in 1988, in the financial services sector, with the arrival of Direct Line, the telesales insurance company. Its success was followed in 1989 by First Direct, the 24-hour telephone bank. Financial services, including direct banking, mortgages and insurance, are still to the forefront, but to them has been added helpline work in a number of products and services, such as utilities companies, airlines, credit card companies and retailers.

The expansion of call centres has not been without controversy. The closure of thousands of branch banks is blamed on their rise. Barclays Bank has closed 723 branches since 1990 (Toyne, 2000). Call centres are typically located in areas of high unemployment, such as Wales and the northeast of England, where wages are low. For workers, conditions in call centres compare unfavourably with work in retail banks. They present an image of rows of identical workstations, battery-hen fashion, not unlike an industrial assembly line. As these are 24-hour operations, workers work flexible shifts. Space per worker, 4–6 square metres, is roughly half that provided in a high street bank. Qualifications are low and training is minimal – as little as three weeks. Career prospects and job satisfaction are low. Consequently, turnover of staff is over 30 per cent annually. Some companies in the industry have upgraded call centre work in terms of skills, prospects and motivation, improving personalized customer service, and thereby reducing the high staff turnover. But what are the trends for the industry generally, which has been labelled as low-skill women's work?

Call centre work, in the long term, may become a casualty of the technology which drove its growth from the beginning. The expansion in internet banking is an example which will have an impact across the financial services sector. Deskilling leading to automation is a familiar occupational pattern that is likely to repeat itself in the call centre industry. By 2001, the trend for call centres to migrate overseas to low-cost countries such as India was gathering momentum.

Sources: Crome, M. (1998) 'Call centres: battery farming or free range?', *Credit Control*, **19**(6); Creagh, M. (1998) 'Call centres – the new assembly lines?', *Credit Control*, **19**(10); Guthrie, J. and Pickard, J., 'Days of call centre jobs may be numbered', *Financial Times*, 11 August 2000; Toyne, S., 'Closures signal end of branch banking', *Sunday Times*, 9 April 2000; Curtis, J., ' … the Indian connection', *Financial Times*, 11 August 2001.

Case questions

In what ways are call centres indicative of changes in industrial society?
In what ways are they likely to evolve?

6.7 Families

Just as the roles of women are changing in modern societies, with the increase in paid employment outside the home, the patterns of families are also changing. The unit of the 'nuclear family', consisting of mother, father and one or more children, has been the basic family unit in European societies. The 'extended family', which also may include grandparents, brothers and their wives and children, has been the pattern in Asian and Southeast Asian societies. In these societies, the extended family, or kinship group, is often an economic unit. The Asian family business built on kinship ties has been an important factor in economic development in Asia. Family relationships translated into business organizations have tended to be hierarchical and based on personal authority. They are also said to be at the core of Asian values, such as frugality and loyalty, discussed in Chapter 4.

Family patterns are changing in all modern societies. A major cause of change is the influence of Western values and culture, with its emphasis on the individual. There are a number of consequences for families. First, whereas in many societies marriages are traditionally 'arranged' by families, the trend now is towards free choice of a partner. Second, the extended family is less cohesive as a unit, partly as a result of urbanization, which brought greater scope for job opportunities further afield. And third, there has been a growing recognition of women's rights to education and careers outside the home.

The result of these trends has been a greater diversity in the nature of families and also a greater likelihood that the composition of families will change over a lifetime. In almost all Western societies, divorce is now accepted as a normal occurrence, and roughly one-third of marriages end in divorce. 'No-fault' divorces are now allowed by law in most Western countries, although countries which are predominantly Roman Catholic (such as Italy) are much less liberal in this respect. A rise in the number of lone-parent families has been brought about largely by divorce. But, in addition, there are growing numbers of people who deliberately opt for lone parenthood. In Britain in 1961, 38 per cent of households were of the traditional type, two parents and dependent children. By 1998–99, this proportion had decreased to 23 per cent (ONS, 2000b). In the US, the percentage of households consisting of a married couple with children under 18 declined from 45 per cent in 1960 to 24 per cent in 2000 (Fields and Casper, 2001).

What are the long-term social implications of changes in family life on the business environment? One in five families with dependent children in Britain today are lone-parent families, and in most of these it is the mother who is the lone parent, whether from divorce (in which women usually obtain custody of children), widowhood, or (rarer) simply never having married. As a growing segment of consumer markets, the lone parent has different needs for goods and services than larger families. Apartments rather than houses may be more suitable. While ready-meals for one are now quite common, package holidays are still typically based on two sharing and holiday operators charge a supplement for single people. For a lone parent, childcare facilities and flexible working hours may be crucial, but while some employers are accommodating, many, especially small organizations, lack the resources. State provision of childcare support has become an important issue as the numbers of lone parents have risen. Single mothers generally fare worse in terms of jobs and pay than other women workers, and a concern of governments is that lone-parent families can become caught in a 'poverty trap', dependent on state welfare.

6.8 Conclusions

1. Modern societies are essentially industrial societies, based on capitalist economic principles. However, there is considerable diversity, including developing and transitional as well as developed industrial societies.
2. Social stratification is a feature of all societies. Classes in industrial society are evolving and becoming more flexibly interpreted, encompassing a new middle class based on consumption and lifestyle.
3. While populations in the industrialized world are growing only very slowly, and becoming greyer, populations in the developing world are growing more rapidly. Ageing populations have implications for governments and businesses, including skill shortages, pressure on healthcare provisions and pension systems.
4. Migration of population from the developing to industrialized regions of the world has become a trend, marked by increasing mobility of labour internationally.
5. Urbanization, while slowing in the developed world, is still a trend in the developing world, where seven out of the world's ten largest cities are located.
6. The shift in industrial structure from manufacturing to services is reflected in reduced membership in trade unions, and also changes in labour relations in response to the changing work environment.
7. Women workers, while closing the gap in pay, in comparison with men, are predominant in low-skilled work and part-time work.
8. The nature of the family is changing in modern society, with a rise in numbers of single-parent families.

Review questions

1. What are the characteristics of 'industrial society', and how are industrial societies changing?
2. It is often said that class no longer has any meaning in modern society. To what extent is this true?
3. What are the effects of the 'demographic time bomb' faced by industrialized societies and what steps can be taken to deal with them?
4. How does the international migration of labour affect businesses in industrialized countries?
5. What are the problems associated with urbanization and why have they become most acute in developing countries?
6. How has the role of trade unions changed in modern industrial societies?
7. What is meant by the 'deskilling' of low-level, white-collar work?
8. The structure of families is changing in almost all societies. What are the changes and how do they affect the ways in which businesses operate?

Assignments

1. To what extent is the changing economic environment affecting social relations in modern industrial societies?
2. Assess the changes in the structure and nature of work in the new information economy.

Further reading

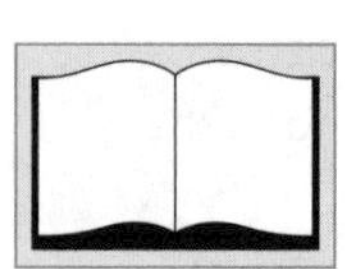

Brown, P. and Lander, H. (2001) *Capitalism and Social Progress* (Basingstoke: Palgrave)

Castells, M. (2000) *The Rise of the Network Society*, 2nd edn, (Oxford: Blackwell)

Giddens, A. (1997) *Sociology*, 3rd edn (Cambridge: Polity Press)

Grint, K. (2000) *Work and Society* (Cambridge: Polity Press)

Chapter

7

The changing political environment: national, regional and international forces

Outline of chapter

LEARNING OBJECTIVES

1. To appreciate the characteristics of nation-states and how these are evolving in the global environment
2. To gain an understanding of political decision-making structures in different national systems and how they interact with business
3. To assess the processes of building democracy and how democratic institutions affect the international business environment
4. To appreciate the dimensions of political risk in business decision-making
5. To understand the changing role of transnational and regional forces in political processes worldwide

7.0 Introduction

Businesses, from global corporations down to family-run enterprises, desire a stable and reasonably predictable environment in which to carry on their activities. As interaction between government and business has grown, the importance of a stable political environment has become more apparent. In the political dynamics of every society, both internal and external factors come into play. First, internal governmental structures and processes form a political system, responsible for containing and channelling conflict and promoting the collective good of the society. Just as no two societies are identical, so no two political systems are identical. The differences can have a profound effect on the attractiveness of a location to business, and on the likely success of any investment, for both home and foreign businesses. Second, regional and global forces outside its territory impact on a country's ability to control its affairs and these considerations also underpin a company's strategy to invest in a particular region. Two themes of this chapter will be the diversity of political institutions and the extent to which political processes at all levels, from the local to the international, are becoming more connected in the wider global environment.

People everywhere wish to see public order maintained, public services function efficiently and government officers carry out their duties. But they want more besides. A police state can offer security, but it hardly offers a conducive environment for a happy life. People also wish to have a good education, a good job and the material prosperity that it brings. A broad trend can be observed in the spread of democracy across the globe, most notably in the past 25 years. Yet democratic systems diverge substantially from one to another and by no means all deliver either stability or the prosperity hoped or expected of them. This chapter will focus first on national political systems and their public policy implications for business, looking in particular at democracy and democratization in its many permutations. Second, we look at the impact of globalization and the growth in transnational political institutions.

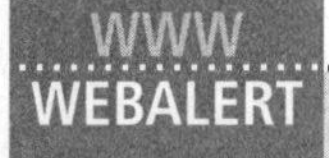

Internet resources on politics

The following site provides links to numerous Web resources on political systems worldwide, international organizations (governmental and non-governmental) and other research resources:
http://www.wcsu.ctstateu.edu/socialsci/polscres.html

7.1 The political sphere and civil society: how political factors affect business

Politics has been defined in numerous different ways, but all highlight the function of conflict resolution in society. Broadly, **politics** refers to processes by which a social group allocates the exercise of power and authority for the group as a whole. Breaking down the definition into three elements, first there is the existence of a social group – the word 'politics' derives from the Greek word *polis*, meaning city-state, a political community. Conflict is inevitable within societies, and politics provides the means of resolving conflict in structured ways. Second, politics concerns power relations. The contesting of power in society arises from groups and individuals with a wide range of viewpoints – ideological, economic, religious, ethnic or simply self-interested opportunistic. In democratic societies political parties are the most high-profile players on the political scene, but political authorities interact with a range of interests in society, including businesses and numerous interest groups, in arriving at policy decisions. Unilever's head of public affairs in the UK has said:

> The pervasive nature of government today means the need for dialogue between business and policy makers has never been greater ... It's absolutely vital that a business like ours keeps close to policy developments, and makes sure we have an input into the policy process. (*Financial Times*, 30 March 2001)

The impact of policy is multidimensional, as shown in the Points to Remember box on political decision-making (section 7.1).

The third element is the terrain of politics, the social group as a whole. While politics occurs in every organization, we are here concerned with agenda-setting for a society as a whole. Its scope is thus public life, rather than particular organizations. For the citizen of ancient Athens, this distinction did not exist: participation in the city-state was both civic and moral in nature, the polis providing the means to the good life. Later developments, especially the growth of secular states in Europe and increasing emphasis on the worth of the individual, led to a separation between public and private spheres. The sphere of politics is public life, institutions of the state, governmental structures and the process by which individuals come to occupy offices of state. The private sphere is often referred to as **civil society**, a term which covers the sphere in which citizens have space to pursue their own personal goals. Private individuals and businesses, trade unions, religious groups and the many subnational associations which exist in pluralist societies are all part of civil society (Linz and Stepan, 1997). Institutions of civil society may be very limited, or even banned, in some states, but the trend in the post-war period has been towards greater **pluralism**, that is, a multiplicity of groups, a development which flows logically from liberalism (Sartori, 1997).

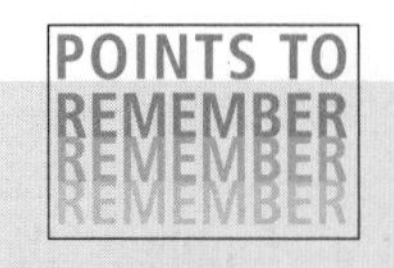

Some areas of political decision-making which impact on business:

- Extent of the welfare state and how it is financed (including health, education, housing, pensions, social security benefits)
- Regional development policies and funding
- Fiscal and monetary policies, such as taxation and currency rules
- Environmental policy and how to enforce it
- 'Law and order' in society
- Reform of the division of power between central, regional and local authorities
- Agriculture and food
- Defence, military establishment and decision to use armed forces in particular situations
- Immigration

Public and private spheres, however, are not as easily separated as the theoretical distinction suggests and their distinction has become blurred with the growth of the welfare state in the major industrialized societies since the Second World War, extending the reach of the state into the private sphere. The liberal's view of the public/private divide is that government interference in civil society should be kept to a minimum. However, the social and economic problems associated with growing inequalities in industrial societies, such as poverty and unemployment, have brought about a revision of this view, to encompass a more interventionist role for the state. The extent to which governments are justified in intervention to promote social welfare is one of the major issues giving rise to political divisions in all societies. It goes hand in hand with the issue of the extent to which governments should intervene in markets. Most governments have undertaken wide-ranging privatization of public enterprises. In addition, we have seen the emergence of public/private partnerships in the provision of public services, such as education, transport, healthcare and prisons (Rhodes, 1996). The Labour Party, re-elected in the General Election in 2001, reiterated its commitment to public/private partnerships, saying in its manifesto: 'Where private-sector providers can support public endeavour, we should use them. A "spirit of enterprise" should apply as much to public service as to business' (Labour Party, 2001). The simple dichotomy of public and private domains, therefore, is being replaced by a less polarized, more interlink ng relationship between the state and civil society. Increasingly, businesses are becoming intertwined with government agencies and processes in activities as diverse as air traffic control and hospitals.

7.2 Nation-states and political framework

The basic unit into which the world's peoples are divided is the nation-state. The concept of the nation-state, introduced in Section 5.2, combines the principle of a people's right to self-determination with the achievement of a territorial state ruled by its own government and subordinate to no higher authority. New nation-states are often born of nationalist movements within existing states. The dismantling of colonial empires following the Second World War gave rise to a large number of new states, as the growing membership of the UN shows (Figure 7.1). Some 17 new states were born out of the break-up of the Soviet Union, falling mainly in the years 1991–92.

The nation-state, or just 'state' for short, may be defined as:

> those specialised institutions that exercise a monopoly of law-making and adjudication over a given territory, and of the organised physical coercion necessary to enforce it. (Beetham, 1991, p. 121)

The definition highlights three defining principles of statehood: territoriality, sovereignty and the monopoly of coercive power. 'State' is a broader term than 'government'. While state encompasses people, territory and institutions, **government** refers to the particular institutions by which laws are made and implemented. It can also refer to the particular individuals in office at a given time, as in 'the government of the day'. The machinery of government may change from time to time, while the state is a more enduring, and unifying, concept.

Figure 7.1 Growth in UN membership

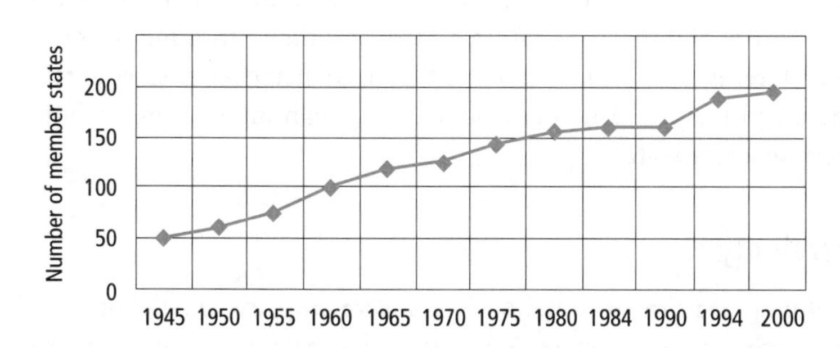

Source: United Nations (2000) *Growth in United Nations Membership 1945–2000*, at http://www.un.org/overview.

7.2.1 Territoriality and the state

The state occupies a geographically defined territory, within whose boundaries it has jurisdiction. Disputes over territory can be particularly bitter and have led to innumerable wars. Maintaining border controls, all would agree, has become more problematic, as territorial boundaries generally have become more permeable with the processes of globalization, such as communications, transport, the internet and the growth of e-commerce. These developments above all, have facilitated the expansion of international business. Although the state is still the legal gatekeeper controlling what crosses its borders, this role has become more daunting with the growing international flows of goods, people, information and money. Importantly from a national economic standpoint, the state also controls access to natural resources, such as mineral reserves and oil, in its territory. It is not surprising that countries such as Venezuela and Mexico, on gaining independence, nationalized their oil industries; but both are now taking steps towards liberalization and privatization. In 2001, the South African government and the mining industry reached a historic agreement: while mineral rights will belong exclusively to the state, the government will bring in a new system of objective criteria for granting licences to companies to exploit mineral rights, with a right of appeal against decisions. Through a stable regulatory regime, it is hoped to encourage overseas investors and also promote smaller mining companies.

The post-colonial states of Africa have generally followed borders inherited from the colonial period, which were artificially drawn and did not reflect ethnic groupings. Except for Rwanda and Burundi, none of the 34 modern African states corresponds to pre-colonial boundaries. Two consequences have followed: historic groupings are divided between states and a state's population may comprise groups which are historic enemies (Hawthorn, 1993). Ethnic conflict has been an inevitable result. In these situations, states struggle to maintain control and a sense of legitimacy over all their inhabitants (see Case Study 7.3 on Nigeria). Internal tensions may lead to secession of national minorities within a state and the re-forming of states. The pictures of refugees fleeing from conflict into neighbouring countries have become a sad feature of modern politics, highlighting the vulnerability and interdependence of states.

7.2.2 Sovereignty

A second defining feature of statehood is **sovereignty**, which denotes the supreme legal authority of the state. Sovereignty has an internal and external aspect. A state has 'internal' sovereignty, in that it possesses ultimate authority to rule within its borders; all other associations within society are subordinate. The state's legal authority is supported by a monopoly of the use of coercive force, in the form of military and police forces. 'External' sovereignty refers to the position of states in the international context, in which all states recognize each other as supreme within their own borders. This principle of mutual recognition, known as the 'sovereign equality of states', has governed the conduct of international relations between states, although the growth of numerous other international actors is now questioning the dominance of state actors, (as will be examined in the section on global politics). Internal and external sovereignty are like reverse sides of a coin. Internal sovereignty declares the state master in its own house, whereas external sovereignty prohibits it from interfering in the affairs of another state.

Sovereignty must be distinguished from the actual exercise of power. In many societies, real power lies outside formal political structures. An example is the ascendancy of military over civilian rulers. Military regimes, arising through violent seizure of power (the *coup d'état*) are inherently unstable and there is a constant threat of social unrest and factionalism within the military leadership. In the 1970s and 80s, Latin America's military regimes gave way to democratically elected governments. Less extreme is rule by co-ordinated political and economic elites which effectively control a country. In such regimes, government and business leaders form links in networks often referred to as 'cronyism'. These personal ties are a major consideration for foreign investors. While some of these states, such as Indonesia, have impressive records of industrialization, they are prone to corruption and instability and are likely to have weak legal systems. They offer location advantages for investors, but may pose high political risk (see Points to Remember box on political risk to international business, section 7.2.3).

In the post-war period, sovereignty has become a live political issue, from national to international level. On the heels of an unprecedented surge in the numbers of sovereign states, there has followed anxiety about whether a state can control its own destiny after all. Regional and global forces increasingly impact on states' governance processes, implying that, while sovereignty is intact in theory, in practice, all states are undergoing shifts in sovereignty. We return to this issue in greater detail in the global politics section.

Attributes of the state

- Defined geographical territory
- Sovereignty, including internal sovereignty, that is, supreme authority within the state and external sovereignty, that is, mutual recognition by states of each other's authority
- Monopoly of coercive power within its borders

7.2.3 Political risk and national security

All states recognize their responsibility to maintain 'law and order' and defend their population against organized military aggression from outside. However, as notions of sovereignty are being revised, so too is the notion of national security. There is virtually no country which has not been the target of foreign attack or invasion at some point in its history. But, however much a government spends on arms, it cannot make its borders impregnable in the modern age. Moreover, most democratic states now recognize the need for international co-operation in order to reduce military threat generally. International conventions such as the Treaty on the Non-proliferation of Nuclear Weapons are part of that effort. While the end of the cold war brought an end to the standoff between the two superpower blocs, threats to peace remain all over the globe, often in regional conflicts which can erupt at any time. States naturally turn to alliances for collective security. The North Atlantic Treaty Organization (NATO), formed in 1949, is perhaps the most influential. NATO became the first peacetime alliance the US had entered. Since 1949, NATO has expanded from 10 to 19 states and now incorporates the former communist states of Poland, the Czech Republic and Hungary, which joined in 1999.

Minifile

NATO

The North Atlantic Treaty is based on collective self-defence: an armed attack on any member is deemed to be an attack on all. There are now 19 members:

Belgium, Canada, Czech Republic, Denmark, France, Germany, Greece, Hungary, Iceland, Italy, Luxembourg, Netherlands, Norway, Poland, Portugal, Spain, Turkey, UK, USA.

Through a Partnership for Peace programme, additional countries, including neutral states (Austria, Finland, Ireland, Switzerland), former communist satellite states, as well as former Soviet republics, have joined existing NATO members in the Euro-Atlantic Partnership Council.

WWW WEBALERT

The NATO website contains links to the institutions of all these states, as well as background and news about NATO itself. It is at http://www.nato.int/

States must also contend with threats such as terrorism, whether originating from disenchanted groups within society or from outside the state. Terrorists have little respect for sovereignty and, indeed, terrorism is used as a political tool by some organizations. Terrorist groups with ample funds are able to tap into global arms markets. Militant Basque separatists in Spain are an example of the destabilizing effects of terrorist tactics for political ends. Terrorist attacks, such as bombings, hijackings and kidnappings, are difficult to control, relatively cheap to mount and can have considerable impact on civil society and business life. They are most likely to occur in countries where there are high levels of political risk, which both local businesses and foreign investors must assess. Indeed foreign investors may be specifically targeted in some regions.

By contrast, politically stable countries, such as the US, have been considered less likely to suffer from terrorist activities. However, the terrorist attacks on New York and Washington in September 2001 were a frightening example of their potential devastation. Armed hijackers crashed civilian aircraft into the World Trade Center in New York and the Pentagon, near Washington, resulting in the loss of thousands of lives and colossal damage to infrastructure. The world's stock exchanges plummeted, giving an early indication of the effects of the attacks on international business. In the immediate aftermath, air travel and cargo shipment were severely disrupted, causing havoc in global transport links. In the longer term, companies will need to reassess the risks of global production networks which involve the transporting of components long distances within tight production schedules. They might decide to manufacture key components in their home country, even if production costs are higher, to limit their exposure to terrorist risks in transport networks. In the wake of the US terrorist attacks, the US and other governments urged the resumption of normal business activities as soon as possible, to avert economic recession. Public confidence, however, depends to a great extent on governments' success in locating the individuals responsible and adopting credible measures to prevent future attacks. Historically, attacks of this magnitude have been inflicted by states on other states, which respond by retaliation, often military, against the perpetrating state. Dealing with the terrorist 'enemy', on the other hand, is peculiarly difficult, as terrorists' shadowy groupings, intricate global financial networks and mobility across national borders make them particularly elusive targets for authorities to control.

Civil war refers to war by groups within the state's borders. A World Bank survey in 2000 found that in the period 1987–97, more than 85 per cent of conflicts were fought within national borders, and of 27 major armed conflicts in 1999, all but two were civil wars (Collier, 2000). Ninety per cent of the deaths were civilian, not military. These conflicts can cripple economic life and divert public money to military expenditure rather than to productive activities. Civil wars and strife are heavily concentrated in the poorest countries, nearly 40 per cent in sub-Saharan Africa (Collier, 2000). Moreover, civil war may spill over into neighbouring countries. The 'capture' and control of resources by those in government or by other groups can fuel civil war, as Case Study 7.1 on the diamond trade shows.

Case study 7.1 Diamond trade and political conflict

Countries rich in diamonds should in theory be guaranteed a rich source of national wealth, but for the nations of Africa the precious gems have brought mixed blessings. Botswana, where diamonds were discovered in 1969, is one of the most stable and prosperous countries in Africa. There, the diamond industry employs nearly a fourth of the country's 1.5 million people and accounts for two-thirds of government income. The industry is run as a 50–50 partnership between the government and De Beers (the company which controls two-thirds of the world's trade in diamonds through probably the largest and oldest cartel in modern international business). The borders of Botswana, unlike the borders of many African countries, make sense. Inside the borders, there is ethnic and linguistic unity. There is also a long history of democratic decision-making. The country's diamond wealth has gone into building roads, schools and clinics. At $3,600 per year, the gross national product (GNP) per capita is seven times higher than the average for sub-Saharan Africa.

For Angola, Congo and Sierra Leone, in stark contrast, diamonds have brought the curse of looting, smuggling and the fuelling of civil wars. In these states, the post-colonial boundaries had produced mixtures of peoples with long-standing hostility to each other and long histories of weak institutions of government. The one-third of the world's diamond trade *not* controlled by De Beers has been sucked into a trading network, where mining is controlled by rebel groups, and the gems find their way into the world's markets, producing profits to fight civil wars. The export of these illicit, or 'conflict', diamonds has been facilitated by other African nations, most notably Liberia. The diamonds then make their way to the diamond exchanges in Antwerp, which handle eight out of ten of the world's rough diamonds. By then it is impossible to say which stones have come from war zones.

The UN has recommended an embargo on all diamonds from Liberia and also a certification system to document the origins of diamonds, in an effort to stifle the lucrative trade between rebels, arms dealers and corrupt African governments. A bill was introduced in the US Congress to require compulsory documentation, to ensure that diamonds sold in the US are not from rebel-controlled mines. But labelling systems would be difficult to implement and the rebel groups could shift their trade through other countries in order to get round the embargo. Such is the aura attached to diamonds in developed countries that the $50-billion-a-year retail diamond jewellery industry is thriving. The political challenge remains for African governments to harness their natural resources to improve the lives of their peoples.

Sources: 'Africa's gems: warfare's best friend', *New York Times*, 6 April 2000; 'Angola's goal: stepping back from the abyss', *New York Times*, 24 December 2000.

Case questions

How is the diamond trade linked to political conflict in Africa?
What are possible solutions?

Political risk to international business

Businesses face political risk wherever they operate, but the risks are greater in locations with a history of political instability. Disruption can take the form of strikes and demonstrations, threats to people and property, and breaks in supplies

Some of the contributing factors are:

- Disaffected groups in society, such as ethnic or religious groups, who feel alienated from the political processes and are likely to resort to violence to make their views heard
- External threats from terrorist groups who wish to destabilize the country
- Armed groups, such as sections of the military, who have a political power base, and pose a threat to the established government
- In federal or other decentralized countries, strong regional states which can threaten the stability of central government and even assert independence from the centre
- Any government whose basis of control is military power rather than the ballot box, as they are liable to fall by the same means that they acquired power in the first place
- Factionalized, political leadership based on personal ties (cronyism), where government assurances may last only as long as the faction holds the ascendancy
- Generally, countries without established democratic institutions to ensure transparency of processes and stable transition between governments

7.3 Sources of authority in the state

In every viable state there is a source of legitimate authority. In a traditional monarchy, such as the Arab state of Saudi Arabia, heredity in the royal lineage is the legitimating principle. In a 'theocracy', religious prerogative is the guiding principle. Iran, which is a Muslim state, while it still has the religious leader (the ayatollah) as supreme leader, now has a dual, religious and secular, institutional hierarchy. Although tensions inevitably arise between secular and religious authorities, Iran's dual structure is widely seen as a step on the way to reform and liberalization. In 'patrimonial states', ruling families are recognized as having authority, but questions of succession and favouritism may cause instability if a power struggle ensues. Patrimonial states, therefore, are potentially unstable. The Suharto regime in Indonesia was overthrown in 1998 by popular uprising. North Korea is, in a sense, a patrimonial state, and its founder, adulated by the population, passed the leadership to his son on his death in 1994. But North Korea is also a communist state; hence, personal rule is reinforced by communist ideology as a legitimating authority.

Ideology as a source of legitimacy is based on a system of beliefs which permeate the whole of society, not just the system of government. 'Ideology' is often used in a broad sense to refer to any set of political beliefs, such as liberalism or conservatism, but both these sets of beliefs embrace political pluralism, whereas the ideological state is monolithic, rejecting any competing belief systems. Fascism, an extreme nationalist ideology, reached its peak in the racist ideology of fascist Germany and Italy. While these fascist states were defeated in the Second World War, fascist groups still form part of the political scene in many states. Historically, communism has been one of the most important ideologies, originating in every case in communist revolution. Since the collapse of the Soviet Union, China has been the leading communist country, followed by a dwindling number of smaller states, such as Cuba and North Korea. Cuba and North Korea are still 'hard-line' communist states, but even these are taking tentative steps to opening their economies. Ideological regimes often rely on charismatic leaders, such as Fidel Castro in Cuba, to maintain ideological fervour. As in other non-democratic regimes, political succession can be a destabilizing event and constitutes an element of political risk for foreign investors.

In most modern states legitimacy is founded on constitutionalism. **Constitutionalism** implies a set of rules, grounded in a society's shared beliefs, about the source of authority and its institutional forms. Constitutionalism stands for the 'rule of law', above both ruler and ruled. Its underlying principle is that the institutions of government, such as president, prime minister and elected assembly, and bureaucracy, derive their power from these pre-existing rules. Actual office-holders will change from time to time and, indeed, a vital function of a constitution is to provide for smooth change in the transfer of power, but the constitution, setting out the ground rules, provides continuity and legitimacy. Inherent in constitutionalism are the control by the civilian authority over the military and the existence of an independent judiciary (court system). Most of the world's constitutions are written, with the exception of the British constitution. However, while the UK has no separate constitutional document, much legislation, contained in Acts of Parliament, is constitutional in nature. This trend towards written constitutional law looks set to continue, with European integration, devolved powers for Scotland and Wales and the impact of the Human Rights Act 1998, which incorporates the European Convention on Human Rights into UK law (see Chapter 8). There are states, such as one-party states, where, despite a written constitution, there is only lip service to the rule of law. The mere existence of a constitution is thus no guarantee of accountable government.

POINTS TO REMEMBER

Sources of authority in nation-states

- *Traditional monarchy* – absolute sovereignty is vested in a hereditary ruler. Most of these states have either been overthrown or gradually democraticized. A remaining example is Saudi Arabia. In Morocco and Jordan, traditional monarchies are making the transition to constitutional monarchy
- *Constitutional monarchy* – the hereditary monarch in these states is little more than a head of state and democratic institutions have taken over government. Examples: Belgium, Japan, Spain, the UK
- *Theocracy* – in these states the religious head is sovereign. The Muslim states come closest to theocratic rule, but all, to a greater or lesser extent, also have secular institutions of state
- *Constitutional republic* – here sovereignty rests with the constitution which guarantees civil and political rights. Examples: Canada, France, Poland (and other post-communist states). In the UK there is a body of republican opinion which supports abolition of the monarchy, in favour of a more modern head of state
- *Communist state* – although communist states typically have written constitutions, in practice sovereignty rests with the communist party, usually through a strong leader. Examples: China, Cuba, North Korea

WWW WEBALERT

A comprehensive guide to the constitutions of the world's nation-states can be found at:
http://www.uni-wuerzburg.de/law/index.html

7.4 Democracy and authoritarianism contrasted

Democracy broadly covers a range of political systems falling under the phrase, 'rule by the people', but popular sovereignty in theory can issue in a great diversity of institutional forms. Democracy is usually placed at one end of a continuum, with authoritarianism at the opposite end. **Democracy** is rule by the people, through elected governments, while **authoritarianism** is rule by a single leader or small group of individuals, with unlimited power, usually dependent on military support to maintain stability. Authoritarian regimes vary: the particularly repressive military regime in Burma (Myanmar) is at one extreme, while other authoritarian states have limited elections among state-approved candidates. Opposition to the regime is seen as a threat and is typically suppressed by military force. In a number of countries, such as Indonesia and Egypt, authoritarian governments have led the drive for economic development, attracting extensive foreign investment (oil riches were an attraction in both Indonesia and Egypt). For international companies which do business in authoritarian states, there is a high level of political risk as security cannot be guaranteed and political dissent and social unrest may destabilize the system as a whole. In such situations the company will find it difficult to remain 'neutral': its co-operation with the government may be seen as support for an oppressive military regime. An immediate concern is that its employees may be at risk if it becomes a target for those opposing the regime. A broader concern is the increasing pressure of international opinion against what is seen as complicity in human rights abuses. For this reason, a number of companies have pulled out of Burma. A further development is that major oil companies are now being pursued in the US courts for alleged human rights abuses in states such as Nigeria, Burma and Indonesia. While such lawsuits may take years to work their way through the legal system, their more immediate impact is the negative images of the companies' global operations.

7.5 Democratic government: the criteria

Most definitions of democracy focus on the formal, institutional aspects of government, such as elections and suffrage, without which there is no democracy. However, as will be seen, even among institutional arrangements there are huge variations and even with elections and universal suffrage many states cannot really be considered democratic. Formal institutions are therefore necessary, but not sufficient, to construct a democracy. This minimal 'electoral democracy' can be distinguished from 'liberal democracy', which stipulates pluralism and political freedoms for individuals and groups (Diamond, 1996). Beyond liberal democracy, lies 'social democracy', which focuses on the broader social and economic spheres in society. Social democracy is concerned with the underlying social and economic conditions in a society which contribute towards deeper participation than the simple exercise of the vote. A sharply divided or unequal society, in which power is concentrated in an entrenched ruling elite, is not a democracy in this substantive sense, even though it may have a constitution and regular elections. When attempting to measure democracy, the requirements of liberal democracy are generally accepted as the key criteria.

'Direct democracy' refers to direct participation in the governance of society. This model, workable only in a small community, is not transferable to a large society. The type of democracy which has evolved in the modern state is 'representative democracy', which can be defined as 'a system of governance in which rulers are held accountable for their actions in the public realm by citizens, acting indirectly through the competition and co-operation of their elected representatives' (Schmitter and Karl, 1993, p. 40). This definition, focusing on the institutional arrangements, is a commonly used measure of democracy. As its roots lie in liberalism and individualism, it is also equated with liberal democracy, although it is now seen as universally applicable, even in countries with very different, often authoritarian, histories. The following is a list of basic principles:

1. *Rule of law*, based on a constitution which establishes representative institutions, accountability of governments and an independent judiciary. Thus, executive power is kept in check
2. *Free and fair elections*, at relatively frequent intervals. These must provide for a choice of candidates and the peaceful removal of representatives from office when they fail to secure enough votes, in accordance with the constitution. Reports of outside monitors are usually seen as guarantee that the election has not been tainted by fraud
3. *Universal right to vote for all adults,* which of course extends to citizens. However, the increasing proportion of resident non-citizens in modern societies poses a problem for democratic participation. Moreover, voting alone is the most minimal form of participation
4. *Freedoms of expression, speech and association* are political rights essential to ensure competitive elections, in which all interests and groups may put forward their candidates. There should be independent media, providing alternative sources of information, to which citizens have access.

These principles are general guidelines; they do not point to one specific type of political system. Democratic systems vary considerably from country to country. All must address constitutional questions such as the division of authority between central and regional or local government, the type of legislative assembly and its relationship with the executive and, importantly, the checks between different governmental authorities.

7.6 Unitary and federal systems

In a **unitary system** authority radiates out from the centre. There may well be local and regional governments, but they are not autonomous actors as their authority is delegated from the centre. Whether a state is unitary or federal has a direct impact on the business environment. Regulatory regimes, such as planning permissions, health and safety and the legal framework generally, may be regionally governed in a federal system, while they will be centralized in a unitary system. On the other hand, the UK is a unitary system with devolved authority to local authorities, and also now with devolved authority to Scotland and Wales. In a **federal system** authority is shared between the centre and local or regional units, which retain autonomy in specific areas, such as education or regional development.

Federalism is often seen as a solution for states with strong local identities which can be incorporated into the larger whole while retaining semi-autonomous status. Thus the separate 'states' of the US have separate legal systems and limited autonomy. However, the power granted by the US Constitution to the federal government 'to regulate interstate commerce' has opened the way for an increase in federal regulation. Separate authorities and inconsistencies in business regulation between states can pose headaches for businesses that operate in more than one state. Germany's constitution, too, provides for state governments, called *Länder*, which, historically, have had strong identities. For countries such as Canada and Belgium, federalism serves to accommodate separate founding nations, who wish to retain separate identities and languages within the federal structure: English and French in Canada; French and Flemish in Belgium. It is often said that a specifically democratic advantage of federalism is shifting decision-making closer to the people affected. The UK, although unitary in principle, in devolving limited authority to a Scottish Parliament and Welsh Assembly, seems to be taking a step in this direction. Federalism is also seen by many as a solution to the governance of the EU, an issue which will be examined later.

7.7 Legislative assemblies

At the centre of any democracy is the **legislative assembly**. It carries the main law-making function, and, through the ballot box, is the one tangible way citizens express a say in the make-up of their government. Many countries have legislatures consisting of two houses (bicameral), where the lower house is the main law-making body. In the US both houses, the House of Representatives (the lower house) and the Senate (the upper house), are directly elected. In the UK only the House of Commons (the lower house) is elected. The upper house, the House of Lords, a combination of hereditary and appointed members, has seen its role gradually reduced to one of a revising chamber. However, conscious of its incongruousness in a modern society, the Labour government elected in 1997 had as part of its agenda reform of the House of Lords, aimed chiefly at abolition of the hereditary members. The first stage of the reform took place in 1999, with the abolition of 600 hereditary peers. Other parliamentary systems have only a single chamber (a unicameral legislature). Sweden and New Zealand abolished the upper chamber.

7.8 Elections

Free and fair elections are a key element in political participation in a democracy. The electoral system may be the traditional first-past-the-post system or one of the more recent proportional representation (PR) systems, which allocate seats in proportion to the votes obtained. While the first-past-the-post system has predominated in the US and the UK, most European countries (and also the European Parliament) have opted for PR. Outcomes in PR systems are seen as representing a broader range of views, friendlier to small parties and perhaps to women candidates. Women worldwide hold just 14 per cent of the seats in national legislatures (Inter-Parliamentary Union,

Table 7.1 Women in national legislatures in EU countries

Country	Percentage of women members
Sweden	42.7
Denmark	37.4
Finland	36.5
Netherlands	36.0
Germany	30.9
Spain	28.3
Austria	26.8
Belgium	23.3
Portugal	18.7
UK	17.9
Luxembourg	16.7
Ireland	12.0
France	10.9
Italy	9.8
Greece	8.7

Note
1. Lower or single house; situation as of 1 July 2001.

Source: Inter-Parliamentary Union (2001) at http://www.ipu.org.

2001). The figures for EU states show wide disparities (seen in Table 7.1), from 42.7 per cent of the seats in Sweden to 8.7 per cent in Greece.

A drawback of proportional representation is that in a multiparty system, if many parties secure seats, it may be difficult to form a government and political instability may result. A common requirement is that a party must obtain a minimum of 5 per cent of the total vote to gain any seats. Poland's first fully free election, in 1991, demonstrates the hazards of extreme PR: 111 parties or groups put up candidates; 29 parties or groups gained seats, including the Beer Lovers' Party, but none gained more than 13 per cent of the total. A series of unstable coalition governments followed, until a 5 per cent threshold was introduced in 1993. Since then, parties have settled into two main blocs.

Increasingly popular is the 'mixed' electoral system, combining first-past-the-post and PR systems. The leading example is Germany. The election of 1998 yielded a coalition between the social democrats (SPD) and Greens, resulting in the gaining of a cabinet post for the Greens in the coalition government. Since then, they have used their voice in government effectively, securing, for example, assurance of the phasing out of nuclear power stations. Italy, which has had 54 different ruling coalitions in the past 53 years, attempted in 2000 to change its voting system from proportional representation to first-past-the-post, in order to reduce the number of parties and bring about stable government. The proposal was required by the constitution to be put to the voters in a referendum, but was rejected (see Minifile on the use of the referendum).

WWW
WEBALERT

Internet resources on parties and elections

The internet has provided political parties and other groups with the means to reach a worldwide audience, even though they may have little or no media freedom in their own states, due to government controls

The following site contains links to political parties, interest groups and other social movements worldwide – international first and then country by country:
http://www.psr.keele.ac.uk/parties.htm

For elections, parties and parliaments, the following are useful:
International Foundation for Election Systems: http://www.ifes.org/
http://www.library.ubc.ca/poli/electoral.htm

Minifile

THE REFERENDUM IN DEMOCRATIC SYSTEMS

The referendum is an example of direct democracy, and has become increasingly popular for governments seeking a mandate for a particularly important issue. In some states (for example Italy) it is a constitutional requirement; in others (for example the UK) it is optional.

Examples of the varied uses of the referendum:

1 Devolution in Scotland and Wales, 1997
2 Rejection of UN membership by the Swiss, 1986
3 The end of apartheid in South Africa, 1992
4 The decision not to join the euro-zone by Denmark, September, 2000.

The advantages of the referendum are that it acts as a check on elected governments, giving citizens an opportunity to express a view on an issue of the day. A drawback, however, is that citizens are typically asked to make a yes/no decision although the issues may be complex. Moreover, ordinary citizens are not as well informed about the ramifications of proposed changes as are elected representatives.

7.9 Political parties

Political parties form the link between voters and legislative assemblies. In democratic states parties perform several functions:

1 They provide candidates for public office, who rely on their organizational machinery and funding to get elected. The independent candidate faces an uphill battle and needs to be very rich.
2 They provide a policy platform on which voters can decide whom to support. Many voters traditionally are party loyalists, not bothered who the individual candidate is.
3 When in office, they provide an agenda for government against which performance can be judged.

Parties vary in their political agendas and in their views of society. Some embrace strong ideological positions, such as communist parties. Others are religious in origin, such as Muslim parties and numerous Christian parties. Many countries have rural-based, or peasant, parties which exist mainly to foster rural interests. Parties may also emerge from interest groups, such as the Green Party, which concentrates on ecological issues. Most of the narrowly based parties have little hope of gaining a majority of legislative seats and forming a government; instead, they seek publicity and political influence for their views. They are more likely to win seats in multiparty systems with PR. In two-party systems, such as the US and UK, the trend has been towards the 'catch-all' party, with weaker ideological underpinning and greater direct appeal to voters via the media, in which personalities are as important as policies. Political parties largely depend on funding from supporters and, although most states attempt to regulate funding, this area is a fertile one for corruption scandals, in which politicians and corporate donors can become enmeshed.

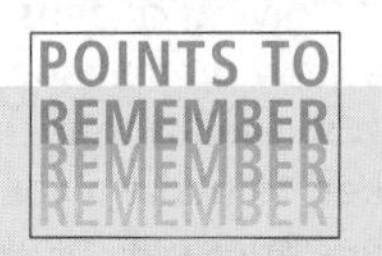

Party systems

- *Two major parties* – examples: the US and UK. The two major parties are catch-all parties aiming to capture the middle ground on the main issues. Both examples have first-past-the-post electoral systems. Third parties, while they obtain electoral support (for example the Liberal Democrats in Britain) are unlikely to gain seats in proportion to their overall support, unless there is a shift to a PR system
- *Multiparty system* – examples: Italy, Poland and other Central and Eastern European countries. In these states, which have PR systems, parties cover a greater range of ideological positions, from left to right. Centre-left or centre-right coalitions are a typical outcome of elections
- *Single dominant party* – examples: Japan, Mexico up to 2000. In these states, while there are numerous smaller parties, the single dominant party has such a reservoir of loyalty that it is extremely difficult to shift from office
- *One-party state* – examples: China, Cuba, North Korea. These communist states differ from the preceding category in that pluralist elections are not tolerated and there is no institutional means of change of government. Clearly, these regimes are not democratic (they are classed as 'not free' in Figure 7.2)

Political parties are usually described in terms of left, right and centre, with the modern catch-all parties falling somewhere near the centre. The modern Labour Party in Britain has shifted from being a left-wing socialist party to a broader-based centre-left party. However, pinning down what these labels stand for in terms of policy can be bewildering, especially as their meanings have shifted over time. Parties to the 'left' generally support high public spending on social services, protection of workers, and trade union rights; they tend to oppose privatization. Parties on the 'right', known almost universally as 'conservatives', generally wish to see a minimum of government intervention in business, reduced public spending and low taxes. They favour more privatization of the economy, reducing the size of government bureaucracy. However, all modern parties, the British Conservatives included, support the welfare state. Nationalist tendencies are associated with the right, but most parties of the right (except extremist right-wing parties) support multiculturalism. With its election in 1997, 'New Labour' in Britain expressly moved closer to business-friendly policies and distanced itself from its ideological, working-class roots. The new social democratic parties across Europe are said to represent the 'third way', between socialism and market liberalism.

7.10 Systems of government: presidential, parliamentary and 'hybrid' systems

It is customary to think of government as comprising three functions or branches: legislative, executive and judicial. The division of functions between the three is known as **separation of powers**. In practice, most systems have considerable overlap between these functions, and the main safeguard that no one branch comes to dominate the others is a system of checks and balances between them. The legislative power, located in an elected assembly, exercises the main law-making function. The executive, although it drafts much legislation and must normally give its assent to legislation, is mainly an administrative authority. The judicial function, located in the court system, interprets the law and thereby keeps a check on the other two branches. Law and policy therefore emanate mainly from the legislative and executive branches and, more specifically, from the political interplay between the two, depending on the balance of power within the system.

A **presidential system** is thought of as producing a stronger chief executive, as presidents are normally directly elected by the people and thus have a personal mandate. The US is the leading example of a presidential system. Checks on executive power are provided by the constitution and also by a vigorous two-party system. The other main proponents of the presidential system have been Latin American countries, for whom a strong presidency is more grounded in political culture, in which nationalism has been a prominent feature. Inherent drawbacks of the 'winner-takes-all' nature of presidential elections are that supporters of the losing candidate may feel alienated, while the winner may overestimate the popular mandate, 'conflating his supporters with the people as a whole' (Linz, 1993, p. 118).

The US presidential election in 2000 was the closest result in the country's history. After five weeks of recounting and several court cases culminating in a decision of the US Supreme Court, George W. Bush emerged the winner. Despite his wish to bring a sense of national unity after such a protracted and bitter episode, his Cabinet and legislative agenda, including major tax cuts, were distinctly rightist, reflecting traditional conservative Republicanism. However, in the 100-seat Senate, which was divided 50–50 between

Republicans and Democrats when Mr Bush took office, one Republican Senator abruptly left the party in May 2001, causing a dramatic shift in power in the Senate to the Democrats, who gained chairmanship of all 20 committees. Suddenly, healthcare reforms, labour rights and the environment came back onto the agenda. Given the system of checks and balances in the US, law-making is likely to be hampered by wrangles, or even 'gridlock', between the president and Congress. Businesses, including those abroad which do business in the US and those who are indirectly affected by US economic and trade policies, look for a clear and coherent legislative agenda on issues such as trade liberalization and regional trade agreements. However, the system seldom delivers the political mandate which elections promise and policies emerge piecemeal through negotiation and compromise among numerous competing interests.

In a **parliamentary system**, the voters elect members of parliament (MPs), from whom a prime minister and Cabinet are selected, usually from the political party with a majority of seats. This is often called the 'Westminster model', as the leading example is the UK. The efficient running of a parliamentary systems depends greatly on the nature and number of a country's political parties. It is usually felt that it works best in a stable two-party system of 'government' and 'opposition' parties, in which the opposition is in effect an alternative government. In contrast to President George W. Bush, Prime Minister Tony Blair, re-elected in June, 2001, may feel he has an overwhelming mandate from the people, as the Labour Party won nearly two-thirds of the seats in the House of Commons (413, in comparison to the Conservatives' 166 seats). However, mainly because of the low turnout – 59.5 per cent of eligible voters – Labour enjoyed the positive support of only about one in four electors. Also worrying is that the turnout among younger voters was particularly low: less than 40 per cent of people under 25 voted. Apart from the obvious conclusion that people are disillusioned with politics, it is also arguable that they are turned off by the mainstream political parties which seem remote. A trend has been the rising profile of various lobby groups and interest groups which seek to *influence* policy on particular issues, rather than play a direct role in politics. Consultation by government with lobby groups of all descriptions – from animal rights groups to railway users – have become routine, arguably sidelining established political parties.

In multiparty systems, a **coalition government**, made up of two or more parties, is the likely outcome. Aware of its power to bring down the government, a minor party in a coalition may demand a 'price' for its co-operation in terms of key policies, to keep it on board. Small right-wing religious parties in Israel are an example of this phenomenon, wielding more political power than their number of seats alone would justify. It could be argued that coalition government is more representative of electoral support, and hence more democratic, but a major disadvantage is its potential instability.

The so-called 'hybrid system' aims to achieve both a stable executive and maximum representation, with an independently elected president and a

Table 7.2 Summary of systems of government

	Presidential	Parliamentary	Hybrid
Advantages	Strong executive based on popular mandate; fixed term of office	Executive reflects electoral support in parliament	Strong executive imparts unity; prime minister co-ordinates parliamentary programme
Disadvantages	Possible disaffection among electorate	Thin majority may lead to breakdown of government	Conflict between president and prime minister
Stability	Stable executive, but legislature may be dominated by the opposing party, stifling the law-making agenda	Stable if prime minister has a large majority; coalition and minority governments can be unstable	Fixed-term president imparts stability; but successive coalition governments can be unstable in multiparty systems

prime minister selected by parliament to head the Cabinet. The model for this system, also known as the dual executive, is the Fifth French Republic. Apart from Hungary, which has a parliamentary system, the post-communist states of Central and Eastern Europe have adopted this model. The theory is that the nationally elected president can foster national unity, playing the role of head of state, while the prime minister plays more of a party-political role, maintaining support for the government in parliament. In practice, these systems may not run as smoothly as envisaged if the two executives are of different parties (called 'co-habitation' in France) or, as is almost inevitable, each sees the other as a rival and political rivalry develops between the two. In new democracies such as Poland and the Czech Republic, where politics tends to focus on personalities, the role of president can be seen as a strong political platform.

7.11 Transitional democracies

Where democratic institutions have become settled, democracy is said to be 'consolidated', meaning that democratic processes have become so routine and internalized in people's attitudes and behaviour that democracy is the 'only game in town' (Linz and Stepan, 1997). Consolidated democracies will still change and evolve, of course, but the overwhelming likelihood is that change will come about in peaceful ways within well-oiled institutions, with minimum risk of system instability. Where states are still putting in place the basic representative institutions, they are referred to as **transitional democracies**, and the process of building democracy, democratization. The earliest democracies were established in the nineteenth century, in the 'first wave'

Figure 7.2 The progress of democracy in independent states, 1972–99

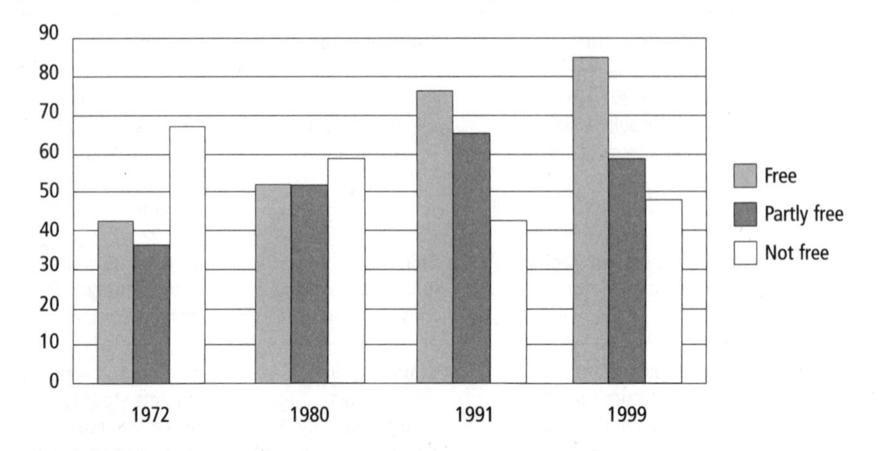

Sources: Gastil, R. (ed.) (1989) *Freedom in the World: Political Rights and Civil Liberties, 1988–89* (New York: Freedom House); Diamond, L. (1996) 'Is the third wave over?', *Journal of Democracy*, 7(3):27; Karatnycky, A. (2000) 'A century of progress' (The 1999 Freedom House Survey), *Journal of Democracy*, **11**(1):187–200.

(Huntington, 1991). A second wave occurred after the Second World War, and a third wave gathered pace in the 1970s, as Figure 7.2 shows. However, some of these democracies may be described as 'shallow', consisting of electoral systems but limited political rights and civil liberties (Diamond, 1996). In Figure 7.2 'free states' are those with a high degree of political and economic freedom and respect for basic liberties. 'Partly free' states offer more limited civil rights, in a context which often includes corruption, weak rule of law and ethnic strife. Countries designated 'not free' deny basic civil and political rights.

7.11.1 Regional divergence in democratic transition

Democratic institutions in Western industrialized states grew in a piecemeal way, out of the social conflicts which emerged with capitalist development, as existing systems came under pressure for greater political participation. The post-communist states in Eastern Europe, by contrast, are making a dual transition, putting in place democratic institutions and a market economy at the same time. In these changing social and economic environments, the success of democracy depends in large part on the new institutions bringing economic prosperity. Those left behind by the new economy are more likely to support anti-reform parties (Kullberg and Zimmerman, 1999). The transition from a collectivist society to one based on individual civil and political rights has been easier for the Central European satellite states than for the former Soviet republics, which had a much longer history of authoritarian rule and have struggled to establish workable democratic institutions.

The states of East Asia and Latin America present a somewhat different picture. These states generally have a history of authoritarian rule. An

WWW WEBALERT

Background information and up-to-date reports on transitional democracies and the general issues related to sustainable democracy can be found on the website of the International Institute for Democracy and Electoral Assistance, at:
http://www.idea.int/

exception has been Costa Rica, which has combined a strong democracy with economic development, as Case Study 7.2 shows. In East Asia, state-led economic development has preceded democratic reforms. Japan was the earliest to democratize, but its parliamentary system was the product of the American Occupation, rather than its own (weak) representative institutions. Since the Second World War, it has been governed almost continuously by a single dominant party, albeit one with much factional infighting. In contrast, changes of political power in South Korea and Taiwan indicate the growth of more pluralist electoral contests.

Single dominant party systems have also been a feature in Latin America, but here the strong state has not produced economic success on the scale of the Asian economies. Ruling elites have done little to heal deep social divisions, deal with land reform or ameliorate extreme poverty. The defeat of Mexico's ruling party in July 2000, after 71 years in power, could mark the beginnings of genuine democratic contests in Mexico, as well as economic liberalization. Mexico's new president sees the North American Free Trade Agreement (NAFTA) as the way to obtain a better deal for Mexicans. An early success was a NAFTA ruling allowing Mexican trucks to carry export goods to US destinations, rather than to reload cargo onto US trucks at the border.

The post-colonial states of Africa have had limited success so far in making the transition to democracy. Social inequalities and ethnic conflict have inhibited the building of viable states. Politics has been largely based on ethnic, religious and tribal loyalties and the ruling elites have been reluctant to accept the notion of competition for power through genuine elections, in which they may face the real possibility of losing power to a rival group. The aid, both bilateral and multilateral, through the World Bank and International Monetary Fund (IMF), that has gone into these weak economies is necessarily channelled through government offices, a process which has enhanced the power of political elites over scarce resources. There are some hopeful signs of democracy gaining ground. Following military dictatorship, Nigeria now has a fragile democracy, but is struggling to control disenchanted groups (see Case Study 7.3). In 2000, the authoritarian regime of President Robert Mugabe in Zimbabwe received electoral shocks despite intimidatory tactics aimed at opposition politicians and their supporters.

Case study 7.2 Costa Rican democracy reaps FDI rewards

Costa Rica was once thought of as simply a 'banana republic', but in the past decade it has attracted impressive flows of foreign direct investment (FDI) which have transformed its economy. Costa Rica now attracts about $517 billion, or 53 per cent of the total foreign investment in Latin America. Schuler and Brown (1999) argue that a major factor in attracting multinational corporations has been the country's political and institutional stability. Costa Rica has established a strong democracy with transparent institutions, competitive elections and a solid social welfare state. The biggest FDI success story has been Intel, whose chip factory now accounts for 37 per cent of Costa Rica's exports. Costa Rica was competing against Mexico for the factory, and both governments offered incentives. The Costa Rican government offered Intel tax-free status for eight years, followed by a 50 per cent discount for another four; a commitment to invest more in infrastructure and education; and a favourable regime on energy prices. Mexico offered enhanced incentives and had the advantage of lower wages than those in Costa Rica. Notwithstanding, Intel opted for Costa Rica. This evidence suggests the decisive role played by a strong democracy, along with membership in a number of international accords (such as General Agreement on Tariffs and Trade (GATT) and World Trade Organization (WTO)).

Schuler and Brown argue that democracy also seems to influence the way that multinationals behave once they have settled in the host country. Lively democratic institutions and interest groups which represent and channel citizens' views can provide valuable feedback to the company and aid it in developing beneficial relationships with the community. For example, Ston Forestal, a US company which invested in a reforestation project in Costa Rica, changed the location of its planned chipping factory after environmental groups had lobbied the government. The company then set up a multiparty watchdog group to monitor its operations. Activities such as this are ways of dealing with society pressures in an amicable way, made possible by transparent and stable democratic institutions.

How does Intel benefit Cost Rica? The company enjoys a tax holiday for eight years, and it brings 90 per cent of its supplies from abroad, as there is no local electronics industry. Still, the enthusiastic workforce at the new factory see the benefits of a constant education in the new economy. One twenty-something employee says chips are far more challenging than bananas, the country's other major export: 'Bananas will be bananas today and bananas tomorrow. When you're making chips ... you always learn something new.'

Sources: Schuler, D. and Brown, D. (1999) 'Democracy, regional market integration and foreign direct investment', *Business & Society*, 38(4): 450–74; 'A silicon republic', *Newsweek*, 2000, 136(9): 42–5.

Case question

Why does democracy reduce political risk for foreign investors in Costa Rica?

7.11.2 Transitional democracies and international business

Transitional democracies are now in the international spotlight, as they represent emerging markets seeking to attract international business. Most of these states are developing economies in which popular governments have replaced colonial rule, which also includes the former Soviet satellite states. In some of these states, in Central and Eastern Europe, multipartyism has

Case study 7.3 Nigeria: political turmoil amidst oil riches

Nigeria, Africa's most populous state with a population of 120 million, is the world's sixth largest producer of crude oil. Yet the 40 years since the country gained independence have seen a torrent of ethnic strife, military government, corruption and widespread poverty. Since 1999, Nigeria has had a democratically elected civilian government, headed by President Obasanjo, who is attempting to unite three traditionally hostile ethnic groups in a federal republic: the Muslim north, the Yoruba people of the southwest and the Ijaw people of the delta region, where the oil fields are situated. Mutual distrust has made it difficult for the federal government to establish a sense of legitimacy needed to bring about stability and economic reform. A leading human rights activist has said: 'Authoritarianism provides a kind of negative stability. Democracy creates space to do a lot of things, sometimes bad things, dangerous things. So democracy brings greater challenges to keep Nigeria together' (Vick, 2000).

In the oil-producing delta region, some of the world's richest multinationals rub shoulders daily with its poorest inhabitants, but the local people see little of the wealth. The major oil companies, including Nigeria's biggest producer, Royal Dutch Shell, operate as joint ventures with the state-owned Nigerian National Petroleum Corporation (NNPC), providing more than 75 per cent of the federal government reserves. Prospects are hopeful for developing more oilfields, as huge oil and gas discoveries have been made by Shell, Texaco, Exxon-Mobil and Elf. Yet communal violence has cost lives, and rebuilding infrastructure and community relations is a task facing both the oil companies and the government. It is likely that the new offshore projects, coupled with onshore construction to revamp oilfield installations, will increase demands for more foreign investment and offer training and jobs to Nigerians.

Privatization is a key to economic development, as well as sociopolitical reform (Hawkins, 2000). Private investment is needed to revive non-energy sectors of the economy and bring greater transparency in Nigeria's institutional structures. It is also needed in order to tackle the rebuilding of the country's infrastructure, especially transport and communications.

Sources: Vick, K., 'A delicate democracy', *Washington Post*, 29 January 2000; Holman, M., and Wallis, W., 'In office but out of power, *Financial Times*, 30 March 2000; Hawkins, T., 'Cornerstone of economic reform', *Financial Times*, 30 March 2000.

Case questions

What are the prospects for Nigerian democracy and what is the role of foreign multinational companies in the country's development?

produced fragile democracies. Because they seem to be on the path to consolidation, they present relative stability for investors. On the other hand, privatization has been subject to political influences of vested interests (EBRD, 2000). At the other extreme are the 'partial democracies', with elected assemblies, but within single-party states where civil and political rights are limited. While these regimes see unity in the single party, their intolerance of opposition makes them closer to authoritarianism. Transitional democracies look to outside sources to provide economic development, through investment and financial aid, and, increasingly their political systems are brought into the economic equation. For foreign investors, they represent new markets, but carry considerable political risk, as businesses cannot be insulated from local political life. Indeed, successful operations often hinge on trust and co-operation with host political authorities. However, if the political risk becomes too high, investors will flee. As the example of Costa Rica has shown, stable and transparent political institutions seem the best long-term guarantee of economic development, a more attractive business environment and a better quality of life for citizens.

7.12 Global politics

It is increasingly recognized by governments that states no longer have the means to deliver national security and material well-being on their own. Interdependence and co-operation have generated numerous alliances and international organizations, the most influential being the UN. Organizations, both governmental and non-governmental, regional and international, have emerged in the post-war period. **Non-governmental organizations** (NGOs) have gained in political influence and become part of the international institutional process in some areas of global concern, such as human rights (for example Amnesty International) and the environment (for example Greenpeace).

Political leaders of the major industrial democracies, known as the **Group of Seven** or **G7** countries, have been meeting annually since 1975 to discuss important economic and political issues facing their societies and the international community generally. The members are Canada, France, Germany, Japan, Italy, the US and the UK. With the addition of Russia at the more recent meetings, they have in practice become the 'G8'. Their discussions provide a forum for setting priorities and highlighting new issues on the international agenda. They cover a wide range of subjects, including macroeconomic policies, international trade, security matters and human rights. While their formal meetings are at ministerial level, they have set up a number of task forces and working groups on specific issues such as money laundering and nuclear safety. The G7 provides a forum for arriving at consensus positions on important global issues. They have also attracted numerous NGOs seeking to influence policies, as well as the more negative and disorderly anti-globalization protesters.

7.12.1 The United Nations

Founded in 1945, the UN has grown from 50 to nearly 200 states. Its institutions and processes have evolved substantially in 50 years, and so too has the body of international treaties and conventions (discussed in the next chapter), which is increasingly recognized in international law. The UN does not constitute a world government, however, as it operates on the basis of intergovernmental co-operation between member states. Its Secretary-General, while having no executive powers that state leaders possess, commands considerable confidence in the international community, and exemplifies the UN's aim of achieving peaceful negotiated settlement of conflicts between states. The General Assembly, in which all member states have one vote, can be contrasted with the Security Council, in which the major post-war powers – the US, the UK, France, Germany and Russia (formerly the Soviet Union) – were made permanent members and given the right of veto. Although the Security Council was therefore less effective than anticipated during the cold war period, the UN was able to provide a forum for international debate and expand its social and economic activities through its many agencies and affiliated bodies. The International Labour Organization (ILO), which actually predates the UN, has set standards for health and safety, workers' rights and child labour; its conventions have been ratified by dozens of states, who, by doing so, show a commitment to be bound by them. Similarly, the human rights covenants have been ratified by over 140 states.

Minifile

CHARTER OF THE UNITED NATIONS

Article 1:

The purposes of the United Nations are:

1 To maintain international peace and security, and to that end:

   To take effective collective measures for the prevention and removal of threats to the peace, and for the suppression of acts of aggression or other breaches of the peace, and

   To bring about by peaceful means and in conformity with the principles of justice and international law, adjustment or settlement of international disputes or situations which might lead to a breach of the peace

2 To develop friendly relations among nations based on respect for the principle of equal rights and self-determination of peoples, and to take other appropriate measures to strengthen universal peace

3 To achieve international co-operation in solving international problems of an economic, social, cultural or humanitarian character, and in promoting and encouraging respect for human rights and for fundamental freedoms for all without distinction as to race, sex, language, or religion

4 To be a centre for harmonizing the actions of nations in the attainment of these common ends

A full text of the UN Charter may be found at: http://www.law.cornell.edu/icj/unchart.htm

While state practice sometimes falls far short of these covenants, ratification does acknowledge a commitment to the principles they contain: the Covenant on Civil and Political Rights (in Article 25) lays down minimum standards for democratic government, including free and fair elections, universal suffrage and secret ballot. The acceptance of states of the principle that these conventions impose on them a 'higher' duty to comply is an indication of a shift away from the pure theory of state sovereignty. The UN itself has taken the lead by giving humanitarian intervention priority over state sovereignty by intervening in states' domestic affairs in cases of human rights violations in Iraq, Somalia and Bosnia. Its peacekeeping operations have expanded and its imposition of economic sanctions, for example against Iraq, has had a direct impact. The UN has approved 12 sanctions' regimes in the past 10 years, in contrast to only 2 in the previous 45 years of its existence.

Looking back over its first 50 years, two parallel trends have emerged: the UN has grown in authoritative stature in relation to states, while state sovereignty has weakened its grip as the sole source of legitimate authority. While there are some who would like to take this process further and make the UN a world government, there are also those who warn that controversial interventions can undermine confidence in its position generally. Any reform of its structure will therefore probably focus on enhancing confidence in its institutions and processes, while retaining the principle of state sovereignty.

7.12.2 The European Union

Regional groupings of states have also grown in numbers in the post-war period. Most of these are trading alliances, but the most advanced, the EU, represents much deeper economic, social and political integration. Originally comprising a group of six states (Germany, France, Belgium, Luxembourg, the Netherlands and Italy) under the Treaty of Rome in 1957, the European Community, as it then was, envisaged a 'pooling' of national sovereignty. When Britain joined in 1973, the erosion of parliamentary sovereignty was a major issue, and it has remained so, particularly among 'Euro-sceptics'. Despite misgivings about national sovereignty, perceived economic benefits have made the EU more popular than ever. It has expanded to 15 members

WWW WEBALERT

EU internet resources can be found at:
http://www.europarl.eu.int/
This site contains links to national parliaments and political groups. The EU's main website is http://europa.eu.int/
The EU institutions website is
http://www.europarl.eu.int/institutions/en/default.htm

and there are 13 applications for membership now being actively considered, most from Central and Eastern European countries. Five had anticipated joining by 2002, but their admission has rather been swept up in the debate over enlargement generally. That debate, in turn, has raised questions about the effectiveness and democratic credentials of EU structures, perceived as unwieldy, over-bureaucratic and lacking in democratic accountability.

The highest law-making authority in the EU is the Council of Ministers, renamed the Council of the EU in 1993. Members are ministers in their own states. Originally, unanimity among its members was required for a proposal to proceed, but this requirement has been relaxed in some key areas (for example agriculture, the environment and transport) by 'qualified majority voting' (QMV). Under this system, which now extends to 80 per cent of its decisions, there is weighted voting based mainly on population. The Nice intergovernmental conference in 2000 proposed reforms to the weighted voting system, shown in Table 7.3. As can be seen, large countries have proportionately more of the votes. The safeguard for smaller countries is a mechanism whereby a majority of countries can block a decision regardless of the weighted vote. The issues which remain outside the QMV process include: trade in services and intellectual property (including TV and film); social security; immigration and asylum; and taxation. The Nice Treaty provides the constitutional basis for EU enlargement and must be ratified by all member states. The process got off to a shaky start, however, when the Irish people voted 'no' to the treaty in a referendum in June 2001, by 54 to 46 per cent. The turnout was barely 30 per cent of the electorate. Ireland has been consistently pro-EU: generous EU subsidies, especially to Irish agriculture, have amounted to 6 per cent of Irish GNP. The No campaign was based on the simple message that 'power, money and freedom' would be jeopardized under the treaty. Worryingly, a week before the referendum, a poll showe that 50 per cent of the voters said they did not understand the treaty (Peel, 2001).

Table 7.3 Reform of the Council and Parliament of the EU

Current members	Current vote in Council	New vote in Council	Current parliamentary allocation of seats	New parliamentary allocation of seats
Germany	10	29	99	99
UK	10	29	87	72
France	10	29	87	72
Italy	10	29	87	72
Spain	8	27	64	50

➤

Table 7.3 (cont'd)

Current members	Current vote in Council	New vote in Council	Current parliamentary allocation of seats	New parliamentary allocation of seats
Netherlands	5	13	31	25
Greece	5	12	25	20
Belgium	5	12	25	22
Portugal	5	12	25	20
Sweden	4	10	22	18
Austria	4	10	21	17
Denmark	3	7	16	13
Finland	3	7	16	13
Ireland	3	7	15	12
Luxembourg	2	4	6	6
Candidate countries				
Poland	8	27	–	50
Romania	6	14	–	33
Czech Republic	5	12	–	20
Hungary	5	12	–	20
Bulgaria	4	10	–	17
Slovakia	3	7	–	13
Lithuania	3	7	–	12
Latvia	3	4	–	8
Slovenia	3	4	–	7
Estonia	3	4	–	6
Cyprus	2	4	–	6
Malta	2	3	–	5

Source: The European Union, in *Financial Times*, 12 December 2000.

The European Commission is composed of 20 appointed Commissioners headed by a President. The 24 Directorates-General of the Commission are the heart of the EU's civil service, responsible for its day-to-day running. Importantly, in addition, the Commission holds a monopoly in proposing legislation and thus enjoys considerable political power in its agenda-setting initiatives, such as the Single Market and Monetary Union.

The European Parliament is composed of members from each state in proportion to the state's population. The EU Parliament has grown in size from 78 to 626 members. Although Members of the European Parliament (MEPs) have been directly elected by EU citizens since 1979, parliament does not play the pivotal role which is customary in national systems. The Treaty of Rome gave parliament little direct say in legislation but, with later treaties, it gained greater influence, with an increase from 15 to 38 areas in which it has 'co-decision-making' powers with the Council (amounting to two-thirds of all EU legislation). These reforms have come in response to criticism that EU institutions lack sufficient democratic accountability and that they are bureaucratic and inefficient.

The enlargement process poses major challenges to achieve a workable union with almost double the number of member nations while establishing a sense of political legitimacy for all the peoples within its compass. In 2000, the German Foreign Minister suggested that a new federal constitution would be needed to set out clear divisions of power between national governments and the EU. He proposed a bicameral parliament, which would include a directly elected lower house and an upper house made up of members of national parliaments. The executive function would rest with a directly elected president, presiding over the commission. This vision of a federal superstate, he argued, would offer greater efficiency in an enlarged Europe, but the federalist principle has proved controversial among other member states, fearful of the weakening of national institutions and greater centralization.

7.13 Conclusions

1. The political sphere concerns decision-making processes for resolving conflict in society as a whole. Interactions between state and private actors are blurring the traditional distinctions between state and civil society.

2. The nation-state is the basic unit into which all the world's people are divided. Sovereignty and territoriality, however, are being eroded with the growing interdependence of states.

3. States vary in their sources of legitimacy. Traditional sources of legitimate authority have given way to constitutionality and democratic forms.

4 Democratic government may take a number of forms: these include presidential, parliamentary and 'hybrid' systems. A stronger executive is associated with presidential systems, while the legislative is predominant in parliamentary systems. The favoured design of new constitutions is the dual executive, or hybrid system.

5 Political parties and pluralistic political debate are characteristic of democratic systems. Two-party systems are associated with the first-past-the-post type of electoral system, while multiparty systems, often leading to coalition government, are characteristic of PR systems.

6 While democracies are increasing in number globally, many of these are transitional democracies, in the process of building institutions of participation and accountability, as well as introducing economic liberalization. The states of Central and Eastern Europe and Latin America are examples.

7 The growth of global political forces has led to a questioning of traditional notions of sovereignty in an interdependent world. In particular the changing structure of the EU towards a supranational body is sparking a reappraisal of the role of nation-states.

Review questions

1. What are the defining characteristics of the nation-state? How is globalization threatening state sovereignty?
2. What are the political risks to international business?
3. What is federalism and what are its alleged advantages? Would it be workable in the EU?
4. List the main defining features of democracy.
5. What are the sources of possible instability in transitional democracies?
6. How do presidential systems compare with parliamentary systems of government? The hybrid system is said to combine the best of both worlds, but does it?
7. How democratic are the main institutions of the EU?
8. What are the proposals for reforming the EU?

Assignments

1. Assume that a company is considering moving production to a location in a developing country (for example Mexico), but is concerned about political

instability. What particular aspects of the country's political structure and processes should it take into account when assessing political risk?

2 What are the links between democratization and economic development? Give two examples and assess how successful they have been.

Further reading

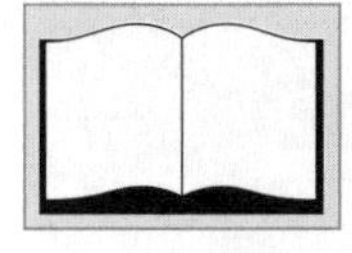

Hague, R. and Harrop, M. (2001) *Comparative Government and Politics: An Introduction*, 5th edn (Basingstoke: Palgrave)

Held, D. (ed.) (1993) *Prospects for Democracy* (Cambridge: Polity Press)

Heywood, A. (1997) *Politics* (Basingstoke: Macmillan – now Palgrave)

McGrew, A. and Lewis, P. (1992) *Globalization and the Nation-State* (Cambridge: Polity Press)

Chapter

The international legal environment of business: moving towards harmonization

Outline of chapter

8.0 Introduction
8.1 How legal systems affect business
8.2 National legal systems
8.3 Legal framework of the EU
8.4 International business transactions
8.5 Resolution of disputes in international business
8.6 Crime, corruption and the law
8.7 The growing impact of international law on business
8.8 Human rights
8.9 Conclusions

1. To understand the interrelationships between national, regional and international legal frameworks in their impact on the international business environment
2. To appreciate the divergence in structures, processes and content between national legal systems
3. To assess the impact of evolving regional, in particular European Union, law-making on enterprises, workers and consumers
4. To apply principles of international law, in particular human rights, to organizations and their workforces

8.0 Introduction

The legal dimension of international business has grown as business relations across national borders have deepened and become more complex. Historically, the legal environment has been determined by national legal systems stemming from state sovereignty. All commercial transactions across national borders, from the simplest export contracts to complex joint ventures, exist within the framework of national legal systems. Globalization of markets and production has provided the impetus for harmonization in the legal systems between states. We now see the dual effects of a weakening of state sovereignty and a burgeoning body of international law. Modern international managers, therefore, require an understanding of the workings of international law, as well as familiarity with different national legal systems.

The speed of some developments such as e-commerce has far outpaced the development of the law to cover them. While governments have slowly woken up to the legal implications of advances in technology, they have also realized their own limitations in regulating international transactions. Lawmakers are now co-operating in international legal reform and the reform of national systems to take account of new ways of doing business. All countries appreciate the need for an efficient, modern, impartial legal system to attract enterprises (both local and overseas investors) and retain their confidence in its processes. They also see the benefits of harmonization of laws to facilitate international transactions. The legal environment can be divided into three interacting spheres, as shown in Figure 8.1: national legal systems; regional law-making authorities, of which the European Union (EU) is the major

Figure 8.1 The three interlocking spheres of the international legal environment

example; and international law emanating from recognized international bodies such as the United Nations (UN) and its agencies. This chapter will set out the 'boundaries' of each and explore the ways in which these overlapping spheres of law impact on international business.

8.1 How legal systems affect business

Law refers to the rules which a society defines as binding on all its members. Whereas groups within a society, such as sports bodies, create rules for their own members, the distinguishing feature of law is that it creates obligations for society as a whole, encompassing individual citizens, businesses and governmental agents. In modern societies law has expanded into almost all aspects of business. While businesspeople are inclined to see legal rules in a negative light, constraining their activities (for example an application for planning permission), in fact much law is of an enabling nature (for example eligibility to apply for public funding). Market-driven economies aim to strike a balance between freedom of enterprise and sufficient regulation to guard the public interest. In the post-war era, with an upsurge in welfare state provisions, the law has extended to areas such as employment protection, consumer protection and health and safety in the workplace. More recently, with advances in telecommunications, data protection for personal details has come into the ambit of legal protection. As can be seen in Table 8.1, legal obligations now cover a wide range of business activities.

Table 8.1 Summary of major areas of law affecting business and relevant authorities

Area of law	Legal authorities
Contract	National; international conventions
Property and planning	National
Employment	National; EU; international conventions
Company	Mainly national; EU
Competition	National; EU
Health and Safety	National; EU; international conventions
Environment	National; EU; international conventions
Intellectual property	National; EU; international conventions
Negligence and product liability	National; EU

Law may be broadly classified into two categories: **public law**, which concerns relations between citizens and the state; and **civil** (or private) **law**, which concerns relations between individuals (including companies). Tax and social security fall within public law, whereas contract law and employment law are areas of civil law. The state plays a significant, although less direct role in the civil law. Legislatures enact laws regulating employment relations for example; and the state's courts may be called on to settle disputes between the parties. In a dispute over a contract or an accident at work, the person who has suffered loss or injury (the 'plaintiff') may bring a claim for money compensation ('damages') or a range of other remedies against the 'defendant' in the state's courts.

A major body of public law is the **criminal law**, under which certain types of wrongdoing are designated by society as criminal offences. In these cases, state authorities initiate proceedings, known as a 'prosecution', in the criminal courts, which, on conviction for a crime, will lead to a fine or imprisonment of the offender. While we tend to think of crime in terms of

Table 8.2 Outline of civil law and criminal law in the English legal system

	Criminal law	Civil law
Concerns	Offences against society	Disputes between private individuals or companies
Purpose of the action	To preserve order in the community by punishing offenders and deterring others	To remedy the wrong which has been suffered
The parties	A prosecutor prosecutes a defendant	A plaintiff sues a defendant
Where the action is heard	The criminal courts, that is, magistrates' court or Crown Court	The civil courts, that is, county court or High Court
Standard of proof	The prosecutor must prove his case beyond a reasonable doubt	The plaintiff must establish his case on the balance of probabilities
Decision	A defendant may be convicted if he is found guilty, or acquitted if he is found not guilty	A defendant may be found liable or not liable
Sanctions	Imprisonment, fine, probation, community service	Damages, injunction, specific performance
Examples	Murder, theft, drunken driving, health and safety violations	Contract, tort, property law

Source: Adapted from Keenan, D. and Riches, S. (1998) *Business Law*, 4th edn, (London: Pitman) p. 5 (reprinted with permission).

individual crimes, such as assault and theft, companies, as well as their directors, can be guilty of criminal offences. Breaches of health and safety law are a common type of corporate crime. In Britain, corporate liability has been extended by new offences of corporate killing, following unsuccessful prosecutions for manslaughter in relation to ferry and train disasters, including a crash at Paddington, London, in 1999, in which 31 people died. Directors cannot hide behind the facade of the company: they may be personally liable for its crimes. On the other hand, enforcement of the criminal law, which is mainly rooted in national systems, poses major challenges as criminal activities have become increasingly globalized and also highly organized. Table 8.2 gives a breakdown of the distinctions between civil and criminal law. Note that the 'burden of proof' is higher in a criminal case, which means that a greater degree of certainty is required for criminal guilt than for the judgment as to which party succeeds in a civil case.

For a business, the bulk of the relevant law stems from national law-making authorities, as each of the world's sovereign states has its own legal system, which has both law-making capacity within its territory (or 'jurisdiction') and capacity to apply its law to legal disputes within its jurisdiction. Before looking at legal institutions, it is important to note that legal systems do not exist in a vacuum, but are influenced by the society's social, political and cultural environment. The legal environment, including the content of law and legal processes, is an indication of attitudes to law in general, as well as the wider values of a society. As is often remarked on, there are over seventeen times as many lawyers per head of population in the US as in Japan (1 for every 400 in the US, compared to 1 for every 7,000 in Japan). People in individualistic societies such as the US make far greater use of the courts to settle disputes (known as **litigation**) than those in the more group-oriented societies. As values change, the law, and people's readiness to use it, may change in harmony. In China's expanding market economy, for example, individuals are now seeking redress in the courts over defective consumer products and workers' rights. China's legal system is becoming more transparent, partly as a result of the influence of foreign investors (McGregor, 2001).

However, reflecting cultural differences as well as the extent of economic development, some areas of legal protection (for example health and safety legislation), while commonplace in industrialized societies, are much less prevalent in the developing world. Although formal legal systems may look much alike between countries, the ways in which they work in practice may be very different. The extent to which a legal system has the capacity to adapt and respond to changes in the environment is a recurring issue in comparisons between national legal systems. Court systems, too, vary enormously in their user-friendliness. The 'wheels of justice' may turn so slowly that a would-be plaintiff, faced with a judicial process lasting years, may decide against litigation. India, for example, in 2000 had some 25 million cases pending. Even if no new actions were filed, the backlog would take an estimated 324 years to clear (Bearak, 2000).

8.2 National legal systems

The pre-eminence of national legal systems derives from the theory of the sovereign state (see Chapter 7). Every legal system may be divided into two main sets of functional institutions. These are legislation (law-making) and adjudication (the settlement of disputes). Legislation, or statute law, is 'law made by a person or institution with the power to make law' (Miers and Page, 1990, p. 3). In democracies, elected legislative bodies link directly with the political system. Much law-making follows the social and political agendas of elected governments. Legislators can get it wrong, of course. The prohibition law in the US in the 1930s, banning alcoholic beverages, met widespread opposition and had to be repealed.

The system of courts, or **judicial system**, interprets and applies the law in particular cases. The extent to which judges thereby shape legal development, overlapping with the law-making function, differs between systems, and, even within systems, is a matter of differing opinions. As will be seen below, 'case law' (judge-made law) is more important in some countries than in others. A general rule is that legal systems attempt to draw a line between law-making and judicial functions. Court systems are designed to prevent the intrusion of political and personal considerations, and judges should be seen to be fair and impartial. This notion of equality before the law is an aspect of the **rule of law**. For transitional democracies, establishing the rule of law and an independent judiciary are as important as instituting a free and fair electoral system.

The world's legal systems can be classified in terms of legal traditions or legal families. The two major Western historical traditions are the civil law tradition and the common law tradition. The civil law tradition, prevalent in Continental Europe, is founded on a comprehensive legal code, whereas the **common law** tradition, English in origin, emphasizes case law. Both have been adopted in a variety of non-Western contexts, as part of modernization processes. Newly independent states have tended to adopt the legal tradition of their former colonial power. For this reason, a lawyer from Ghana will find it much easier to understand a lawyer from Kenya or England, than one from the Ivory Coast just next door, which falls within French colonial influence (Zweigert and Kötz, 1998).

8.2.1 Civil law tradition

The civil law tradition is by far the older of the two and has its origin in the ancient Roman *ius civile*, which in the sixth century was codified in the Justinian Code. Civil law relies on a legal code for the basic groundwork of the system, on which further law-making is built. The legal code is a comprehensive, systematic setting out of the basic law for a country. The modern models of codified law are the French Civil Code of 1804, known as the Napoleonic Code, and the German Civil Code of 1896. Codified law is in fact divided into a number of different codes, depending on the subject matter. The civil code, which contains the body of private law (that is, between citizens), is complemented by a Commercial Code and a Criminal Code. These codes have demonstrated their adaptability by providing models for numerous other countries in Europe, Latin America, Africa, Asia and the Middle East. They are adaptable in federal systems, as in Germany itself, or in unitary systems, as in France. In the UK, Scotland falls in the civil law tradition. Japan's choice of the civil code model coincided with the country's initial industrialization and modernization policies in the late nineteenth century. The attraction of the civil law model lies in the supremacy of the single authoritative source of the law. The principles and concepts contained in the codes form the basis of legal reasoning. Although the accumulated decisions of judges are useful as guidelines, they are not in themselves a

Table 8.3 Selected civil law and common law countries

Civil law	Common law
Argentina	Australia
Brazil	Bangladesh
Chile	Canada
China	Ghana
Egypt	India
France	Israel
Germany	Jamaica
Greece	Kenya
Indonesia	Malaysia
Iran	Nigeria
Italy	Singapore
Japan	England
Mexico	United States
Sweden	Zambia

source of law. This is the major distinction between the civil law and common law systems. The distinction has been described as one between different legal styles. The urge to regulate and systematize has dominated Continental European legal thinking, whereas English lawyers have tended to improvise, not making a decision until they have to, on the view that 'we'll cross that bridge when we come to it' (Zweigert and Kötz, 1998, p. 70).

8.2.2 Common law tradition

The common law tradition originated in England some 900 years ago – long before Parliament had become the supreme law-making authority. Common law is essentially judge-made law, known as case law. In deciding a particular dispute, the judge creates a 'precedent' to be followed in similar cases in the future. The body of law builds up through the accumulation of precedents in decided cases. The system has both flexibility and rigidities in practice. Precedents may be applied more loosely or more strictly in later cases, lending flexibility. However, as the court system is hierarchical, the decisions of higher courts form precedents which must be followed by lower courts. Faced with what a judge feels is a bad precedent, the judge in a lower court has little choice but to follow it. The growth in statute law, in the form of Acts of Parliament, mainly in the past 100 years, has come about largely in response to the complexities of economic and social changes. Modern judges spend a great deal of their time interpreting and applying statute law, including, it should be added, European law. The growing importance of statute law (also referred to as enacted law) suggests a convergence with the civil law tradition, although, when it comes down to interpreting the law in particular factual situations, which is what matters to litigants, the judge still holds a good deal of power.

Common law systems have been transplanted to countries as diverse as the US and India. Like all legal systems, the tradition has been adapted to the local environment. The US, with its division between federal and 50 state jurisdictions, has evolved a particularly complex system, with overlapping jurisdictions that can be confusing to outsiders (and even insiders). Each state constitutes a system within a system; Louisiana even has remnants of French codified law from its own colonial past. The individual states have made efforts to achieve consistency in the law in key areas that affect business, notably through the Uniform Commercial Code, which has been adopted by all the states (although only partially in Louisiana). The American Law Institute has spearheaded the efforts to bring about consistency by producing its restatements of the law in areas such as contract and product liability (see Case Study 8.3 on Firestone). These restatements resemble codified law in all but name, but they do not have the status of a statute as they are not passed by Congress. Their aim is clarify the law and act as guidance to lawyers and judges.

Table 8.4 Summary of civil law and common law traditions

	Civil law tradition	Common law tradition
Sources of the law	Comprehensive legal codes	Judge-made law and statutes
Role of case law	Guidance, but not binding	System of binding precedent
Legal style	Systematized application of principles	Pragmatic and piecemeal

8.2.3 Non-Western legal systems

The growth in commercial law has reached almost all countries, aware that economic development depends on a sound legal framework and an efficient and accessible court system. As has been seen, the groundwork for modern legal systems in much of the world was the legacy of colonial regimes. Legal traditions in many countries, which are based on customary law, predate Western systems and continue to form an important part of the overall legal environment. In many countries, therefore, we now find a mixture of pre-modern customs, colonial forms and newer codes designed to keep up to date with business needs. The study of evolving legal systems in developing countries reveals much about the relationship between law and social change.

Non-Western legal traditions include Islamic, Chinese and Hindu law. Of these, Islamic law, called the *Shari'a* (God's rules), is perhaps the most highly developed. Islamic law can have a direct impact on the way business is conducted in Muslim countries, such as Saudi Arabia and Sudan. Because the *Shari'a* prohibits 'unearned profits', the charging of interest is forbidden. Financing through banks can still be arranged, by devising alternative legal forms to cover transactions, such as profit-sharing and loss-sharing by a lending bank. Islamic countries have introduced codes for the secular regulation of activities such as the formation and enforcement of contracts, foreign investment and the employment of foreign workers. Accordingly, most now have secular tribunals for these areas.

Both Western and non-Western legal traditions have evolved and adapted to different cultural contexts, in response to two related forces. First, there has been a perceived need to modernize national legal structures as societies have become more complex, and legal relations, such as consumer and employment contracts, have become more common. Most of this development has come through legislation, such the Consumer Protection Act 1987 and Employment Rights Act 1996 in the UK. Second, the growth of global markets has led to increasing international efforts to achieve uniformity and standardization of laws across national borders. Much of this latter effort has come through multilateral international conventions signed by a number of sovereign states, which, when ratified by national authorities, become incorporated into the domestic law of the state. In particular, international conventions have played an important role in bringing common legal frameworks for international trade in goods (discussed below). Within the EU harmonization has gone further, putting in place supranational legal structures for both law-making and adjudication (Denza, 1999).

WWW
WEBALERT

General international law sources:

A good source for the legal environment generally, including both national and international materials, is
http://www.law.cornel.edu/world/

A site for international trade and commercial law is
http://www.jus.uio.no/lm/index.html
This site has been expanded to include electronic commerce, environmental law, human rights, Islamic law and much more

8.3 Legal framework of the EU

For each member state, the EU provides a growing source of law, which has become intertwined with their own national law. The foundation Treaty of Rome 1957, referred to as the EC Treaty, has been greatly expanded, with articles renumbered, as a result of the Treaty of Amsterdam 1997. The law of the EU is still technically referred to as EC law. The current constitutional structure is the product of the Treaty of European Union 1992 (TEU), also known as the Maastricht Treaty. EU law-making touches a wide range of areas, including:

- Elimination of trade barriers between member states
- A common agricultural policy
- A common commercial policy
- A common transport policy
- Harmonization of competition law
- Harmonization of social policy
- Economic and monetary union (EMU).

The UK recognizes the supremacy of European Community law in the European Communities Act 1972 (as amended in 1986, 1993 and 1998). The European Court of Justice (ECJ) is the sole interpreter of European law and can override national legislation in cases of conflict. Although national supreme courts (such as the House of Lords in the UK) have ultimate authority in domestic matters, in issues involving EU institutions and EC law, the ECJ is the ultimate authority. Case Study 8.1 highlights the importance of European law for business.

Case study 8.1 **Legal battle between Tesco and Levi Strauss**

In legal battles that have gone to the High Court in England and the ECJ, Tesco is attempting to establish a right to sell Levi jeans in its supermarkets at prices undercutting those in high street shops. The case has wide implications for stores which sell popular designer brands at discount prices. The issue is whether the brands, which are registered trade marks, should be allowed to control which retailers sell their products. In a practice known as 'parallel imports', Tesco and other retailers had been able to buy branded goods cheaply in, say, Southeast Asia, bypassing the brand owners' official distribution channels in Europe. The law is clear that, within Europe, manufacturers cannot prevent a retailer from buying goods in one country and selling them in another. In a 1998 decision seen as a victory for brand owners, the ECJ held that retailers could not import goods from outside Europe without the manufacturer's consent.

In 1999, the UK courts delivered conflicting decisions in the case of perfume imports, in the Davidoff case (in England) and the Joop! case (in Scotland). In the climate of uncertainty, brand owners such as Levi were tempted to sue parallel importers such as Tesco. Tesco then sued the jeans company for 'groundless threats', with a claim for damages. An initial ruling by the ECJ in 2001 left the legal position unclear, saying that the decision should go back to the national courts and that they should take account of the interests of parallel importers.

From the consumer's point of view it has been argued that parallel imports put pressure on prices and give the consumer more choice. Levi jeans bought at Tesco cost considerably less than those bought at Levi's stores. Levi argued that the issue was not essentially about price, but that supermarkets could not provide the expert sales staff needed: 'Customers need advice on what's on offer and the difference between loose and baggy, straight and slim ... We're not saying you need a university degree to sell jeans, but if a person is cutting bacon and filling shelves one minute, it's not possible for them to sell jeans as well.' Levi said that Tesco had never met the standard to become a licensed outlet and lack of training was one of the main reasons. Tesco replied, 'It's not rocket science to sell jeans ... we don't think giving five minutes extra training than our staff get justifies an extra £20 on the price and neither do our customers.'

Sources: Hargreaves, D. 'Showdown in the supermarket', *Financial Times*, 22 January 2001; Hargreaves, D. 'Levi puts case for "special" sales skills', *Financial Times*, 16 January 2001; Eaglesham, J., Voyle, S. and Hargreaves, D., 'European Court leans to Levi over cheap imports', *Financial Times*, 6 April 2001.

Case questions

What is the essential issue of the Tesco–Levi case?
What are the wider implications for retailers of branded goods?

EC law and institutions

- *Treaties* creating the EU, which must be ratified by member states
- *Law-making* by the Commission and Council (plus co-decision procedure with the European Parliament):
  - Regulations – directly applicable throughout the EU; incorporated automatically into the law of each member state; create individual rights and obligations
  - Directives – require member states to implement their provisions, usually within a given period of time, for example two years; may have direct effect, allowing individuals to enforce rights directly, if the member state does not implement the directive in the required time limit
- *European Court of Justice* (situated in Luxembourg): interprets the treaties and other legislation; modelled on courts in the civil law tradition, in that it is not bound by its previous decisions, but its case law has in fact shown consistency

8.4 International business transactions

Laws covering trade between businesses in different countries have existed since the medieval period, when the *law merchant* was born of customary rules used by the merchants of the period. These rules, relating to the sale of goods and the settlement of disputes, were gradually incorporated into national bodies of law, codified in the case of the civil law countries and part of the common law in common law countries. In England, the law became enacted in the Sale of Goods Act 1894, and in the US the Uniform Commercial Code (1951) harmonized the law between the 50 states. Impetus to achieve international harmonization has come from a number of initiatives.

8.4.1 International codification

Set up in 1966, the UN Commission on International Trade Law (UNCITRAL) attempted to devise a framework to satisfy the needs of businesses from trading nations of all continents. The result was the Convention on Contracts for the International Sale of Goods (CISG) of 1980 (the Vienna Convention), which came into force in 1988. The CISG does not apply automatically to international sales. The convention must be ratified by individual states, becoming incorporated in their domestic law. The number of countries which have ratified the convention (59 by August 2001) continues to rise and they now account for two-thirds of the world's trade. Among major trading nations, the US, Germany, France and China have ratified, but neither the UK nor Japan has done so. The convention applies to contracts falling within its scope which are concluded by firms in countries which have ratified, or to contracts whose performance is carried out in a country which has ratified. For transactions between firms in non-ratifying countries, the rules of private international law apply (these are discussed below).

Where the CISG makes a major contribution is in harmonizing rules to do with the formation of contracts for the sale of goods, obligations of the parties and remedies. It attempts to bridge the gap between civil and common law jurisdictions on questions such as the 'meeting of minds' between the parties over the existence of an agreement and its particular terms. These are the key areas in which disputes arise and the CISG attempts to compromise between countries which require certainty and those which allow greater flexibility. For example, the requirement that a contract must be in writing is traditional in common law countries (although of diminishing importance), whereas civil law countries tend to have no writing requirement. The CISG allows ratifying countries the option, in keeping with their own national law. China, for example, has preserved its writing requirement.

WWW
WEBALERT

The UN's main international law website is
http://www.un.org/law/

The UNCITRAL home page is
http://www.uncitral.org/en-main.htm

Texts of the conventions can be found at
http://www.uncitral.org/english/texts/sales/index.htm

The UNIDROIT principles are available in full at
http://www.jus.uio.no/lm/unidroit/contract.principles.1994/index.html

The International Institute for the Unification of Private International Law (UNIDROIT) has complemented the CISG, and approached the need for unification from a different perspective. The UNIDROIT Principles of International Commercial Contracts, published in 1994, offer general rules for international contract and are broadly similar to the CISG, but of wider application. The Principles are not confined to the sale of goods. Moreover, as they are not embodied in any binding international convention, they can be incorporated into contracts by firms from any country, not just those that have ratified the CISG. It has been suggested that they come closest to 'the emerging international consensus' on the rules of international trade (Moens and Gillies, 1998, p. 81). Because the Principles do not themselves have any force of law, they can be adopted and modified as needed, and have even provided models for national legislators as diverse as Mexico, Quebec and Holland. In particular, they have facilitated the growing trade between Australia and its Asian neighbours.

8.4.2 Cultural factors in international contracts

Negotiation of international contracts usually involves use of a foreign language for at least one of the parties. Apart from problems of translating technical terms, the cultural context of negotiations varies considerably. High-context and low-context languages will have different styles of negotiation. Attention to detailed terms and confrontational bargaining are far more significant in the Anglo-American context than in Asian contexts, for example. The formally agreed contract may be in one language, with an unofficial translation in another, which clarifies the terms. Alternatively, the contract may have two official versions in two different languages. An inescapable difficulty is possible misunderstandings in the translation process. The CISG exists in six languages (Arabic, Chinese, English, French, Russian and Spanish) and unofficial translations into other languages must be made for negotiators who need them. Interpretation of terms, even between speakers of the same language, can differ from country to country. For example, the French word *droit* can mean either 'law' or 'right' in English, giving significant scope for misunderstanding. Hence, it should be remembered that while the contract creates legal obligations, these are not necessarily interpreted in exactly the same way by all parties, and, in case of dispute, an arbitrator or judge faces an unenviable task of finding out what the parties intended in a particular situation.

The role of the contract itself is viewed differently in different cultures. In individualistic cultures the detailed formal contract governs business relationships, whereas in the more group-oriented societies, such as Japan and Southeast Asia, business relies more on informal, personalized relationships. **Relational contracting**, as the latter is known, is rooted in societies where personal ties built on trust, often over a number of years, matter more than formal written documents. In these societies, the preferred method of settling disputes is out of court, rather than through litigation. In more individualist societies, **arm's length contracting** (in which the agreement is paramount) is more the norm. With the growing numbers of joint ventures and expanding markets across cultural boundaries, an understanding of cultural sensitivities is essential in cross-border contracts. While written contracts are now part of the modern legal systems that have been adopted in non-Western societies, the underlying cultural environment is still influential in their negotiation and interpretation. It goes without saying that a 'meeting of minds' over both the terms and the working relationship that flows from the agreement is good insurance against a breakdown which could lead to the courts.

8.5 Resolution of disputes in international business

Every international business, sooner or later, becomes involved in a dispute with a foreign element. The exposure to legal risk is greater for international businesses than domestic ones, mainly because of multiple jurisdiction (see

Points to Remember box on international business and legal risk in section 8.5.1). Disputes are likely to arise over contractual terms, licence agreements and in the area of tort, in which the firm either alleges wrongdoing or is the defendant in a negligence or product liability claim. The area of the law concerned is **private international law**, defined as the law applying to the private law between individuals and firms in more than one country. Also referred to as conflict of laws, private international law seeks to establish rules for deciding which national law to apply to a particular situation. The rules of private international law give guidance on three broad issues:

1 the choice of law governing transactions
2 the choice of forum, that is, the country in which a case should be heard
3 the enforcement of court judgments.

The harmonizing of private international law has been an important aim of international conventions. The Rome Convention on the Law Applicable to Contracts 1980 and the Brussels Convention on Jurisdiction and Enforcement of Judgments in Civil and Commercial Matters 1968 have both been incorporated into English law.

Both arbitration and litigation involve choice-of-law rules, depending on the type of dispute. We look at two types of dispute: contractual disputes and those involving negligence or product liability claims.

8.5.1 Contractual disputes

In the basic transaction of buying or selling goods, at least one of the contracting firms is likely to find its rights governed by foreign law, thereby adding to the legal risk in a number of ways. First, there is the question of what contract law in the foreign jurisdiction actually stipulates. Then there is the possibility of having to go through the courts in that country to obtain redress. Finally, the firm may face problems of getting a judgment of the foreign court enforced in its own country.

Litigation is costly, time consuming and may bring unwanted publicity if the case is a high-profile one. Added risks in international disputes are the distance, unfamiliarity of the law and unfamiliar legal cultural environment. While US businesses have become accustomed to a culture of litigation, the costs in damages can be astronomical, and the high cost of liability insurance is a consequence. In contract disputes, the incentives to find other means of dispute resolution are therefore strong. Practising lawyers, far from suggesting litigation in all cases, emphasize the benefits of 'alternative dispute resolution'. Alternatives to litigation are:

- *Settlement* by the parties 'out of court'

- *Mediation*, in which the parties agree to bring in a third party, who attempts to settle their differences
- *Arbitration*, the submission of the dispute to a named person or organization in accordance with the agreement. Arbitration is not a cheap alternative and can be lengthy, but on both counts is usually thought to be preferable to litigation. It has become popular in licensing disputes and international construction contracts.

Contracts between firms based in different countries may specify a 'choice of law' to govern their contract. Normally this choice will also govern the forum in which any disputes will be heard. Most countries recognize choice-of-law clauses. For EU member states the Rome Convention provides that if the parties have not made a clear choice of law, then the contract is governed by the law of the country with which it is most closely connected. In practice, this is likely to be the law of the party who is to carry out performance of the contract. The Brussels Convention provides that jurisdiction depends on whether the defendant is 'domiciled' in the EU (which, for a firm, means that it must have a 'seat' of business there). In employment contracts, the employee can sue where he/she carries out his/her duties. In consumer contracts, the Brussels Convention (now an EU regulation) gives the consumer the right to sue in local courts. This regulation will have profound implications for online traders, who may be liable to be sued in national courts of any EU member state where their business activities are directed. For enforcement of judgments, most states will recognize the judgment of a foreign court, if the foreign law and procedure are broadly compatible with its own. Within the EU this recognition is automatic, as it is between states within the CISG.

Whereas the Brussels and Rome Conventions envisaged international contracts to be almost all business-to-business, the growth in e-commerce has greatly expanded the numbers of consumer deals across national borders. An online trader, even a small or medium-size enterprise, may sell goods to consumers in many states from one website. A survey in 2000 found that over 50 per cent of European online traders are accessed in ten or more countries (Landwell, 2000). Thus the online trader needs to be familiar with the relevant national law, such as the consumer's right to cancel. Moreover, the online trader may be liable to be sued in the courts of all the states in which its website is accessed. In 2000, a Directive on Electronic Commerce recognized the need for a uniform legal framework across Europe, balancing the desire to encourage e-commerce with the need for protection of consumers. Part of the solution is to provide alternative ways of solving disputes. In the US, Dell Computers has been selling its products online since 1996, and now sells to consumers in 85 different countries. The company has devised a system whereby, in cases of complaint, the consumer has redress from a local office.

International business and legal risk

International businesses may be exposed to legal risk in a number of ways:

- Contractual risks in overseas markets: for example in France and Portugal consumer contracts must be in the local language in order to be legally binding
- Protection of intellectual property: trade marks require registration both at home and in other countries where customers are located; copyright materials, such as software, also require protection; lax enforcement is a problem in many countries
- Risk of liability for injuries or defective products and subsequent litigation in a foreign jurisdiction
- Risk of infringement of data protection requirements, designed for protection and security of personal data
- Risk of dealings with local officials, especially where local regulation is complex and the possibility of corruption arises; a firm could incur criminal liability under home country laws (for example, the US Foreign Corrupt Practices Act)

8.5.2 Negligence and product liability

While obligations under contracts are defined by the particular agreement, obligations in **tort** arise from a range of broadly defined obligations owed by those in society to fellow citizens generally. The plaintiff may suffer personal injury or damage to property in an accident caused by the activities of the defendant. If the plaintiff's reputation has been damaged by something the defendant has said publicly, the claim is in libel. There are many different areas of tort law, but the areas which are of greatest relevance to business are negligence and product liability. In a **negligence** claim, the defendant is alleged to have failed to take reasonable care and so caused the plaintiff's injuries or loss. **Product liability** claims impose a duty which is much nearer to 'strict' liability, in which the defendant (usually the producer) is made liable for defective products that cause harm to consumers. The development of tort law in these areas parallels the growth of modern consumer society. Factory-produced goods, mass transport, advanced pharmaceutical products and medical procedures and industrialized food production have all carried risks of accidents and injury, sometimes on a wide scale. All industrialized countries have in place laws protecting consumers and other victims in these cases. In the EU, product liability laws have been harmonized by a Directive in 1985, which has been incorporated into national law (in the UK, by the Consumer Protection Act 1987). The Directive, which includes a 'development risks defence' providing an escape route for producers who have achieved an industry-standard level of product testing, is perceived to be less consumer-friendly than US law.

In the US product liability litigation has developed into a booming industry. While product liability laws vary from state to state, the legal climate has facilitated litigation in three key ways: (1) the use of the **'class' action**, whereby a group of plaintiffs may come together to bring legal proceedings; (2) the award by courts of 'punitive' damages (intended to punish the defendant for the wrongdoing) to plaintiffs, in addition to compensatory damages. Huge sums have been awarded by American juries as punitive damages (although often reduced on appeal, it should be added; and punitive damages are capped in some states); and (3) the 'contingency' fee system for lawyers' fees, also known as the 'no-win-no-fee' system, whereby the legal fees are an agreed percentage of the damages. With this prior arrangement, the potential plaintiff without huge resources can still bring a claim. In a Florida case, three sick smokers brought a class action on behalf of 500,000 Florida smokers. At the end of the two-year trial in 2000, they were awarded $12.7 million in compensatory damages and $144.8 billion in punitive damages against the five major tobacco companies.

Clearly, the successful plaintiff in a negligence or product liability claim in the US stands to gain greater damages than his or her equivalent in most other countries. Plaintiffs, like all consumers of services, shop around and 'forum shopping' is a continuing issue in the international legal environment. The rules of private international law provide guidelines on where claims in tort should be brought (choice of forum), which hinge on where the damage suffered by the plaintiff took place. In Bhopal, India, in 1984, a chemical disaster resulted in the deaths of 2,000 to 4,000 people and injuries to several hundred thousand others. The victims attempted to sue the parent company, Union Carbide, in New York, arguing that negligence in the design of the plant caused the accident, in which a massive escape of poisonous gases occurred. Their claim failed, as much of the design and engineering that went into the plant was carried out by local engineers in India. The plaintiffs then sought damages in India. Undeterred, foreign plaintiffs from poorer countries have continued to press claims against defendant corporations in richer countries. South African residents have sought to bring claims for asbestos injuries in the English courts, the details of which are given in Case Study 8.2. In the US courts, a recent development has been an upsurge in claims from plaintiffs abroad, who allege that their injuries from pollution accidents and sweatshop conditions fall within international human rights law, allowing them to establish jurisdiction in the US. Indians in Ecuador have sued Texaco in a federal court in New York for an alleged dumping of crude oil in the Ecuadorian jungle.

Case study 8.2 South Africans sue in English courts: targeting the multinationals

Workers in South African asbestos factories and nearby residents have overcome the first hurdle to bringing claims in the English courts for their asbestos-related illnesses suffered before 1979. This would be a group action involving about 3,000 plaintiffs. In a landmark decision in summer 2000, the House of Lords, England's highest court, decided that the plaintiffs would be able to sue Cape plc, the parent company, in the English courts. Cape owned a number of subsidiaries in South Africa, all of which are now closed. The plaintiffs claim that the parent company, 'knowing (so it is said) that exposure to asbestos was gravely injurious to health, failed to take proper steps to ensure that proper working practices were followed and proper safety precautions observed throughout the group' (*Lubbe* v. *Cape* plc, p. 1550).

The grounds for allowing cases to proceed in England were based on arguments that the plaintiffs would not be able to obtain justice in South Africa. First, because legal aid would be unobtainable and many of the plaintiffs are poor. Second, the country had little experience of group claims on this scale; and third, the necessary legal expertise and the technical evidence needed in this case would be very difficult to obtain in South Africa. The case can be distinguished from the Bhopal disaster, where the US courts decided that, as a matter of public policy, claims would have to be made in India.

The Cape case has significant implications for multinationals with subsidiaries in developing countries. The greater the control exerted by the parent company in areas such as health and safety, the more likely it could be held directly liable to claims in English courts. The same argument would apply to joint-venture arrangements. The lesson may be, according to one expert: 'Either step back completely from their subsidiaries, so that if something goes wrong they do not owe a duty of care, or take a really hands-on role' (Eaglesham, 2000).

Sources: Lubbe v. *Cape* plc [2000] 1 WLR 1545; Eaglesham, J., 'Litigation that looms from lands far away', *Financial Times*, 22 August 2000.

Case question

What are the legal risks of liability for transnational companies and what are the possible solutions?

When a consumer suffers harm as a result of a product defect, a manufacturing company can find itself on the end of product liability claims, where the damage may be multiplied in relation to the number of consumers. The large corporation which manufactures for global markets may face claims from millions of consumers worldwide, as Case Study 8.3 shows. The product recall is a means of limiting the damage which is effective in some cases, such as the Tylenol case, in which contamination of painkilling tablets resulted in the deaths of eight people and the removal of the product from retailers' shelves. The recall in the Firestone case has been on a much larger scale.

Case study 8.3 Firestone recalls 6.5 million tyres

Firestone, the US tyre company taken over by Bridgestone of Japan in 1997, announced to US consumers in August 2000 that it would replace free of charge about 6.5 million tyres, most of them fitted on Ford Explorers, a sports utility vehicle (SUV). The product recall announcement was the culmination of investigations that are continuing into injuries and an estimated 148 deaths that have been linked with the tyres since the late 1990s. At least 100 lawsuits have been filed against Firestone, and two national class-action lawsuits, in Texas and Florida, have been filed. In one case, a child was killed in Florida, when the tyre on her mother's Ford Explorer blew out and the vehicle flipped over two and a half times. (SUVs require more reliable tyres than ordinary cars, because they are more likely to roll over when they lose a tyre.) It appears that the tyres were inclined to split in hot weather, and the majority of the lawsuits are in southern states. Bridgestone recalled the same tyre in a number of overseas markets in 1999, including the Middle East, Thailand, Malaysia, Venezuela and Columbia, apparently confirming the tyre's weakness in hot climates.

If Firestone and Ford knew of the problems and did nothing, they could face heavy fines in federal criminal proceedings. The companies and their executives could also face criminal charges by state prosecutors. Ford has maintained that it did not know of safety problems with the tyres until they managed to extract the information from Firestone. The tyre crisis has damaged the relationship between the two companies which goes back nearly a century. Congressional investigations in both House and Senate are looking into what Firestone and Ford knew, and when they knew it. More damaging than the cost of the recall is the damage to the reputation of the companies and the loss of confidence in their products and brands. Moreover, in today's global markets, the scale of the damage is far greater than would have been conceivable in the days of the two business partners and friends, Henry Ford and Harvey Firestone.

Sources: Bradsher, K., 'Documents portray tire debacle as a story of lost opportunities', *New York Times*, 11 September 2000; Rohter, L., 'Bridgestone agrees to recall 62,000 tires in Venezuela', *New York Times*, 5 September 2000; Grimaldi, J., 'Tiremaker moves to settle suits', *Washington Post*, 10 August 2000.

Case questions

What are the lessons which should be learnt from this case? Once the faults had emerged, should the companies involved have handled the situation differently?

8.6 Crime, corruption and the law

A body of criminal law forms an important part of every national legal system. However, societies differ markedly on which activities are designated as crimes and crime prevention and enforcement vary from society to society. Moreover, attitudes towards corruption also differ among countries. What is seen as criminal dealing in one society may be accepted as normal in another. For international businesses, the robustness of criminal law enforcement and the society's attitudes towards corruption are aspects of the location which form part of its legal risk. Foreign direct investors seeking a stake in the privatization projects of transition economies may find themselves in a grey area, required to make payments to officials which seem to be of doubtful legality, but in cultures where a certain level of corruption is tolerated.

Criminal activities, such as smuggling, trafficking in goods and people, and 'money laundering' of the illicit gains, are all areas of considerable business involvement, which generate huge sums of money. Globalization, while it has opened up enormous opportunities for good, has also provided unprecedented scope for transnational crime, which national authorities struggle to contain or prosecute. The illegal drug trade is estimated to be worth $400 billion per year, amounting to 8 per cent in value of world trade, greater than that in motor vehicles. The UN agency for crime prevention estimates that well-organized criminal organizations with trafficking infrastructure in place can shift any product line at will – from human beings or body parts to cultural artefacts and nuclear products (UN Office for Drug Control and Crime Prevention, 1999). Criminal justice systems, by contrast, are national in scope and, although they co-ordinate their crime detection efforts, the differing systems and laws make it difficult to control transnational crime.

Also lucrative is the 'grey' area of business activity, which handles a variety of goods and services through informal channels, outside national regulatory systems. The underground or 'black' economy is the market in goods which are being bought and sold illegally. An example is the trade in products that are much in demand, such as alcohol and cigarettes, which when traded illegally avoid payment of customs duties. Other products traded include pirated goods such as software, counterfeit designer goods and counterfeit pharmaceutical products, all of which find buyers eager to avoid the higher prices charged through legitimate markets. While most would agree that illegitimate trade harms legitimate businesses as well as consumers, efforts to control such trade have encountered difficulties in an environment where there seems to be steady consumer demand, coupled with cross-border supply networks.

8.7 The growing impact of international law on business

International law covers the body of rules recognized by the international community as governing relations between sovereign states. It is also referred to as public international law, to distinguish it from the rules of private international law discussed above. The world's sovereign states, while recognizing international law, have not (as yet) created a supranational legal system with enforcement mechanisms mirroring those at national level. The functions of law-making and dispute settlement, therefore, rely on the co-operation of states and the willingness of state authorities to submit to international law as a matter of obligation. Since the Second World War there has been an accelerated growth in international law, which has coincided with the processes of globalization described in Chapter 2. While states are still inclined to see national interest as paramount, they increasingly recognize that, in the long term, state interests are interdependent. The growth in international law has been largely due to a growing awareness of the following:

- The need to protect the global environment
- Global security and the need to control nuclear and other weapons
- Human rights as transcending national law.

8.7.1 Treaties and conventions

Most international law comes about through treaties and conventions, and most of these are the result of initiatives by UN-affiliated bodies. **Treaties** may be multilateral, involving many countries, or bilateral, between two countries. An extradition treaty is an example of a bilateral treaty, requiring states to co-operate on the handing over of persons accused of crimes. Major multilateral treaties may take years in the drafting stages and do not become law until ratified by a given number of individual states specified in the treaty itself. There is no cut-off date; additional states may ratify indefinitely. However, even when a state does ratify, there is no guarantee that it will abide by treaty obligations, especially if they seem to conflict with national interest. It is in these circumstances that the effectiveness of international law

Minifile

GLOBAL COMPANIES UNDER FIRE

1984: Union Carbide

Escape of poisonous gases from pesticide plant in Bhopal, India, kills 2,000–4,000 people

1989: Exxon

The supertanker, *Exxon Valdez*, spills 10 million gallons of crude oil into William Sound, Alaska

1995: Shell

Campaigners criticize Shell for failing to influence the Nigerian government over the execution of dissidents

1997: McDonald's

Company wins a long libel case against two UK anti-globalization campaigners, who accused it of destroying rain forests, but McDonald's attracts considerable adverse publicity in the process

1997: Nike

Protests against Nike in 50 US cities and 11 countries, for sweatshop conditions in factories in Asia is tested. International public opinion, encouraged by the many non-governmental organizations (NGOs) plays an important role in putting pressure on governments. The UN can impose **sanctions** on individual states which are in serious breach of international law. Sanctions against Iraq for its failure to co-operate with UN weapons inspectors are an example. Alleged breaches of international law can also be subject to judicial proceedings in a variety of legal settings, considered in the next section.

8.7.2 Environmental law

A rapidly growing area of treaty-making has been environmental law. A number of environmental disasters, such as the *Exxon Valdez* oil spill off the Alaskan coast in 1989 and the Chernobyl nuclear plant disaster in 1986, have dramatically raised public consciousness of the need for co-operation between states. The United Nations Environment Programme dates from 1972. The UN Conference on Environment and Development, at the Rio Summit in 1992, adopted the concept of sustainable development, which refers to 'meeting the needs of present generations without compromising the ability of future generations to do the same' (Wallace, 1997, p. 197). The conference produced the Declaration on Environment and Development (the Rio Declaration), which includes the 'polluter pays' principle, although, when it comes to dispute resolution (discussed below), the polluting state will seldom consent to international adjudication or arbitration. The Rio Summit also adopted the Convention on Biodiversity and the Convention on Climate Change. The Biodiversity Convention aimed to protect and sustain biodiversity by a number of measures, including national monitoring of biodiversity, environmental impact assessments and national progress reports from individual countries. Transboundary pollution and the effects of transboundary industrial accidents are also the subject of international conventions. Widespread pollution of the atmosphere or seas is an international crime. State responsibility for the environment is an established principle, but it has been flexibly interpreted, particularly in relation to developing countries which cannot reach international standards for protecting the environment overnight. Moreover, the responsibility of the large transnational corporations (TNCs) as important global players in environmental issues is increasingly recognized (this theme is revisited in Chapter 12).

WWW
WEBALERT

A website on environmental treaties and resource indicators is http://sedac.ciesin.rg/pidb/pidb-home.html

The Biodiversity Convention (and many other documents) can be found at http://www.biodiv.org/Index.html

8.7.3 Settlement of disputes in international law

Despite the fact that there is no overarching international legal system equivalent to a national one, there are judicial means available for settling disputes in international law. First, national courts interpret and apply international law, thereby acknowledging its binding force. In Belgium in 2001, four Rwandans were found guilty and given lengthy prison sentences for war crimes in Rwanda. This landmark trial was the first ordinary jury trial for crimes committed in another country. Other countries could follow suit, including France, Germany and Switzerland, which all allow ordinary courts to try war crimes. Second, the International Court of Justice (ICJ), which sits in The Hague, in the Netherlands, hears a limited range of international cases. The ICJ is a UN body, whose authority derives from its governing Statute, attached to the UN Charter. While the ICJ's prestige is acknowledged, its effectiveness is limited by the restrictions to its jurisdiction. The major one is that it hears only disputes between sovereign states. A non-state organization cannot apply to it, although cases can involve activities of individuals and companies. Examples are the cases brought by Libya against the UK and US over the handing over for trial of two Libyans accused of planting the bomb which caused the explosion over Lockerbie, Scotland, of a Pan American jet in 1988, in which 270 people lost their lives. An agreement was reached under the auspices of the UN for the accused to be tried in a Scottish court sitting in the Netherlands in 2000, at which one was acquitted and the other found guilty of the bombing.

WWW
WEBALERT

The home page of the International Court of Justice is
http://www.icj-cij.org/

Informative documents about the ICJ can be found at
http://www.icj-cij.org/icjwww/ibasicdocuments.htm

Third, other international tribunals have been set up in the area of criminal law. Beginning with the Nuremberg trials after the Second World War, those who are alleged to have committed war crimes and genocide have been subject to international criminal proceedings. In the 1990s the ICJ set up an International Criminal Tribunal for Rwanda and also one for Yugoslavia. Beyond these special tribunals, considerable international effort has gone into establishing a permanent international criminal court to hear cases of crimes against humanity, from any country. A UN Conference in Rome in 1998 agreed a convention, the Rome Statute of the International Criminal Court. As of September 2000, 112 countries had signed and 20 had completed ratification. The very large number of signatories, representing a majority of the world's nations, suggests strong support, although the US and China remained opposed to the principle.

Fourth, there is the dispute settlement procedure established by the World Trade Organization (WTO) for member states, in its capacity to oversee world trade. This process will be examined in Chapter 9.

8.8 Human rights

Human rights may be defined as basic, universal rights of life which transcend social and cultural differences. The first general enunciation of human rights came in the Universal Declaration of Human Rights, adopted by the UN General Assembly in 1948. It did not have the legal authority of a convention or treaty, but it did give expression to a consensus on fundamental freedoms, including social, cultural, political and economic rights. These took more concrete form with the adoption of two conventions in the 1960s: the International Covenant on Civil and Political Rights and the International Covenant on Economic, Social and Cultural Rights. These conventions take a broad view of the content of human rights, stretching the concept from principles such as freedom from slavery and torture to the right to vote for governments and bargain collectively in the workplace. A majority of the world's states have ratified both covenants, committing themselves to implementation. However, subscribing to these goals in principle does not readily translate into practice, especially for developing countries, where economic development has often taken precedence over human rights issues. For example, child labour is tolerated in many developing countries and large TNCs which have affiliated manufacturers in these countries have been criticized for failing to take a stronger stand against the practice.

Other UN conventions cover specific areas of human rights. These include:

- Convention on the Elimination of All Forms of Racial Discrimination, 1966
- Convention on the Rights of the Child, 1989
- Convention on the Elimination of Discrimination Against Women, 1979
- Convention against Torture and Other Cruel, Inhuman or Degrading Treatment or Punishment, 1984
- Convention Relating to the Status of Refugees, 1951.

A trend in the increasing global awareness of human rights issues has been to place responsibility on companies to answer for their practices and policies, irrespective of the national laws in host countries. What standards should the company apply? While it was once thought that local standards suffice, this view is no longer considered to be tenable. Companies are now expected to maintain consistent standards and policies across their operations, whatever the location. Both legal and ethical issues are involved. As

The International Covenant on Civil and Political Rights

- Right to life
- Right not to be held in slavery
- Right against arbitrary arrest or detention
- Freedom of movement and freedom to choose place of residence
- Freedom of thought, conscience and religion
- Right of peaceful assembly

Covenant in full can be accessed at
http://www.tufts.edu/departments/fletcher/multi/texts/BH498.txt

The International Covenant on Economic, Social and Cultural Rights

- Right to just and favourable conditions of work
- Right to fair wages and a decent living
- Right to join trade unions
- Right to medical attention in the event of sickness
- Right to free primary education
- Right to take part in cultural life

Covenant in full can be accessed at
http://www.tufts.edu/departments/fletcher/multi/texts/BH497.txt

WWW
WEBALERT

Internet sources of human rights law:

The Universal Declaration of Human Rights is at
http://www.un.org/Overview/rights.html

The Convention on the Rights of the Child is at
http://www.unicef.org/crc/convention.htm

The website of the UN High Commissioner for Human Rights is at
http://www.unhchr.ch/

The Charter of Fundamental Rights of the European Union (draft) is at
http://www.europarl.eu.int/charter/en/default.htm

we have seen, companies can be sued in their home countries for alleged wrongdoings in foreign operations. Importantly, too, companies are now perceived as having a duty of social responsibility to the local communities in which they are located. The strategy implications for companies are examined further in Chapter 12.

The European Convention on Human Rights (ECHR) was produced by the Council of Europe in 1950. Its permanent legacy was the establishment of the European Court of Human Rights (in Strasbourg), which hears cases of alleged breaches of its provisions brought by individuals in member states. The rights defined in it are similar to those in the Covenant of Civil and Political Rights. The UK government, while not a party to the convention, has recognized decisions of the Strasbourg court brought by UK citizens, and has now incorporated the convention into UK legislation, in the Human Rights Act 1998, which took effect in October 2000. The new statute has far-reaching implications, giving the right to sue public bodies for breaches, and stating that courts and tribunals are obliged to interpret all legislation, past and future alike, in light of the convention. In addition, the EU has stepped into the human rights arena with a draft 'fundamental charter', which would enshrine 50 basic rights. This document would seem to overlap with the ECHR, and confusion could arise over whether grievances should go to national courts, the European Court of Human Rights, or the EU's ECJ. The debate on the new charter is part of the wider debate on the constitutional future of European institutions.

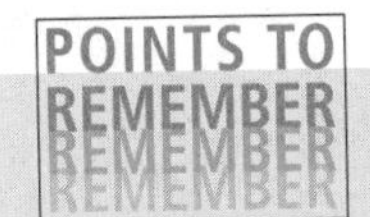

The European Convention on Human Rights (ECHR), now enacted in the Human Rights Act 1998

- Right to life
- Prohibition of torture, slavery and forced labour
- Right to liberty and security
- Right to a fair trial
- No punishment without lawful authority
- Right to respect for private and family life, home and correspondence
- Freedom of thought, conscience and religion
- Freedom of expression
- Freedom of assembly and association
- Right to marry
- Right to an effective remedy
- Prohibition of discrimination on any ground

The Act may be found at http://www.homeoffice.gov.uk/hract

IMPLICATIONS FOR BUSINESS OF THE HUMANS RIGHTS ACT 1998

1 All public bodies, including any company or organization performing a public role, can be sued for breach of the convention. Hence privatized utilities could be sued for breach of the Act, for example, by objectors claiming that proposed electricity pylons or airports interfered with home and family life.

2 Tribunals such as employment tribunals must take account of the Act, so that, in deciding whether a firm had acted fairly and reasonably with respect to an employee it had dismissed, the new right to privacy must be taken into account. Therefore companies need to review their policies on monitoring internet usage and surveillance of employee emails.

3 Businesses, as well as humans, have rights under the Act. When they appear before numerous regulatory bodies such as the Financial Services Authority and the Takeover Panel, new, more stringent standards of a fair and impartial hearing and respect for property must be observed. This far-reaching provision would affect, for example, decisions to withdraw or refuse licences in many different contexts, from pharmaceutical products to bus routes.

8.9 Conclusions

1. The legal environment of international business may be depicted as interacting spheres, consisting of national legal systems, regional authorities and international structures.
2. Most of the law affecting business transactions emanates from national legal authorities, but an increasing amount is international in scope, and, for EU member states, products of EU law-making.
3. Civil law and common law legal traditions have been established all over the globe, in many cases existing alongside non-Western legal systems, such as Islamic and Chinese.
4. EU law-making increasingly penetrates the national legal systems of EU member states, taking precedence when there is a conflict between EU and national laws.
5. While commercial transactions across national borders are governed by national law, harmonization of national laws through international convention and codification is moving forward apace, in recognition of the global interconnectedness of modern business.
6. Resolution of disputes in contract and tort can lead to lengthy (and costly) litigation. Settlement 'out of court', mediation and arbitration are alternatives to litigation.

7 Law-making and enforcement in the area of criminal law has increasingly encountered the globalization of criminal activity. Levels of corruption, which are higher in some countries than in others, can deter investors and create an uncertain legal environment.

8 International law focuses on relations between sovereign states, enshrined in treaties and conventions. Increasingly, nonetheless, individuals and organizations are being brought within their scope, in human rights and environmental law.

Review questions

1. What is meant by the interlocking spheres of national, regional and international law? Which is the most important in the business environment and why?
2. What are the differences between civil and criminal law?
3. What are the main functions of a national legal system?
4. How do codified legal systems differ from common law systems? What are the difficulties for a federal system such as the US?
5. What international conventions exist for harmonization of national trade law?
6. Distinguish between arm's length contracting and relational contracting. What are the consequences for joint ventures across the two traditions?
7. What factors account for the global growth in negligence and product liability claims?
8. List the factors involved in 'legal risk' for an international business.
9. What is the impact of treaty activity in environmental law on business operations?
10. Name at least three examples of human rights law. How does the law on human rights impact on business?

Assignments

1. 'For international business, while national legal systems provide the detailed legal framework as well as the structures for dispute settlement, significant areas of harmonization are facilitating cross-border transactions.' Assess the extent to which this is a fair statement of the changing international legal environment.

2 Assess the impact that the human rights law – now enshrined at international, regional and national levels – will have on the ways businesses operate.

Further reading

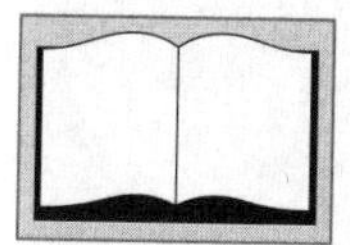

Adams, A. (1999) *Law for Business Students*, 2nd edn (London: Longman)

Akdeniz, Y., Walker, C. and Wall, D. (eds) (2000) *The Internet, Law and Society* (London: Longman)

Keenan, D. and Riches, S. (1998) *Business Law*, 5th edn (London: Pitman)

Schaffer, R., Earle, B. and Augusti, F. (1999) *International Business Law and its Environment*, 4th edn (Cincinnati: West)

Wallace, R. (1997) *International Law*, 3rd edn (London: Sweet & Maxwell)

Chapter

World trade and the international competitive environment

Outline of chapter

1. To appreciate the contributions of theories of international trade to an understanding of the ways in which companies, industries and nations compete in the global environment
2. To understand the rationale and mechanisms of national trade policies
3. To understand the evolution of the multilateral trading system, in terms of its structures, processes and issues to be resolved
4. To assess the impact of regional integration on the business environment

9.0 Introduction

Across the ages, businesses seeking markets have looked to trade beyond their home country. Growth in international trade has been a major contributor to the rise of the major industrialized countries, stretching back to the Industrial Revolution. Indeed, when we look at the flourishing trade between Asia and Europe as far back as the medieval era, we are tempted to think that globalization has been happening for a long time. However, both the volume and the patterns of trade between nations have changed greatly over the years. The post-war era has seen trade grow at a remarkable rate: between 1950 and 1998 the volume of world exports increased ×18, while production went up ×6.5. The forces propelling this growth are the industrialized economies of the three major trading areas, the Americas, Europe and Asia (see Figures 9.1 and 9.2). Expansion and deepening of trading relations, along with increased regional integration, have become important globalizing trends in the world economy.

This chapter aims to look first at why trade takes place, examining some of the theories which help to explain patterns of world trade. A second aim is to analyse the divergent views on the issues of free trade and protectionism. Finally, the chapter looks at the recent developments in the patterns of world trade, with the growth of regionalism and the changing role of the World Trade Organization (WTO). In respect of each of these aims, it should be borne in mind that world trade involves a number of different perspectives.

Figure 9.1 Leading exporters in world merchandise trade, 1998

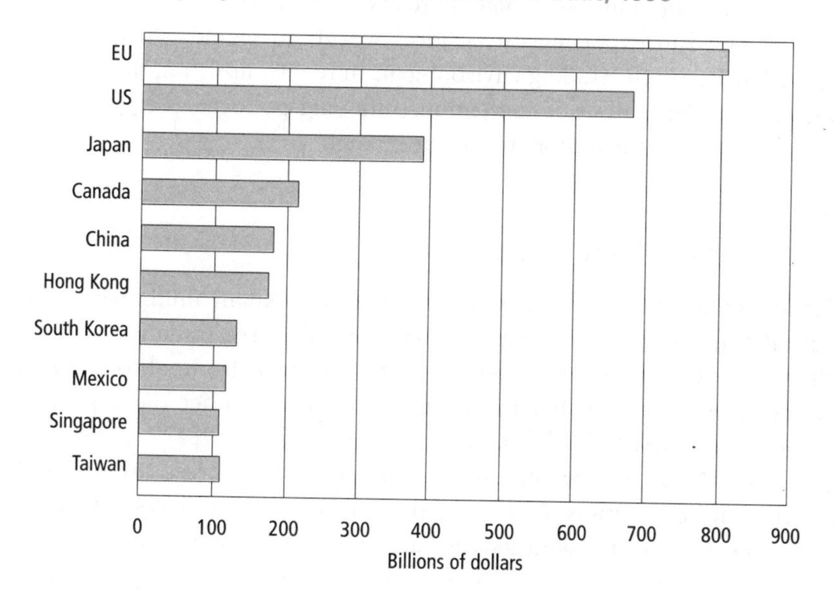

Source: World Trade Organization statistics (2000) at http://www.wto.org.

Figure 9.2 Leading importers in world merchandise trade, 1998

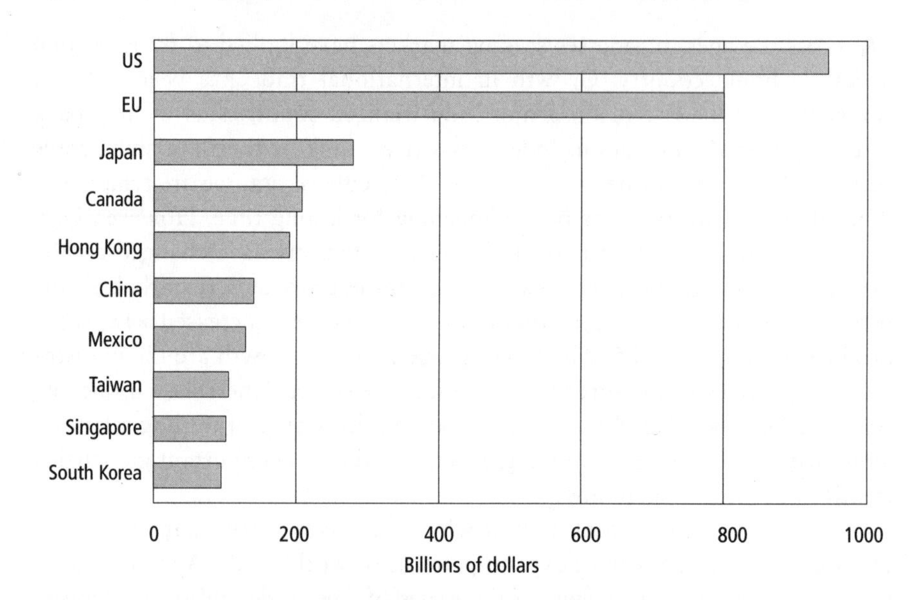

Source: World Trade Organization statistics (2000) at http://www.wto.org.

There is the perspective of the ndividual business wishing to expand beyond its home market. Then there are national governments focusing on national interests. Third, there are the consumers, looking for a variety of goods and services, both domestic and imported. And, of course, consumers are themselves workers in industries which, in today's world, are more likely than ever to be engaged in exporting. In an ideal world, all would benefit and none would lose out in the trading environment. In reality, however, the issues have become complex and even contentious, drawing political, social and ethical issues into the global competitive environment.

9.1 International trade theories

The first major theorist of international trade was Adam Smith, who believed that all countries benefit from unrestricted trade. Free trade is said to exist where citizens can sell abroad (export) and buy from abroad (import) without restrictions, or barriers by governments of either the exporting or importing country. In his book, *The Wealth of Nations* ([1776]1950), Smith argued in favour of the 'invisible hand' of market forces, as opposed to government intervention. When countries produce the products in which they are the most efficient producers, they are said to have an 'absolute advantage' in these products. A country may then sell these goods overseas and purchase goods from overseas which are produced more efficiently elsewhere. Thus, both countries benefit from trade.

9.1.1 The theory of comparative advantage

Starting from the principle of absolute advantage, David Ricardo ([1817]1973), writing some 40 years after Adam Smith, developed his theory of **comparative advantage.** His theory contends that, if Country A is an efficient producer of wheat and Country B an efficient producer of clocks, it pays A to purchase clocks from B, even if it could itself produce clocks more efficiently than B. According to Ricardo, if countries specialize in the industries in which they have comparative advantage, all will benefit from trade with each other, consumers in both countries enjoying more wheat and more clocks than they would without trade. According to Ricardo's theory, therefore, trade is not a 'zero-sum' game, that is, where one side's gain is the other's loss, but a 'positive-sum' game, that is, one in which all parties benefit.

In reality, most countries do not specialize in ways envisaged by Ricardo's theory. Furthermore, the model does not allow for the dynamic changes that trade brings about. Economists base the benefits of free trade on 'dynamic gains' that lead to economic growth. Free trade leads to a increase in a country's stock of resources, in terms of both increased capital from abroad and greater supplies of labour. In addition, efficiency may improve with large-scale production and improved technology. Opening up markets and creating more competition can provide an impetus for domestic companies to become more efficient. Trading patterns are also influenced by historical accident, government policies and the importance of transnational corporations (TNCs) in the global economy, all of which have been incorporated into newer trade theories. The impact of government policy can be seen in Case Study 9.1.

Case study 9.1 The impact of oil in world trade

The two oil crises of the 1970s, which saw the price of oil increase tenfold, left an enduring impact on patterns of world trade. In 1973, the Organization of Petroleum Exporting Countries (OPEC), the oil producers' cartel whose members controlled 85 per cent of the world's oil, decided to raise the price of oil fourfold and limit the amount of oil produced. OPEC member countries are Saudi Arabia, Iran, Venezuela, Iraq, the United Arab Emirates, Kuwait, Nigeria, Libya, Indonesia, Algeria and Qatar. The seemingly endless supply of cheap oil, which had fuelled industrial growth, mainly in the US, in the previous decades, came to an abrupt halt. Further price rises were to follow, culminating in the 1979 crisis brought about by the Islamic revolution in Iran and the Iran–Iraq war. For a time, OPEC countries grew rich from oil revenues, but their market dominance (and their oil wealth) was to decline in the 1980s, as demand fell. The crises led to world recession, the search for alternative energy supplies, reduced demand for OPEC oil and increased output by non-OPEC countries, notably Norway, Mexico and Russia.

In the period 1997–98, both OPEC and non-OPEC oil-producing countries saw prices fall as a result of the Asian financial

Case study 9.1 continued

crisis, down to $10 a barrel in 1998. Some, including Saudi Arabia and Iran, then decided to cut production drastically. By then, the Asian recovery was under way, demand surged and the result was a trebling of oil prices, bringing fears of another oil crisis. Could there be a repeat of the 1970s crises? The largest producer, Saudi Arabia, with the largest reserves, derives 75 per cent of its state revenues from oil. But, with one of the world's fastest-growing populations and a generous welfare state dating back to the oil-rich 70s, it now has domestic debt of $133 billion, more than 100 per cent of gross domestic product (GDP). When the price reached $30 a barrel, the Saudis agreed to release more oil, as fears of shortages spread across the US. Saudi Arabia depends on the US as its biggest market and also for its defence in the volatile Middle East. The world is less dependent on oil than it was in the 1970s – oil accounted for 53–4 per cent of energy needs at the start of the 1980s and is now 40 per cent. Gas and coal prices, unlike oil, have remained stable. It has been said that the world now runs on information, not oil, but business decisions based on $20 a barrel look very different if the price becomes $30 a barrel, or more. While a repeat of the 1970s oil price shocks is not on the cards, assumptions about a new era for the world economy may be premature.

Sources: Gause III, G.F. (2000) 'Saudi Arabia over a barrel', *Foreign Affairs*, 79(3): 80–95; Crooks, E., 'A barrel of woes', *Financial Times*, 26 January 2000; 'The end of opaque?', *The Economist*, 22 April 2000; 'Lifting the veil', *The Economist*, 8 July 2000; 'Oil's taxing times', *The Economist*, 16 September 2000.

Case questions

How does the price of oil affect world trade?
What is the role of the OPEC governments in influencing the price of oil?

OPEC's website is http://www.opec.org
The site has links to member countries

9.1.2 Newer trade theories

More recently, theorists have turned their attention to the growing importance of TNCs in international trade, taking into account the globalization of production and trade between affiliated companies (see Chapter 2). Krugman, in his book *Rethinking International Trade* (1994), emphasized features of the international economy such as increasing returns and imperfect competition. More precisely, he went on, 'conventional trade theory views world trade as taking place entirely in goods like wheat; new trade theory sees it as being largely in goods like aircraft' (Krugman, 1994, p. 1). For companies, innovation and economies of scale give what are called **first-mover advantages** to early entrants in a market. This lead cumulates over time, making it impossible for others to catch up. For firms able to benefit in this way, an increased share of global markets has led to oligopolistic behaviour in some industries, such as the aircraft industry. For countries, there are advantages to be gained from encouraging national firms which enjoy first-mover advantages. There are clear implications here that government intervention can play a role in promoting innovation and entrepreneurship, thereby boosting competitive advantage of nations.

9.1.3 Porter's theory of competitive advantage

In his book, *The Competitive Advantage of Nations*, published originally in 1990, Michael Porter (1998b) developed a theory of national **competitive advantage**. His considerable research, which is set out in the book, attempts to find out why some countries are more successful than others. Each nation, he says, has four broad attributes that shape its national competitive environment. They are:

- *Factor conditions*. The nation's position in factors of production, such as skilled labour or infrastructure, necessary to compete in a given industry
- *Demand conditions*. The nature of home demand for the industry's product or service
- *Related and supporting industries*. The presence or absence in the nation of supplier industries and related industries that are internationally competitive
- *Firm strategy, structure and rivalry*. The conditions in the nation governing how companies are created, organized and managed, and the nature of domestic rivalry. (Porter, 1998b, p. 71)

The four attributes, or determinants, form a diamond shape, as shown in Figure 9.3. Porter stresses that the four determinants are interdependent. Favourable demand conditions, for example, will contribute to competitive advantage only in an environment in which firms are able and willing to respond. Advantage based on only one or two determinants may suffice in natural resource-dependent industries, or those with lower technological input, but to sustain advantage in the modern knowledge-intensive industries, advantages throughout the diamond are necessary. Porter adds that there are two additional variables in his theory. They are chance and government. Chance can open up unexpected opportunities in a variety of ways: new inventions, external political developments and shifts in foreign market demand. (The fall of communism and the opening up of Central and Eastern Europe is an example.) Government policies which Porter highlights include a strong antitrust policy, which encourages domestic rivalry, and investment in education, which generates knowledge resources.

Figure 9.3 Porter's diamond: the determinants of national advantage

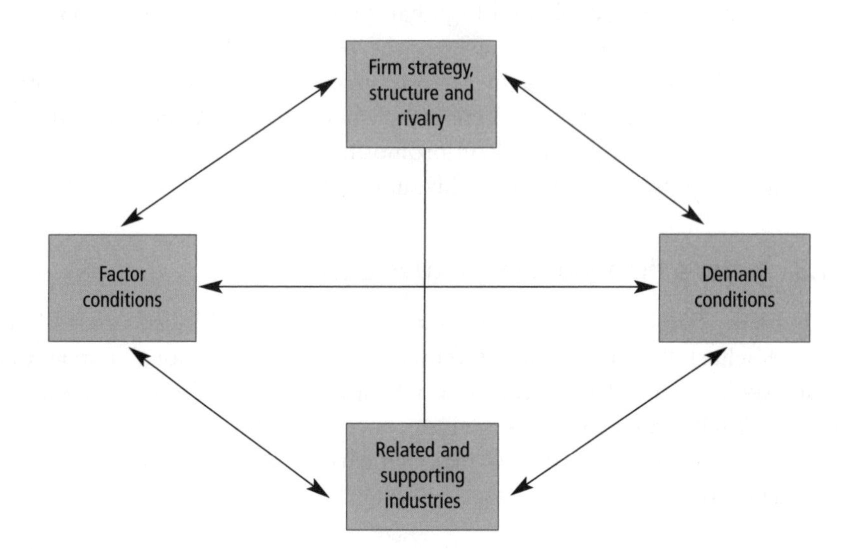

Source: Porter, M. (1998b) *The Competitive Advantage of Nations* (Basingstoke: Macmillan – now Palgrave) p. 72 (reproduced with permission).

Minifile

DIAMOND CONDITIONS OF THE JAPANESE VCR INDUSTRY

Access to specialized inputs (factors)

- Japanese manufacturers had prior expertise in audio and video technologies through the production of home audio equipment, tape recorders and TVs
- Pool of talented electrical engineers
- Internal funding within diversified companies and low-cost loans from banks allowed large-scale capital investment.

Japanese home demand

- High demand for compact, high-performance units from sophisticated domestic buyers.

Local Japanese rivalry

- Fierce domestic competition between the VHS (JVC) and Beta (Sony) camps led to constant innovation and upgrading.

Related and supporting industries

- VCR makers worked closely with parts makers to develop high-precision, high-performance parts
- Competitive Japanese suppliers of magnetic heads, tuners, tape decks, volume regulators, other electronic parts, machine tools and robotics.

Source: Porter, M., Takeuchi, H. and Sakakibara, M. (2000) *Can Japan Compete?* (Basingstoke: Macmillan – now Palgrave) p. 137 (reprinted with permission).

Porter emphasizes that the diamond is a tool not just for explaining past competitive advantage, but also for predicting how industries will evolve in the future. The theory is useful in demonstrating the interaction between different determinants of national competitive advantage, but it probably underemphasizes world economic integration. For example, both capital and managers are now likely to be mobile. Similarly, related and supporting industries are increasingly internationalized, thanks largely to cheaper transport, reductions in import duties and the advances in communications technology. By the 1990s, an estimated one-third of all manufacturers' trade involved parts and components (World Bank, 2000a). Business-to-business e-commerce has further opened up opportunities for sourcing components and materials globally. Growth in the export of commercial services is similarly linked to e-commerce developments.

Hirst and Thompson (1999) remind us of the essential difference between comparative advantage, which pertains to the national *economy*, and competitive advantage, which pertains to the *companies* that make it up. Competitive advantage in areas such as manufacturing and services can be deliberately created and maintained (through government policy and corporate strategy), whereas comparative advantage obtains where natural factor endowments are paramount, as in agricultural and extractive industries (Hirst and Thompson, 1999; Gilpin, 2000). Hirst and Thompson go on to suggest that, on the whole,

Minifile

GLOBAL COMPETITIVENESS RANKINGS

Two 'league tables' of competitiveness are compiled annually. They are the *Global Competitiveness Report*, published by the World Economic Forum (WEF) in Geneva, and the *World Competitiveness Yearbook*, published by the International Institute for Management Development (IMD) in Lausanne. They use somewhat different indicators and arrive at somewhat different rankings. The WEF is weighted towards economic indicators, including economic creativity, while the IMD criteria are broader, including quality of life and cultural values.

Perhaps surprisingly, the US, ranked first in 1999, slipped to second in the global competitiveness table in 2000, behind Finland, home of Nokia, the world's largest mobile phone manufacturer. In WEF's other indexes, growth competitiveness and economic creativity, the US still came top. One notable discrepancy between the two league tables is that the UK is ranked 8 by WEF and only 15 by IMD.

Rankings for 2000:

	Global Competitiveness Index (WEF)		*World Competitiveness Scoreboard (IMD)*
1	Finland	1	US
2	US	2	Singapore
3	Germany	3	Finland
4	The Netherlands	4	The Netherlands
5	Switzerland	5	Switzerland
6	Denmark	6	Luxembourg
7	Sweden	7	Ireland
8	UK	8	Germany
9	Singapore	9	Sweden
10	Australia	10	Iceland
11	Canada	11	Canada
12	Belgium	12	Denmark
13	Austria	13	Australia
14	Japan	14	Hong Kong
15	France	15	UK

Sources: World Economic Forum and Harvard Institute for International Development (2000) *Global Competitiveness Report 2000* (Geneva: WEF); International Institute for Management Development (2000) *World Competitiveness Yearbook* (Lausanne: IMD).

it makes more sense to speak of companies, rather than countries, competing with each other. Countries do compete in, for example, attracting foreign direct investment (FDI), but here, as was seen in Chapter 2, location advantages often focus on particular regions and cities, rather than on whole countries. And the competition is based on many aspects of the business environment, such as social and cultural values, which are not measurable in the same ways that relative cost structure, productivity and exchange rates are measurable (Hirst and Thompson, 1999, p. 122). Nonetheless, international competitiveness 'league tables' do attempt to rank countries (see Minifile).

WWW
WEBALERT

Highlights of global competitiveness league tables may be found on the following websites:
http://www.imd.ch/wcy/wcy/cfm
http://www.weforum.org/

9.1.4 Product life cycle theory

Raymond Vernon's theory of the international product life cycle explains trade from the perspective of the firm. Vernon's theory dates from the 1960s, a period when, owing to the size and prosperity of the American consumer market, a new consumer product was likely to begin life in the US. In Phase I, the firm produces only for the American market. Products which began life in this way include televisions, fridges and washing machines. In this early phase, demand at home leads to expansion, and demand overseas, which is limited to high-income groups, is satisfied by exports. As the market matures in Phase II, and overseas demand grows, foreign producers begin to produce for their own home markets, limiting the appeal of US imports. At the same time, cost considerations take on greater importance, and the product becomes more standardized. US producers are likely to shift production overseas, first to the higher income markets (such as Europe). In Phase III, producers in these countries, where labour costs are lower than in the US, will begin exporting to other countries, and even to the US (Phase IV). Finally, in Phase V, production shifts to low-cost environments, such as Asian industrializing economies. Over the cycle, production has moved from the US to other advanced countries and finally to developing countries.

The product life cycle model assumed that most innovations would originate in the US, a view which reflected US manufacturing dominance in consumer durables up to the 1970s. While many products did follow the pattern described by Vernon, the model has become less valid as globalization has evolved. Global companies with dispersed production (as discussed in Chapter 2) may use components from various locations and choose yet another for assembling the final product. Because of the rapid pace of technological innovation and short product life cycles, a company in industries

Figure 9.4 Vernon's product life cycle theory

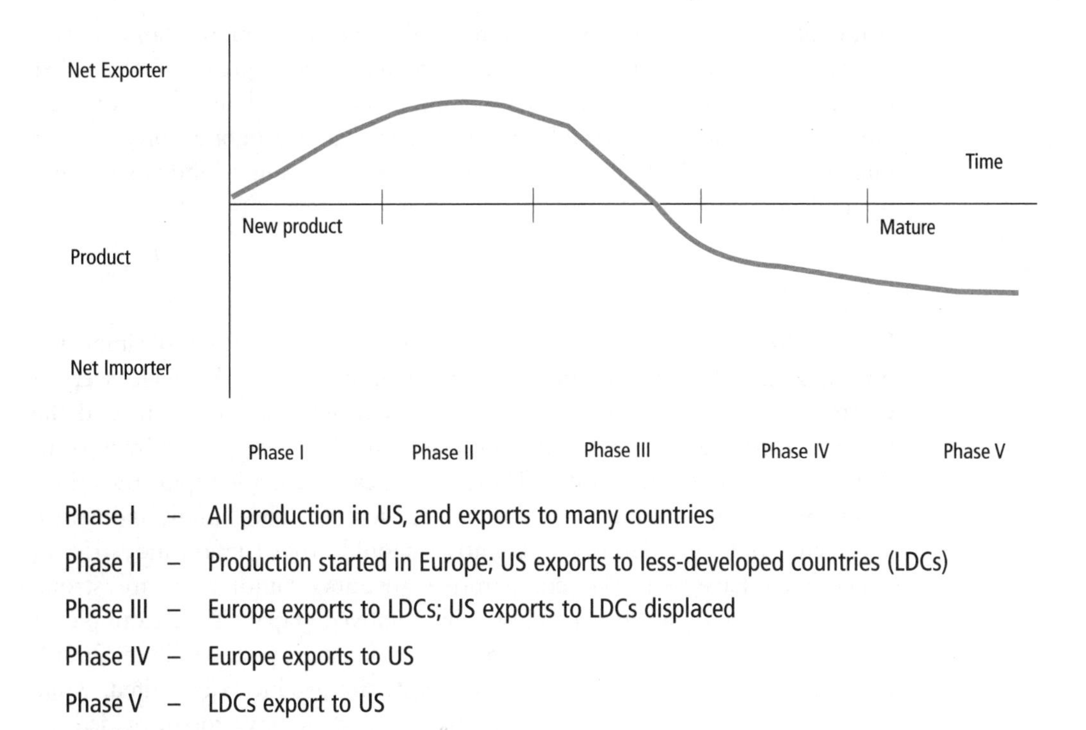

Source: Reprinted by permission of Harvard Business School Press, from Wells, L.T. (ed.) (1972) *The Product Life Cycle and International Trade* (Boston, MA) p. 15. Copyright © 1972 by the Harvard Business School Publishing Corporation, all rights reserved.

such as consumer electronics may well introduce a new product simultaneously in a number of markets, wiping out the leads and lags between markets. (This point will be explored further in Chapter 10.) The model is useful in explaining production patterns for some types of products, such as standardized consumer goods, but is less useful in predicting future patterns, especially in industries dominated by a few global players.

The Institute of International Economics website is http://www.iie.org
It contains numerous resources and links for all trade issues

A comprehensive website on US trade issues is http://www.mac.doc.gov/
This is the US Department of Commerce Market Access and Compliance site

The International Trade Administration of the US Department of Commerce also has an extensive website at http://www.ita.doc.gov/

The ITA offers an information service on 'big emerging markets' at http://www.ita.doc/gov/bems

9.2 Trade policy and national priorities

National economic prosperity for almost all countries is more than ever tied in with international trade. However, benefits are not spread evenly, either between countries or between groups within individual countries. Governments face innumerable political, social and economic pressures to intervene in trade. In this section we look at the reasoning behind government policy. The major policy areas are listed below:

Promoting industrialization

Industrialization may be promoted by restricting the flow of imported products, thereby encouraging domestic manufacturing. We have seen in Chapter 3 that industrialization in many countries, such as Japan and the newly industrialized countries of Southeast Asia, has been guided by government, through industrial policy. These countries have made rapid transitions from mainly agricultural to industrial economies. The 'infant industries' argument holds that developing countries should protect infant industries in which they have potential comparative advantage until they are strong enough to survive when protections are removed. Japan is an example of both successful infant industry support and industrial policy (Gilpin, 2000). In the cases of Japan and South Korea, domestic producers benefited, while for Singapore and other tiger economies, foreign direct investors provided the impetus of development. Industrialization may focus on **import substitution**, that is, producing goods for domestic consumption which otherwise would have been imported. Domestic industries nurtured through protective measures in this way do not always become competitive in world markets. Export-led development, by contrast, focuses on growth in export-oriented goods. Industrialization in Taiwan and South Korea has taken this route.

Protecting employment

By restricting imports, governments aim to safeguard domestic jobs. However, the situation is seldom as simple as it seems. A common fear of US workers in manufacturing jobs is that their jobs have gone to lower paid overseas workers. Work in lower skilled jobs, as in the textile industry, is particularly vulnerable to being lost to low-cost imports. However, proponents of trade liberalization would argue that protectionist measures are damaging to the economy in the long term. They argue that restricting imports may lead to retaliation, so that a country's exporters in profitable sectors may suffer, causing job losses in those sectors. Import restrictions may also have a dampening effect on *foreign* workers' incomes, which translates into a decrease in jobs in domestic export industries. Workers in industrialized countries who are displaced by global competitive forces are usually those without the skills to benefit from the newer job opportunities. Payment of

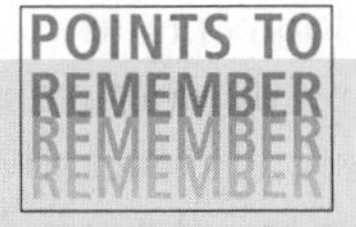

Free trade and protectionism: the pros and cons

'Free trade' as a term is misleading. There has never been 'free' trade in the sense of no barriers at all. 'Trade liberalization' is therefore more accurate, to indicate measures *towards* free trade

Those in favour argue:

- Free trade benefits all countries
- Capitalism is driven by competition. A country risks falling behind if it cuts itself off from competition
- Costs of protecting industries can be high. Protecting *infant* industries can be justified, but too often protection is for *senile* industries

Opponents of free trade argue:

- Protection of national industries promotes independence and security
- Levels of domestic employment can only be maintained through protectionist measures
- National industries, if aided by government, can compete globally, increasing national wealth. After all, other countries will aid *their* industries

unemployment and other benefits for displaced workers fall on the public purse, and whole regions can suffer decline as a result. In the long term, it could be argued, governments need to look at the education and training needs of the economy to enhance competitive advantage. Nonetheless, protectionist pressures are very strong: special interests' regional strongholds are often effective in mobilizing political support.

Protecting consumers

Conventional wisdom holds that consumers benefit from free trade, in that competition in markets brings down prices and increases choice. More recently, consumer interest has shifted somewhat, to focus on issues of health and safety. The industrialization and globalization of the food chain have resulted in agricultural produce and livestock being transported hundreds, even thousands, of miles to markets. Contamination such as bovine spongiform encephalopathy (BSE) in beef can thus have global ramifications. Governments have at their disposal a variety of regulatory measures on consumer products such as food and medicines, whether produced at home or abroad. Often they target imported products through an outright ban, or through labelling and packaging requirements. Restrictions raise controversy if they are perceived as simply a device for controlling imports under the guise of safety. However, the issue is often not straightforward. In the area of new developments in food production, scientific evidence may be incomplete or apparently conflicting, and consumer perceptions may understandably be cautious, or even negative. Hormone-treated beef from the US was banned in the EU, but found not to be in breach of WTO rules. The use of genetically modified (GM) foods, also originating in the US, while not totally banned, is under consideration, and is resisted by many European consumers. For governments, it is therefore difficult to distinguish genuine safety concerns from protectionist pressures. As will be seen later in this chapter, WTO rules focus on the product, not on its production methods, but this stance is one of the current controversial issues facing the WTO.

Promoting national interests

National interest covers a number of considerations. First, it is thought that the strategic sensitivity of defence industries dictates that domestic suppliers are preferable to foreign ones, and thus should be protected. The strategic necessity argument can be extended to a great number of products. It was used to provide federal funding for the semiconductor industry in the US in the 1990s, as semiconductors are crucial to defence systems. Food production is one of the most heavily protected industries, because of the strategic importance of safeguarding food supply and also agricultural employment. On this reasoning, subsidies and import restrictions have long benefited Japanese farmers, while Japanese consumers have paid well above world prices for their food. These barriers are only slowly coming down.

Second, national governments have evolved strategic trade policies, by which they target industries in which national competitive advantage can be gained. Strategic trade policy holds that governments can assist their own firms in particular industries to gain competitive advantage. This theory mainly applies to oligopolistic industries such as the aerospace industry, in which the US helped Boeing by providing it with lucrative defence contracts, while European governments helped Airbus through subsidies.

Third, trade policies may be linked to foreign policy objectives, as was clearly demonstrated during the cold war, when trade followed political and military alliances. Government overseas aid packages to developing countries may be tied to trade. Trade policies are often based on historical relationships between countries, such as those between the former colonial powers of Europe and their former colonies. The dispute between the EU and US over banana trade has its roots in the preferential treatment that former colonies in the Caribbean have continued to receive, which, the US has argued, contravenes WTO rules (see Case Study 9.2). The US has used trade sanctions against Iran and Libya, both considered dangerous to US national interests. Although sanctions are generally thought to be ineffective, it is estimated that the US has imposed sanctions 61 times on 35 countries (Gilpin, 2000). A controversial piece of US trade legislation has been the Helms-Burton Act, under which US

Why governments intervene in trade

- To nurture infant industries and promote industrialization
- To protect domestic employment, especially in low-skill jobs, from low-cost imports
- To protect consumers from unsafe products
- To safeguard national interests:
  - through government purchasing in strategic industries
  - through strategic trade policy for globally competitive industries
  - in pursuit of foreign policy
  - in maintaining national culture and identity

firms can sue (in US courts) foreign firms which deal with Cuba, which has been subject to a US trade embargo since the communist revolution of 1959. Among trading partners of the US there has been much hostility to this statute. A thaw in US–Cuba trade relations has been evident from 2000, with relaxation of the embargo on shipments of food and medicines to Cuba.

Fourth, national interest concerns the maintaining of national culture and identity, for which cultural products such as literature, film and music are particularly important. The growth of the internet and global media have led to fears of cultural globalization, prompting some national authorities to limit foreign content and foreign ownership in these sectors.

9.3 Tools of governmental trade policy

Government policies affect trade in numerous ways, both directly and indirectly. Of direct impact is the manipulation of exchange rates. Devaluing a country's currency will have the immediate effect of making exports cheaper and imports more expensive (see Chapter 11). However, governments now have less room to manipulate rates in increasingly interlinked currency markets. Similarly, most governments are now party to multilateral and regional trading arrangements which curtail their ability to control trade. Therefore we will look at government policy options in the context of changing global and regional contexts. The traditional tools for controlling trade are tariffs, quotas, subsidies and other non-tariff barriers to trade.

The classic tool of trade policy is the **tariff**, or duty payable on imported goods. When we think of protectionism, that is, the deliberate policy to favour home producers, we think naturally of tariff barriers. The tariff raises the price of an imported product, thereby benefiting domestic producers of the same product. Japanese whisky producers have been protected in this way, by huge import duties levied on foreign whisky. The sums collected also swell government coffers. The main losers are the consumers, who pay higher prices for the imported product. While tariffs on manufactured goods have diminished dramatically, thanks to the multilateral GATT (to be discussed later), tariffs on agricultural products are still common.

The **import quota** limits the quantity of an imported product that can legally enter a country. Licences may be issued annually to a limited number of firms, each of which must stay within the amounts specified in its import licence. Limits are set so as to allow only a portion of the market to foreign goods, thus protecting the market share of domestic producers. Restricting supply in this way is likely to result in higher prices for consumers. Import quotas are sometimes evaded by companies shipping their goods via other countries with quota to spare when their home country's quota is used up. An exporting firm may ultimately set up production in a country to avoid the imposition of quotas.

An alternative to the import quota is the **voluntary export restraint** (VER), which shifts the onus on the exporting country to limit its exports, or possibly risk the imposition of quotas or tariffs. A leading example of the VER has been Japanese car exports to the US. In the 1980s, when the Japanese motor industry was growing apace and making rapid inroads in the American market, the US government persuaded Japan to agree to a VER. A way round these restrictions is to set up local production, which Japanese manufacturers have done in the US and other markets. The protectionist urge, however, is still strong, as governments have imposed **local content requirements** to ensure that local component suppliers gain. Japanese motor manufacturers have responded by locating associated Japanese component manufacturers near to assembly plants in the overseas location, thus facilitating just-in-time operations and maintaining high local content.

Government **subsidies** are payments from public funds to domestic producers. For advocates of strategic trade policy, the line of reasoning is that the extra funds will boost the local company's competitive position in the global market. Funds in the form of research and development (R&D) grants are intended to give competitive advantage to the local producer over foreign competitors. Export subsidies are a means of ensuring that domestic producers can sell abroad at competitive prices. In general, subsidies benefit domestic producers by enabling them to compete with low-cost imports in the home market, and by helping them to compete in export markets. Besides direct funding, there are other types of subsidies, including loans at preferential rates and tax concessions. Countries in the 'strong-state' tradition, such as France, Germany, and other Continental states, have tended towards higher state subsidies, whereas those in the more laissez-faire, 'weak-state' tradition, such as the US and UK, have tended towards lower subsidies. However, in the US, individual state governments have provided lavish incentives to German and Japanese car assembly and component plants (Dicken, 1998, pp. 272, 333).

Advocates of trade liberalization criticize subsidies on several grounds. Subsidies work against a 'level playing field' for trade, as unsubsidized

Figure 9.5 Producer support estimate for agriculture (per farmer) 1996–98

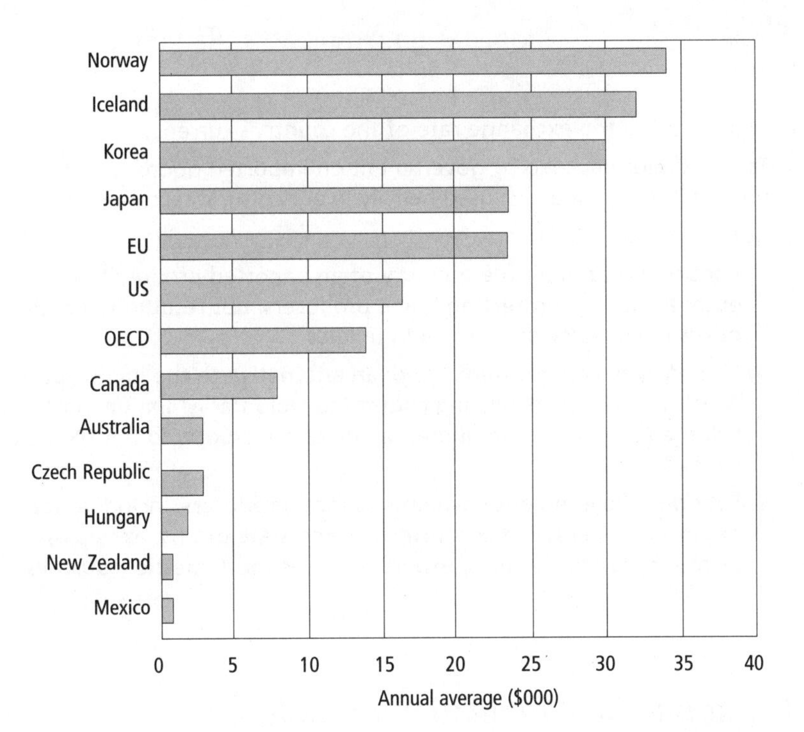

Source: Financial Times, 19 November 1999.

foreign firms argue that they face unfair competition. And, although they aim to increase the competitiveness of domestic firms, they do not encourage local firms to be more efficient. Often, they protect inefficient producers (and jobs), creating a culture of dependence on subsidies. Agriculture is a traditionally heavily subsidized sector (see Figure 9.5). The EU, through the Common Agricultural Policy (CAP), has provided substantial subsidies for farmers since 1962, creating considerable trade friction with other nations. The extent of EU support has diminished in the 1990s, but agriculture continues to be a highly politically sensitive sector.

As trade in the post-war period has expanded, tariff barriers have generally come down, largely as a result of multilateral initiatives (discussed below). On the other hand, many non-tariff barriers, described above, have proliferated, in both developed and developing countries. Trade disputes between countries have led to a good deal of tension in international relations. This trend reflects the fact that trade issues, as the discussion above has shown, have become enmeshed in numerous other areas of policy, including industry, investment and employment. At the same time, national trade policy, once seen as a defining attribute of the nation-state, is becoming embedded in an international regulatory framework We look next at the changing institutional environment of trade at international level.

Tools of government trade policy

- Manipulating the exchange rate of the country's currency
- Tariffs: duties imposed by government on imported goods, which protect home producers; used heavily in agricultural sector
- Non-tariff barriers:
  - *Import quotas:* limit the quantity of an imported product that can enter a country, protecting home producers, but resulting in higher prices to consumers; common in textiles
  - *Voluntary export restraint (VER):* an alternative to the import quota, which obliges the exporting country to 'voluntarily' limit exports, or risk the imposition of a quota; Japanese car exports to the US are an example
  - *Subsidies:* government payments to local producers, including loans at preferential rates, tax concessions and state grants; examples: price support for farmers; export subsidies for domestic industries

9.4 International regulation of trade

Institutional arrangements put in place in the immediate aftermath of the Second World War have played a major role in establishing a global trading order. The preceding era, scarred by the Great Depression of 1929–30, had seen protectionism and a decline in world trade. Under the **Bretton Woods** system designed at a conference of the allied nations in 1944, exchange rate stability would be achieved by pegging every currency to gold or the US dollar (see Chapter 11). Negotiators also laid plans for an international trade organization (ITO) to bring down tariff barriers, but the charter eventually drawn up in 1948 met with little enthusiasm from nations, still reluctant to endorse free trade. Instead, a more modest set of proposals for a weaker institutional framework was formulated, in the **General Agreement on Tariffs and Trade (GATT).** Under GATT successive rounds of negotiations have brought about global trade liberalization, leading to the establishment in 1994 of the **World Trade Organization (WTO),** reminiscent of the stronger body envisaged in the early days after the war. The WTO now has over 140 member states. Two other institutions set up as a result of post-war initiatives were the International Monetary Fund (IMF) and the International Bank for Reconstruction and Development (the World Bank) (discussed in Chapter 11). The Bretton Woods system disintegrated in the early 1970s, bringing about a resurgence of protectionism. The period 1945–70 has been called the 'golden age of capitalism' (Kitson and Michie, 1995).

The WTO website is http://www.wto.org
The International Monetary Fund (IMF) website is http://www.imf.org
The World Bank's website is http://www.worldbank.org

9.4.1 GATT principles

GATT provided the principles and foundation for the development of a global trading system which were carried forward into the WTO. Perhaps the most important of these is non-discrimination, or the **most-favoured-nation (MFN)** principle. There are two aspects to this principle: (1) favourable tariff treatment negotiated with one country will be extended to similar goods from all countries; (2) under the principle of 'national treatment', imported goods are treated for all purposes in the same way as domestic goods of the same type. MFN status is negotiated between countries, and while it is the norm among trading partners, there are exceptions. US legislation has linked MFN treatment with human rights record. Because of its poor human rights record, China was granted only temporary MFN status from 1980 onwards, which was renewed annually. Unconditional MFN status came in 2000, paving the way for WTO membership.

Other GATT principles include reciprocity, requiring tariff reductions by one country to be matched by its trading partners; and transparency, ensuring that the underlying aims of all trade measures are clear. The principle of fairness allows a country which has suffered from unfair trading practices by a trading partner to take protectionist measures against that country. Defining fair practice is at the heart of many trade disputes, as countries naturally have differing perspectives on what is and is not fair. An example is **dumping**, or the sale of goods abroad at below the price charged for comparable goods in the producing country. The GATT anti-dumping agreement of 1994 allows anti-dumping duties to be imposed on the exporting country by the importing country, in order to protect local producers from unfair competition.

The Uruguay Round, culminating in the 1994 GATT, laid the groundwork for future trade liberalization, while allowing countries to take limited steps to safeguard national industries. It resulted in worldwide tariff reductions of about 40 per cent on manufactured goods. Less spectacularly, it made strides in the more difficult areas of reducing trade barriers in agricultural products and textiles. It also initiated agreements on intellectual property rights and services, both crucial areas in growing world trade. Finally, the GATT 1994 created the WTO as its successor institution.

9.4.2 WTO and the regulation of world trade

Whereas GATT in 1947 created only a weak institutional framework, the WTO, which came into being in 1995, was designed on a firmer legal footing, with a stronger rule-governed orientation. This approach is reflected in its organizational structure. A Ministerial Conference, consisting of trade ministers of all member states is the main policy-making body, which meets every two years. A Dispute Settlement Body oversees the dispute settlement procedure for specific trade disputes between countries. This new legal procedure for resolving disputes marks a sharp departure from the GATT procedure, which had no power of enforcement.

The WTO's dispute settlement procedure aims to resolve trade disputes through impartial panels before they escalate into damaging trade wars in which countries take unilateral action against each other. A country which feels it has suffered because of another's breach of trading rules may apply to the WTO, which appoints an impartial panel for hearing the case within a specified timetable. A country found to be in breach of trade rules by a panel may appeal to the Appellate Body. If it is again found to be in the wrong, the WTO may authorize the country whose trade has suffered as a result, to impose retaliatory trade sanctions. In the long-running dispute between the US and EU over banana exports from the Caribbean, the WTO authorized sanctions by the US in 1999. Much has been at stake in terms of wider trading relations (see Case Study 9.2).

For the WTO's procedure to succeed, countries must adhere to its decisions, even when they disagree with them. All countries enjoy a recognized right to safeguard national interests, but this principle, as well as the interpretation of WTO rules themselves, is subject to considerable latitude in interpretation. If countries impose unilateral sanctions, bypassing WTO, then WTO procedures, and the authority that underlies them, could be eroded. The US law known as Section 301 is such a provision. Originally enacted in the Trade Act 1974, it authorizes the US to retaliate unilaterally against other countries (as opposed to specific companies) which it judges are violating a GATT provision or unfairly restricting the import of US goods or services. Section 301 was strengthened in 1988, authorizing the US Trade Representative to identify 'priority trade practices' of other countries that pose the greatest barriers to US trade, and to single out particular countries with a history of trade discrimination. Under this legislation a country could lose access to the entire US market, not merely that of the offending product. The legislation has been criticized for its aggressive unilateral approach which, some argue, is in breach of WTO rules (Sell, 2000). In February 2000, a WTO panel ruled, in what was seen by a number of developing countries as an unsatisfactory decision, that Section 301 is not incompatible with WTO rules, so long as the US refrained from taking unilateral action.

Case study 9.2 The US–EU dispute over bananas

The damaging trade dispute between the US and EU over banana imports has threatened to undermine both US–EU trade relations and the WTO's dispute settlement procedure. The roots of the dispute go back to the Lomé Convention, an agreement between the EU and former colonies of the African, Caribbean and Pacific regions (the ACP countries), to provide trade and aid. Most of the 71 members are developing countries. The convention, renegotiated in 2000, is now shifting gradually to free trade agreements, in order to come into line with WTO's trading rules. The immediate cause of the dispute was an agreement signed in 1993, which gave the ACP countries preferential treatment in EU markets, which represent 40 per cent of the global market for bananas. This preferential regime was objected to by the US and Latin American banana-producing countries, which alleged discrimination. (Although the US grows no bananas, a major owner and producer, Chiquita Brands, is based in the US.) Latin American bananas are much cheaper than those from the small plantations of the Caribbean, where cost of production is about three times higher.

A WTO panel found against the EU in 1997. The EU modified the banana regime, but the US still objected, claiming the right to impose trade sanctions amounting to $520 million to a range of products, from bubble bath to chandeliers. The WTO, while it authorized retaliatory sanctions of $200 million in 1999, ruled that the US had violated international trade rules by imposing sanctions unilaterally. The EU Commission then devised another set of proposals to open the market gradually. From the US perspective, the EU seemed to be using delaying tactics. The EU, on the other hand, has had the difficult task of balancing protection of ACP countries, where many communities are economically dependent on banana exports, against compliance with WTO obligations. The bitter dispute with the US has tested the relatively new WTO dispute settlement process to the limit. A compromise agreement was negotiated in 2001, although it is likely that opposition to the deal from vested interests will rumble on.

Sources: de Jonquières, G., 'Trade goes bananas', *Financial Times*, 26 January 1999; de Jonquières, G., 'A partnership in peril', *Financial Times*, 8 March 1999; Smith, M., 'Brussels backing for new banana regime', *Financial Times*, 5 October 2000.

Case questions

What are the essential elements of the banana dispute and why did it become so protracted and so bitter?
What are the implications for the dispute resolution procedure in future?

WWW WEBALERT

The website on EU–ACP co-operation is http://www.ue-acp.org

9.5 Issues facing the WTO

Although only six years old, the WTO has made a dramatic impact in focusing international attention on issues of world trade and it has also sparked controversy. Most members anticipate a new round of multilateral trade negotiations, but there are major policy issues on which they diverge sharply. These include labour standards, environmental protection and competition policy.

9.5.1 Labour standards and environmental protection

Awareness of humanitarian and environmental goals has impacted on both companies and governments. But whether trade policy should take these areas into account has become a controversial issue. Those in favour of trade liberalization argue that these issues, important as they are, should be kept separate from trade and that bringing them into trade negotiations will increase protectionism. Burma, which is a WTO member, has drawn condemnation from the ILO and other bodies for its persistent use of forced labour. In 1997, the US banned investment in Burma, but the US remains the biggest market for its exports, particularly clothing – up 400 per cent between 1997 and 1999. The US could not impose restrictions on Burma's clothing exports without violating WTO rules as they now stand. Human rights groups have pressed for a 'social clause' in WTO trade agreements to allow a ban on both trade and investment against Burma.

Environmentalists argue that if issues such as global warming and protection of the rain forests are not brought into the equation, commercial goals will win out and the environment will suffer. Trade unionists in industrialized economies, fearful of job losses, argue for the inclusion of labour standards in trade policy. Moreover, labour standards, including practices such as child labour, have come to be included in human rights principles generally. These issues have crystallized over China's application for WTO membership, as shown in Case Study 9.3: its growth as a trading power suggests it can no longer be left out, but its poor human rights record has been a major hurdle to smooth entry.

The WTO's planned ministerial meeting in Seattle, USA in December 1999 had to be abandoned in the midst of heated divisions among the delegates within the meeting and violent demonstrations by anti-globalization protesters on the streets of Seattle. The meeting was intended to initiate a new trade liberalization round. Areas targeted were services and agriculture, which had been brought onto the agenda in the Uruguay Round, but on which progress had been limited. Divisions emerged between the triad powers – the US, EU and Japan – and the many developing countries who are the majority of the WTO's members. While industrialized countries urged core labour standards and environmental policy to be linked with trade policy, developing countries argued that these are a pretext for legitimizing

Case study 9.3 China and the WTO

China is the world's most populous country and seventh largest economy. Since liberalization reforms began in 1979, its exports have climbed on average 15 per cent per annum, making it now the world's fifth largest exporter. While it would seem obvious on the surface that China should be within the WTO, there have been a number of hurdles to overcome. The main obstacles have been its closed economy; protected state industries and agriculture sectors; less than transparent legal and administrative structures; and poor human rights record. After 14 years of negotiations, agreements were reached in 2000 with the US and with the EU, paving the way for WTO membership. Under these agreements, China is committed to:

- Cut average tariffs to 17 per cent
- Reduce the tariff on vehicles from 80–100 per cent to 25 per cent by 2006
- Open up its telecommunications markets by allowing 49 per cent investment by foreign telecoms providers, increasing to 50 per cent after two years
- Cut tariffs on agricultural products to 14.5–15 per cent.

The dismantling of China's protectionist regime should quicken the pace of foreign investment, possibly doubling FDI over the next five years. According to forecasts, exports could double by 2005, adding a percentage point to economic growth for the next five years. Opening markets, and the economic changes they entail, will have deeper effects on China's society which are less easy to predict, as the painful adjustments are likely to increase unemployment. Moreover, China's joining the WTO has come at a time of challenges for the organization itself, which is becoming embroiled in areas once considered the preserve of domestic policy, such as labour standards, intellectual property rights, competition policy and food safety rules. The real progress of trade liberalization and the integration of China into WTO structures is likely to be a longer and more painstaking process of accommodation than envisaged by the optimists at the time of the breakthrough agreements.

Sources: 'China and the WTO', *The Economist*, 20 November 1999; Kynge, J. and Hill, A., 'Foreign investors see safer future', *Financial Times*, 16 November 1999; de Jonquières, Guy, 'Beijing's hard bargain', *Financial Times*, 26 May 2000; Kynge, J., 'Deal with Brussels clears way for China's WTO membership, *Financial Times*, 20 May 2000.

Case questions

What are the implications of China joining the WTO for international export business? What are the doubts about China's ability to deliver on trade liberalization commitments?

WWW WEBALERT

The Chinese Ministry of Foreign Trade & Economic Co-operation is at http://www.moftec.gov.cn/moftec/main.html

The Business Coalition for US–China Trade is at http://www.business4chinatrade.org/

protectionist measures against their exports. Demonstrations in the streets reminded everyone that global economic integration, while it was previously seen as an issue mainly between governments, is now seen as one mobilizing ordinary consumers, worried about issues such as food safety. Non-governmental organizations (NGOs) have been instrumental in vocalizing environmental and human rights issues and the 1999 meeting provided a high-profile occasion for intensive lobbying. The disintegration of multilateral negotiations tarnished public perception of the WTO and also probably set back efforts to initiate a further round of multilateral talks.

9.5.2 International competition policy

Competition policy, which as we saw in Chapter 3 is subject to varying national frameworks, has become a thorny issue at WTO panels. In 1997 the EU threatened to impose trade sanctions on Boeing, objecting to its merger with McDonnell Douglas on the grounds that it adversely affected the competitive position of Airbus, the European aerospace manufacturer. In another case the US claimed, on behalf of Kodak, that Fuji of Japan benefited from restrictive practices in the Japanese market, which discriminated against Kodak products. To the dismay of the US, the panel decided that Japan had not violated WTO rules, as there had been no connection between government action and Japan's market structure. Clearly, however, countries differ enormously on competition policy, including merger regulation and scope for restrictive practices (see Chapter 3). National competition regimes can amount to institutional barriers to trade and foreign investment.

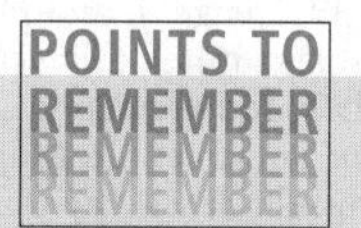

Agenda of issues facing WTO, 2000–04

- Review dispute settlement procedure
- Review food safety rules
- New round of negotiations on services liberalization
- Start negotiations on further liberalization of agricultural trade
- Attempt to resolve tensions between world trade rules and environmental agreements (multilateral environmental agreements, or MEAs)
- Explore possible role for WTO in competition policy
- Revitalize efforts to negotiate an agreement on FDI policy
- Review possible insertion of core labour standards clause in trade agreements
- Review policy on regional trade agreements

There are two proposals under consideration for regulating competition policy. One is to devise an international code, aimed at harmonizing competition policy, to be overseen by the WTO. This approach is favoured by the EU, but has so far been resisted by the US, as it entails giving the WTO powers to override national competition authorities. The US Justice Department's Antitrust Division would seem to favour bilateral co-operative agreements as an alternative, while stressing the need for controlling international cartels. Between US and EU competition authorities, co-operation in pursuing international cartels has progressed and could lead to some form of multilateral antitrust organization in the future.

9.6 Regionalism

While the WTO, like GATT, represents a **multilateral** approach to trade liberalization, **regional trade agreements (RTAs)** have grown in importance in the post-war period. These are formed between countries in a broad geographic area, such as the continents of Europe and North America. They are designed to bring down trade barriers among their member states, thus opening up regional markets for national producers. However, their impact can be much broader, as strong regional markets can have a significant impact on world trade patterns. Political considerations also play a key role, as economic integration is inseparable from the political power balance within any region, and regional trading blocks are influential in global politics. We begin by looking at the categories of regional groupings, expanded from the one originally devised by Bela Balassa in *The Theory of Economic Integration* (1962). They can be categorized accordingly:

- *Free trade area.* Member states agree to remove trade barriers among themselves, but keep their separate national barriers against trade with non-member states
- *Customs union.* Member states remove all trade barriers among themselves and adopt a common set of external barriers
- *Common market.* Member states enjoy free movement of goods, labour and capital
- *Economic union.* Member states unify all their economic policies, including monetary, fiscal and welfare policies
- *Political union.* Member states transfer sovereignty to the regional, political and law-making institutions, creating a new 'superstate'.

There are now nearly 180 regional trade groupings. Regional trade agreements must be notified to the WTO, and GATT provides that they are allowable provided they do not harm non-members or the global trading system as a whole. Although there does seem to be inbuilt discrimination against non-members, the review of these agreements to date has been lenient (Gilpin, 2000). Their numbers have grown dramatically in the 1990s, as shown in Figure 9.6. This upsurge can be explained by their appeal as a collective counterbalance against globalization. They provide an enlarged 'domestic' market and offer a platform for global competitiveness. Most of the world's nations belong to at least one regional grouping, the vast majority of which fall into the first two categories of free trade area and customs union (see Table 9.1). The categories can be seen as successive steps towards deepening economic integration. Only the EU has reached the stage of economic union; political union is in the formative stages, but many issues are outstanding, including the relationship between member nations and EU institutions. In the Americas, NAFTA has been followed by the South American common market but, as yet, no hemispheric economic integration. Asian nations in ASEAN have increased their co-operation, while APEC

Table 9.1 Regional trade groupings

Region	Group	Member countries	Date of formation	Type of agreement
South America	ANCOM (Andean Common Market)	Bolivia, Colombia, Ecuador, Peru, Venezuela	1969	Customs union
Asia-Pacific	APEC (Asia-Pacific Economic Co-operation Group)	18 countries, including the US, Japan, Australia, New Zealand, Canada, South Korea, China, Mexico, Chile	1989	Free trade area (to be in place by 2020)
Southeast Asia	ASEAN (Association of Southeast Asian Nations)	Indonesia, Malaysia, the Philippines, Singapore, Thailand, Brunei	1967	Co-operation agreement, free trade by early 2000s
Caribbean	CARICOM (Caribbean Community)	13 English-speaking Caribbean nations, including Antigua, Bahamas, Barbados, Belize, Guyana, Jamaica, Trinidad and Tobago	1973	Common market
Europe	EU (European Union)	Austria, Belgium, Denmark, France, Finland, Germany, Greece, Ireland, Italy, Luxembourg, The Netherlands, Portugal, Spain, Sweden, UK	1957	Economic union, moving towards political union
South America	MERCOSUR (Southern Common Market)	Argentina, Brazil, Paraguay, Uruguay	1991	Common market
North and Central America	NAFTA (North American Free Trade Agreement)	Canada, Mexico, US	1994	Free trade area

Figure 9.6 Regional trade agreements notified to GATT/WTO

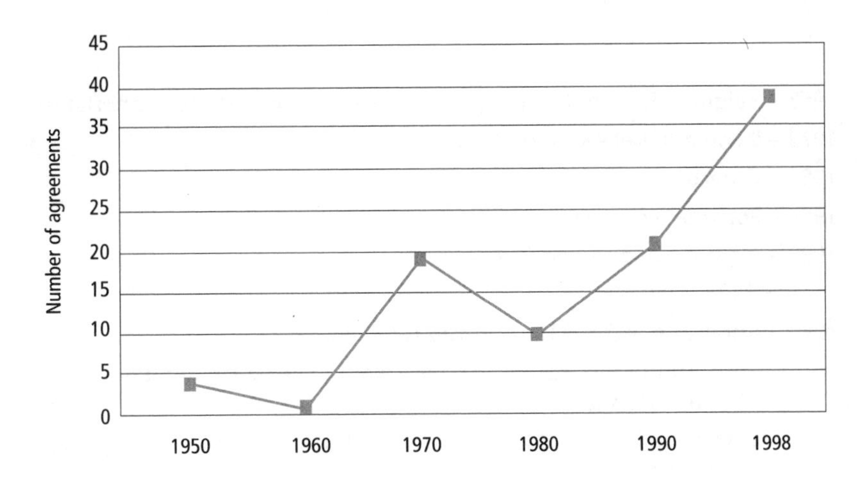

Source: WTO, in *Financial Times* survey: 'The World Trade System at 50', *Financial Times*, 18 May 1998.

countries, embracing all of the Pacific region, have set their sights on a free trade regime by 2020. We look at differing examples of regionalism in Europe, North America and Asia.

9.6.1 The EU

As early as the Treaty of Rome in 1957, the six founding members of the European Economic Community envisaged both economic and political integration. The institutions set up, dominated by the Commission and Council, have remained the structural foundations, and the European Court of Justice (ECJ) has established its legal supremacy (see Chapters 7 and 8). No other regional grouping begins to approach this level of structural autonomy. European Monetary Union (EMU), discussed in Chapter 3, to which 12 of the 15 current member states have subscribed, will encourage further cross-border trade. However, the goal of the Single European Market, which was the cornerstone of European economic integration, has come about only gradually, amid a good deal of political and bureaucratic stalemate. The Single European Act of 1987 aimed to dismantle internal barriers and establish a single market by 1992. Businesses would be able to move seamlessly from one member country to another, without bureaucratic frontier procedures. Product standards would be recognized between member states. Financial services would be liberalized, so that firms such as banks and insurance companies could compete across national borders.

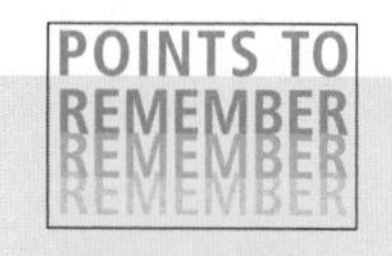

EU enlargement

1957 – Belgium, France, Germany, Italy, Luxembourg and the Netherlands

1973 – Denmark, Ireland and the UK

1981 – Greece

1986 – Portugal and Spain

1995 – Austria, Finland and Sweden

Total = 15

1998 – Applications from 13 countries received:

Front runners – Cyprus, Estonia, Poland, The Czech Republic, Slovenia, Hungary

Other applicants – Bulgaria, Latvia, Lithuania, Romania, Slovakia, Malta and Turkey

Possible overall total = 28

In reality, progress in internal liberalization has been neither as swift nor as easy as many predicted back in 1987. Liberalizing of financial services began in the mid-1990s and the aim is to meet a 2005 deadline. Banks and investors urge speeding up the necessary legislation, which has taken years. Telecommunications deregulation and deregulation of utilities such as water, gas and electricity have been uneven. Histories of protected industries and varying degrees of state ownership have slowed progress. Deeply rooted national cultural differences were underestimated, and domestic political considerations have loomed large. The latter have sparked continuing debate on principles of sovereignty and national identity and also the economic interests of groups of workers affected by liberalization. For agriculture, the effect of the GATT Agriculture Agreement of 1994 was to reduce the CAP budget, but it still amounts to half the EU's annual budget. Liberalization has taken on renewed urgency in negotiations on EU enlargement, as the countries waiting in the wings are concerned to protect farming interests, creating more strain on the CAP in propping up relatively inefficient agriculture.

WWW WEBALERT

The NAFTA website is http://www.nafta-sec-alena.org/english/home.htm

APEC's home page is http://www.apecsec.org.sg/

MERCOSUR is at http://www.americasnet.com/mauritz/mercosur

The ASEAN Secretariat is at http://www.asean.or.id

The EU Commission's main website is http://europa.eu.int

9.6.2 NAFTA

The North American Free Trade Agreement (NAFTA), which came into effect in 1994, comprises the US, Canada and Mexico. While NAFTA does not envisage the degree of economic integration of the EU, its provisions and future developments raise similar issues, including political concerns and the question of sovereignty. In contrast to the EU, NAFTA is centred on one dominant power, the US, whose GDP is 10 times that of Mexico, a much bigger gap than that between the rich and poor EU members. Fear of economic dependence on the US has bred nationalism in both Canada and Mexico, although rather more virulent in nature in its Mexican form. In the post-war period their economies became increasingly integrated into that of the US, as US companies set up branch plants and subsidiaries to export to US markets. A free trade agreement, securing free access to markets, offered advantages to all three countries. The US looked for advantages of low-cost labour in Mexico; the opening of Canada and Mexico to US financial services; and improved access to oil in Canada and Mexico. For the two smaller states, advantage consisted of negotiated rules to put their access to US markets on a more secure footing, replacing the informal relationships of the past.

Market access provisions are the main substance of NAFTA, by which the parties agreed to eliminate tariffs on most manufactured goods over a 10-year period. NAFTA's investment rules allow investors from any of the three countries to be treated in the same way as domestic investors. These rules apply to both FDI and portfolio investment. For matters other than investment, NAFTA introduced a dispute settlement procedure. While it aimed to satisfy the worries of smaller partners that the stronger partner always has the upper hand, nonetheless, there is the problem for smaller countries that US pressure may be backed up by retaliatory measures such as anti-dumping measures to restrict imports into the US. Two 'side accords' of NAFTA concern labour standards and environmental standards, stemming from concern in the US over firms moving production to Mexico in order to avoid the higher US standards. Commissions were set up in both areas to monitor and enforce national standards (rather than ILO standards), but enforcement procedures are weak (Porter, 2000).

Unlike the EU, NAFTA operates no common external trade policy and has no institutions for dealing with exchange rates. The Mexican peso crisis of the mid-1990s was left to individual governments to resolve. NAFTA aimed to increase exports between partners, who already traded heavily with each other, and create jobs in all three countries. By 1996, the US president reported to Congress that trade between the US and its NAFTA partners had grown 44 per cent since the agreement was signed (Schaffer et al., 1999, p. 457). US and Canadian citizens had feared that their jobs would be lost to Mexico, a fear articulated by American trade unions in particular. Presidential candidate, Ross Perot, in the 1992 campaign, warned Americans of 'a giant sucking sound going south' if the border with Mexico was opened. However,

Case study 9.4 NAFTA and the blessings of free trade for Mexico

Mexican trade has flourished since the launch of NAFTA in 1993. Exports to the US, which account for 80 per cent of Mexico's exports and one-third of its GDP, have risen from $40 billion in 1993 to $110 billion in 1999. This increase reflects the rapid growth of FDI in Mexico, reaping the advantages of duty-free access to the US market. Industries ranging from plastics to cars are concentrated in areas known as *maquiladoras*, or free trade zones, where assembly plants produce goods for export. Until 2000, *maquiladora* plants paid no import duties on components destined for re-export. By then, these factories were no longer dependent on customs concessions for survival, but had become well established, buying many of their inputs from Mexican suppliers and exporting to growing Latin American markets. There is also evidence of clusters of suppliers. Volkswagen, which invested in Mexico in 1989, originally to meet Mexican demand, now exports 340,000 of the 400,000 cars it makes annually. Its plant in Pueblo is the company's only North American base. Moreover, Volkswagen relies on 60 locally based suppliers for many components for the Pueblo plant.

Mexican hopes that NAFTA-induced trade and FDI would raise their living standards have not as yet been fulfilled. Hourly rates of wages and benefits for a production worker in Mexico remain very low at $1.75, compared to over $17 in the US. As a result, some 300,000 Mexicans risk emigrating illegally to the US every year. Mexico's new president, who is committed to raise living standards, wants to reopen the immigration issue, which was kept out of the original NAFTA negotiations.

Looking beyond its American neighbours, Mexico entered a free trade agreement with the EU in 1999, the first between the EU and a Latin American country. The agreement covers manufactured and agricultural goods and services, and would bring in phased reductions in tariffs.

Sources: Parkes, C., 'Mexico's free trade zone may be victim of its own success', *Financial Times*, 14 May 1999; Tricks, H., 'Economists urge strategy for industry', in Survey on Mexico, *Financial Times*, 5 October 1999; Tricks, H., 'Border crossing', *Financial Times*, 21 August 2000.

Case question

Why do Mexicans have mixed feelings about NAFTA?

there seems to be a rough balance between employment gains in the US and Canada due to NAFTA and job losses due to imports from Mexico (Schaffer et al., 1999). On the other hand, despite the benefits of NAFTA investment, living conditions in Mexico have remained poor, as Case Study 9.4 illustrates.

9.6.3 Regionalism in Asia

Regionalism has proceeded more slowly in the Asian and Pacific regions than in either Europe or the Americas. One explanation is the extreme socio-cultural, political and economic diversity that has inhibited the development of a shared regional identity or sense of shared 'destiny'. ASEAN comprises the newly industrialized economies of Southeast Asia, while APEC encompasses the entire Pacific region (see Table 9.1). While economic integration has grown, impetus towards a free trade area has been weak among the major powers of the region – Japan, China and the US. Japan's multinationals have pursued a strategy of Asian expansion, investing heavily in 'regional production alliances' and increasing their Asian trade. By the 1990s, Pacific Asia had overtaken the US as Japan's largest export market. Production networks in Asian countries have enabled Japanese companies to retain competitive advantage in Western markets, by exploiting the comparative advantages offered by neighbouring low-cost economies. Japan's economic leadership in the region, however, has been set back by its own economic woes (discussed in Chapter 3), as well as by the Asian financial crisis.

Meanwhile, China's star has risen rapidly, causing alarm among ASEAN countries, which see the FDI which they had hoped to attract going to China instead. The issue of China's membership in the WTO has caused divisions in APEC (see Case Study 9.3). One group, consisting of the US, Canada, Australia and Singapore, wishes to bring down trade barriers, while the less developed countries, notably Malaysia and China, have been reluctant to endorse free trade. Japan, meanwhile, has established bilateral talks on free trade with South Korea and Singapore. This seems to indicate that Japan is seeking to reassert its position as the economic centre of the region. A new collaboration has been agreed between the ASEAN countries and Japan, China and South Korea, called 'ASEAN plus three'. However, Lee Kuan Yew, Singapore's founding father, feels that 'three plus ASEAN' would be more accurate and Japan is the most important of the three (*Financial Times*, 10 October 2000). Shifting power balances in Asia are therefore affecting regional economic integration and the prospects for future trade liberalization.

9.7 Developing countries and world trade

The World Development Report 1999/2000 stated that 'for developing countries, trade is the primary vehicle for realizing the benefits of globalization' (World Bank, 2000a, p. 5). Trade as a percentage of GDP in developing countries has increased at a much faster rate than in the developed world (see Figure 9.7). However, trade itself does not guarantee development. Countries in sub-Saharan Africa, which export mainly low-value primary commodities, remain poor. While developing countries' share in world trade in manufactured goods increased from 6 per cent in 1965 to 20 per cent in 1995, developed economies still predominate. And the dominance is particularly strong in the high-value, high-tech products (Castells, 2000a). The benefits of technical knowledge to be gained by low-cost producers has largely been confined to the newly industrialized economies of Southeast

Figure 9.7 Growth of trade, as percentage of GDP

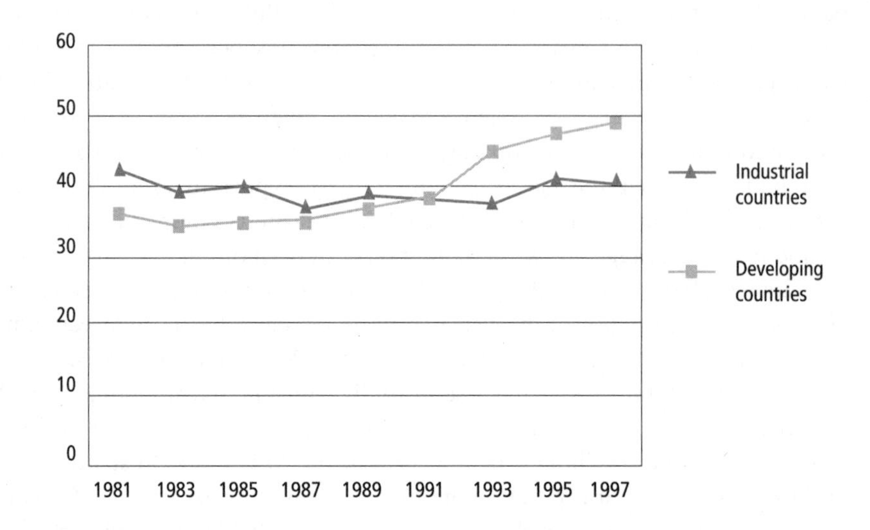

Source: World Bank (2000) *World Development Report 1999/2000* (Oxford: Oxford University Press) p. 5.

Asia. In the increasingly important trade in services, all countries, developed and developing alike, stand to gain. Services now account for about 70 per cent of GDP in industrialized countries and about 50 per cent in developing countries. In the 1990s growth rates in exports of commercial services were highest in East Asia and Pacific, growing at about 18 per cent annually (World Bank, 2000a, p. 34). Poorer developing countries have been keen to attract foreign investors to improve infrastructure services, such as telecommunications and banking, which underpin modern economic activities.

While developing economies have huge potential for trade expansion, they often complain that the world trade system is stacked against them. They make up more than three-quarters of the membership of the WTO, but the organization, like GATT before it, does not operate on democratic principles, but on the rule of consensus. This means that no decision can be approved without the consent of the main trading nations. Developing countries point to the fact that GATT barely touched barriers to developed countries' markets in products such as textiles and agricultural products. On the other hand, developing countries have slowly gained expertise in trade matters, enhancing negotiating skills. The dispute resolution procedure has been used extensively by developing countries, for example by India against the US on textiles. The WTO estimates that the Uruguay Round resulted in tariff reductions of 37 per cent on industrial products relevant to developing countries, which is slightly less than the average. Developing countries have won a number of concessions over longer transition times to comply with WTO rules, but even so, the administrative resources and technical expertise entailed by compliance procedures are beyond the means of the poorest developing countries. The broadening WTO agenda to include labour standards and environmental measures is resisted by many developing countries, as disguised protectionism. However, the fact that, on the contentious issues, developing countries are now taking an active part is indicative of the impact of globalization.

9.8 Globalization and the world trading system

Trade, as this chapter has highlighted, involves both political and economic considerations. Nation-states have traditionally relied on tariffs, quota restrictions and other policies which rested on the assumption that protection and economic development naturally went together. In modern economies, the level of productivity, technological innovation and investment are more than ever dependent on participation in the global economy. Participation no longer simply means increasing trade, although expansion of trade has been one of the major trends of the post-war era. Increasingly, through the global strategies of TNCs, foreign investment has been the driver of trade. The processes of globalization in integrating national economies can largely be attributed to TNCs' global production networks. Global competition, as has been seen in this chapter, has led to growing interdependence of states and a strengthening of multilateral institutions. Protectionist voices still abound, but governments are now constrained by numerous multilateral agreements designed to liberalize trade.

The 1980s and 90s, however, saw a tension between two apparently contradictory trends: trade liberalization, sponsored by the WTO, on the one hand, and growing regional trading blocs on the other. In this context, regionalism has served two purposes. First, regional trade agreements have permitted firms to build a better competitive base in the 'internal' market. Second, it has allowed groups of states in region l trade blocs to enhance their political and economic power. Economists have argued that regional agreements put up barriers to free trade with outsiders, but predictions of a regionalized economy have not yet come to fruition (Castells, 2000a). As we have seen, few of these groupings are homogeneous or cohesive. Apart from the EU, institutional structures are limited. Even in the EU, which is the most economically integrated, nation-states have not yet been superseded as defining units for a population's economic interests. But those interests are now played out in regional, as well as multilateral, institutions. Moreover, bilateral free trade agreements are a continuing trend. Economic integration has thus become more extensive as well as more complex, encompassing national, regional and multilateral links.

9.9 Conclusions

1. The post-war period has seen a growth of international trade and a trend towards liberalization of the world trading system. Although trade, both exports and imports, is predominantly between the three main trading powers – the US, EU and Japan – other countries, notably the industrialized nations of Southeast Asia, are now important players.

2. International trade theories offer explanations of why countries, as well as companies, compete and how comparative and competitive advantages can be exploited.

3. Government policy, highly influential in international trade, rests on concerns of national producer and consumer interests.

4. Tools of government trade policy include exchange rate manipulation, tariffs and non-tariff barriers to trade. However, the growth of the multilateral trading system, initiated by GATT, has limited the scope of governments to act unilaterally in managing trade.

5. The WTO, successor to GATT, has strengthened the rule-governed system of international trade regulation, particularly in regard to dispute settlement. Nonetheless, tensions remain over the decision-making and implementation of WTO decisions in trade disputes.

6. Outstanding issues facing the WTO are whether to link issues such as core labour standards and environmental protection to trade policies. There is considerable difference of opinion between developed and developing countries over these issues.

7. The post-war trend towards RTAs represents growing regional economic integration. However, regional groupings differ considerably in their internal cohesiveness and structures, the EU being the most integrated.

8. World trade can best be viewed in the context of globalization, in which the large TNCs with globalized production capacities have been major players.

Review questions

???

1 How relevant is the theory of comparative advantage to modern trade patterns?

2 What are the main contributions of Porter's theory of competitive advantage?

3 What is meant by strategic trade policy?

4 Outline the motivations underlying government trade policy.
5 Summarize the arguments for and against free trade.
6 What are the main tools of government trade policy?
7 Define the GATT principles of most-favoured nation and national treatment.
8 In what ways does the WTO represent a step on from GATT?
9 What are the outstanding issues facing the WTO and why has it struggled to arrive at a consensus?
10 Why have regional trade groupings become popular, and in what ways, if any, do they undermine multilateral trade liberalization efforts?
11 Contrast the EU and NAFTA in terms of regional integration.
12 Why do developing countries have ambivalent feelings about trade liberalization?

Assignments

1 Assess the contrasting perspectives and interests of developed, industrializing, and developing countries with respect to global trade liberalization.
2 Is regionalism a 'stepping stone' or 'stumbling block' to free trade? Compare the progress of regional integration in three regions: Europe, North America and Asia.

Further reading

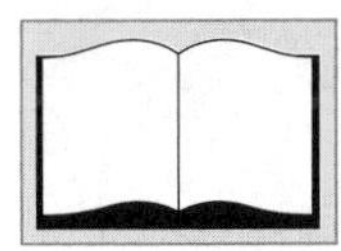

Berry, B., Conkling, E. and Ray, D. (1997) *The Global Economy in Transition*, 2nd edn (Englewood Cliffs, NJ: Prentice Hall)

Gilpin, R. (2000) *The Challenge of Global Capitalism* (Princeton: Princeton University Press)

Hirst, P. and Thompson, G. (1999) *Globalization in Question*, 2nd edn (Cambridge: Polity Press)

Mattli, W. (1999) *The Logic of Regional Integration: Europe and Beyond* (Cambridge: Cambridge University Press)

Michie, J. and Grieve Smith, J. (eds) (1995) *Managing the Global Economy* (Oxford: Oxford University Press)

Chapter

10 Technology and innovation

Outline of chapter

1. To appreciate the role of technological change in economic progress
2. To gain an insight into the ways in which innovation is generated and diffused in different societies
3. To understand the interactions between national systems of innovation and processes of globalization and technology transfer
4. To gain an overview of the impact of the rapidly changing technological environment on business processes and structures

10.0 Introduction

Technology is a key driving force in the world economy. Technological innovation and the capacity to sustain a technological lead are crucial to success in the competitive environment, for both companies and countries. No longer the preserve of engineering and design departments, technology now penetrates every aspect of business, linking research and development (R&D), design, production and distribution in global networks. In particular, advances in computing, telecommunications and transport have had widespread implications in all sectors, from manufacturing to media. Moreover, technology changes have impacted on the ways in which organizations operate, both internally and, increasingly, in interdependent global networks. The declining cost of transport and communications, shown in Table 10.1, gives an indication of the changes that have taken place. The result has been a host of wide-ranging changes in the ways in which we live and work, taking in all manner of developments, from convenience food to the internet.

Cutting-edge technology can be an important source of competitive advantage. However, the relationships between knowledge, technological innovation and markets are now recognized to be more complex than was once thought. The growth of international markets has focused attention on differences between national systems of innovation and differences in organizational structures that can promote or inhibit innovation. Social, cultural and political factors in national environments can influence the creation and adoption of technological know-how. Globalization processes have raised

Table 10.1 Declining cost of transport and communications (1990 US$)

Year	Sea freight (average ocean freight and port charges per ton)	Air transport (average revenue per passenger mile)	Telephone call (3 minutes, New York to London)	Computers (index, 1990=100)
1920	95	–	–	–
1930	60	0.68	245	–
1940	63	0.46	189	–
1950	34	0.30	53	–
1960	27	0.24	46	12,500
1970	27	0.16	32	1,947
1980	24	0.10	5	362
1990	29	0.11	3	100

Source: IMF, World Economic Outlook 1997, in UN (1999) *Human Development Report 1999* (Oxford: Oxford University Press) p. 30.

these questions particularly in relation to technology and knowledge transfer. Thus, while organizations see the need for a strong focus on technological innovation, they are becoming increasingly aware that technology must be viewed in the context of the wider business environment. This chapter aims, first, to explain the broad processes of technological innovation and diffusion, in the context of national and organizational environments. Second, key developments in information technology (IT) and biotechnology will be examined, highlighting trends of technological globalization. Finally, some conclusions on the future impact of technology on the competitive environment will be put forward.

10.1 Concepts and processes

Technology can be defined as the methodical application of scientific knowledge to practical purposes. It is a concept at the intersection of learning and doing. Throughout history there have been talented, imaginative individuals, able to assimilate scientific knowledge and transform its principles into practical inventions. An **invention** is a product or process which can be described as 'new', in that it makes a significant, qualitative leap forward from the state of existing knowledge. The term **innovation** is broader in its scope, in that it covers not just inventions, but a range of technical improvements to products and processes that are commercially exploitable. While many inventions, including patented ones, are never commercially produced, innovations, by definition, are economically valuable. Technical innovation has thus been described as the matching of new technology to a market, or 'the first commercial application or production of a new process or product' (Freeman and Soete, 1997, p. 201). Inventions can be legally protected by a patent, which gives the inventor (or more often, a company) 'ownership' of its rights of exploitation. An innovation may be a less dramatic step forward, for example an improvement that speeds up an industrial process. While not patentable, it is nonetheless significant in that it can lead to scale economies. Scientific knowledge plays a crucial role in technical innovation. There are, however, many steps along the way from turning a scientific discovery into a workable invention which can be commercially exploited.

Historians puzzle over two key questions in relation to technology. First, why science and invention flourish in particular societies during certain eras, but not in others. And second, why some societies, with high levels of learning, scientific knowledge and creative inventors, still seem unable to convert learning into invention, or invention into technological advancement at the level of society. David Landes points to two examples. Islam, in its golden age 750–1100, 'produced the world's greatest scientists, yet a flourishing science contributed nothing to the slow advance of technology in Islam' (Landes, 1998). More remarkable were the Chinese, with a long list of inventions, including the wheelbarrow, compass, paper, printing, gunpowder and porcelain. In the twelfth century, the Chinese were using a water-driven machine for spinning hemp, anticipating English spinning machines by some 500 years. Yet technical progress made little impact on the Chinese economy. The Chinese, it seems, had the scientific knowledge to produce the steam engine but, for some reason that still baffles historians, failed to do it. Summarizing the debate, Landes points to China's lack of 'a free market and institutionalized property rights' as key factors that discouraged initiative (Landes, 1998, p. 56).

POINTS TO REMEMBER

Concepts and processes

- *Technology* is the methodical application of scientific knowledge to practical purposes
- *Innovation* is the creation or improvement of products or processes, including incremental improvements, which bring commercial benefits
- An *invention* is a new product or process which is industrially applicable. Many inventions fall by the wayside for lack of commercial exploitation
- *R&D* is the systematic search for new knowledge in specific academic disciplines (basic research) and also new knowledge for specific applications (applied research)

We generally assume that, in societies where learning is valued, a high level of science education will lay the foundations for people with technological talent to flourish, and, further, that their skills will feed into the country's industries, fostering economic prosperity. However, the relative importance of 'demand-pull' and 'science-push' is debated. Both forces play a role in technological innovation. Emphasis on demand-pull factors, as in product life cycle theory, has been criticized as one sided. How, it might be asked, can consumers judge a revolutionary new product of which they have no knowledge (Freeman and Soete, 1997, p. 200)? Many of the early inventors, with their scientific backgrounds, had little idea of the economic potential of their innovations, or of the many possible applications of their technology. Science-push was clearly important among the early inventors and entrepreneurs, who formed new companies in order to exploit their inventions. However, there were instances where demand predominated and these certainly became more prevalent when innovation became 'routinized' within large firms. It is arguable that, even today, whereas large firms with vast R&D expenditure account for the bulk of innovations, radical innovations often come from small firms.

While it is easy to see that technical innovation plays a key role in economic development, the processes and environmental factors that generate innovation are complex. A simple linear model depicting the flow of ideas from science to applied research and then to development for commercial application is now seen as too simplistic, overlooking many factors and interactive influences.

10.2 Theories of technological innovation

Theories of technological innovation start from the assumption that innovation is a key to economic progress. In terms of competitive advantage, technological innovation, as Porter has pointed out, can create first-mover advantages, which governments can promote (see Chapter 9). The importance of 'improvements in machines' was recognized by Adam Smith at the outset of his *Wealth of Nations* ([1776]1950). However, for a long period, economic theorists tended to see technological change as an 'exogenous variable', that is, outside the traditional inputs of labour and capital. Against this background, Schumpeter stands out for his analysis of technological innovation as central to economic development.

10.2.1 Schumpeter's theory of industrial waves

Schumpeter's work spanned the period from 1912 to 1942. As industrial economies developed during that period, his analysis of the role of technological innovation evolved. From the outset in 1912, he stressed the importance of the individual entrepreneur in the innovative process. Schumpeter saw that innovation can encompass not just technical but also marketing and organizational innovations. The key actors in the Industrial Revolution were both talented inventors and entrepreneurs, who often went into production making (and improving) their own inventions. The cotton-spinning industry, for example, was transformed by the inventions of Arkwright, Hargreaves and Crompton in the late eighteenth century. Richard Arkwright, for one, embodied important qualities as inventor and entrepreneur, protecting and exploiting his patents, with a partner, Jedediah Strutt, providing the necessary capital for further investment. Large-scale machine production dramatically increased output and brought down prices.

Schumpeter saw the shift in technical innovation from the individual inventor to R&D specialist professionals within firms. Two developments were of particular importance. The first was the increasing importance of scientific research as the basis of innovation, and the second was the growing bureaucracy of large organizations, with their specialist R&D departments. 'The romance of the earlier commercial adventure', he said, 'is wearing away', replaced by 'just another office worker' (Schumpeter, 1942, p. 132).

Table 10.2 Summary of long waves of technical change

Approximate timing	Kondratieff waves	Science, technology, education and training
First 1780s–1840s	Industrial Revolution: factory production for textiles	Apprenticeship; learning by doing, scientific societies
Second 1840s–1890s	Age of steam power and railways	Professional mechanical and civil engineers; institutes of technology, mass primary education
Third 1890s–1940s	Age of electricity and steel	Industrial R&D labs, national laboratories
Fourth 1940s–1990s	Age of mass production ('Fordism') of automobiles and synthetic materials	Large-scale industrial and government R&D, mass higher education
Fifth 1990s–	Age of microelectronics and computer networks	Data networks, R&D global networks, lifetime education and training

Source: Adapted from Freeman, C. and Soete, L. (1997) *The Economics of Industrial Innovation*, 3rd edn (London: Cassell – now Continuum) p. 19 (reprinted with permission).

He viewed the changes that take place within capitalism as involving 'creative destruction'. New products, new methods of production and new forms of organization emerge, 'revolutionizing economic structure, *from within*' (Schumpeter, 1942, p. 83).

He used the notion of business cycles, devised by the Russian economist Kondratieff, to describe successive 'waves' of economic development, in which technological innovation played a crucial role. The first long wave is the Industrial Revolution and development of factory production (1780s–1840s). The second wave is that of steam power and the growth of the railways, lasting until the 1890s. The third wave, which lasted until the Second World War, was dominated by electricity and steel. Following Schumpeter's death shortly after the war, theorists have added a fourth wave, that of Fordist mass production (1940s–1990s) (see Chapter 2), and a fifth, that of microelectronics and computing, from the 1990s (see Table 10.2). Each Kondratieff wave is based on technological changes and their widespread diffusion in the economy, creating changes in investment opportunities and employment. While Schumpeter could not have foreseen the pace of technological change of recent decades, an enduring contribution of his analysis, echoed in more recent theorists, is the interdependence between technological innovation, economic progress and the social environment.

10.2.2 Product life cycle theory reconsidered

According to product life cycle theory (outlined in Chapter 9), the introduction of a new product by a firm depends on a large market in the firm's home country, which will bear the costs and risks of R&D. Demand from high-income consumers in the US in the 1950s and 60s thus resulted in a lead in consumer durables. The theory holds that this monopoly advantage is gradually whittled away as the product becomes standardized and production moves to less advanced countries. Maintaining competitive advantage requires continually introducing new products. The theory can be criticized for its static view of technology. More recent consideration of the product life cycle model points out that it overemphasizes consumer demand and misses the dynamic implications of technology development (Cantwell, 1989). As technology accumulates, innovation becomes diffused and the 'technology gap' closes. A further shortcoming of the product life cycle model is its focus on products independently of each other, with each new product seen as a radical innovation (Freeman and Soete, 1997). In reality, product innovations are interrelated and technological changes evolve across a range of products. Hence, the narrow focus of product life cycles does not capture the dynamic quality of innovation processes.

Theories of how innovation is generated now take into account the diffusion of technology across the globe. Competitive positions of countries and firms may shift over relatively short timespans, as technological changes play out in markets (see Case Study 10.1). The technological lead of European countries before 1900 was eroded as the US (and later, Japan), caught up and eventually surpassed European countries. European countries were then in the position of catching up. The geographic expansion of transnational corporations (TNCs) has led post-war technological change, reshaping the competitive environment between firms and between countries. It is clear that industrial 'latecomers' have benefited from technology transfer, although the evidence is that the diffusion of technology differs between different national environments. Foreign direct investment (FDI) has brought about the globalization of production, but whether this has led to globalization of technological innovation is open to debate. Large companies have tended to concentrate their R&D activities in their home countries, but there are now indications that specialized R&D is being decentralized to overseas locations, in order to benefit from different areas of excellence in different localities (Patel and Pavitt, 1991; Archibugi and Michie, 1997b). Much current debate on the generation and diffusion of technological innovation, and its relation to economic growth, highlights the importance of national innovation systems on the one hand and forces of globalization on the other.

Case study 10.1 A tale of two companies

In the mobile phone industry, Nokia of Finland is young, sexy and 'with it', while Ericsson of Sweden is the conservative, middle-aged engineer. This characterization might help to explain the relative success of the two companies in selling mobile phones. There are similarities between the two: both are over 100 years old and symbols of Nordic industrial success. But while Nokia's share of the global mobile phone market rose from 22.5 per cent in 1998 to 27 per cent in 1999, Ericsson's declined from 15 to 10.5 per cent. Ericsson, on the other hand, is the global market leader in mobile telecommunications infrastructure.

No one in 1980 could have possibly predicted that Nokia would become the world's leading mobile phone company. Started as a paper mill in 1865, by the 1980s it had grown to become an industrial conglomerate, making everything from boots to TVs. At one point, Nokia was the biggest toilet paper manufacturer in Europe. Spotting the potential of Global Systems for Mobile Communications (GSM) technology in mobile phones, it then decided to divest itself of its mature businesses and focus on mobile telephony. Nokia's phones became icons of the whole industry, combining an understanding of the technological revolution, an eye on fashion trends and a strong brand. To maintain its cutting edge, Nokia has launched a venture capital arm, to foster new business ideas by investing in start-ups. And it has developed a division devoted to e-commerce solutions for corporate customers.

Ericsson, with its emphasis on infrastructure systems, has traditionally relied on selling its equipment to the large telecommunications companies around the world, often government controlled. It entered the mobile phone market only incidentally and has been slower to adopt a consumer orientation. The company is now trying to become more responsive. It too has gone into the mobile internet market, forging an agreement with Microsoft to form a joint venture to develop wireless internet applications.

Both Nokia and Ericsson are now looking over their shoulders, as competitors are gaining on them rapidly in 3G (third generation) technology, including Japan's Matsushita and Fujitsu and Korea's Samsung Electronics.

Sources: Fox, J., 'Nokia's secret code', *Fortune*, **141**(9), 1 May 2000; Harbert, T., 'A tale of two mobile telephone makers,' *Electronic Business*, **26**(5), May 2000; 'Star turn', *The Economist*, 8 May 2000.

Case question

What are the similarities and contrasts between Nokia and Ericsson in their corporate approaches to technology and innovation?

WWW WEBALERT

Nokia's website is http://www.nokia.com

Ericsson's website is http://www.ericsson.com

10.3 National systems of innovation

First Britain, then the US and later Japan and Germany have all been able to achieve high levels of technological innovation coupled with economic growth. It has long been recognized that national environment is important in stimulating or inhibiting innovation. Writing in 1841, Friedrich List addressed ways in which Germany could catch up with England. Significantly, he emphasized the importance of both social and cultural factors and government policy in, for example, the protection of infant industries and setting up technical training institutes (Archibugi and Michie, 1997a). Indeed, List anticipated many of the aspects of national environment which were later to be grouped together under the term 'national system of innovation'. There is now a considerable body of literature on national systems, their different approaches to innovation and how they interact (Lundvall, 1992).

A national **innovation system** is broadly defined as the structures and institutions by which a country's innovation activities are encouraged and facilitated, both directly and indirectly. The term 'system' might imply that these institutions and policies are co-ordinated, when in fact levels of co-ordination vary between countries. The word 'network' has been used to describe the relevant linkages between companies, disciplines and institutions (Patel and Pavitt, 2000). Summing up these threads, Mowery and Oxley define the national innovation system as 'the network of public and private institutions within an economy that fund and perform R&D, translate the results of R&D into commercial innovations and effect the diffusion of new technologies' (Mowery and Oxley, 1997, p. 154).

10.3.1 Key aspects of a national innovation system

The key aspects, outlined by Archibugi and Michie (1997a), are: education and training; science and technology capabilities; industrial structure; science and technology strengths and weaknesses and interactions within the innovation system. Each is now discussed in turn.

Education and training

In general, governments are responsible for formal provision of education. Achieving high rates of participation at all levels, from primary through to higher education, is a key to national economic growth. Clearly, too, qualitative issues are important and governments are keenly aware of the need to maintain high-quality graduates in the new technologies, such as IT and biotechnology. The German government is concerned that it is producing too few graduates too slowly. The average German graduate is 28 years old on graduation and only 16 per cent of Germans in the same age group graduate from university (see Figures 10.1 and 10.2). To make up for the skills shortage in the short term, Germany, like the US and UK, has offered work permits to

Figure 10.1 Percentage of same age group with a university-level degree

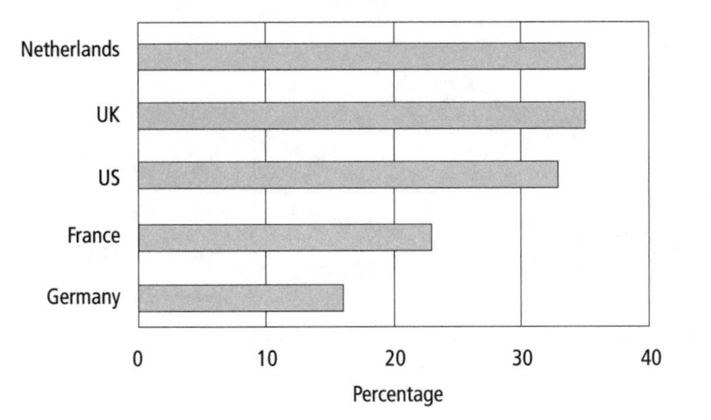

Source: OECD (2000) Education at a glance 2000, in *Financial Times*, 26 October 2000.

Figure 10.2 Average years of study until graduation

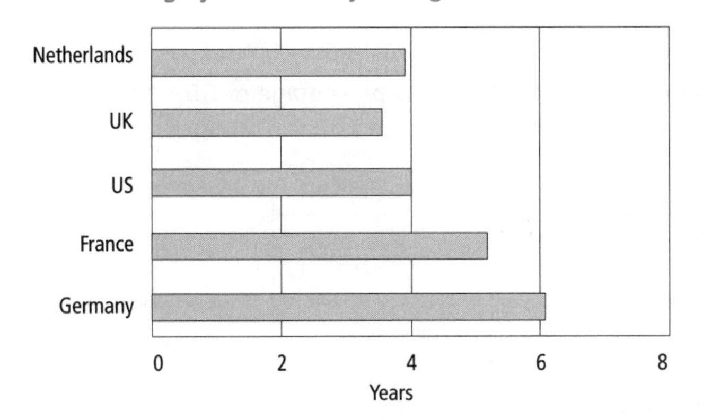

Source: OECD (2000) Education at a glance 2000, in *Financial Times*, 26 October 2000.

foreign IT specialists. In the long term, Germany is facing the problem that, in science and engineering, it has less than half the Organization for Economic Co-operation and Development (OECD) average number of graduates per 100,000 employees (*Financial Times*, 26 October 2000). Learning includes a number of processes, including learning-by-doing and interactive learning, which are influenced by social and cultural factors. Technological innovation relies on both institutionalized scientific research and interaction between people with different kinds of knowledge (Lundvall, 1992).

Science and technology capabilities

Countries differ in the resources devoted to R&D activities, in both public funding and business expenditure. The richer countries devote about 3 per cent of gross domestic product (GDP) to R&D activities, while for most

Figure 10.3 Business-funded R&D as a percentage of GDP, 1981–99

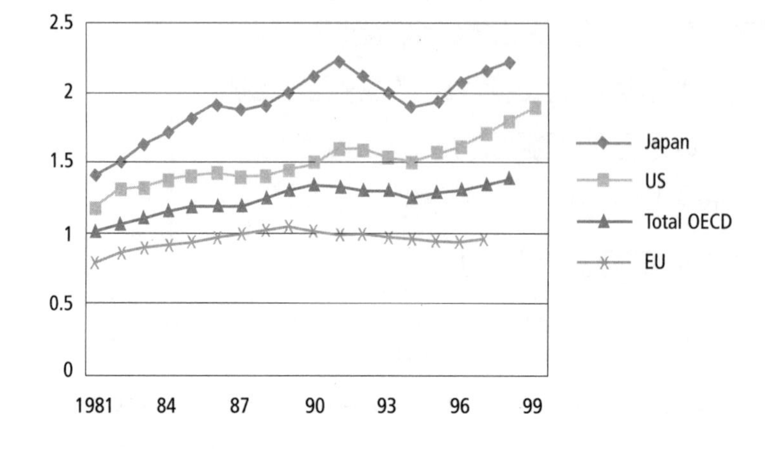

Source: OECD (2000) Main Science and Technology Indicators, in *OECD Observer*, September 2000.

Figure 10.4 Government-funded R&D as a percentage of GDP, 1981–99

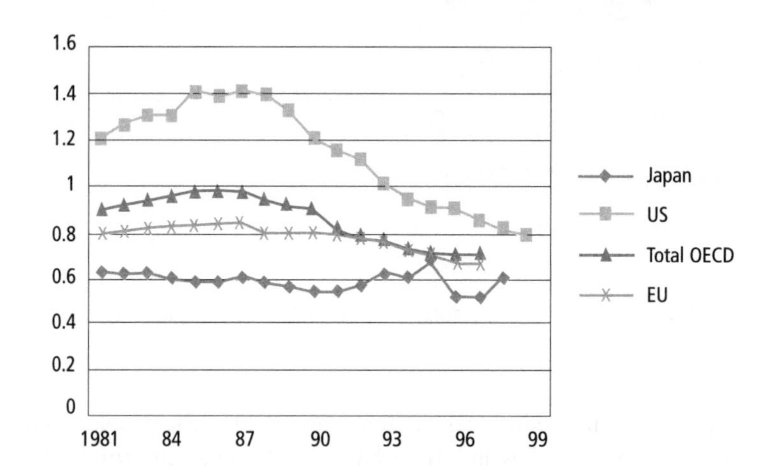

Source: OECD (2000) Main Science and Technology Indicators, in *OECD Observer*, September 2000.

countries the percentage is much lower and developing countries hardly figure. Government funding of R&D declined in the 1990s, while business investment in R&D increased, as shown in Figures 10.3 and 10.4. Government spending is often linked to defence objectives. In the US, high levels of defence R&D during the cold war declined in the 1990s. As was pointed out in Chapter 9, supporters of the 'new trade theory' in the US generally favour greater government spending to enhance competitive advantage (Tyson, 1992).

Industrial structure

Large-scale investment in R&D is borne mainly by a country's large firms, as only they are able to undertake the long-term R&D programmes and the accompanying risks. Research has shown that the share of large firms is on average about 49 per cent, but it varies considerably between sectors (Patel and Pavitt, 1994). Of course, simply spending a lot of money on R&D does not ensure successful innovation. Inter-firm rivalry and competition in home markets can lead to 'imitative' increases in R&D in particular product fields (Patel and Pavitt, 1994). Small firms can play a role, as has been the case in high-tech areas. The small start-up is flexible and less bureaucratic than the large established firm and may be a rich source of ideas. Microsoft and many other high-tech companies began life as start-ups. In the US, venture capital for start-up firms has been more developed than in either Europe or Japan. The rapid growth of biotechnology start-ups in the US in the 1980s owed much to funding by venture capital. By 1999, the attraction had worn off and almost half of all venture capital investment in the US in 1999 was in internet-related companies (OECD, 2000d).

Science and technology strengths and weaknesses

Countries differ in their areas of specialization and the intensity of R&D activities. Where a country pursues a particular technological strength in an area of growing global importance, it stands to gain competitive advantage. Japan's intense investment in R&D in the fast-growing consumer electronics industry in the 1970s and 80s is an example. Japanese electronics firms overtook both European and US firms in taking out patents, both at home and in the US (Freeman, 1997). India's growth in software development is a more recent example of building competitive advantage, as shown in Case Study 10.2.

Interactions within the innovation system

Interactions, whether formal co-ordination or informal networking, contribute to innovation activities within a country and to their diffusion. Government guidance differs substantially from country to country. The co-ordinating role of Japan's Ministry of International Trade and Industry is often cited for its crucial role in the country's economic development. Strong state guidance in the Soviet Union, by contrast, was much less successful and the separate research institutes for each industry sector had only weak links with each other. The Soviet Union's concentration of R&D expenditure on military and space projects (3 per cent of gross national product (GNP)), coupled with the rigid command economy, left little scope for civilian innovation links to develop (Freeman, 1997). A more recent trend globally has been growing interaction between academic researchers and firms, as scientific research is playing a more important role in the development of many new technologies, such as life sciences.

National systems of innovation

Definition of a national system of innovation:

- 'the network of public and private institutions within an economy that fund and perform R&D, translate the results of R&D into commercial innovations, and effect the diffusion of new technologies.' (Mowery and Oxley, 1997, p. 154)

Elements of a national system of innovation:

- Education and training, including learning-by-doing and interactive learning
- Science and technology capabilities, involving public and business sectors
- Industrial structure, including investment in R&D
- Science and technology strengths and weaknesses, whereby countries' national specialisms differ
- Interactions within the innovation system, including government–business links and inter-firm collaborations

10.3.2 Some conclusions on national innovation systems

There is no one model of innovation system that can be said to be superior in generating and diffusing technological innovation. While it is clear from the example of the industrialized countries that innovation is linked to economic growth, countries show a good deal of diversity in their national innovation systems. Simple quantitative comparisons of R&D expenditure tell only a partial story. Social, cultural and historical differences have an influence on the ways in which learning, scientific curiosity and entrepreneurial flair are allowed to flourish in national environments (Lundvall, 1992). Government initiatives are more influential in some countries than in others. Huge investment in industrial R&D in Germany and Japan in the post-war period was crucial in their efforts to catch up economically. The ability to assimilate and imitate innovations from elsewhere as the basis of further local innovative developments has been a particular feature of Asian economic development. This process of technology transfer holds out to all nations the possibility of benefiting from innovation. However, technical change has proceeded unevenly among countries. Adaptation of technology and use in local environments is still dependent on diverse national systems. Diffusion of technology is in part governed by ownership structures of intellectual property, which have tended to be heavily concentrated in the producing countries. Hence, control of the ownership of technology can limit the extent of the benefits of technology transfer enjoyed by firms in industrializing countries.

Case study 10.2 India: a new tiger economy?

In just ten years, India has become established as a centre of the global software industry, employing an estimated 280,000 software engineers in about 1,000 companies, and sending many more to work overseas in California's Silicon Valley and elsewhere. The reasons behind this IT boom include the following factors:

- government deregulation of the internet in 1999
- entrepreneurial flair
- soaring demand for low-cost, high-quality software and services
- availability of highly skilled, relatively low-wage, English-speaking professionals
- geographic position, giving a time zone advantage with both the US and Europe, whereby outsourced software services can be provided overnight

Software exports have grown at a rate of about 50 per cent a year, the US being the biggest customer, accounting for about 61 per cent of Indian software exports. India's software exporters have moved up the value chain, from low-value maintenance work to design and development work increasingly focused on internet solutions.

But is India on the way to becoming a new tiger economy? Some observers are sceptical. They point to the fact that the Asian tigers were strong in manufacturing and, in particular, manufacturing exports, whereas India is much weaker. Poor quality infrastructure, unreliable electricity supplies, bureaucracy and weak support services such as banking hamper growth. Well-educated, basic workforces in the Asian tiger economies can be contrasted with the uneven situation in India, where there is a highly educated elite, but an overall literacy level of only 60 per cent. Thus it is difficult for companies to find the skills to compete in manufacturing. The Indian government plans to double enrolments in engineering colleges to meet demand for IT workers, in an effort to sustain India's competitive advantage in knowledge-based industries, including IT and pharmaceuticals. India is thus embracing the new economy, while still wrestling with some familiar problems of the old economy.

Sources: India: Information Technology (Financial Times Survey), *Financial Times*, 1 December 1999; Gardner, D., 'Weighed down by an old economy', *Financial Times*, 17 October 2000; 'India plans to double IT workers to meet global demand', *New York Times*, 5 August 2000.

Case question

To what extent does India's embrace of the new economy provide an engine for economic growth?

10.4 Patents and innovation

Patents are often referred to as a type of 'industrial' property, and patent activity is an indicator of levels of innovation. We should be cautious, though, not to read too much into patent statistics, as many innovations, such as informal and incremental improvements, fall outside patent activity. That said, patent statistics are an often-cited barometer of innovative activities.

Protection of property which exists in inventions and other products of human intellect have been the subject of heated policy debates from the days of the Industrial Revolution through to the present. Many would argue that technology should be freely available for anyone anywhere to use. Governments of industrialized countries, on the other hand, have long established policies for protecting intellectual property, in the belief that only by doing so will the incentive be provided for people to devote time and resources to innovation. From research and design through to testing, a new product can take many years before it reaches consumers. Companies, it is felt, would be unwilling to commit resources in the absence of a system for granting exclusive rights over the product for a reasonable period of time. It is acknowledged that limited monopolies are created, restricting competition, but it is argued that this is a price that must be paid to ensure technical progress (Bainbridge, 1996). Many in developing countries, on the other hand, argue that they are effectively frozen out by these policies because of the concentration of intellectual property ownership in the industrialized countries. This is a recurring issue in relation to innovation policies, to which we will return when we look at technology transfer. In this section, we look at the nature of intellectual property (IP) rights and how they come into being.

Minifile

WHERE WOULD WE BE WITHOUT ... ?

- *Self-adhesive tape*, invented in 1929, by a lab worker in 3M
- *Paper tissues*, invented in 1924 by Kimberley Clark and launched in 1930 as Kleenex
- The *power drill*, invented in 1895 by Wilhelm Fein of Stuttgart, Germany. Black & Decker's first portable drill was produced in 1910
- The *contact lens*, originally made of glass, was fitted to six patients by Dr Rudolf Frick in 1888. The first plastic contact lens was made by I.G. Farben in Germany in 1936
- The *ring-pull*, first used on canned beer by the Iron City Brewery of Pittsburgh in 1962
- The *paper cup*, created by Hugh Moore in 1909, for his water cooler with disposable cups
- The *Post-it note*, invented by Art Fry at 3M in 1975, now sold in over 200 countries

Source: Financial Times Business, 18 December 1999 and 2 December 2000.

10.4.1 What is a patentable invention?

The patentable invention is a new product or process which can be applied industrially. These basic requirements are similar across most countries, with some variations. In Europe, the main source of law is the European Patent Convention 1973 (EPC), which member states have incorporated into national law (These are EU states plus Switzerland, Monaco, Liechtenstein and Cyprus.) A European Patent Office was set up under the convention. In the UK, the relevant law is the Patents Act 1977. US patent law requires that the invention be 'useful' rather than 'industrially applicable', as required by the EPC. The requirement that the invention must be an industrial product or process rules out discoveries, scientific theories and mathematical methods, as they relate to knowledge and have no technical effect. Mere ideas or suggestions are also excluded, as a complete description of the invention must be submitted as part of the patent application. Moreover, the invention must not have been disclosed prior to the patent application, as once disclosed, it

Case study 10.3 Quest for the blockbuster drug

Waves of consolidation among the large pharmaceutical companies reflect the drive to put more money into R&D, in the search for the elusive blockbuster drug that will guarantee financial success. Sir Richard Sykes, Chairman of GlaxoSmithKline, said:

> You can't discover drugs with a man and a dog. It requires really big expenditure to pull together a lot of knowledge coming from different areas. There are some things we want to do today but can't, even with a £1.2 billion R&D budget. (Cookson, 2000)

R&D spending in the global pharmaceutical industry rose from $39 billion in 1998 to $43 billion in 1999. Newly merged GlaxoSmithKline, like its rival Pfizer-Warner Lambert, are likely to spend up to $4 billion a year on R&D.

The decoding of the human genome, the 100,000 genes that provide the blueprint for the human being, has resulted in opportunities to exploit key information on the causes of disease, which, it is argued, smaller companies are not in a position to do. On the other hand, large bureaucratic companies may be stifling innovation. Sidney Taurel, Chairman and CEO of Eli-Lilly, with its $2.3 billion R&D budget, says: 'We still do not believe that size per se matters ... There is no proof that the combined entity grows faster than the two entities separately. In fact, the reverse seems to be true' (Pilling, 2000).

GlaxoSmithKline announced in 2000 that the company would be separating R&D into eight competing centres around the world, in order to encourage innovation. The research would be broken down into therapeutic areas, such as anti-virals, asthma and cancer. The stakes are high. In 2000 Eli-Lilly lost a legal case in the US on a secondary patent for its biggest-selling 'lifestyle' drug, Prozac, while Pfizer lost a case on a secondary patent for its impotence drug, Viagra. These were seen a minor setbacks for the drugs concerned. Eli-Lilly has a new once-a-week patent for Prozac in the pipeline, as well as a rival to Viagra. More significant in the long term for drug companies is that any dilution of their patent protection would open the way for competition from generic producers, which charge a fraction of the branded product's price and would inevitably eat into their profits.

Sources: Cookson, C., 'Double size, double complexity', *Financial Times*, 6 April 2000; Pilling, D., 'Size isn't everything for Lilly', *Financial Times*, 4 July 2000; Michaels, A., 'Eli Lilly falls 31% after patent ruling on Prozac', *Financial Times*, 10 August 2000.

Case question

What is the importance of patent protection for drug companies and how is it being eroded?

becomes 'prior art' and can no longer be said to be new. Most inventions are not totally new products, but improvements on existing products. For a pharmaceutical drug, for example, a new patent can be obtained for a new dosage of one-a-week, rather than one-a-day. This can be a means of extending the life of a patent (see Case Study 10.3). While we tend to think of only the most formal inventions as patentable, in fact the scope of potentially patentable inventions is expanding all the time, extending to software, micro-organisms and business methods.

Computer software and business methods are both patentable in the US, but only to a limited extent in Europe. In Europe a software-based invention is patentable if it has a 'technical effect'. This means that a new program which affects how the computer operates is patentable, whereas a computer game is not. The game, like most software, is protected by copyright, but the expansion of software patents has been a trend in the US since they were recognized as patentable by the Supreme Court in 1981. In the US a 'way of doing business' is patentable, whereas it would not be in Europe, although there are ways of getting round this restriction. The US has seen growing numbers of business methods patent applications, especially for e-commerce patents, such as Amazon.com's 'one-click' shopping method in 1999. The European Commission is considering widening European law, but many believe that the US has gone too far in granting monopoly protection where there is little justifiable case. They argue that it is difficult to see how a miracle cure for AIDS and an online retailer's system for repeat orders are at all comparable. On the other hand, US companies are seeking to extend their coverage to Europe, where they accounted for 52 per cent of business methods applications to the European Patent Office (EPO) in 1999 (Amazon.com was among them) (*Financial Times*, 26 October 2000).

WWW
WEBALERT

The website of the UK Patent Office is
http://www.patent.gov.uk

The US Patent and Trademark Office is at
http://www.uspto.gov

The European Union's site for intellectual and industrial property is
http://europa.eu.int/comm/internal_market/en/intprop/indprop/index.htm
Latest proposals, directives and reports are all available here

10.4.2 Patent rights

The **patent** gives its owner an exclusive right for a limited period to exploit the invention, to license others to use it and to stop all unauthorized exploitation of the invention. Eighty per cent of patent holders are companies, not the actual inventors. The duration of a patent in the UK is four years, renewable for up to 20 years. Renewal fees become steeper over time and most inventions have been superseded by new technology long before the 20 years have expired. In the US, the normal duration is 20 years at the outset, with 'maintenance' fees payable at intervals. Being able to license the technology to other manufacturers entitles the patent holder to collect royalty fees agreed with the licensee. Much FDI relies on the licensing of technology. A patent may also be sold outright ('assigned') to someone else, who is then entitled to exploit it commercially. In common with other IP rights, 'exhaustion of rights' applies to patents. Under this principle, once the patent holder has consented to the marketing of the product in specific countries, he or she cannot prevent 'parallel imports', that is, importation of the product from another country, usually a lower cost one. A consequence is that the owner of a patent for a product which is sold in a number of countries might find it difficult to maintain price differentials between them.

Legal requirements for a patentable invention

The four legal requirements for a UK patent are that the invention must:

- be new, that is, not part of the 'state of the art'
- involve an 'inventive step', that is, not obvious to a person skilled in the art
- have an industrial application, either a product which can be made industrially, or a process which is a means of achieving a concrete result
- not be excluded from patentability. Excluded categories are scientific discoveries, literary works (for which copyright is available) and transgenic animals

Categories which *may* be patentable if the invention has a 'technical effect':

- computer software
- business method

For an inventor, the process of applying for a patent can be complicated, long and expensive. The process of patent office 'examination' of a patent application typically takes from two to four years. The help of expert professionals is almost always needed, stacking the odds against the individual inventor-entrepreneur. The simplest route for the inventor is to apply for a patent in his or her home country but, in that case, the patent granted will cover only that country, which most nowadays would find inadequate. There is no such thing as a global patent! For the multinational company with

Table 10.3 Comparison of costs and fees (in euros) for obtaining a patent in the EU, the US and Japan

	Filing and search fees	Examination fees	Grant fees	Renewal fees	Translation costs	Agent's fees	Total
EPC (typical application, eight member states)	810 + 532	1,431	715	16,790	12,600	17,000	49,878
US	690	–	1,210	2,730	n/a	5,700	10,330
Japan	210	1,100	850	5,840	n/a	8,450	16,450

Source: European Commission (July 2000) 'Commission proposes the creation of a Community Patent', at http://www.europa.eu.int/comm.

global markets, there are means available to alleviate the need to make separate applications in every country. The EPO in Munich (established by the EPC) provides one route. Application to the EPO allows the applicant to designate particular countries, typically eight, in which the patent will be valid. However, the grant will be a bundle of individual national patents, each of which must be translated into the national language and enforced in national courts. The expense of translation into several languages adds to the overall expense, making European patents several times more expensive than US or Japanese patents (see Table 10.3). Clearly, expense and bureaucracy can discourage innovation. Despite appeals from European businesses, attempts to create a single European patent have foundered for three decades. The most recent proposal, a European Commission proposal of July 2000, would allow a single application submitted in one language, making the process much more efficient and cheaper. Disputes would be settled under the European Court of Justice (ECJ), rather than in the many national legal systems. However, because the proposal would require treaty amendment, reform is likely to be slow.

An alternative route is offered by the Patent Co-operation Treaty (PCT) procedure, which covers over 100 countries. Under the PCT, the applicant makes one application to a regional office and the process is divided into an 'international' phase and a 'national' phase. For the applicant with a global market in mind, there are considerable savings to be made in comparison with multiple individual country applications. The process is overseen by the World Intellectual Property Organization (WIPO) in Geneva. There were 2,625 PCT applications in 1979, each designating on average 6.66 countries. By 1998, the total number of applications had grown to 67,007, and the average number of countries designated on each had leapt to 71.74 (WIPO, 1999). This would amount to 3.5 million individual national applications. It is possible to use multiple routes to gain competitive advantage. For example, an initial application may be filed through the national route, obtaining a filing date, or 'priority date', and then application is made to the EPO, which takes the same priority date if done within twelve months of the original application. This apparent 'backdating' can be a crucial advantage to an application, as the priority date is used for determining the prior art relevant to the application.

The US Patent Office receives the largest number of applications – over 250,000 in 1998 and 270,000 in 1999 (US Patent Office, 1999). It issued 143,686 patents in 1999. Strongest growth is in the information and communications technologies (ICT). Every national patent system receives a significant number of applications from abroad every year. These are an indication of levels of R&D activity and innovations in the pipeline. The US Patent Office granted 32,119 patents to Japanese applicants in 1998, a 32 per cent increase from the previous year, and an indication of activity in many areas of technology (Paul and Kano, 1999). In the UK in 1999, 63.9 per cent of the patents issued were to foreign residents (see Table 10.4). This implies that a substantial proportion of R&D is controlled by foreign firms, which are potentially more likely to migrate to other locations than home-based firms.

Table 10.4 UK patents granted in 1999, by leading countries of residence

Country of residence	Number of patents
United Kingdom	2,883
Canada	123
France	150
Germany	708
Japan	1,281
South Korea	533
Taiwan	181
USA	1,380
Total of other countries	756
Total	7,995

Source: The Patent Office Annual Report 1999–2000, Annex 1 (2000) (Newport, South Wales: Patent Office).

10.4.3 The Trade-Related Aspects of Intellectual Property (TRIPS) agreement

There have been significant efforts to harmonize national laws on intellectual property rights through multilateral agreements. Following the Uruguay Round of GATT, the agreement on **Trade-Related Aspects of Intellectual Property (TRIPS)** attempted to bring national legal regimes into harmony. Obligations of national treatment (equal treatment for foreign and domestic individuals and companies) and most-favoured nation (MFN) treatment (non-discrimination between foreign individuals and companies) apply. These provisions took effect from 1996 for most countries, with transitional periods allowed for developing countries to comply. Most developing countries had a further five years, but the least developed countries have ten years to comply (that is, until 2006). TRIPS does not aim to make all countries conform to a single system, but to set certain 'minimum standards', with latitude for national variations. In the controversial area of plants and animals, TRIPS provides that plant varieties must be patentable, but members may exclude certain types of plants and animal inventions. The TRIPS Council of the WTO monitors national laws for conformity. Disputes under TRIPS are settled through the WTO dispute settlement procedure.

TRIPS has come in for a great deal of criticism from developing countries. Industrial countries hold 97 per cent of all patents worldwide and global corporations hold 90 per cent of all technology and product patents (United Nations, 2000). Critical areas for developing countries are new drugs to fight diseases such as AIDS and new seeds for crops. Both areas rely on research in biotechnology, or life science technology. In industrial countries, the trend away from publicly funded research to private funding has brought the increasing domination of a few large multinationals in these areas. Many developing countries have either a weak patent system, or none at all. In pharmaceutical drugs, India allows patenting of processes, not products. The result has been a booming local industry producing generic drugs for sale to many poor countries, where inhabitants cannot afford the prices charged by the multinational drug companies. The TRIPS agreement will therefore require much tighter regulation of IP rights, as it provides 20-year protection of both process and products. More than 80 per cent of the patents granted in developing countries go to residents of the industrial countries (United Nations, 1999b). The TRIPS agreement therefore seems to consolidate the hold of the multinationals from industrial countries over intellectual property rights.

WWW
WEBALERT

Text and discussion of TRIPS may be found at
http://www.wto.org/english/tratop

The website for WIPO is
http://www.wipo.int/ Information on the PCT may be found here

10.5 Technology transfer

Acquiring technology from other countries is known as **technology transfer**. While the term usually refers to transfers from the advanced economies to industrializing economies, it also covers transfers between industrialized countries. Technology transfer has been crucial to the processes of industrial growth and global integration. It is now recognized that technology transfer is not a simple one-way process, but more interactive and complex. Research has reopened basic issues of how knowledge and skills are acquired and how imitation and innovation are interlinked.

10.5.1 Channels for international technology transfer

The post-war period has seen the emergence of four main channels of technology transfer. These are FDI, joint ventures and strategic alliances, licensing and trade in capital goods (Mowery and Oxley, 1997). We look at each in turn.

FDI

FDI investment by TNCs is a major source of technology for developing countries. For the host country, the benefits derive from observing, imitating and applying the technologies, including the management methods. Spillover effects can include linkages developed with domestic suppliers, but to exploit spillover effects requires incentives for local firms to adopt the new technologies. A recent trend among TNCs has been to relocate R&D activities from the home country to overseas locations, enhancing the parent company's overall innovative capacity (United Nations, 1999a). The late industrializing countries of Asia and Latin America have benefited from FDI flows, mainly from the US and Japan. From the 1980s, outflows from newly industrialized countries, mainly South Korea, Taiwan, and China, have also increased, reflecting a successful build-up of technological capabilities.

Joint ventures and strategic alliances

Collaborative innovation is a growing trend among firms in industrialized countries and also between firms in industrializing and advanced economies. As costs of innovation have increased and companies have become more specialized in R&D activities, companies see the benefits of marrying expertise and sharing costs. OECD research shows that numbers of new strategic alliances grew over the 1990s, from just over 1,000 in 1989 to over 7,000 in 1999 (OECD, 2000d).

Technology licensing

The owner of a patent may license a foreign manufacturer to produce the product under licence, in return for royalties. Many late industrializing countries have relied significantly on licences for technology, particularly from the US and Japan. South Korea's spending on licences increased tenfold in the period 1982–91 (Mowery and Oxley, 1997). The age of technology transferred through licensing, however, is significantly older than that through FDI.

Capital goods trade

Sometimes called 'embodied' technology transfer, the importation of machinery and equipment provides a means to assimilate the technology. By 'reverse engineering', discovering how a product has been made, it is possible to develop and refine the technology further. Japan's post-war industrial development is a good example of the benefits of imported technology, which were assimilated and complemented by local R&D and engineering capabilities. Japanese firms similarly benefited from licensed technology, building on substantial investments in R&D and engineering (Bell and Pavitt, 1997). Importing foreign technology is not limited to imitation, but part of a larger process of technological accumulation.

Channels for international technology transfer

- FDI, whereby opportunities to apply and adapt advanced technology can provide a foundation for local technological innovation
- Joint ventures and strategic alliances between firms in different countries, bringing together expertise in different disciplines
- Technology licensing, which allows a manufacturer to produce another's patented product, in return for royalties
- Capital goods transfer provides a means, by 'reverse engineering', of learning how a product is made and then to adapt and refine the technology further

10.5.2 Technology diffusion and innovation

Technological diffusion was once thought to be the simple acquisition and adoption by developing countries of the technologies of developed countries, akin to adopting a set of 'blueprints', without any further creative contribution. It is now recognized that this view is oversimplified, in that the processes of diffusing technology are more dynamic, involving technical changes and adaptations to specific local conditions. Technological learning, or 'absorptive capacity', is at the heart of these processes. Formal education and training clearly play a part, but much learning is also acquired by doing, as in 'on the job' training. To benefit from technological accumulation, firms need to develop skills and know-how to improve the technology acquired from abroad. Japan and Germany are examples of countries that have combined imported technology with development of local technological capabilities. On the other hand, late industrializing countries, while they have been able to increase productive capacity, have varied in their capacities for technological innovation.

Some economies may seem to have become locked into sectors where competitiveness depends on low-wage production and are unable to break into the more knowledge-based sectors. Examples are the Latin American economies. A scale-intensive motor industry grew up in Argentina in the 1950s and 60s, along with the beginnings of specialist supplier industries, but these seemed not to have progressed further in the 1990s (Bell and Pavitt, 1997). To the extent that this is the case, economies are said to be 'path-dependent'. By contrast, some of the Asian late industrializing economies have moved from labour-intensive sectors (which are supplier dominated) to sectors such as cars and consumer durables and then to specialized equipment. Singapore is an example of this trajectory. Certainly, while technological innovation would seem to have become more difficult for late-industrializing countries, there are even greater gaps between these and other developing countries, despite increasing access to international higher education and training. It has been suggested by Bell and Pavitt, that for today's developed countries, productive capacity and technological capacity developed in parallel. Doing and learning went hand in hand. By contrast, in the current, fast-moving world of technical change, 'the skills needed to use and operate technologies, and those required to create and change technology' have become separated (Bell and Pavitt, 1997, p. 123).

Activities of global companies in expanding their global reach through FDI and licensing have been major forces behind the diffusion of technology. Processes of technology transfer can thus be viewed from different perspectives. While they can be seen as part of a larger picture of globalization, they can also be seen as nation-specific, that is, dependent on national systems of innovation, rather than superseding them. It follows that national action, including government policies, can give needed impetus, as has happened in India in the software industry. Less developed countries, where well-trained workforces earn much lower salaries than in developed countries, may exploit opportunities in an area such as IT, for which geographic location is not a key issue (recall Case Study 10.2).

10.6 Information and communications technology (ICT)

The IT revolution has been compared to the industrial revolution in its pervasiveness, amounting to a further long wave, to use Schumpeter's terms. It began just after the Second World War, when, with army sponsorship, a team at the University of Pennsylvania produced the first electronic computer, a monster weighing 30 tons and using so much electricity that it caused Philadelphia's lights to flicker. The 1950s saw the commercial development of mainframe computers, spearheaded by IBM.

10.6.1 The technology revolution

In the early post-war period, many in the industry did not see the huge potential of computing. Those who did felt it would be a very long time before computer-based automation would bring about the 'automatic factory', and many feared it would bring mass unemployment. Diffusion of computer technology in the 30 years after the war rested on clusters of both radical and incremental innovations, such as computer-aided design (CAD) and software engineering. Economic factors also played a crucial role in diffusion, in that technical advantages were combined with falling prices. The arrival of microelectronics in the 1960s and the microprocessor in the early 1970s made possible the diffusion of computer technology across industries, ultimately extending to small to medium-size enterprises (SMEs). The spread of the microcomputer started with Apple Computer in 1976, followed by IBM's 'personal computer' (PC) in 1981, whose name has become the generic name for microcomputers. IBM's PC relied not on its own software, as Apple's machine had done, but on Microsoft's MS-DOS operating system. The number of PCs leapt from 2 million in 1981 to 5.5 million in 1982, due in large part to cloning, which served to diffuse the technology all over the world and create a common standard.

Microprocessors have been described as the 'fundamental building block of the new technology', making it possible to produce better products more cheaply and efficiently (Baily, 2000). A single memory chip now holds 250,000 times as much data as one from the early 1970s. In 1970 a state-of-the-art computer cost about $4.7 million, which was equivalent to 15 times the lifetime wages of the average American worker. Now, a personal computer with more than ten times as much computing power can be purchased for less than two weeks' wages for an average worker. The average cost of processing information fell from about $75 per million operations in 1960 to one-hundredth of a cent in 1990.

Table 10.5 Numbers and percentages of the population on the internet in 20 selected countries (2000)

Country	Number of people (millions)	Percentage of population
Australia	7.77	40.54
China	16.9	1.34
India	4.5	0.45
Japan	27.06	21.38
South Korea	15.3	32.31
Czech Republic	0.35	3.4
Denmark	2.3	43.1
Finland	2.27	43.93
France	9	15.26
Germany	18	21.74
Iceland	0.14	52.11
The Netherlands	6.8	42.79
Norway	2.2	49.57
Poland	2.8	7.25
Russia	9.2	6.3
Spain	4.6	11.5
Sweden	4.5	50.72
UK	19.47	32.72
US	148.03	53.72
Canada	13.28	42.8

Source: Nua Internet Survey (2000) at http://www.nua.ie/surveys.

10.6.2 The internet and e-commerce

Further networking capacities were opened up with the creation and rapid development of the internet. Like computing technology, the internet was a product of military research, the first network dating from 1969. Initially, the US Defense Department and university research centres, including the National Science Foundation, were able to communicate via the network, but commercial exploitation and corporate use were not far behind, eventually, in 1979, being able to link up computers through ordinary phone lines. From military-inspired innovation, the internet became available to anyone, anywhere, with a PC, decreasing in price all the time.

The diffusion of computer technology led to reorganization of factories and increases in productive capacity. Changes in the workplace required both new skills and new management structures. The pervasive effects on social and economic organization brought about by technical changes have been termed a new 'technological paradigm'. These changes are the basis of the 'new economy', or the 'knowledge economy', whose fundamental features are that it is 'informational, global and networked' (Castells, 2000a, p. 77). In the process referred to as 'technological convergence', telecommunications technology is now integrated with information processing technology. Innovations in ICT can thus be major drivers of globalization, making possible a networked, interdependent global economy traversing nation-states.

WWW
WEBALERT

The European Union e-commerce unit's website is
http://www.ispo.cec.be/ecommerce/
This is a comprehensive site for information on technology, policy, trends and international developments

Internet trends can be found on the Nua website at
http://www.nua.ie/surveys

Internet trends are also available from IDC, an internet research firm, at
http://www.idcresearch.com/default.htm

E-commerce, which is the use of the internet to replace traditional paper transactions, has been one of the major recent developments in the rapidly growing world of communications technology. While the major centres are still the industrialized countries, where there is the highest density of internet users, e-commerce is expanding in other parts of the world as well, particularly in Asia. E-commerce has opened up enormous opportunities for both business-to-consumer and business-to-business commerce. E-retailing has grown as PC density has increased, mainly in the industrialized countries, as shown in Table 10.5 on internet penetration.

Following the dotcom start-up retailers, which were conceived as internet businesses, e-retailing is now seen as integral to traditional bricks-and-mortar businesses. Services too, including banking and other financial services, have expanded rapidly. Much 'e-tailing' is substitution, shifting business from high street retailers and banks to online equivalents. Nonetheless, e-tailing has dramatically increased the potential not just for sales, but also for marketing, advertising and customer relations. There are still drawbacks to online purchases of goods and services. A major one is security. Although the tech-

Case study 10.4 A quiet revolution in manufacturing

Although rather overlooked in the frenzy of dotcom start-ups, the internet is transforming key operations in the manufacturing sector. Four main areas identified by Ken Vollmer, Research Director at Giga Information Group are:

- Product design, in which information may be shared over the internet
- Procurement, through business-to-business e-marketplaces
- Customer service, improving customer support for products
- Supply chain innovations, which can be critical in the competitive environment, in which product life cycles become shorter.

Fujitsu Siemens has invested 30 million euros in a programme to improve manufacturing and streamline the supply chain, aiming to reduce the build cost of its PCs by 40 per cent and cut distribution costs by 25 per cent. It is not just high-tech companies that are using the internet. Caterpillar, which manufactures construction equipment, is creating an internet-based marketplace, which it hopes will save $100 million in the first year. Targeted improvements are faster product introduction cycles, more efficient design collaboration with suppliers, improved inventory management and more cost-effective ordering.

Some of the more imaginative internet applications are in the design process. New software tools make possible the access of CAD files on the Web. Online services can link designers and engineers in online meetings, publish design data on the Web, and drag content from manufacturers' websites to drop it into online drawings. Virtual meetings and design reviews can thus be conducted on the Web by engineers and designers working in different countries.

Internet technology is also invading operations, allowing production control managers to link into factory equipment and view real-time production data. In a *Financial Times* review, Geoffrey Nairn concludes: 'Experts see a day when every controller and piece of factory equipment will have a unique internet protocol (IP) address and can thus be directly linked into an internet-based supply chain'.

Source: Nairn, G., 'Ripples from a quiet revolution bring net gains for manufacturing sector', *Financial Times*, 1 November 2000 (reprinted with permission).

Case question

In what ways is the internet transforming manufacturing and what are the implications for the future?

nology of security systems is improving, security breaches are a serious threat in e-commerce. Research by the Department of Trade and Industry (DTI) in the UK suggests that more than half of firms experience security breaches, but only one in seven has a formal security management policy (*Financial Times*, 7 June 2000).

The biggest opportunities are taking place in business-to-business commerce, which could well reach growth rates of 60–80 per cent a year (see Figures 10.5a and 10.5b). These developments provide opportunities for worldwide sourcing for all sectors, including raw materials, components and services. The internet can save costs by streamlining purchasing, distribution and marketing. While the benefits have been apparent to multinationals above all, SMEs too have benefited. SMEs are able to form networks linked to multinational companies, opening up new avenues for co-operative development of technology as well as markets. The transnational 'web' of global production networks is transforming supply chains. In 1999, General Motors and Ford announced plans to develop online trading exchanges for supplier transactions. Again, there are social and labour implications of these developments. Developing countries may gain from the new economy, as software centres in India and the Philippines have demonstrated, but whether these gains will close the 'digital divide' between rich and poor countries remains an issue (to be discussed further in Chapter 12).

WWW
WEBALERT

The UK Government sponsors a global information network for SMEs at http://www.open.gov.uk/g7/sme/

Figure 10.5 Composition of worldwide internet commerce

(a) 1997 total: $15 billion

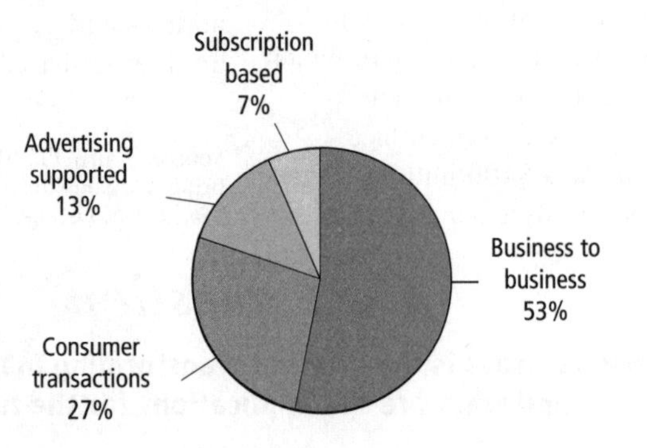

(b) 2002 total: $1,053 billion

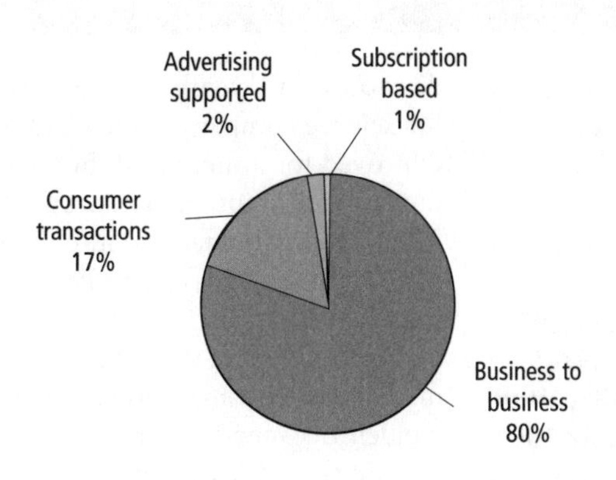

Source: Information Technology Survey, *Financial Times*, 19 January 2000, p. vi.

10.7 Biotechnology

Biotechnology is 'the application of scientific and engineering principles to the processing of materials by biological agents to provide goods and services' (OECD, 1999). Because biotechnology is concerned with the manipulation of living organisms, it is often called 'life science' technology. Practical applications extend from primary sectors (such as agriculture and forestry) to secondary industries (such as food, chemicals and drugs). The growth in biotechnology is a further aspect of technological convergence, made possible by the advances in computing. Research on the genetic make-up of living organisms has led to 'genetic engineering' or genetic modification. The research is relatively young, having begun only in the 1980s. Genetically modified (GM) bacteria producing human insulin for treatment of diabetes was approved in 1986, as was the first vaccine using deoxyribonucleic acid (DNA). The use of vaccines to prevent disease is one of the greatest potential benefits from the new science of microbiology. Whereas treatment for many diseases is expensive and inaccessible, vaccines offer an affordable alternative. In developing countries in particular, the death toll from preventable diseases, especially the childhood killer diseases, could be dramatically reduced (Freeman and Robbins, 1995).

Biotechnology research has not been without controversy. Scientists have inserted foreign genes into animals in their efforts to study human diseases and possible cures. A company based in Scotland, PPL Therapeutics, created Dolly the sheep and was successful in obtaining a patent from the EPO. Researchers in the US have created a cloned monkey, the first GM mammal.

Case study 10.5 A food revolution?

The production of genetically engineered plants to endow them with various qualities, such as the corn that produces its own pesticide, is altering farming and food systems, but there are doubts about long-term effects in both developed and developing countries. In 1996, GM crops were planted on just over 4 million acres worldwide. In 1999, GM soya, corn, cotton and other crops were grown on nearly 100 million acres, most of it in the US, Argentina and Canada. The US is far ahead of other countries. It is estimated that as much as 70 per cent of the foods on the shelves of US supermarkets contains GM ingredients, although it is difficult to tell, as there is no mandatory labelling in the US. While farmers and consumers in the US have appeared to be untroubled by worries about food safety, there are signs of consumer uneasiness. McDonald's and other companies have asked suppliers to stop shipping GM potatoes.

European consumers have been sceptical about GM foods. Many supermarkets and fast-food outlets guarantee GM-free products and products with GM ingredients are required to be labelled. GM crops are produced as trial crops only and the accidental inclusion of GM seeds in consignments of non-GM seeds from Canada generated adverse publicity. The incident also highlighted the difficulties of preventing GM crops from mingling with non-GM crops. In the US in 2000, Kraft Foods announced a nationwide recall of taco shells which contained bioengineered corn, developed by Aventis CropScience, a large life science company, which had been approved for animal feed, but not for human consumption. The corn, milled in Texas and manufactured into shells in Mexico by a subsidiary of PepsiCo, proved impossible to trace.

For developing countries, research has made possible a high-protein maize and 'golden rice' enriched with vitamin A, which can aid the estimated two million children vulnerable to diseases related to vitamin A deficiency in poor countries. Both were invented by Western scientists, funded by research institutes, but IP rights have been acquired by global life science corporations, Monsanto (now part of Pharmacia & Upjohn) and AstraZeneca. In Third-World-friendly gestures, they are giving developing countries' farmers free access to the grain. Sceptics question the use of golden rice as a 'quick-fix' remedy, pointing to more low-tech, cost-effective alternatives, such as the reintroduction of the diverse food plants which farmers used to grow before the 'green revolution' of the 1960s brought high-yield hybrid plants, also produced by Western laboratories.

Sources: Barboza, D., 'Farmers scaling back genetically altered crops', *New York Times*, 1 April 2000; Marquis, C., 'Monsanto plans to offer rights to its altered-rice technology', *New York Times*, 4 August 2000; Pollack, A., 'On the trail of genetically altered corn flour from Azteca', *New York Times*, 30 September 2000; Pollack, A., 'Kraft recalls taco shells with bioengineered corn', *New York Times*, 23 September 2000.

Case question

What are the benefits and risks of GM crops for developing countries?

Under the Biotechnology Patents Directive, neither DNA nor the human genome can be patented, as they are discoveries. However, an invention based on gene sequences, requiring the isolation and manufacture of genes, can be patented, as human intervention is involved, assuming the process is capable of industrial application.

WWW
WEBALERT

Among many biotechnology websites are the following:
http://www.bubl.ac.uk/biotechnology
http://www.oecd.org/ehs/biolinks.htm

The Biosafety Information Network is at
http://www.binas.unido.org/binas/index

Research has made possible the breeding of high-yield, disease-resistant plants, with reduced reliance on pesticides and herbicides. However, it has given rise to ethical questions which have generated heated debate, centred on food safety and the environmental impact. One of these concerns is doubts over the research underpinning GM foods, including food safety and environmental effects. North American consumers have so far been relatively unperturbed about GM foods, whereas European consumers have been much more sceptical, as shown in Case Study 10.5. Some experts argue that scientific advances hold out genuine prospects of revolutionized food production to feed the growing populations of developing countries. This raises a second ethical concern, which is the powerful position of the few global companies, all based in industrialized countries, that now dominate the world's agribusiness sector. The expansion of the use of patents to cover seed varieties has helped to consolidate their economic power, but also raised questions of public policy and accountability. Farming communities in developing countries fear the risk to local ecosystems from GM crops, while reducing their scope to produce alternative crops.

10.8 Globalization and technological innovation

Howells and Wood pose the question:

> How is the global shaping of production (in terms of overall corporate structures) influencing the distribution and character of R&D and technical competence? Corporate, and consequently national, performance is at the interface between research/technical know-how and production. (Howells and Wood, 1993, p. 7)

We have seen in this chapter that globalization of production has led to a diffusion of technology, but also that technological capacities still depend to a large extent on national innovation systems. It is also true that technological innovation increasingly depends on links between scientific research and industrial R&D, both of which differ between national technological environments. The R&D strategies of global companies aim to draw on sectoral specializations offered by specific countries. Archibugi and Michie observe that 'Nations are becoming *increasingly* different and the international operations of large firms are exploiting and developing this diversity' (Archibugi and Michie, 1997b, p. 191).

Globalization processes in both generating innovation and exploiting its fruits therefore highlight the continued role of national government policies. Providing incentives to companies for innovative activities and supportive infrastructure such as industry–university partnerships, they can attract the innovative activities that generate competitive advantages. It is for this reason that Michael Porter and others stress the importance of government in fostering innovation. Technological innovation thus has a national as well as global dimension. Countries which have concentrated on low-cost, labour-intensive manufacturing industries have been less successful in developing the more technologically advanced production systems. It is arguable that businesses in these countries may find opportunities in the knowledge-intensive industries of the new economy, where geographic location is less important. On the other hand, poor developing countries risk falling further behind, opening up a 'digital divide' between rich and poor countries. We will return to this issue in Chapter 12, with discussion of the challenges facing international businesses.

10.9 Conclusions

1. Technology is central to economic development and prosperity. Technological innovation can lead to competitive advantages in the world economy.

2. Innovation is a broad term, ranging from seemingly modest improvements in operations to radical new inventions that transform the way we live.

3. Technological development can be seen in terms of 'long waves' or cycles, each wave denoted by its dominant new technology, which transforms both methods of production and organizational structures. The current wave is that of microelectronics and computer networks.

4. The national system of innovation is defined as the institutions by which a country's innovation activities are encouraged and facilitated. Education and training, as well as industrial structures, are important components. Interactions, both formal and informal, are increasingly seen as contributing to innovation networks.

5	Patents are an indication of the amount of formal innovation in a society, and also the sources of innovation. Both products and processes, if new and industrially applicable, can be patented. Patent law regimes are still essentially national.
6	For developing countries, technology transfer represents a variety of means for acquiring technology from other countries. They include FDI, joint ventures, licensing and trade in capital goods. The diffusion of technology is increasingly seen as an interactive process, in which host countries can develop independent innovative capacities over time.
7	ICT has led to transformational change in all aspects of business life. The growth in business-to-business e-commerce, in particular, is bringing about greater efficiencies in design, production and distribution.
8	The impact of globalization of production on the generation of global technological innovation is much debated. R&D activities of TNCs are becoming more dispersed, benefiting from nation-specific specialisms.

Review questions

???

1. Explain science-push and demand-pull in the development of new technology.
2. What is Schumpeter's view of technological innovation and waves of economic development?
3. Outline the elements of a national system of innovation. How relevant is the educational and training environment of the country?
4. Which countries have evolved particularly successful national innovation systems and why?
5. Why are patents crucial to technological lead?
6. What are the conditions which must be satisfied before a patent may be obtained for a process or product?
7. Why is the TRIPS agreement said to be disadvantageous to developing countries?
8. Describe briefly the four ways in which technology transfer takes place, pointing to the advantages and disadvantages of each.
9. In what ways has the revolution in IT transformed business?
10. Assess the possible benefits and the ethical issues of biotechnology research.

Assignments

1. Assess the differences in national innovation systems and the ways in which government policies are relevant to technological innovation.
2. How do businesses and societies benefit from technology transfer? Assess the difficulties for developing countries in closing the 'technology gap'.

Further reading

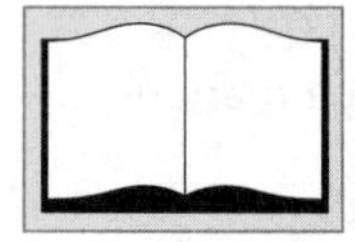

Archibugi, D. and Michie, J. (1997) *Technology, Globalisation and Economic Performance* (Cambridge: Cambridge University Press)

Castells, M. (2000) *The Rise of the Network Society*, 2nd edn (Oxford: Blackwell)

Freeman, C. and Soete, L. (1997) *The Economics of Industrial Innovation*, 3rd edn (London: Cassell)

Landes, D. (1998) *The Wealth and Poverty of Nations* (London: Abacus)

Pearce, R. (1997) *Global Competition and Technology* (Basingstoke: Macmillan – now Palgrave)

Chapter 11

International financial markets

Outline of chapter

LEARNING OBJECTIVES

1. To gain an overview of the evolving structures and processes that make up the international financial system, including the extent and implications of financial globalization for international business
2. To analyse the ways in which shifting patterns of global finance have impacted in diverse economic environments, including developed, industrializing and developing countries
3. To gain an insight into the role of transnational corporations (TNCs) in driving globalization through strategies of acquisition and control

11.0 Introduction

Smoothness and efficiency in financial transactions are valued by all businesses, whether local, national or international. For business dealings which are entirely within national boundaries, these aims are much more easily achieved than they are when dealings are across national borders. With globalization, many more firms, including small to medium-size enterprises (SMEs), are internationally active. There is therefore a growing need for businesspeople to grasp essential aspects of the international financial environment. Growing trade networks lead to a demand for cross-border financial services. These include currency exchanges, stock exchanges, banks and other financial intermediaries by which money transfers take place and credit is arranged. Like international trade in goods, cross-border financial flows have existed for centuries. However, the twentieth century saw major changes in international finance. Growing overseas investment, as well as trade, led to the growth of global capital markets and global financial institutions. Facilitated by improvements in communications technology, cross-border capital flows have become more extensive and national financial systems have become more deeply enmeshed than ever before in global financial networks.

Global financial markets are now 24-hour-a-day, fast-moving and complex processes, whose operations are on a scale which dwarf many national governments: world foreign exchanges deal with an average $1,490 billion every day. This chapter will attempt to demystify these processes as they impact on businesses. A major aim is to explain in relatively simple terms how international financial institutions interact with businesses, investors and national financial systems. As will be seen, sharply differing perspectives have emerged between enterprises, consumers and governments. The growth of international financial institutions, raising broad questions of stability and control in financial markets, has drawn both praise and criticism. From the business point of view, there are huge benefits from integrated markets, which have been particularly evident in emerging markets, but there are also risks of instability and vulnerability to financial shocks. TNCs have been major drivers of financial globalization. A second aim of the chapter, therefore, will be to explore the role of TNCs in global financial markets. Shifting patterns of corporate control, now evident on a global scale, have revealed the differing perspectives of corporate management, shareholders, lenders, consumers and governments. With globalization has come greater awareness of the interactions between market, national and international forces that increasingly impact on international business.

11.1 International capital markets

Access to capital is essential for every company. Firms may turn to banks and other institutions for loans, raising capital by debt financing. Or they may

Figure 11.1 Numbers of US and European IPOs

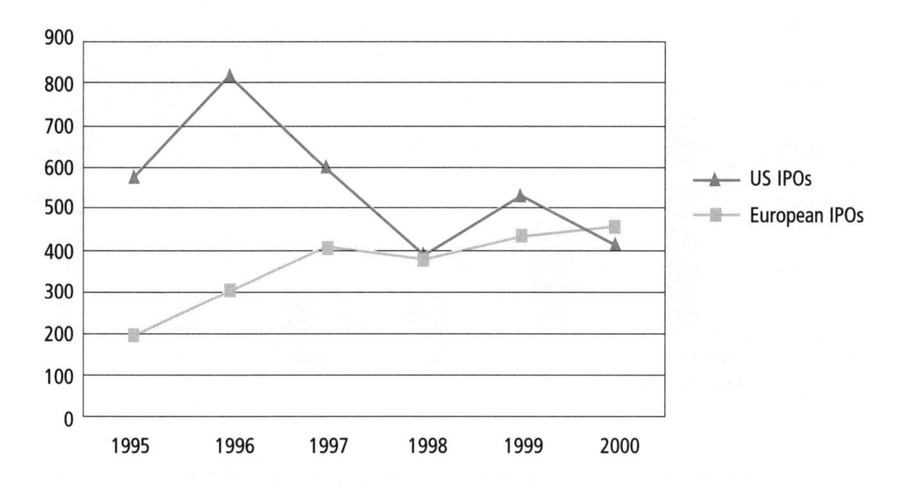

Source: Financial Times, 24 November 2000.

raise capital through share offerings, known as 'equity financing'. In practice, companies rely on both equity and debt financing. When share prices have been buoyant, investors have flocked to purchase shares. With high-tech shares in particular, investors became accustomed to dramatic increases in share prices in the 1990s, but these giddy heights could not be sustained and prices tumbled in 2000. When a company is publicly 'floated', it is listed on a stock exchange, and its shares are offered through an **initial public offering** (IPO). In the 1990s, European countries saw a steep rise in the number of IPOs, largely because of privatizations in major industries such as telecommunications (see Figure 11.1). The largest in 2000 was the flotation of Deutsche Post, Europe's biggest postal service operator, in a market capitalization of 23.4 billion euros. By contrast, as can be seen from Figure 11.1, US IPOs lost momentum towards the end of 2000, as IPO shares disappointed investors expecting dazzling early gains which had typified internet IPOs a year earlier.

11.1.1 Stock exchanges

By 2000, the total capitalization of the world's publicly traded equity was over $20 trillion (New York Stock Exchange, 2000). Capital markets refer to flows of capital, including equity investments (portfolio investment) and also government securities. They are handled through stock exchanges. **Stock exchanges** facilitate the buying and selling of shares and other securities, in an increasingly integrated global economy. Companies may apply for a 'listing' on a stock exchange, allowing their shares to be traded publicly in equity

Figure 11.2 Turnover value on leading stock exchanges

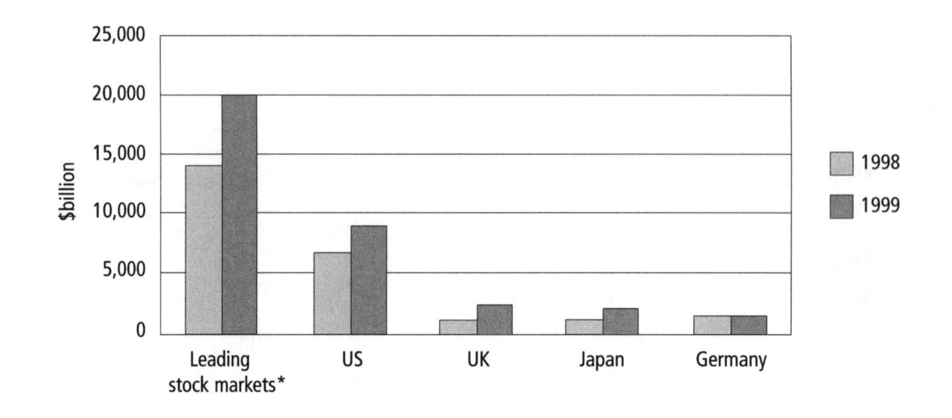

Note
* Includes US, UK, Japan, Germany, Sweden, France, Spain, Italy, Switzerland, Netherlands, Canada, Hong Kong, Australia, Singapore, Finland, Denmark, Belgium, Norway, Malaysia, Austria, New Zealand.

Source: Financial Times, 19 May 2000.

markets. Stock exchanges are located in financial centres around the world. Along with traditional exchanges, such as the New York and London Stock Exchanges, there are rapidly growing newer exchanges, such as the Nasdaq (National Association of Securities Dealers Automated Quotations system) in New York. Founded in 1971, the Nasdaq focuses on technology and other 'new economy' stocks. In Europe, the Frankfurt Neuer Markt, founded in 1997, has also grown rapidly. There are many indices following the movement of share prices, including the Dow Jones Industrial Average and Nasdaq Composite in New York and the FTSE 100 index in London. The indices, which represent baskets of shares, give only a performance benchmark and have been criticized as not reflecting true market performance (Coggan, 2000). The typical picture of frantic trading on the floor of stock exchanges is now becoming outdated, with the rise in electronic trading systems, which facilitate global trading. The New York Stock Exchange now handles 40 per cent of its volume through SuperDOT, its computerized trading system (New York Stock Exchange, 2000).

While stock markets historically served the needs of investors within their national borders, global companies now often seek listings outside their home countries in order to attract more international investors. The New York Stock Exchange estimates that US investors, who traditionally invest in US companies, are likely to double the non-US component of their equity portfolios from 5 per cent to around 10 per cent over the next few years (NYSE, 2000). While this may not seem very significant, it could amount to $350 billion shifting into foreign equity markets (Cochrane et al., 1995). An important trend in capital markets has been the growth of institutional investors, such as pension funds and other investment funds. Investment institutions have broadened their horizons from their national markets to international markets. The largest are the US institutional investors, who have assets six times the size of their European counterparts. The US-based index fund managers lead the world in international investment, accounting for about 70 per cent of the entire market for internationally traded equities (Conference Board, 1999). Some of these institutional shareholders, such as the California Public Employees (Calpers) with $24.3 billion holding of foreign equities, are noted for their shareholder activism. Their greater participation in international markets is likely, as the *Institutional Investment Report* points out, to lead to greater pressures on company boards to increase shareholder value.

WWW
WEBALERT

World stock exchanges have informative websites on how they function

The New York Stock Exchange is at
http://www.nyse.com

New York's Nasdaq exchange is at
http://www.nasdaq.com

The London Stock Exchange is at
http://www.londonstockexchange.com

The Tokyo Stock exchange is at
http://www.tse.or.jp/

The German Stock Exchange is at
http://www.exchange.de

There are two sites that offer links to all the world's major exchanges:
http://www.nyse.com/international/globalmarketplace.html
http://www.nasdaq.com/reference/onlinemarkets.stm

Stock exchanges are subject to national regulation. Regulatory systems aim to establish transparency and 'market integrity, that is, ensuring that the market is fair and efficient and warrants public confidence' (OECD, 2000a). Cross-border markets present new challenges to national systems of regulation. Integration in capital markets has not been matched by integrated regulatory frameworks. The advent of e-commerce, which facilitates almost instantaneous securities transactions around the globe, benefits investors, but is also vulnerable to market abuse. Protection of the investing public is a major concern of stock market regulators. In the US, the Securities and Exchange Commission provides oversight. In the UK, the regulation of financial services was reformed by the Financial Services and Markets Act 2000. Under the new framework, the Financial Services Authority (FSA) took

Minifile

THE UK FINANCIAL SERVICES AUTHORITY

The expanded role of the FSA under the Financial Services and Markets Act 2000 includes:

- Authorization and supervision of stock-brokers and financial advisors
- Oversight of the new offence of 'market abuse', aimed at protecting the investing community
- Banking supervision
- Regulation of building societies
- Protection of investors, taking over from the Investment Management Regulatory Organization and Personal Investment Authority
- Supervision of insurance services, taking over from the Insurance Directorate

over from nine former regulatory authorities, acquiring wide powers of regulation of insurance, investment business and banking.

Most stock exchanges have gone through a period of liberalizing, 'big bang' reforms, dismantling restrictions on trading and opening up markets. Although most of the EU has adopted a single currency, it has been much slower to integrate financial markets. The persistence of home-country supervision has allowed fragmentation in financial markets to persist, with the result that investors have not as yet been able to take advantage of the full benefits of the single currency. One stumbling block has been the contentious issue of harmonizing tax rules, which has been highly sensitive politically. Businesses within the EU have urged government finance ministers to speed up the integration of financial regulatory systems, in order to enhance the efficiency (and investor appeal) of its capital markets.

WWW WEBALERT

Financial regulators

The UK FSA is at
http://www.fsa.gov.uk
This site provides a summary of the Financial Services and Markets Act 2000

The US Securities and Exchange Commission is at
http://www.sec.gov/

11.1.2 Bond markets

Debt financing has given rise to an international bond market which facilitates trade in a variety of loan instruments. A **bond** is a loan document promising to pay a specific sum of money on a fixed date and pay interest at stated intervals (Held et al., 1999, p. 205). Bonds are marketable securities which can be issued in different currencies. An 'external bond' is one issued by a borrower in a capital market outside the borrower's own country. The external bond may be a foreign bond, which is issued in the currency of the country in which it is issued. **Eurobonds**, by contrast, are issued in currencies other than those of the countries in which they are issued. Dollar-denominated bonds issued outside the US are examples of eurobonds. Their attraction has been that they escape official regulation. Global bonds are the most flexible of bonds, as they may be sold inside as well as outside the country in whose currency they are denominated. Dollar global bonds are regulated by the US Securities and Exchange Commission (SEC). The World Bank is the leading issuer of global bonds. Governments have also raised money in this way, with the recent addition of developing countries. Of the international bond market, eurobonds account for about 70 per cent, while foreign and global bonds amount to 30 per cent (Kim and Kim, 1999, p. 276). The largest category of borrower is banks, followed by corporations and governments.

Companies must listen to bondholders as well as shareholders when taking strategic decisions. As can be seen in Figure 11.3, corporate bonds became more popular in the latter half of the 1990s, largely because share performance over the period weakened. In particular, telecommunications companies have relied heavily on the issue of bonds to pay government authorities for third-generation mobile phone licences. In 1998, telecoms companies issued $65 billion of debt globally, whereas the figure for 2000 was $155 billion. As of December, 2000, the biggest-ever multi-currency corporate bond issue was that of Deutsche Telekom in June, 2000, amounting to $14.6 billion of debt.

Figure 11.3 Corporate bond issues in the US and UK, 1995–99

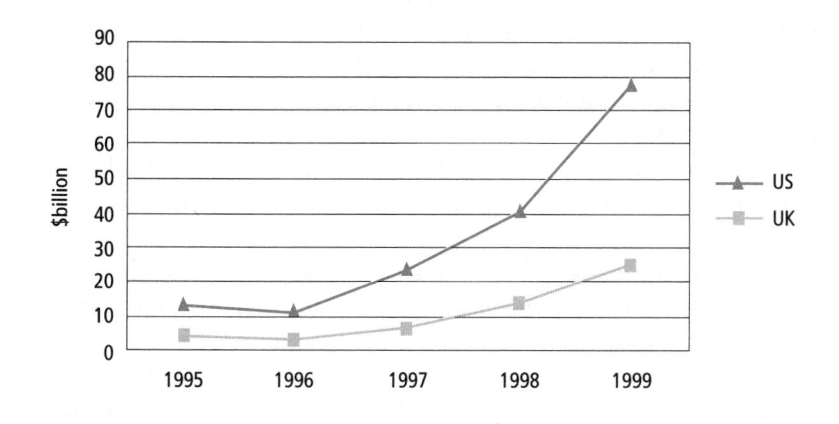

Source: The World in 2000 (1999) (London: *The Economist*) p. 140.

11.2 Development of the international monetary system

Besides equity investment and debt financing, global finance also includes the important element of cross-border flows of money, via money markets. Currencies are generally controlled by national central banks, although the European Central Bank is more akin to a 'supranational' institution. Currencies, however, are linked in global financial networks, which have become more integrated as trade and foreign direct investment (FDI) have grown. The growth in global financial flows has outpaced both trade and output (Held et al., 1999, p. 203). For businesses, consumers and governments, stability in international finance is a priority. However, achieving an effective international system has relied on co-operation between sovereign states, which has encountered numerous hurdles. In order to understand the challenges currently confronting international financial institutions, we need to look briefly at how they have evolved.

11.2.1 The gold standard

The rise in trade and financial flows from the late nineteenth century led to growing internationalization of finance. To facilitate these movements, the world's major trading nations adopted a global **gold standard** system, which lasted from the 1870s to 1914, a period in which Britain was the strongest trading nation. Under the gold standard, all currencies were 'pegged' to gold, which removed the uncertainty of transactions involving different currencies. For each currency, a conversion rate into gold ensured stability. The system required countries to convert their currency into gold on demand and did not restrict international gold flows. Governments willingly endorsed the system, even though, in theory, it reduced their control over their own economic policy. In practice, governments did not always play by the 'rules of the game', and there was more national monetary autonomy than supposed (Eichengreen, 1996, p. 28). Significantly, national interest rates, while they showed some convergence, were largely influenced by domestic conditions. Nonetheless, the gold standard period represented the emergence of a global financial order.

The maintenance of the gold standard depended on central banks' continuing commitment to external convertibility. Eichengreen comments:

> The essence of the pre-war system was a commitment by governments to convert domestic currency into fixed quantities of gold and freedom for individuals to export and import gold obtained from official and other sources. (1996, p. 46)

This system broke down with the First World War, when governments used precious metal to purchase military supplies and restricted movements in the gold market, thus causing currencies to float. The system collapsed, despite efforts to resurrect it in the inter-war period, during which government priorities had shifted from exchange rate stability to domestic economic concerns. Moreover, the domination, or hegemony, that Britain had exerted over capital markets had declined and the rise of American commercial and financial power did not lead to its taking on a similar role in the international system (Eichengreen, 1996, p. 92).

11.2.2 The Bretton Woods agreement

The Bretton Woods agreement at the close of the Second World War was meant to usher in a new international financial order and a restoration of stable foreign exchange. It was not, however, simply a revamped gold standard system. It differed from the gold standard system in three ways. First, currencies were pegged to the dollar, with the dollar fixed in terms of gold at $35 an ounce. This was an 'adjustable peg'. A country could alter its currency only if it was in 'fundamental disequilibrium', which was not fully defined. Second, controls were permitted, to limit private financial flows. Third, a new institution, the **International Monetary Fund** (IMF) was created to monitor national economic policies. The IMF could also help out countries with balance-of-payments difficulties. The Bretton Woods system has been described as 'a compromise between the free traders, who desired open global markets, and the social democrats, who desired national prosperity and full employment' (Held et al., 1999, p. 201). It aimed to liberalize world trade, but also took into account governments' wishes to maintain systems of social protection and other domestic objectives. This meant that governments had considerable autonomy to pursue domestic economic policies.

During the 1950s and into the 60s, international capital flows were low, largely because of national capital controls and also because of the limited infrastructure for private international capital flows. This situation was about to change dramatically. Events in the 1960s and 70s led to the collapse of the Bretton Woods system. Three factors can be highlighted. First, in the 1960s the US was gripped by inflation and a mounting trade deficit, fuelled by increasing imports, largely from the growing economies of Europe. Second, there rose the 'Euromarkets', which were systems for taking foreign currency deposits, such as dollar deposits, in European banks (Kapstein, 1994, p. 32). The source of the dollars could be individual investors, central banks or firms. From the 1950s, a Eurocurrency market grew, as funds flowed into European banks, and European economies were growing. European banks were able to expand their Eurocurrency business, unrestrained by the national regulations and capital controls. Third, the Organization of Petroleum Exporting Countries' (OPEC) quadrupling of the price of oil (see Case Study 9.1) had the effect of transferring huge sums from the oil-importing countries to the oil-exporting countries. The oil exporters, with their mounting surpluses, invested in international money markets, swelling the funds of international banks. Much of this OPEC surplus was recycled to developing countries, thus contributing to the expansion of global financial flows. The effects of a booming Eurocurrency market, combined with US inflation and a growing trade deficit, led to speculative activities against the US dollar, the linchpin currency of Bretton Woods. In 1971, President Nixon announced that the dollar would no longer be convertible to gold, heralding the collapse of the Bretton Woods system, with its system of fixed exchange rates. This brought about extreme volatility in exchange rates.

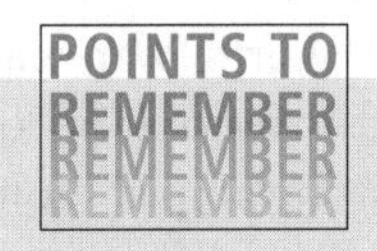

Stages in the development of an international monetary system

The gold standard (1870s to 1914):

- Exchange rates fixed to the value of gold
- Freedom to export and import gold

The Bretton Woods system (1944–71):

- Currencies pegged to the dollar, in turn fixed to the value of gold
- Controls on private financial flows permitted
- Establishment of the IMF, to oversee stable foreign exchange

Post-Bretton Woods:

- Countries determine exchange rates, under oversight of the IMF
- By Jamaica Agreement of 1976, the IMF allows greater exchange rate flexibility

11.3 Foreign exchange in the contemporary environment

When firms carry out transactions across national borders, the need to convert from one currency to another arises. The mechanisms for paying in other currencies are referred to as **foreign exchange.** The 'exchange rate' is the number of units of one currency that are needed to purchase one unit of another currency. The strength of the US dollar has made it a base currency for much international business. The US dollar is therefore said to be 'fully convertible', or a 'hard' currency. This means that it can be exchanged by both residents and non-residents without exchange controls, that is, with no limits on the amount. Many of the world's currencies, by contrast, are 'weak' and not fully convertible.

11.3.1 Exchange rate systems

Exchange rate systems vary from fixed exchange rates at one extreme to floating exchange rates at the other. A **fixed exchange rate** may be set by government, whereas a **floating exchange rate** allows the value of the currency to be determined by day-to-day trading in the foreign exchange markets. An alternative is the **'pegged' exchange rate**, by which a country's currency is tied to another currency, such as the US dollar, and moves up or down in accordance with the other currency. With the collapse of the Bretton Woods fixed exchange rate system, the IMF altered its rules to allow greater exchange rate flexibility. Accordingly, countries can maintain their own exchange rate policy. Exchange rates pegged to the dollar, which allow only limited flexibility, are often cited as one of the causes of the Asian financial crisis (which is discussed below), as governments struggled to maintain the peg.

Floating exchange rates can allow rapid movements in value, which may hamper governments' wishes to maintain low inflation. In practice, most systems allow for 'managed' exchange rates allowing fluctuation within specified bands. In 1979, the European Community set up the Exchange Rate Mechanism (ERM), which limited fluctuations within a target zone of 2.25 per cent either side of an agreed value. The British pound and Italian lira were both forced out of the system in 1992, largely, it is thought, because of the activities of well-known hedge fund managers (see next section). After these events, the bands were widened to 15 per cent. In 1999 the ERM was superseded by European Monetary Union (EMU). This is a fixed exchange rate system, using a common currency (see Chapter 3 for a fuller description of EMU).

Determination of exchange rates

- *Fixed exchange rates* – determined by government or other agreement, for example the member states' national currencies within the euro-zone
- *Pegged exchange rates* – value of the currency is linked to the value of another currency, or basket of currencies, for example the Danish currency is pegged to the Deutschmark
- *More flexible arrangements* – allow the currency to float according to supply and demand, with limited government intervention. The major industrial countries fall into this category, including the US and Japan. The euro also falls into this category

11.3.2 Money markets

Companies which do business internationally are directly affected by foreign exchange rates. Their transactions thus expose them to financial risk. To protect them from adverse currency fluctuations, they may turn to trading in currency markets. The 'currency futures contract' allows a business to buy or sell a specific amount of foreign currency at a designated price in the future. They are therefore said to have a **hedge** against future fluctuations which can adversely affect their business. For TNCs, importers, exporters and others, dealings on the currency markets are incidental to their main business. If a firm's main business is to buy and sell currencies with a view to profit, it engages in 'arbitrage'. This is a type of speculation, in which the buying and selling of a commodity, such as currency, contains considerable risk, but also a chance to make handsome profits. A wide range of financial instruments, known as 'derivatives', have been devised, so named because they are derived from primary dealings in equities, commodities and currencies. Derivative contracts allow companies to transfer financial risk between parties, although not to eliminate it (Brown, 2000).

Trade in derivatives grew enormously in the 1990s. Hedge funds are associated with fund managers such as George Soros, who acquired a 'troublemaker' image from the point of view of governments, fearful of speculation against their currencies. The downfall of the fund, Long Term Capital Management (LTCM), is often highlighted as the most spectacular example of the risks of hedge funds. LTCM was based on what was thought to be a low-risk arbitrage strategy built on an efficient market model. Founded in 1994, it seemed like a 'money machine' at the time, so masterful were its managers (Stulz, 2000). But a collapse in bond markets, triggered by Russia's debt default in 1998, brought LTCM to the brink of bankruptcy, threatening to destabilize world financial markets. It was rescued by a consortium of 14 financial institutions, which provided $3.63 billion at short notice. The failure of LTCM was a graphic lesson that risk management is not an exact science. Since then, hedge funds have become more cautious, and closer to mainstream investments. Moreover, the global economy has changed and developing countries in particular have seen the risks in adopting currency pegs.

11.4 The IMF and World Bank

Although the Bretton Woods system of fixed exchange rates disintegrated in the 1970s, the IMF and World Bank, which were created in the 1940s by the Bretton Woods agreement, have continued to grow and become important actors in international finance. Both organizations have grown from the original 44 member states to over 180 today, most of these developing countries. The changes that have taken place in the world economic environment over their more than 50 years in existence have led to very different roles for both organizations from those intended by their founding agreement. Moreover, both have come in for a good deal of criticism in recent years. We concentrate here on how their roles have changed.

The IMF was originally designed to promote exchange rate stability. It had a pool of money contributed by member countries and could provide short-term loans to members suffering from balance-of-payments deficits. The aim was to allow a country to maintain imports, avoid the imposition of controls and thus reduce pressure on its currency and restore equilibrium. The IMF would consider a devaluation of more than 10 per cent if a country's currency was in 'fundamental disequilibrium', according to its Articles of Agreement. Changes in the IMF's functions have come about as developing countries have increased participation in global financial flows. The IMF's role has shifted to providing assistance to developing countries, aimed at achieving long-term development objectives. It has also been called on for assistance in financial crises, in three Asian countries in 1997 and in Brazil in 1998 – a role much broader than that envisaged by its founders. Further, in giving assistance, it imposes strict monetary and fiscal conditions on recipient countries, which have given rise to criticisms of its role as contributing to the problems (Mikesell, 2000). The IMF has shifted 'from being an overseer of the Bretton Woods system to being a key player in poor countries' development' (Harris, 1999, p. 200). The IMF's monitoring role has also changed. While traditional monitoring has focused on countries' macroeconomic policies, a broadened 'surveillance' role takes in the country's entire financial structure, including the soundness of its banks, in keeping with a role of lender-of-last resort (Harris, 1999, p. 207).

WWW
WEBALERT

The IMF website is at
http://www.imf.org

The World Bank website is at
http://www.worldbank.org

The **World Bank**, or, to give it its full name, the International Bank for Reconstruction and Development (IBRD) has also undergone changes in its role. From the outset, the World Bank was envisaged as assisting in development, beginning with post-war reconstruction. The money would be channelled through governments towards specific development projects. As the organization has evolved, however, it has gone in more for financing broad programmes, rather than specific projects, bringing it closer to the IMF's changed role of making general purpose loans. It has funded programmes in Africa, Asia and in the transition economies of Central and Eastern Europe – all areas in which the IMF is also active. Like the IMF, the World Bank now imposes a range of conditions attached to loans, including institutional changes, such as privatization of banks; legal reforms, including property rights; and conditions regarding foreign investment (Mikesell, 2000). Thus there is overlap between the IMF and World Bank, not envisaged by the Bretton Woods agreement, as both organizations have become involved in general economic and social development.

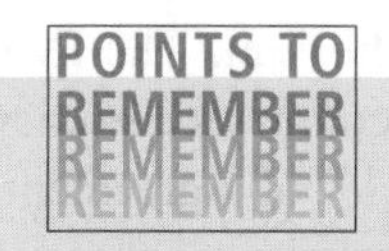

The IMF and World Bank

International Monetary Fund (IMF) – founded in 1947, under the Bretton Woods agreement. Its members now number 182, and the fund, contributed by member states, is administered by a board of executive directors. Its defined purposes are:

- to help members suffering from balance-of-payments difficulties
- to maintain stable exchange rates

The World Bank (International Bank for Reconstruction and Development – IBRD) – also founded by the Bretton Woods agreement, the World Bank began operations in 1946. It is funded by member states and also by the issue of bonds. Its purposes are:

- to help to fund development projects, for example power generation projects
- to help to fund broad development programmes

11.5 The Asian financial crisis

The financial crisis that struck three Southeast Asian countries and South Korea in 1997 was to generate a general rethinking of international finance, the relationships between national and international institutions and the role of the IMF. The crisis that spread from Thailand to South Korea, Malaysia and Indonesia startled the world, largely because it occurred in high-growth economies, against a backdrop of seemingly stable economic conditions, with neither the large budget deficits nor the inflation commonly associated with financial crisis, as had occurred in the peso crisis in Mexico. Interpretations of why it occurred differ widely, but it is generally agreed that there was no single cause, but a mixture of both national domestic conditions and global financial movements.

11.5.1 Genesis of the crisis

The roots of the crisis lie partly with the nature of economic development within what has been called the 'Asian model' of capitalism (see Chapter 4), which was based on 'guided capitalist development' rather than on market forces (Singh, 1999, p. 11). In all the Asian economies, government links with banks and investors had led to 'cosy' relationships, in which banking regulation was weak.

Policies of liberalization and deregulation in the 1990s led to inflows of capital, as investors were attracted to high rates of interest and trusted that governments would not allow their banks to fail. Net capital inflows more than doubled between 1994 and 1996 in the four countries (Singh, 1999). The investment boom was largely financed by borrowed money, much of it in US dollars. As in other developing countries struck by financial crisis, banks and businesses across Southeast Asia borrowed in dollars and then either loaned in local currency or invested in local assets. Asian currencies were pegged to the dollar and interests rates on dollar loans were generally lower than on local currency loans. The collapse of the Bangkok Bank of Commerce in 1996 started a bank run which led to a banking crisis in Thailand. Thai financial institutions had engaged in imprudent lending on local property development and found themselves at risk of defaulting on dollar-denominated debt to international financial institutions. The Thai government attempted to defend the currency, the baht, by increasing interest rates and buying baht with its own foreign currency reserves, but this effort exhausted the reserves of the central bank. Under increasing pressure, the baht was floated in 1997 and immediately dropped 20 per cent in value (see Figure 11.4). In summary, overinvestment had been followed by a swift deterioration in confidence. Declining confidence caused investors to flee. Banks and businesses found the burden of dollar debts increasingly crippling. The

Figure 11.4 Exchange rates of Asian currencies against the US dollar

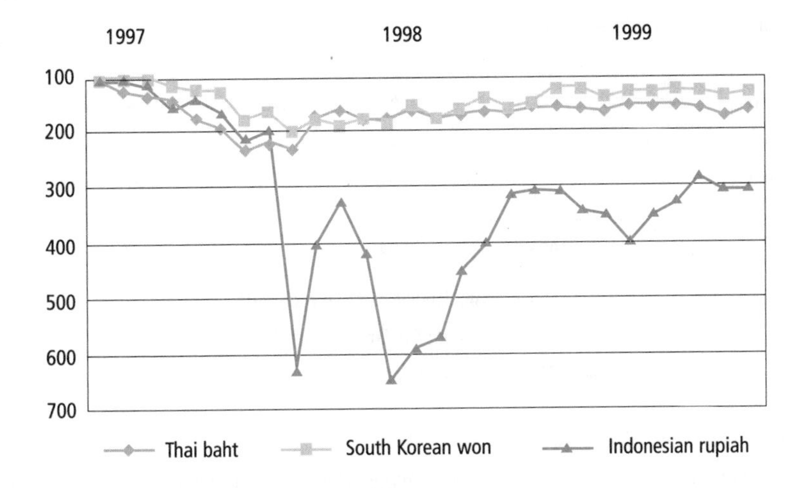

Source: The Economist, 9 October 1999, p. 106.

banking crisis was thus directly related to the currency crisis, the combined effect of which was to send the economy into meltdown (Krugman, 1999).

Authorities were surprised by the rapid spread of the crisis to neighbouring countries, in a process that has been described as 'contagion' (Krugman, 1999, p. 96). Before long, the currencies of the Philippines, Malaysia, Indonesia and South Korea were also under pressure, as the flight of capital continued. For the Southeast Asian region, an inflow of capital of the order of US$93 billion in 1996 turned into an estimated outflow of US$12 billion in 1997 (Bhagwati, 1998; Griffith-Jones, 1999). A major factor was the interconnectedness of their economies, as much of the money that flowed into the region was through 'emerging market funds', which grouped all of them together. The enthusiasm of investors for the region as a whole had been based on a perception of the Asian 'miracle'. When one stumbled, investors lost faith in all of them (Krugman, 1999, p. 97).

11.5.2 Aftermath of the crisis

Thailand, Indonesia and South Korea applied for IMF help. Large sums by way of credits were made available by the IMF to the three countries, to support their currencies and meet external debts. IMF conditions to strengthen fiscal and monetary stability were imposed, in the hope that confidence in capital and foreign exchange markets would be restored. As can be seen from Figure 11.4, with the exception of Indonesia, the affected currencies gradually recovered. Foreign bank lending, which had nose-dived, did not recover so well, as Figure 11.5 shows. FDI flows into the affected countries, with the

Figure 11.5 Foreign bank lending and FDI flows for Indonesia and five Asian economies

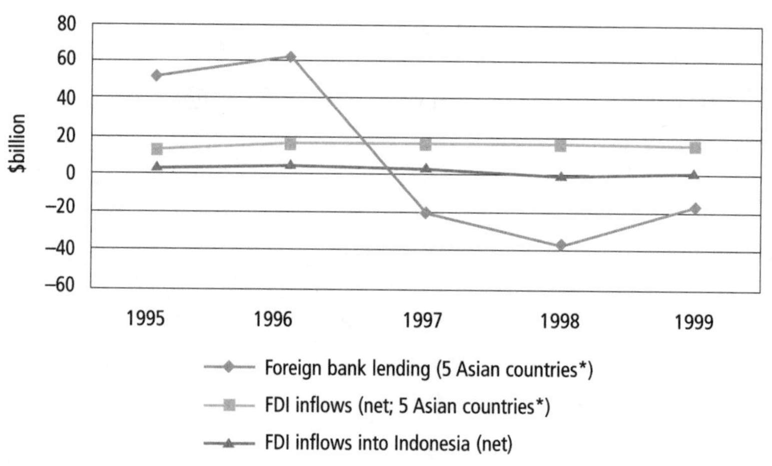

Note
* Indonesia, South Korea, Malaysia, Philippines, Thailand.

Sources: United Nations (1999) *World Investment Report 1999* (Geneva: United Nations) pp. 56 and 479 (Table B.1); *Financial Times*, 10 April 2000.

Case study 11.1 Economic problems in Indonesia

Indonesia was particularly severely affected by the Asian financial crisis, which was compounded by social and political turbulence. With a population of 212 million people, Indonesia is the world's fourth most populous country. It is also one of the most geographically dispersed and ethnically diverse. While nearly 90 per cent of its people consider themselves Muslims, there are some 300 ethnic groups clustered on about half the 3,000-mile-stretch of 13,000 islands that make up the country. Indonesia's colonial legacy was a mixture of Dutch, Portuguese and British, leaving a fragmented structure which is still evident. The 32-year military regime of President Suharto brought national unification and economic growth, but in a regime dominated by patronage and corruption. Following the currency and banking crisis of 1997, the IMF launched a $43 billion assistance programme conditional on austerity measures, but the economy deteriorated alarmingly, violent unrest erupted and Suharto was forced out of office. The IMF suspended its assistance until a new interim government could be established in 1998.

The transitional government paved the way for democratic elections in 1999, but economic and political stability still seem a way off. Some 300 political parties having participated in the general election, the government is a coalition of the main Muslim parties. It has faced extreme problems of tackling entrenched interests in pushing through reforms of the banking system, the legal system and corporate governance – all of which have been slower than hoped. Because of the slowness of reform, the IMF briefly suspended lending in 2000, but then altered its policy to one of greater flexibility, recognizing that developed world systems of governance were not realizable instantly, and efforts to bring about reforms too quickly could actually deter investors. Among the government's worries are threats to stability posed by numerous separatist movements, unleashed following the overthrow of the Suharto regime. Formerly Portuguese East Timor has broken away and is now administered by the UN. Gas-rich Aceh threatens separatism, as do the 'Spice Islands', the Moluccas, half of whose population is Christian. The central government is striving to preserve national unity and democratic institutions, but much depends on its delivery of economic reforms.

Sources: Mydans, S., 'Indonesia's many faces reflect one nation, divisible', *New York Times*, 5 September 1999; Montagnon, P. and Thoenes, S., 'Indonesia in a hole', *Financial Times*, 8 June 1998; Montagnon, P. and McCawley, T., 'Boxed in', *Financial Times*, 16 May 2000.

Case question

In the aftermath of the financial crisis, what reforms have taken place in Indonesia and what are now the advantages and disadvantages of Indonesia as a business location and investment?

exception of Indonesia, held their ground. According to the *World Investment Report 1999*, the reasons lie in the integrated production networks of TNCs which were established in the region; in some cases, they increased their stakes by buying out weakened joint-venture partners (United Nations, 1999a,

p. 56). Moreover, the more attractive FDI regimes that have been instituted seem to have encouraged investors. In 2000, businesses of the insolvent South Korean conglomerate, Daewoo, were slowly being sold off. The South Korean government's proposal, in 2000, for forming a state-run holding company to take over its still-troubled banks met with scepticism from the IMF, as its three-year, $58 billion rescue plan for the country was coming to an end. Indonesia's plight, highlighted in Figure 11.5, was compounded by social and political instability, as is shown in Case Study 11.1.

In its Asian rescue packages, the IMF has been criticized for exacerbating the problems, rather than curing them. In particular, its one-size-fits-all market-oriented solutions, administered as shock therapy, have been criticized as not taking into account varying national conditions from country to country. This view is expressed by Joseph Stiglitz, former chief economist at the World Bank, who has pointed in particular to the fact that recession in ethnically divided Indonesia could potentially contribute to social and political strife (Stiglitz, 2000) (see Case Study 11.1 on Indonesia). An important lesson from the Asian experience is that financial crises may have multiple causes, some of which stem from specific aspects of the national environment. Solutions therefore need to address the realities of specific national conditions.

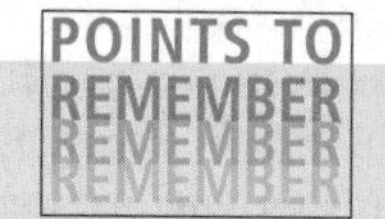

The Asian financial crisis, 1997–98

Causes:

- Rapid liberalization of national financial systems, bringing in greater trade and investment, but with the risks of volatility
- Weak banking systems, characterized by imprudent lending for development
- Flight of capital caused by departure of large inward investors

Lessons to be learnt:

- Financial crises may arise from a mixture of causes, some rooted in the specific national environment. Solutions should therefore be tailored to national conditions
- Liberalization of the national financial system requires a sound, independent banking system to maintain confidence
- Vulnerability of pegged exchange rates when waning confidence leads to pressure on the currency
- Risks in short-term capital flows, which are more volatile than long-term investment

11.6 Global markets for corporate control

The opening of markets to flows of private capital has been a trend of the post-war period, one which has accelerated with the fall of the communist states of Central and Eastern Europe. Through FDI, TNCs have been the major players in this process. As has been seen in earlier chapters, FDI is associated with a number of processes: globalization of production (Chapter 2); increases in world trade (Chapter 9); and the diffusion of technology (Chapter 10). An often-cited characteristic of TNCs is their ability to 'shop around' between countries, taking advantage of different investment regimes in different countries (Tolentino, 1999, p. 171). The main vehicle for FDI has become merger and acquisition activity (M&A) (OECD, 2000b). *The World Investment Report 1999* commented:

> the increased competition brought about by liberalization and globalization and the special needs and conditions of particular industries leading to a consolidation on a global scale, especially in developed countries, are driving cross-border M&As. (United Nations, 1999a)

11.6.1 Mergers and acquisitions

A **merger** occurs where two or more companies agree to come together to form a new company. An example of a merger is that of Grand Metropolitan and Guinness to form Diageo. In the case of an acquisition, or **takeover**, a stronger company takes over a weaker one. The company may simply buy the weaker one if the smaller company is a private company. If the smaller company is a public one, however, the shareholders become involved and a majority of their shares must be acquired by the bidding company. Their board of directors may recommend selling out to the bidder, but in the case of a hostile takeover, the bidder bypasses the board and makes an offer to the shareholders of the target company directly. A further type of acquisition is the **leveraged buy-out** (LBO), by which a group, usually managers of the company, make an arrangement, through a loan or venture capital finance, to buy out the company's equity. The leveraged buy-out is thus a means for achieving corporate restructuring, often financed by venture capitalists. According to the Centre for Management Buy-Out Research (reported in Rivlin, 2000), buy-outs rose 62 per cent from 1998 to 1999 in Europe, from 20.1 billion euros in 1998 to 30.4 billion euros in 1999, much of this focused on restructuring. The bulk of these deals were in the UK, one of the biggest being the sale of United Biscuits to a group of trade and finance bidders.

Mergers and acquisitions (referred to as M&A activity) are key to companies' growth strategies. A major driving force has been the enhancement of shareholder value, bringing cost savings and efficiencies. M&A activities may be **horizontal integration**, that is, between companies in the same industry, often referred to as 'consolidation'. In the late 1990s there were waves of consolidation in the pharmaceuticals and chemicals sector, for example, the main rationale being the increasing returns of economies of scale in R&D. **Vertical integration**, that is, between firms in successive stages of production or distribution, can also be strategically valuable, bringing benefits of internalization (see Chapter 2). An example is the $182 billion takeover of Time Warner by AOL in 2000. In this megadeal, an internet provider took over a media and entertainment company, exemplifying a new economy predator taking over an old economy conglomerate. The deal required approval of the US antitrust authority, the Federal Trade Commission, which imposed stringent conditions.

Some large companies have grown by diversification, acquiring subsidiaries in businesses only loosely related to each other. Diageo, formed from a merger of Grand Metropolitan and Guinness, is an example. Diageo's divisions include wine and spirits, beer, packaged food and burger restaurants. A recent trend has been for highly diversified companies to slim down

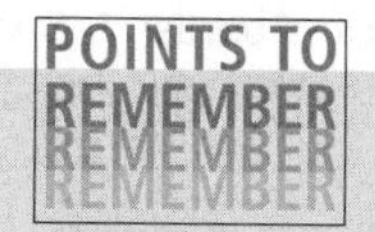

Mergers and acquisitions

- *Merger* – the coming together of two or more companies to form a new company
- *Acquisition* – the takeover of a company by another company. Acquisitions also include the takeover of a state-owned enterprise by a private sector company (privatization)
- *'Hostile' takeover* – situation in which a company targets a prospective acquisition, but the board of directors of the target company reject the acquisition proposal. The would-be acquiring company therefore makes an offer directly to the shareholders of the target company
- *Demerger* – the spinning off of a part of a company's business, such as a division, which is viable on its own. Demerger is usually part of a corporate strategy to refocus on the core business
- *Leveraged buy-out (LBO)* – a group, often managers of a company, obtain finance to buy out part or all of the company's equity

to what is conceived to be their core business and 'demerge', or spin off, the non-core businesses. In the case of Diageo, wine and spirits seem to be the core business, although the company owns a range of strong brands in other businesses, including Guinness beer, Haagen-Dazs ice cream and Burger King, the world's second-largest burger chain.

Table 11.1 Global acquisitions

Target	Acquirer	Value ($billion)	Sector
Mannesmann (Germany)	Vodafone AirTouch (UK)	198.9	Telecoms
Time Warner (US)	AOL (US)	181.9	Internet/media
Sprint (US)	MCI Worldcom (US)	127.3	Telecoms
Warner-Lambert (US)	Pfizer (US)	87.9	Pharmaceuticals
Mobil (US)	Exxon (US)	86.4	Oil
SmithKline Beecham (UK)	Glaxo Wellcome (UK)	78.4	Pharmaceuticals
Citicorp (US)	Travelers (US)	72.6	Banking/financial services

Source: Financial Times, 5/6 February and 30 June 2000.

11.6.2 Trends in cross-border mergers

Historically, there have been periods of heightened merger activity generally, resulting in the rise of large conglomerates, as happened in the 1960s in the US and Europe. From the 1980s onwards, waves of privatizations in former state-owned industries, such as telecommunications and utilities, have accounted for much acquisition activity, attracting foreign investors, usually global companies keen to expand into new markets. The telecommunications industry accounted for 20 per cent of the world's total M&A activity in 1999, with the chemical industry second, and petroleum and gas exploitation third (OECD, 2000b). The oil industry saw a radical transformation of the competitive environment with the $57 billion merger between BP and Amoco, which was followed three months later by a deal between Exxon and Mobil worth $80 billion. Ironically, the Exxon–Mobil merger reunited two offshoots of Standard Oil, forced to be dismantled under antitrust law by the US Supreme Court in 1911. In today's global economy, these major players in the oil and gas industry are aiming to secure partnerships with national oil companies in the world's major oil-producing countries.

While M&A activity has a long history within national economies, in 1999, cross-border mergers had grown in number, to half of all reported mergers in the US, the EU and Asia (Paul, 2000). In the 1990s cross-border M&A activity increased fivefold in Organization for Economic Co-operation and Development (OECD) countries. What is even more striking, though, is the increase in the average deal value, which rose from $29 million in 1990 to $157 million in 1999 (OECD, 2000b). Research suggests that 95 per cent of

Case study 11.2 Vodafone's takeover of Mannesmann

In February 2000, the chairman of the German engineering group, Mannesmann, finally conceded defeat in the three-month-long battle to prevent a takeover by the mobile phone operator, Vodafone of the UK. Vodafone's victory marked the first time that a foreign company had succeeded with a hostile bid for a large German group. The deal became the largest takeover of all time, at just over £100 billion. The new company became Europe's largest publicly traded company and the world's largest telecommunications group. The bid came in the context of a rapidly expanding global mobile telecommunications market, in which both companies had experienced rapid growth. Mobile phones, expensive luxuries in the late 1980s, are now owned by nearly half the population of the EU. Vodafone, controlling 35 per cent of the British mobile phone market, broke into the American market in 1999, with the acquisition of AirTouch of the US. Meanwhile, Mannesmann, essentially an engineering and automotive group, entered the mobile phone business only ten years previously and greatly boosted its position by its acquisition of Orange, which controls 17 per cent of the British market.

Vodafone's success in overcoming an inherent hostility to takeovers in German corporate culture can be put down to its winning over Mannesmann's shareholders. Unusually for a German company, 70 per cent of Mannesmann's shareholders are foreign, including some large US institutional investors, who were persuaded the deal would be in shareholders' interests. To their voices was added that of the chairman of DaimlerChrysler, Jürgen Schrempp, who was an influential member of Mannesmann's supervisory board and also the head of Hutchison Telecom, Mannesmann's largest single shareholder thanks to its 44 per cent stake in Orange. Opposed to the deal were the strong trade unions, including IG Metall, which, under German corporate structure, are represented on the supervisory board. The German government was also opposed, arguing that the deal risked upsetting Germany's stakeholder culture, which valued employees before shareholders. In response, the Vodafone CEO, Chris Gent, gave assurances to the trade unionists. The engineering and automotive businesses, employing 100,000 workers, could be floated off. The deal had to clear the EU competition authorities, which required Orange to be sold off. Orange has been acquired by France Telecom.

Vodafone's victory is seen at one level as a triumph for the Anglo-American style of capitalism, at the expense of the consensual German stakeholder model. At another level, as John Plender has commented: 'Germany's "insider" financial system, in which the banks have played a dominant role, has been opened up to a genuine market in corporate control' (Plender, 4 February 2000).

Sources: Plender, J., 'Whirlwinds of change', *Financial Times*, 4 February 2000; Atkins, R. and Lewis, W., 'Triumph for Vodafone as Mannesmann gives in', *Financial Times*, 4 February 2000; Lorenz, A., 'Mobile mania', *Sunday Times*, 9 January 2000; Lorenz, A., 'V for Victory', *Sunday Times*, 6 February 2000.

Case questions

What were the key factors that enabled Vodafone to take over Mannesmann?
What are the implications which company directors should note for future merger activity generally?

UK TNCs that expanded abroad during the late 1980s did so via acquisitions (Hubbard, 1999). The UK overtook the US in 1999 as the most active source of M&A investment and remained in that position in 2000. The 1999 figures were swelled by Vodafone's acquisition of AirTouch in the US (for £41.25 billion) and the 2000 figures are boosted by Vodafone's takeover of Mannesmann (for £101.2 billion) (Office for National Statistics, 2000a). Like banking and public utilities, telecommunications have been dominated in many countries by state-controlled companies, but are experiencing rapid changes in the competitive climate, as Case Study 11.2 indicates.

11.7 Regulation and TNCs

The sheer size of many newly merged TNCs has renewed the debate on the concentration of economic power in corporate hands and the domination of some global industries by only a few powerful companies. The Vodafone–Mannesmann deal, as the *Financial Times* (5 February 2000) noted in an editorial, 'is on a par with the gross domestic product of Denmark'. But whereas countries are enmeshed in international regulatory regimes, such as those for international trade by the World Trade Organization (WTO) and international monetary issues (the IMF and World Bank), there is no regulatory framework for TNCs at international level. Industrialized countries have all enacted competition (or antitrust) legislation, designed to curb monopolists (see Chapter 4 for a fuller discussion). Within the EU, there are both EU and national regulatory frameworks to comply with, which, it is intended, will become harmonized across the EU. However, in the wake of the Vodafone–Mannesmann deal, the EU Parliament added amendments (opposed by Britain and Ireland) to the proposed EU takeover directive, to give workers a greater say in takeover situations.

Mergers must be notified to national authorities, as well as to the EU Commission, for clearance, and can be blocked under competition law if they constitute an abuse of a dominant market position, or allowed through with conditions attached. Indeed, national rules have become more complex and the list of countries with merger regulations is growing. Merger notification regimes are in place in 57 jurisdictions and, of these, between 1994 and 2000, 35 have enacted new or substantially revised rules, creating a 'daunting landscape' for companies contemplating cross-border mergers (Paul, 2000).

Competition policy, like company regulation generally, is subject to wide variations of interpretation and also changing public perceptions about big business in general. A 'national champion' is seen as enhancing competitive advantage for the home nation, and some governments welcome consolidation of companies within some sectors in order to create a single entity stronger than its former constituent parts, fit to compete globally. A shift of attitudes towards greater acceptance of takeovers, especially hostile ones, has taken place in a number of countries, such as France and Germany, opening up the market for corporate control and bringing a greater focus on shareholder value. This shift stems from the growing equity culture and a move away from the stakeholder model. In Germany, the number of shareholders grew from 5 million in 1992 to 8 million in 1999, while trade union membership fell from 12 to 10 million (*The Economist*, 20 November 1999). Notwithstanding Germany's legislation on corporate governance, which is stacked against the hostile takeover, Mannesman shareholders, in supporting the Vodafone deal, went 'in favour of shareholder value and against national champions' (*The Economist*, 20 November 1999).

As globalization processes have encompassed more countries, developing and transitional economies have run the risk of becoming dependent on foreign capital, as well as technology. Thus, while TNC investments have brought benefits to societies, they have also created concentrations of economic power which in many ways are perceived as not accountable to governments. Foreign-owned companies in Hungary accounted for 80 per cent of manufacturing investment in 1996, providing a third of the country's employment (United Nations, 1999b). National authorities typically offer incentives to attract foreign investors. Regulatory frameworks for FDI serve two purposes: to control the activities of TNCs in the interests of host countries; and to protect TNCs in overseas locations from, for example, arbitrary seizure of assets (Tolentino, 1999). From 1995, a Multilateral Agreement on Investment (MAI) has been under consideration, under the auspices of the OECD. Such a treaty would aim to regulate FDI at international level, balancing the interests of host countries and foreign investors. However, the negotiation process has been dominated by the developed countries and thus perceived by developing countries as flawed in the area of control of TNCs (Tolentino, 1999). While MAI negotiations seemed to stall, countries have proceeded with bilateral agreements, tailoring agreements to fit particular needs on a country-by-country basis. A shortcoming of this piecemeal approach, however, is that it does not cover as many countries as a multilateral agreement would cover, bypassing especially the poorest developing countries.

11.8 The global financial environment and developing countries

Globalization of production and FDI have led to increases in capital flows from advanced countries to many developing countries, but their benefits have been distributed unevenly. Only a relatively small group of developing countries attract the lion's share of private capital flows. Asian and Latin American countries have been successful in attracting investment, whereas African and Middle Eastern countries have been much less so. Where FDI has contributed significantly to economic growth, fluctuations in these flows and changes in exchange rates have brought financial instability and even crisis in

Asian industrializing countries, Mexico, Brazil, and Russia. Thus, globalization has brought problems of overinvestment in some countries, but underinvestment in others.

Case study 11.3 Dancing to the IMF tune in Kenya

Kenya's economy held out prospects of industrial development in the decade following independence from Britain in 1963. Optimism turned to disappointment, however, as economic decline set in, leading to reliance on aid from Western donors and the institutions of the IMF and World Bank. Kenya's problems, it is generally agreed, have stemmed mainly from government corruption and inefficiency, squandering aid funds and leaving public finances in a perilous state. The population doubled from about 15 million in 1979 to about 30 million now, while economic growth has steadily declined, from 6.6 per cent per annum during 1964–73 to 1.8 per cent in 1998. The proportion of the population below the poverty line increased to 50 per cent. In 1997, after years of broken promises by the Kenyan government to clean up corruption, the IMF finally grew impatient and cut off funds, soon followed by the EU, which withheld an aid package. The result compounded Kenya's woes, as external investors repatriated $250 million, forcing a 20 per cent depreciation in Kenya's currency, the shilling. The government was forced to increase borrowing. By 1997–98, it was spending 40 per cent of its current revenue in servicing its debts.

President Daniel arap Moi, re-elected in 1997, but without an outright majority in parliament, appointed a new finance minister who was committed to decreasing government expenditure, reducing salaries of civil servants (including teachers) and raising new taxes. Not surprisingly, these measures led to social and political unrest, interwoven with ethnic and tribal conflict. Adopting a new tactic in 1999, Moi brought into government the renowned wildlife conservationist, Richard Leakey, to root out corruption in government ministries. The IMF and the donors were persuaded that things were changing, but, in giving a new 3-year, $198 million loan, imposed the toughest conditions ever imposed on a recipient government. A new anti-corruption law, largely dictated by the IMF, must be passed by parliament and government finances will be open to daily inspection by IMF officials. The notoriously inefficient port of Mombasa, East Africa's biggest port, is to be privatized, as are the state-owned telecommunications and railway companies. Rooting out corruption and inefficiency still has a long way to go, and political uncertainty hangs over the end of Moi's term of office in 2002, but Kenyans are hopeful that reforms will ultimately lead to a stronger economy and a brighter future.

Sources: Southall, R., (2000) 'Dilemmas of the Kenyan succession', *Review of African Political Economy*, 27(84): 203–20; Southall, R. (1999) 'Reforming the state? Kleptocracy and the political transition in Kenya', *Review of African Political Economy*, 26(79): 93–109; 'Fund dance', *The Economist*, 5 February 2000; 'Dancing in Kenya to the donors' tune', *The Economist*, 5 August 2000.

Case question

For a company contemplating investing in Kenya, in what ways has the business environment improved under the current reforms?

For the first group of countries, in Asia and Latin America, *The World Development Report 1999/2000* (World Bank, 2000a) examined ways to capture the gains from financial globalization without running the risks of volatility in capital markets. Liberalizing the domestic financial environment, it recommends, needs to be complemented by strengthening bank regulation and stabilizing the macroeconomic environment. These aims have been echoed in IMF rescue packages in the crisis-struck Asian economies. The second group of countries, in Africa and the Middle East, have yet to see sustained economic development and present greater long-term problems. In 1997, Africa received only 2 per cent of the world total of FDI. For this reason, many countries have had to rely on assistance from the IMF and World Bank. Loans and grants from rich nations now account for 10 per cent of all economic activity in Africa. Despite this help, these countries remain poor, amassing a huge debt burden that, many argue, has made matters worse. Case Study 11.3 on Kenya illustrates that structural reforms are needed in order to use funds efficiently. A general problem seems to be that countries become dependent on the IMF, making it even more difficult for them to attract private capital. The situation has been likened to that of individuals who become dependent on welfare aid. A study found that of 89 less-developed countries that received IMF aid between 1965 and 1995, by 1998, 48 were no better off than they were before receiving the loans and 32 were actually worse off (Longman and Ahmad, 1998).

Debate on changing the role of the IMF has thus focused on the different functions it fulfils in the different types of developing country. While Asian programmes are seen as rescue packages in countries which have dynamic economies, aid to sub-Saharan African countries has taken on the quality of permanence. It has been argued that the IMF and World Bank should co-ordinate their roles in countries which have yet to develop the basic systems for growth, including legal structures, public administration and social services. Alternatively, there are those who say that the IMF should revert to short-term loans and dealing with financial crises, allowing the World Bank to concentrate on development programmes in poor countries. Attention has also focused on easing the debt problems of the poorest countries and opening up more export opportunities for crops and textiles produced in these countries. Granting debt relief would at least ease the burden of interest payments. Among the 41 countries eligible for debt relief in 2000, the average debt load was 125 per cent of their GDP (*New York Times*, 1 October 2000). Debt relief, like trade reforms, relies on the will of authorities in wealthy countries. The IMF's Managing Director, Horst Köhler, has said: 'We have to tackle the selfishness of wealthy countries. This is a question of morals' (*New York Times*, 1 October 2000).

11.9 Conclusions

1 All business requires access to capital. A firm may borrow funds or raise capital by issuing shares, known as an initial public offering (IPO).

2 Stock exchanges handle flows of publicly traded shares in systems which are becoming increasingly globalized. Moreover, investors, especially institutional investors such as pension funds, are seeking advantageous investments abroad.

3 Foreign exchange refers to currency dealings across national borders. Exchange rates can be determined in a number of different ways, including fixed exchange rates, 'pegged' exchange rates and more flexible arrangements.

4 With the collapse of the Bretton Woods fixed exchange rate system in the early 1970s, volatility in exchange markets set in. The IMF, founded under the Bretton Woods agreement, has responsibility for maintaining stability in the international monetary system.

5 The IMF and World Bank have evolved considerably since they were established in the 1940s, particularly to address problems of financial crisis, as in the Asian crisis of 1997–98, and the many problems of developing countries.

6 The Asian crisis highlighted the risks of volatile capital flows and posed challenges for the Asian economies in restructuring, in order to attract foreign investors in a more stable financial environment.

7 TNCs have become drivers of financial globalization, largely through M&A activities. The benefits of global integration, however, must be weighed against the concentration of economic power enjoyed by merged global companies, especially in relation to host economies.

8 Problems of heavily indebted poor countries have come to be recognized as major challenges for the developed world, sparking a debate among all players, including corporate leaders, the IMF and government authorities.

Review questions

1. How have capital markets become globalized and what are the implications for listed companies?
2. How can a company benefit from the issuing of bonds and how do bondholders differ from shareholders?

3 Explain the benefits that were enjoyed under the gold standard system.

4 What were the aims of the Bretton Woods agreement? What were the reasons behind its collapse in the 1970s?

5 Explain the differences between fixed, floating and pegged exchanged rates.

6 Summarize the initial aims of the Bretton Woods institutions – the IMF and World Bank. How have their roles evolved since their formation?

7 What were the causes of the Asian financial crisis of 1997–98?

8 How have the Asian economies been restructured and reformed since the crisis and what has been the role of the IMF? To what extent have their combined efforts been a success?

9 Mergers and acquisitions have become increasingly important in the markets for corporate control. What is the driving force behind them?

10 In what ways are developing countries' economies vulnerable to global financial movements?

Assignments

1 Globalizing capital markets have provided opportunities for companies for corporate finance, but have also posed financial risk. Discuss the extent to which this statement is true.

2 Many feel that, given the continuing risk of financial crisis, the international financial system as regulated by the IMF and World Bank is in need of reform, but there is little consensus on what shape reforms should take. What are the possibilities for reform that would stand a greater chance of reducing volatility and also aiding development in the poor countries, which has so far eluded the World Bank?

Further reading

Eichengreen, B. (1996) *Globalizing Capital: A History of the International Monetary System* (Princeton: Princeton University Press)

Harwood, A. (ed.) (1999) *Financial Markets and Development: The Crisis in Emerging Markets* (Washington: Brookings Institution Press)

Kapstein, E.B. (1994) *Governing the Global Economy: International Finance and the State* (Cambridge, MA: Harvard University Press)

Krugman, P. (1999) *The Return of Depression Economics* (Harmondsworth: Penguin)

Kuttner, R. (1991) *The End of Laissez-Faire: National Purpose and the Global Economy After the Cold War* (New York: Alfred A. Knopf)

Michie, J. and Grieve Smith, J. (eds) (1999) *Global Instability: The Political Economy of World Economic Governance* (Andover: Routledge)

Global change and challenges of the international environment

Outline of chapter

LEARNING OBJECTIVES

1. To gain an overview of how each of the dimensions of the international business environment fits into a dynamic overall picture
2. To focus on some of the primary challenges facing all societies, such as environmental protection and climate change, and on how businesses are placed to respond positively and in socially responsible ways
3. To grasp the pros and cons of how globalization impacts in differing national environments, offering broadening opportunities for international businesses, as well as benefits for host societies

12.0 Introduction

Preceding chapters have each presented a key aspect of the international environment which impacts on businesses. While individual aspects are identifiable as possessing their own characteristics, they do not function independently, but as facets of an overall picture of the environment, rather like pieces in a jigsaw. For a business, therefore, an understanding of how the 'pieces', such as economic, cultural, social and other inputs, are put together is essential to long-term success. This chapter shifts the focus, first, to an overview of how the parts interact in the changing environment and, second, to the challenges and opportunities that are emerging for businesses in the future.

The themes of globalization and local diversity have run throughout the preceding chapters and they are taken up here again in the context of challenges that lie ahead. Attention will be given to the wider issues in the world economy: global inequalities, environmental issues, social responsibility and the new frontiers of the information age. Questions about the impact that economic activities have on societies and the environment for present and future generations are generating debate, not just in the business community, but in the international community generally. The opportunities are immense, but so are the threats. Businesses, from the small firm to the global company, are uniquely placed to take proactive approaches in a rapidly changing environment, and an understanding of the multisided nature of the issues will enhance their ability to meet the challenges ahead.

12.1 Global and national environments: an overview

Two themes have recurred throughout this book. First, globalization, defined as the expansion and deepening of ties across national borders, has gained ground in all aspects of the business environment. Second, national differences, rather than melting away, seem to have persisted and adapted in the changing environment. These themes are presented in Table 12.1, which, in a simplified form, gives an indication of how organizations (such as the World Trade Organization (WTO)) and processes (such as economic integration) fit into the larger picture. The headings, global and national environments, are not used here to represent separate 'containers', but as aids to help to visualize relationships. In reality, these categories are increasingly shading into each other, in dynamic interactive processes that are redefining their contours. In all these categories, global changes have brought improvements valued by people in their immediate national and local situations. Of course, change can have numerous effects, both beneficial and detrimental, on businesses, governments, consumers and societies generally. From a firm's point of view, one of the major advantages of understanding the forces that go to

Table 12.1 Global and national environments

Dimension	Global environment	National environment
Economic	Global and regional economic integration; globalization of production	National economic systems
Cultural	Media and internet penetration; consumer society and global markets	National and sub-national cultural, including linguistic and religious, groupings
Social	International division of labour; international migration	National and sub-national social groupings, for example family and ethnic groups
Political	International and regional political interdependence and integration	National political systems; political parties in pluralist states
Legal	International law and practice (in for example human rights and environment); international tribunals	National legal systems, including national legislative processes and national judicial systems
Trade and competitive	Multilateral trade agreements (for example GATT); multilateral organizations (for example WTO); regional trade groupings	National strategic trade policy; bilateral trade agreements
Technological	Global R&D by transnational corporations and international bodies	National innovation systems
Financial	Global capital markets; international institutions (for example IMF and World Bank)	National financial systems, including banks and other financial institutions

make up the environment is to be able to assess more accurately the ways in which change will affect its activities, and thus by managing change, to reduce the risks.

12.2 Change in the business environment

The preceding chapters have each focused on a selected aspect of the business environment. Each has emphasized the changes that are currently taking place and the ways in which businesses are both responding to and bringing about changes themselves. The pace of change clearly varies from place to place and, of course, not all change is for the better. Change is almost universally perceived as involving winners and losers. Technological innovation has brought untold benefits in quality of life, healthcare and the working environment, but has also resulted in the displacement of low-skilled workers in advanced economies, as their jobs migrated abroad to low-cost locations. Industrialization of production has also produced harmful side effects, such as pollution, and it has depleted the world's non-renewable energy resources. Much depends on the viewpoint of the speaker. In the case of foreign direct investment (FDI), for example, host-country perspectives may differ markedly from those of the home country of the foreign investor.

Changes in the business environment can largely be attributed to processes of globalization and liberalization. Globalization encompasses processes of technological innovation, deepening FDI and expanding trade and financial networks. Indeed, improvements in technology, including transport and communications, have been instrumental in bringing about the other developments just listed. They make up the flows of money, goods and information that characterize modern society. The countries whose populations have benefited to the greatest extent are the advanced economies of the world which have been at the f refront of technological innovation and its commercial exploitation. These developments have owed much to liberalization, opening economies to market forces, which have had a broad impact across the whole spectrum of the business environment, including cultural and social environments, and legal and political systems. For many countries, mainly the advanced Western economies, individualist cultures fostered capitalist enterprises, along with legal systems to protect property, and democratic national political systems responsive to citizens. The defining characteristics of the market economy, stemming from the early industrializing Western economies, have come to be identified with liberal market reforms in the context of nation-states.

By contrast, the histories and cultures of the countries of Asia, Latin America and Africa represent an array of differing environments, commonly featuring the pre-eminence of community and family values over individual values. Changes, including more open markets and social mobility, have come less from indigenous forces and more from external forces, specifically growing FDI, reflecting the globalization of production. While liberalization in these countries offers manifold opportunities for business enterprises, it has also had a 'downside' of market volatility and inequalities, which have posed challenges for good governance. The experiences of these countries demonstrate the importance of understanding how changes in one sphere have repercussions in others.

Globalization and liberalization have brought opportunities for economic development and technological diffusion, but also instability, as changes occur in established ways of doing things and established structures in society. Asian countries in particular have welcomed the opportunities brought by technological innovation and have set out to adapt them to existing social and cultural values. In this way, nations have aspired to grasp the best of both worlds: stability from established systems and economic growth from FDI and imported technology. Foreign investors that have succeeded in establishing themselves, often with local partners, have demonstrated the value of co-operation through cross-cultural management approaches, which work within the local environment, rather than trying to recreate the home-country structures in the foreign location. Even during the financial crisis of 1997–98, these long-term investors provided an element of stability amidst the volatility of short-term capital movements.

China is an example of a transitional economy, in which market reforms are taking place in a rapidly changing business environment. Daily it is becoming easier for Western businesses to enter China, as barriers come down, but changes in other aspects of the business environment are moving more slowly. An independent legal system, private property rights and intel-

Case study 12.1 Volvo in South Korea

In the wake of the Asian financial crisis in 1998, Volvo acquired the Samsung building machinery operations, formerly part of the vast Samsung conglomerate and one of the five largest makers of earth-moving machines. Volvo was convinced that, in spite of its economic problems, the region would provide a vast market for construction equipment as economic development gathered pace. Faced with the task of turning round the loss-making enterprise, Volvo quickly introduced drastic measures. It cut employment at the plant plus ancillary services from 2,300 to 1,700. It introduced a Western style of management, forming a new 12-strong management team, half of whom are Koreans. It has transformed production methods based on teamwork, boosting responsibility to employees. A range of initiatives has been introduced to base pay on capabilities rather than on how long employees have been with the company. Volvo has also recognized trade unions, something Samsung had previously avoided, as a way of putting relations with employees and managers on a more clearly defined basis. A former Samsung employee who has been promoted to plant manager said: 'The main thing I find is that people lower down the organization are encouraged to take on greater responsibility'.

An unexpected bonus from Volvo's point of view has been that, in trials comparing their machines with Caterpillar (US) and Komatsu (Japan), they came off surprisingly well in technical performance. The Koreans had thought of their machines as low-price products, but Volvo has raised the machines' selling price to reflect their true worth. Last year, the excavator division just about broke even. Volvo has transferred the head office of its heavy excavator operations to South Korea, closing its main excavator plant in Sweden. The company will need to sell 8,000 excavators a year globally, but this figure does not seem out of reach now.

Source: Marsh, P., 'Volvo digs deep in Korea', *Financial Times*, 13 June 2000 (reprinted with permission).

Case question

What were the obstacles facing Volvo and what are the elements of the Swedish company's success in turning around Samsung's excavator operations?

lectual property rights are still underdeveloped by Western standards. Also political decision-making is still closer to authoritarianism than democracy. Whether marketization of the economy will lead to social and cultural change, and ultimately a peaceful transition to democracy, has become a tantalizing question for observers of China. There are the beginnings of democratic forms in China. Many point to the fact that at the height of the cold war, few would have predicted the relatively peaceful overthrow of Soviet communist regimes in Central and Eastern Europe. On the other hand, the post-communist transitions have varied considerably, from the relatively smooth progress of Poland and Hungary to the erratic progress of Russia. In general, countries with deep legacies of authoritarianism, as in the former Soviet republics, have found the path to economic reforms more difficult than countries with stronger civil society, such as those in Central and Eastern Europe. Economic reforms, it seems clear, do not take place in isolation from other dimensions of the national environment. They can stimulate change in social and cultural spheres and also come about as a result of pressures within societies.

12.3 Left behind? The least-developed nations

It was once thought, optimistically, that globalization would spread economic growth and prosperity from the advanced countries to the developing countries, eventually bringing the benefits of a better quality of life to all. Since 1980, not only has the gap between rich and poor within countries widened, but the gap between rich and poor countries has grown, as shown in Figure 12.1. Global integration has proceeded unevenly, delivering benefits to some nations, but leaving others marginalized, with little prospect of catching up.

12.3.1 The plight of poor countries

For 59 poor countries, the 1980s and 90s saw declining gross national product (GNP) per capita (United Nations, 1999b). For Sub-Saharan Africa and South Asia, the share of the population living in poverty rose over the 1990s. According to the World Bank, about half of Africa's 600 million people live on $0.65 a day (World Bank, 2000b). The poor are likely to be undernourished and lack access to clean water and sanitation. The UN's Food and Agriculture Organization estimates that about 826 million people are undernourished – 792 million people in the developing world and 34 million in the developed world. Asian countries, the report says, have made greater progress in reducing poverty, due to their economic expansion and slowing population growth, while the poorest countries of Africa, which have experienced the greatest depth of hunger, are not progressing so well (see Figure 12.2). The reasons highlighted by the UN are 'instability and conflict, poor governance, erratic weather, poverty, agricultural failure, population

Figure 12.1 Widening gap between rich and poor countries

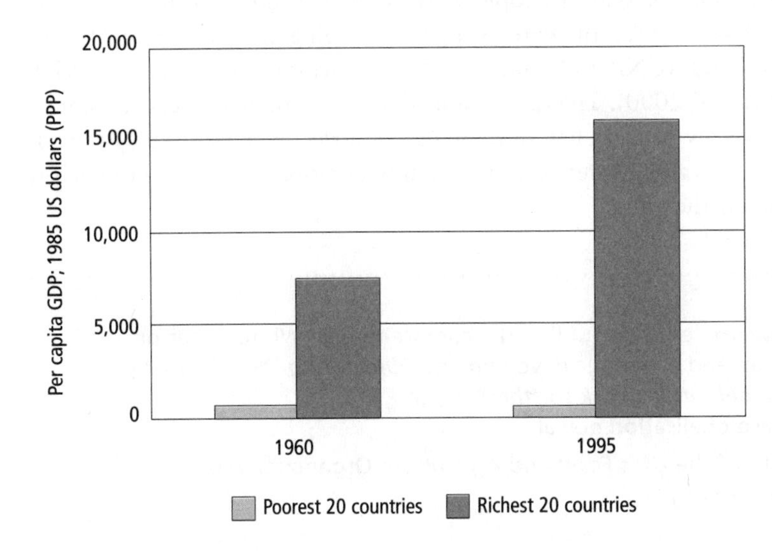

Source: World Bank (2000) *World Development Report 2000–2001* (Oxford: Oxford University Press) p. 51.

Figure 12.2 Food deprivation: proportion of the population undernourished, 1996–98

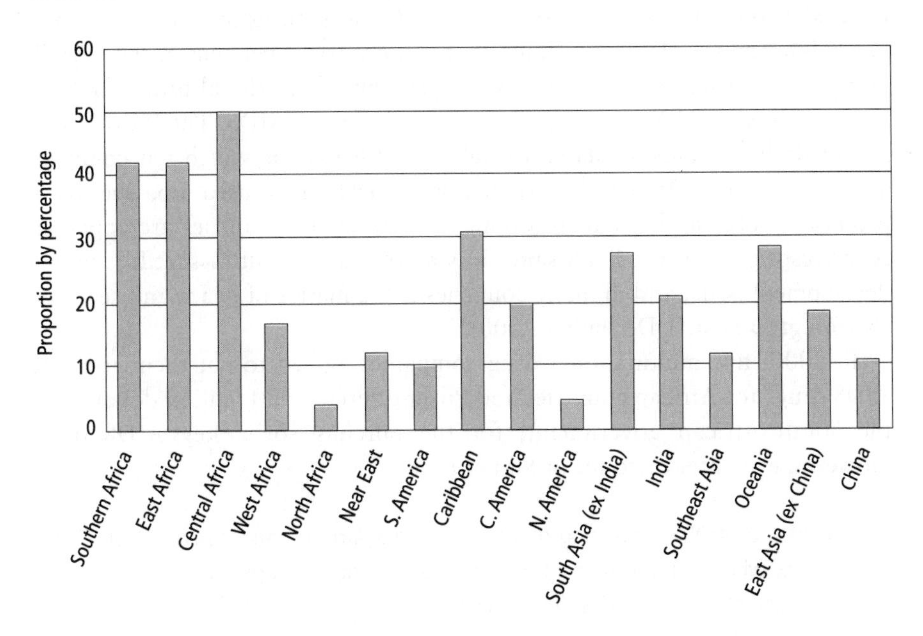

Source: UN Food and Agriculture Organization (2000) *The State of Food Insecurity in the World.*

pressures, and fragile ecosystems' (UN Food and Agriculture Organization, 2000). In 2000, 2.4 billion people were without sanitation and 1.1 billion without a fixed source of water supply, according to a report by the UN Children's Fund (UNICEF) and the World Health Organization (WHO) (WHO/UNICEF, 2000). The report adds that where there *is* access to water, it is not necessarily safe, as few developing countries have modern systems for treating waste water. Water scarcity is a now a global problem, in which the poor come off the worst.

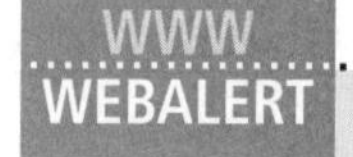

The UK Government has published a comprehensive White Paper on globalization and economic development, *Eliminating World Poverty: Making Globalisation Work for the Poor,* at http://www.globalisation.gov.uk

The website of the UN's Food and Agriculture Organization is http://www.fao.org

Hunger and lack of clean water make the poor particularly vulnerable to natural disasters and disease. The effect of the AIDS/HIV epidemic in sub-Saharan Africa has been devastating, more difficult to cope with in poor countries lacking the money for medicines, which are supplied by global pharmaceutical companies. The WHO estimated that, by the end of 2000, the rate of new infections in the region was stabilizing. From 4 million newly infected people in 1999, the figure for 2000 was an estimated 3.8 million newly infected people. For a region that is home to 10 per cent of the world's population, Africa still accounts for 70 per cent of the global total of people living with AIDS/HIV and 80 per cent of deaths from AIDS. The World Bank has made loan funds available to fight the disease, for which ten countries applied in 2000. When the $1 billion allocation is used up, the Bank promised more would be forthcoming, as another 13 countries are applying. A spokesperson for the Bank said: 'It is more than a health issue. It is now a development issue, and in many countries it is a matter of peace and security' (*Washington Post*, 1 December 2000).

In 2000, five multinational drug companies agreed to cut their prices of AIDS drugs for African countries and Pfizer offered a $50 million donation to the South African government, for the purchase of a key AIDS drug. However, even at a discount of 90 per cent:

> a cocktail of AIDS-suppressing drugs for a single African patient might cost $2,000 per year, which is more than four times the average per capita income in many of the worst-afflicted countries. (Kahn, 2000)

The broader issue is that of drugs patents generally. The TRIPS agreement (discussed in Chapter 9) strengthened the grip of patent holders globally. Still, it made provision for countries in emergency situations to bypass patent rules. The South African government could argue that, with 10 per cent of its population estimated to be infected, the AIDS crisis counts as such an emergency. It would then be able to buy non-licensed 'copycat' generic drugs from India (India will be required to enforce patents under TRIPS by 2005–06) (Ward, 2001). Moreover, there are signs that some large pharmaceutical companies have introduced flexibility in their pricing policies: in 2001 Merck agreed to discounts on two AIDS drugs sold in Brazil, when the Brazilian government was on the verge of allowing a local generic manufacturer to make a copy of one of them.

12.3.2 Development prospects for Africa

For the poorest countries of Africa, whose economies are mainly agricultural, trade has not delivered the hoped-for gains. As shown in Figure 12.3, share of world trade in exports grew only in tea and tobacco (the latter gains mainly due to diminishing production in the US). Although Africa accounts for less than 2 per cent of world trade, its countries are deeply integrated in the world economy. Sub-Saharan Africa has an export to gross domestic product (GDP) ratio of 29 per cent, which is higher than that of Latin America (15 per cent). The problem for African countries is that their exports are primary commodities, which are vulnerable to swings in commodity markets. Economic diversification would help to reduce this dependency. Moreover, the World Bank has called on the developed world to open markets to African agricultural produce. The Organization for Economic Co-operation and Development (OECD) subsidies for agriculture total $300 billion a year, about the equivalent of Africa's GDP (World Bank, 2000b). The IMF's programme of debt relief for heavily indebted poor countries (HIPCs), founded in 1996, has been behind schedule, due in part to the fact that eligible countries must provide detailed programmes for how the freed-up money will be used. By April, 2000, only five countries had qualified for relief. In 2000, France announced that it was writing off up to $7 billion of debts owed by Africa's HIPCs, setting an example to other industrialized nations (*Financial Times*, 5 April 2000).

Debt relief by international financial institutions and donor countries can provide an opportunity to target resources at the problems of human deprivation. Political instability and corruption have inhibited progress, and, as the international institutions now stress, restructuring of political and social institutions are an essential part of the process, if sustainable improvements are to be made. The World Bank's report, *Can Africa Claim the 21st Century?*, stresses that African countries have a 'window of opportunity', requiring action in four main areas: 'conflict resolution and improved governance; more investment in people; increasing competitiveness and diversifying economies; and better support from the international community' (World Bank, 2000b).

These are very broadly defined areas and the emphasis seems to be on the internal restructuring that is needed, rather than on help from outside. It is generally true that in low-income countries, growth in per capita income has a noticeable effect on the speed of poverty reduction (Dollar, 1999). A more stable environment will encourage business, economic growth and diversification. Foreign investors, as in Asia and Latin America, can provide much-needed impetus, provided that the necessary infrastructure can be built and maintained in relative peace and security.

WWW
WEBALERT

Websites on Africa

A general site is http://www.africa.com

For news, policy, economic information and business links: http://www.allafrica.com

The site for the Common Market for Eastern and Southern Africa (COMESA) is http://www.comesa.int/home

Figure 12.3 Africa's share of world trade for its main export crops

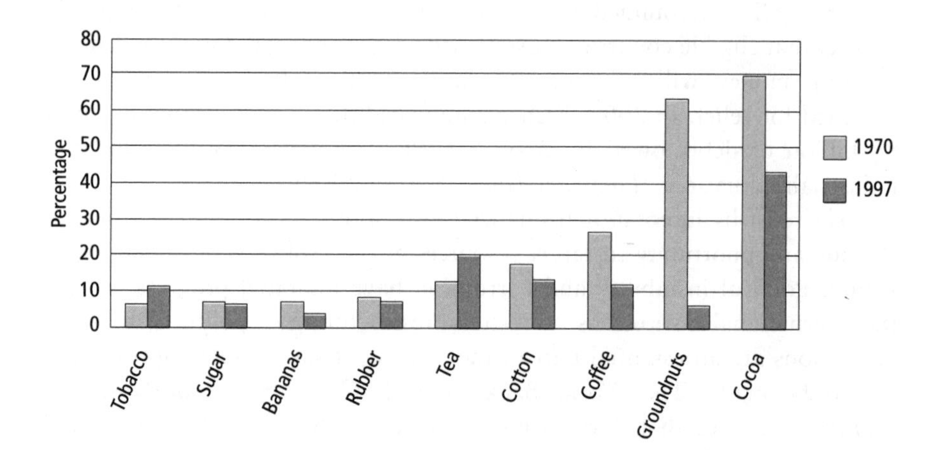

Source: FAOSTAT 2000, in *Financial Times*, 1 June 2000.

Case study 12.2 Unilever in Tanzania

Unilever Tanzania is a two-year-old subsidiary of Unilever that manufactures a range of basic goods, such as soap powder and soap, in the country. Tanzania's distribution system has been dominated by wholesalers. Unilever has decided to bypass this system and go direct to the outlets. This has been a large-scale undertaking, as the country is dotted with some 100,000 retail outlets, in 9,000 villages. With half the population living below the poverty line, consumers buy rice, maize and flour in tiny quantities every day from mini-kiosks in lanes that are too narrow for vehicles.

While Unilever delivers goods by van to large shops in towns, it had to find an alternative form of distribution for inaccessible villages. It came up with the 'bicycle brigade'. Salesmen are given bicycles with large boxes welded to the back, to transport small packs (50g) of detergent powder, margarine, soap and oil. Each salesman visits about 20–30 shops. At present, the salesman heads back to a central distribution point when he has delivered all his goods, but in future Unilever plans to locate vans with stocks at strategic points to make distribution more efficient.

Under the system, shopkeepers have more stock available and do not have to travel to wholesalers. The system has improved sales fivefold over five months. Small Omo detergent packs and Blue Band margarine have become market leaders. It is thought that in the longer term the system could also be used as a pipeline to convey socially beneficial items, such as pesticide-treated mosquito nets to combat malaria. Rajendra Aneja, Unilever Tanzania's Managing Director says: 'a systematic distribution operation is crucial to the success of any company in a developing economy'. He believes that 'with a little innovation, even the poorest economies offer a wealth of opportunities'.

Source: Turner, M., 'Bicycle brigade's mission', *Financial Times*, 16 August 2000 (reprinted with permission).

Case questions

What were the difficulties posed by the economic and social environment in Tanzania and how were they overcome?

Under what circumstances would this system be transferable to other countries?

12.4 Social responsibility of the firm

TNCs have been the drivers of globalization and the beneficiaries of liberalization policies of national governments. Should expanding freedoms to pursue corporate goals be balanced by greater social responsibility for corporate players? **Social responsibility** refers to a group of related issues, including human rights, human development and environmental protection ('green') issues. In the past, they have been seen as public policy matters falling within the ambit of governments, which formulate laws and policies. So long as businesses adhered to existing legal obligations, they were free to focus on 'the bottom line', that is, profits and shareholder value. This simplistic view, which separates social responsibility concerns from business has now become outdated, giving way to the view that the power that companies enjoy entails duties of social responsibility in the community. As was seen in Chapter 8 on the legal environment, there is a growing body of law in areas of human rights, workers' rights and environmental protection, both national laws and international treaties. The company, as employer and producer of goods and services for global markets, is directly involved in the employment conditions and operating processes. Thus it is in the 'driving seat' in relation to upholding human rights, improving working conditions and protecting the environment. Therefore, it is argued, corporate leaders should take a more proactive role in moving ahead of the minimal standards required by law.

Two factors can be highlighted in bringing about this change in the approach to social responsibility. First, while markets have delivered economic results, they have left out of the equation considerations of human and environmental values. The insertion of these concerns in the social market economies is a recognition of market limitations. The human rights and environmental questions posed daily for large corporations, such as oil companies in developing states, also show the inadequacy of viewing business in isolation from the community. No longer can a TNC doing business in a developing country remain disengaged from the live community issues in its places of operation. Second, the sheer size of the world's global corporations now dwarfs many national economies. Questions of how they are using this power in socially responsible ways are now being addressed to companies, as well as to governments. Critical natural resources, such as water, are now privatized, and the trend is continuing. Two large transnational water companies, Générale des Eaux and Lyonnaise des Eaux, now operate in 120 countries, some of which, such as those in the Middle East, have chronic problems of water scarcity. As water is now seen as a big business opportunity, questions of social responsibility inevitably arise, as the public interest may conflict with that of the shareholders of water companies. It has been said that, once a company passes a certain size, it ceases to be seen as entrepreneurial (a good thing) and starts to be seen as too powerful (a bad thing).

For global companies, social responsibility raises the basic question, 'what is the company for?' **Stakeholder** theory points to the many different interests that company directors must address. Some of these, such as shareholders and employees, are internal to the company, while those of suppliers, customers and the community in general are outside the organization itself, although these relationships may come to be seen as integral to the company's strategy. An emphasis on social responsibility is not unlike the stakeholder approach, but in place of separate (and possibly conflicting) interests, there is substituted the more integrative concept of social responsibility, which goes beyond the idea of balancing specifically defined interests. This newer approach, reflecting growing international opinion that companies are now expected to 'do good' and not just generate profits, is increasingly seen as striking a more favourable chord with shareholders, who are now more informed and potentially more critical of lax social and environmental standards than in years gone by. An area in which this tendency for shareholders themselves to drive the social responsibility agenda has become evident is protection of the environment.

Social responsibility

Social responsibility comprises a group of issues, including:

1. *Human rights*, including rights such as freedom from torture and right to privacy (see Chapter 8)
2. *Workers' rights*, such as the right not to be discriminated against on grounds of race, sex, religion or nationality; and also working conditions (for example health and safety measures) (see Chapter 6)
3. *Environmental protection*, including reducing pollutants, protecting ecosystems, and reducing demands on non-renewable natural resources

While there are national and EU laws, as well as international treaties, laying down minimum standards in all these spheres, the socially responsible company will go beyond the minimum required by law

TNCs are often criticized, especially by numerous watchdog groups, when their operations in developing countries do not come up to international standards and when they are perceived as exploiting cheap labour, rather than behaving as good 'corporate citizens'

12.4.1 Raising corporate standards

Large TNCs operate in a huge range of national cultural environments. While it was once thought that local standards sufficed, companies are now expected to maintain consistent standards and policies across their operations, whatever the location. In many countries, however, practices such as child labour are commonplace. Accurate data on the extent of child labour are difficult to obtain, but it is estimated that there are about 250 million children aged 5–14 engaged in economic activity, mainly in developing countries. Of these, about 120 million work full time, while the rest combine work with schooling. In terms of regional breakdown, 60 per cent of child workers are in Asia, 32 per cent in Africa, and 7 per cent in Latin America. It should be noted, however, that in terms of participation rate, Africa has the largest proportion of child workers, as Table 12.2 shows.

Many companies have introduced voluntary codes of conduct, outlining their principles on legal and ethical standards. Levi Strauss, which relies on

Table 12.2 Economic activity participation rate of children 5–14 years of age, by region and sex, 1995

	Both sexes %	Boys %	Girls %
World	24.7	27.0	22.3
Regions			
Africa	41.4	46.0	36.7
Asia (excluding Japan)	21.5	22.5	20.4
Latin America and Caribbean	16.5	21.8	11.1
Oceania (excluding Australia and New Zealand)	29.3	32.7	25.8

Source: ILO (1998) *Statistics on Working Children and Hazardous Child Labour in Brief* (ILO: Geneva).

more than 400 subcontractors overseas, discovered that 25 per cent of the local subcontractors were abusing the workforce. As part of its programme to stop such practices, it devised new sourcing guidelines for the future, which address legal, ethical, environmental and employment standards (Schaffer et al., 1999). Such codes have now become accepted practice. While they are doubtless part of a public relations exercise to deflect criticism, they underline the sense in which the modern corporation is aware of its responsibility as a good corporate citizen. These codes tend to be worded in general terms and most lack mechanisms for external monitoring and audit. Nike has 700 contract factories in 53 countries, with varying legal, social and economic environments. Having been a target of protesters, Nike has issued a code of conduct which is complemented by internal and external monitoring and has begun to involve non-governmental organizations (NGOs) in its monitoring processes.

12.4.2 Reaching for international standards

On an international level, there are three initiatives which have addressed ethical issues. The first is from the OECD. Its Guidelines for Multinational Enterprises, first issued in 1976, have recently been strengthened. The 2000 version includes standards for corporate governance, workplace conditions, environmental safeguards, bribery and protection for whistleblowers. While they are not binding, these guidelines are supported by the OECD's considerable ability to publicize abuses and bring pressure to bear on governments and corporations. The OECD's 1976 version prompted changes in national law in member states.

Second, the International Labour Organization (ILO), which dates from 1919, sets standards and provides monitoring of working conditions. Now a UN agency, its organization includes representatives of government, labour and employers from each member state. It aims to set up national mechanisms for employment protection and monitoring and, in addition, it aims to promote the recognition of basic rights, including freedom of association.

Third, the UN has initiated a Global Compact between governments, corporations and NGOs. The Compact lists nine key principles from the Universal Declaration of Human Rights, the core standards of the ILO and the Rio Declaration. They include support of human rights, the elimination of child labour, free trade unions and the elimination of environmental pollution. These are 'aspirational' rather than binding in their effects. The significance of the initiative is the bringing together of the major players in a single forum for debate about the issues. Nike, DaimlerChrysler, Unilever and Royal Dutch Shell were among the corporations that signed the accord, as were Amnesty International and the World Wide Fund for Nature. The UN Secretary General said:

> Companies should not wait for governments to pass laws before they pay a decent wage or agree not to pollute the environment ... If companies lead by example, the governments may wake up and make laws to formalize these practices. (*New York Times*, 27 July 2000)

The launch of the Global Compact illustrates three points that are indicative of the current global legal and ethical environment:

- The line between what is ethical and what is legal has become blurred. What is legal in a particular country may not pass muster by international ethical, and often legal, standards
- Global corporations, with a presence in all continents, are often in a stronger position than governments to take a lead in implementing higher ethical standards
- The bringing together of corporate, governmental and NGO representatives in an, as yet, embryonic framework under the auspices of the UN emphasizes that the changing environment encompasses both state and non-state players.

12.5 Challenges of environmental protection and climate change

Land, water and air are the components of the physical environment which have been affected by industrial processes associated with economic development.

It is generally acknowledged that industrial processes cause environmental damage, altering ecosystems. While it is also now recognized that human activities contribute to climate change, there is a diversity of views on what solutions should be adopted. Managers have become accustomed to dealing with local pollution problems arising from their operations, entailing interaction with local community authorities. However, wider issues such as climate change and biodiversity, while nonetheless real, seem remote, complex and unsusceptible to the usual means of resolution. What is more, scientific evidence is not always clear cut and regulatory regimes are still in doubt, partly over difficulties of measurement and enforcement. It is largely down to the lobbying – and more recently, active involvement of 'green groups' – that environmental issues and climate change are now seen as urgent issues on the global agenda, engaging governments, corporations and consumers alike.

12.5.1 Environmental protection

Businesses are becoming more conscious of the need for new, cleaner technologies, partly because of growing social and ethical considerations, and also because international regulations agreed by governments are growing in number (see Chapter 8). Companies now take a broader view of their 'environmental footprint', looking at all phases of their operations, from production processes to the nature of the products they sell, to assess whether they can be made more environmentally friendly. Consumers have been a source of pressure, creating new demand, for example, for products which are recyclable. Environmental protection and economic efficiency, once seen as posing a dilemma of choice, are now seen as merging together, in that protecting the environment is now a primary object of the business, and not seen, as in the past, as a constraint on business.

WWW
WEBALERT

In the UK, the Department for Environment is located in the new Department for Environment, Food and Rural Affairs (DEFRA) (created in 2001) at
http://www.defra.gov.uk

There are many websites run by NGOs. They include:
The National Environmental Trust at
http://www.environet.policy.net/

Friends of the Earth at
http://www.foe.org.uk

Greenpeace at
http://www.greenpeace.org

World Wide Fund for Nature at
http://www.panda.org

Environmental management, that is, assessing environmental impact and devising suitable strategies, is now seen as central to companies' operations, especially in the industries which are by nature more pollutant. These include chemicals, mining, pulp and paper, iron and steel, and refineries. For the large TNCs which use subcontracting and licensing arrangements, there is a question of how much control can be exerted on subcontractors in terms of environmental management. This question is often posed for TNCs operating in developing countries with weaker environmental protection regimes. Although it is difficult to assess the impact of industries in different locations, research suggests that the ratio of pollution-intensive industries in FDI stock is higher than in domestic investment (United Nations, 1999a). FDI to many countries that have relied on mineral exports has increased as a result of liberalization and privatization. Historically, state-owned production was highly pollutant, partly because of obsolete technology, whereas the flow of new investment has brought cleaner technology and greater environmental protection.

Developing countries with weak environmental policies and weak enforcement are also host to manufacturing industries, in which they enjoy traditional comparative advantage due to low-cost labour. Where these plants are export-oriented, consumers in developed countries' markets can be a source of

POINTS TO REMEMBER

Aspects of environmental management

Processes:

- *Air*
  - Emissions of gases, particle matter, metals, organic chemicals and odours
  - Risks of fires and explosions
- *Water*
  - Use of process water and emission of process water
  - Emissions of water contaminated, for example, by metals or oil
  - Contamination of surface water or underground water
- *Land*
  - Waste disposal, including hazardous waste
  - Extraction of raw materials
  - Soil contamination by metals
  - Surface disturbance, such as erosion or subsidence
- *Products*
  - Contaminating components, such as metals, chemicals, pesticides
  - Recyclability, including recyclable packaging

pressure for environmental protection. The International Organization for Standardization (ISO), which produces ISO standards, has developed a certification for standards of environmental management (ISO 14000). Although research suggests that foreign affiliates in manufacturing industries might have higher environmental standards than domestic manufacturers, the adoption rate of ISO 14000 certification does not show any noticeable differences between foreign and domestic firms (United Nations, 1999a, p. 302). However, limited research to date does show marked differences for energy efficiency (United Nations, 1999a, p. 302). TNCs are finding that, in the new context of social responsibility, it is advantageous to integrate systems of environmental management across all their corporate activities globally, wherever the location.

12.5.2 Climate change

Climate experts generally believe that a slow process of '**global warming**' is occurring, caused by the build-up of heat-trapping gases, or 'greenhouse gases', produced mainly by the burning of fossil fuels. The evidence emanates from a panel of hundreds of scientists, the Intergovernmental Panel on Climate Change, who have published reports in 1990, 1995 and 2000. Most feel that this process threatens ecology and human well-being, causing extreme effects such as severe flooding in some places and desertification in others. Island nations and low-lying regions, such as Bangladesh, risk submerging beneath the sea, while the Sahara Desert in Africa is expanding. Experts say that curtailing emissions is needed to slow down the warming process. This view was incorporated into the UN's Kyoto Protocol in 1997. This treaty set targets for the reduction in carbon dioxide (CO_2) emissions, mainly by the industrialized countries. The overall target was that by 2008–12, industrial countries would reduce their combined greenhouse gas emissions to 5 per cent below 1990 levels. The treaty was signed by over 150 countries, but has not come into force as it has not been ratified by any of the industrialized nations. (It will not come into force until countries accounting for 55 per cent of greenhouse gas emissions have ratified.) The treaty itself was in some ways unsatisfactory, as it left open important questions of how these targets were to be achieved.

WWW
WEBALERT

Websites with specific content on climate change

The Intergovernmental Panel on Climate Change is at
http://www.ipcc.ch/

The UN Framework Convention on Climate Change, which includes the Kyoto Protocol, is at
http://www.unfccc.de
http://www.panda.org/climate/summit/

The fate of the Kyoto Protocol seemed to hinge on the US position, as US emissions amounted to 36 per cent of the world total in 1990, the benchmark year used by the Kyoto Protocol. The Kyoto Protocol required the US to reduce its emissions by 7 per cent from 1990 levels by 2008–12. Its emissions in 1998 were up nearly 22 per cent on 1990 levels. Detailed rules for implementation of reductions in emissions were intended to be agreed in a follow-up meeting in The Hague in 2000, attended by delegates from 170 countries. At that meeting, the US took the view that two policies, emissions trading and the use of carbon 'sinks', should be taken into account in meeting the targets. Emissions trading, which is recognized in the Kyoto Protocol, would allow countries to buy emission 'credits' from other, less polluting, countries in order to meet their targets without actually cutting emissions in their domestic economy. Individual companies, too, would have permits to emit greenhouse gases, which they could trade like any other commodity (see Minifile). The inclusion of carbon 'sinks' allows forestation and agricultural land, which absorb carbon dioxide, to be set against emissions targets. Critics of this policy fear that biodiversity will be threatened by encouraging sink projects which clear native forests in order to plant industrial plantations. Both policies were opposed by EU representatives and the meeting in The Hague ended without agreement.

Minifile

THE MARKET IN EMISSIONS TRADING

The principle behind emissions trading is that companies which reduce their carbon emissions beyond their allotted targets at relatively low cost can sell 'credits', equivalent to permits, to other companies that face higher costs in reaching their targets. A market similar to a commodity market can thus be established in emissions trades that potentially is worth billions of dollars. Although the extent that this market will be allowed to grow will depend on the rules laid down in international treaties, the market is already under way. As discussions in the The Hague were collapsing without agreement in 2000, a group of 35 large energy companies gathered for an inaugural meeting of the Emissions Market Development Group, launched by consultant Arthur Andersen, the bank Crédit Lyonnais and Natsource, a new broker dealing in emissions trading. The group intends to establish an emissions 'bank', which would exchange credits generated by corporate and national trading schemes.

Meanwhile, the launch of an online marketplace for emissions trading, CO2e.com, was announced by PricewaterhouseCoopers (PwC). PwC is confident that 'the emissions reductions now can be offset against those which can be made in the future', even though at the time of launch, the Kyoto Protocol had not been finalized. The portal will be 'a single point of entry for corporations which need to understand and cope with their duties in terms of climate change'. Its aim is 'to help companies establish what their position is and what they need to do now or in future' (*The Telegraph*, 19 November 2000).

Sources: Houlder, V., 'Accord at The Hague would boost market in emissions trading', *Financial Times*, 23 November 2000; Houlder, V., 'Business sees green controls as a prospect, not just a cost', *Financial Times*, 18 November 2000; Fagan, M., 'PwC to launch online CO_2 exchange', *The Telegraph*, 19 November 2000.

Prospects of reaching agreement seemed to recede even further when President George W. Bush announced in March 2001 his rejection of the treaty on the grounds that it would be harmful to the US economy. Notwithstanding the non-participation of the US, representatives of 185 nations resumed negotiations on the Kyoto Protocol and reached a compromise agreement in Bonn in July 2001. The agreement approved the two policies of emissions trading and carbon sinks, giving the go-ahead for the market in emissions trading (see Minifile).

12.5.3 Implications for business

Despite the differing positions of national negotiators on how to respond to global warming, the raised profile that these negotiations have now acquired has impressed on business the need to look at the green implications of its operations, and especially at levels of emissions. One consideration is that reductions are likely to be required under future treaties and it is preferable to get a head start. Another is that companies are in a position to take the lead in positive action to alleviate potentially harmful global warming, especially in industries that have high levels of emissions (see Case Study 12.3). Cutting pollution, while it can be seen as a cost, is also a business opportunity. Large car makers, such as General Motors and Ford, have committed considerable research to less polluting cars, run on fuel cells. Thus they have an advantage over less sophisticated rivals. Low-emission technologies have opened opportunities in the energy industry and also a range of manufacturing industries. Clean technology can also be exported to countries in the developing world. The Kyoto Protocol built in considerable flexibility, adopting a number of possible approaches, including emissions trading, which in turn give businesses a variety of tools for meeting the climate change challenges. Business leaders at the World Economic Forum meeting in Davos in 2000 voted global climate change the most pressing issue confronting the business community. Companies are in a position to act, while political leaders have often appeared to get embroiled in political bargaining that has rather diverted attention from the overall purpose of negotiations.

Europeans have learned to live with high fuel taxes and green politics. The UK and Germany are roughly on target to meet Kyoto targets. UK emissions of the basket of greenhouse gases are expected to be about 13.5 per cent below 1990 levels in 2010 and emissions of carbon dioxide (which comprises about 80 per cent of the total greenhouse gas emissions) about 7 per cent below (DEFRA, 2000). The distribution in reductions across the UK economy are shown in Figure 12.4.

In the UK, the March 2000 budget introduced a number of environmental tax reforms, including a climate change levy on business to encourage energy efficiency, which has met with criticism from businesses that jobs and production will suffer (see Minifile). Although discounts will be available for heavy energy users, a report for the Engineering Employers' Federation showed that

Case study 12.3 Business initiatives in cutting gas emissions

A number of leading companies, including DuPont, Shell and BP, have joined a growing list of businesses committing themselves to substantial voluntary reductions in the release of heat-trapping greenhouse gases. DuPont has already cut greenhouse emissions to 50 per cent below 1990 levels. It has found ways to end emissions of nitrous oxide, a greenhouse gas that was emitted in the production of nylon. Aluminium companies are focusing on both energy savings and eliminating the powerful greenhouse gas, perfluorocarbon, by changing their smelting process.

In other initiatives, Johnson & Johnson and IBM entered commitments with the World Wide Fund for Nature and the Center for Energy and Climate Solutions. Under these commitments, the companies would reduce emissions over the next decade to well below 1990 levels.

What is particularly striking about these commitments is that the companies have taken voluntary moves, with

> no guarantee that they will get credit for the cuts they make now under future regulations or in future systems set up to allow trading of credits given to companies that reduce their output of gases below required levels. (Revkin, 2000)

A former head of the US Department of Energy's energy efficiency programme, Joseph J. Romm, commented: 'Many companies figured out in the 1990s that when an environmental issue reaches a certain level of public consciousness and seriousness, it's better to be proactive than reactive' (Revkin, 2000).

In the UK, a scheme is being planned by DEFRA by which firms may voluntarily agree to targets for reducing greenhouse gas emissions, concentrating initially on carbon dioxide. Participating organizations would agree to reduce emissions to a particular level each year and would be given a permit accordingly. If, by the end of the year, they have reduced their emissions below the target level, they could sell on their remaining unused permits to companies in the scheme which have not met their own targets. The hope is that the financial incentive will help to reduce emissions.

Source: Revkin, A., '7 companies agree to cut gas emissions', *New York Times*, 18 October 2000; UK Department for Environment, Food and Rural Affairs (2001) *A Greenhouse Gas Emissions Trading Scheme for the UK*.

Case question

In what ways is the voluntary, proactive approach adopted by these companies preferable to a reactive approach?

more than 3,000 UK companies have annual energy bills of over £100,000, but will be ineligible for the discount. Particularly hard hit when the climate levy starts to bite will be small or medium-sized companies, some of whom, according to one British managing director of a US-owned company, may consider shifting production to the US if productivity suffers (*Financial Times*, 21 November 2000).

Minifile

PROTECTING THE ENVIRONMENT: THE UK BUDGET 2000

The following is a summary of key provisions in the green budget of 2000:

Tackling climate change:

- extension of reduced vehicle excise duty (VED) rate to existing cars with engines up to 1,200cc
- introduction of graduated VED system for new cars based primarily on their carbon dioxide emissions
- an additional £280 million allocated to tackling congestion hot spots and modernizing public transport
- further encouragement for emissions trading
- implementing the climate change levy to encourage energy efficiency in the business sector

Improving air quality:

- a fiscal incentive to encourage the take up of cleaner ultra-low sulphur petrol
- lower rates of tax for vehicles which use less polluting fuels

Regenerating our cities and protecting our countryside:

- introduction of an aggregates levy to tackle the environmental costs of quarrying and encourage recycling
- pre-announced increases in landfill tax to encourage waste minimization and recycling
- consultation on possible stamp duty relief for new developments on brownfield land to encourage an urban renaissance
- further discussions on a voluntary package to reduce the environmental impact of pesticide use

Source: HM Treasury (2000) *Budget: March 2000,* at http://www.hm-treasury.gov.uk/budget2000.

Figure 12.4 UK greenhouse emissions in 1990 and projections for 2010

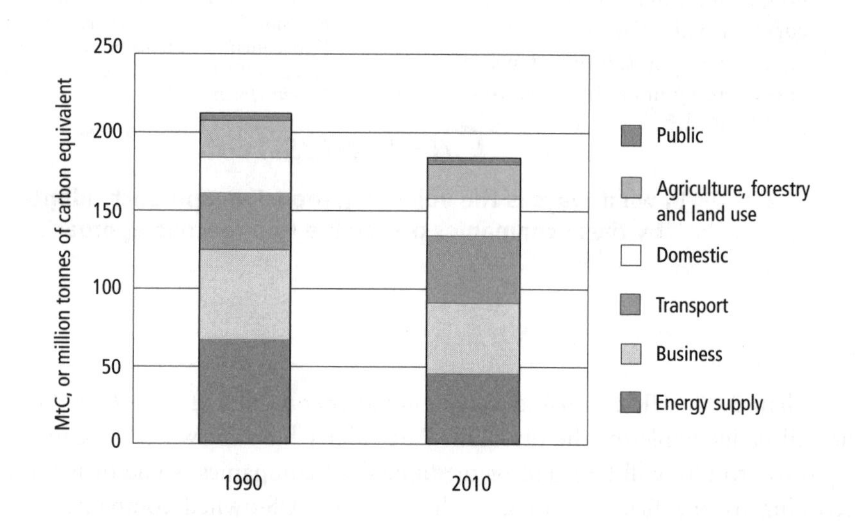

Source: UK Department of Environment, Food and Rural Affairs (2000) *Climate Change: Draft UK Programme* at http://www.defra.gov.uk/environment.

12.6 Challenges of the new information age

The last two decades of the twentieth century have seen the explosion of information technology (IT) and the spread of networked information systems to virtually all types of industry. The internet has been described as 'globalization on steroids' (World Bank, 2000c). Advances in IT, and especially telecommunications and internet technology, have been crucial to the emergence of what is called the 'new economy', based on electronic networks (see Chapter 10). Combined with deregulation of financial markets, globalization has brought enormous opportunities for investment and hastening market integration, but it has also exposed serious risks, which threaten to undermine the undoubted benefits. There is no doubt that near-instantaneous electronic trading in capital markets has facilitated the radical movements in capital flows that have contributed to financial crises, in Mexico in 1994, in Asian countries in 1997, in Russia in 1998 and Brazil in 1999 (Castells, 2000b, p. 52). While investors flocked to join the rush to emerging markets, financial collapses brought hardship and suffering to millions of innocent victims in stricken economies (see Chapter 11).

The new economy has tapped wellsprings of entrepreneurial energy all over the globe, as internet start-up companies leapt onto the bandwagon. Here too, investors were not lacking. Some of the dotcom companies saw amazing growth, on a scale of 400–500 per cent rise in share prices almost overnight, following glittering initial public offerings. In the US in 1997, a higher proportion of households' assets were in securities than in real estate (Castells, 2000b, p. 54). These inflated values were bound to come down to earth, however, when the realization that the business foundations of many of the dotcom enterprises were unsound and that 'virtual' retailers face all the familiar problems of the old economy, such as product quality and prudent accounting. The surviving dotcoms and the more recent arrivals have been more realistic in their expectations.

Has the globalized world of the internet left behind the national borders of the old economy? In *The Invisible Continent*, Kenichi Ohmae describes the new borderless world of the emerging internet-based economy, which he calls the 'invisible continent' of cyberspace, or 'Cyberia' (Ohmae, 2000). While he speaks of leaving behind the national borders of the 'old world' environment, he does envisage nations, companies, individuals and regions moving at different paces towards the new continent. He offers a scorecard of national readiness to move into the invisible continent (Ohmae, 2000, p. 238). Not surprisingly, the US is at the forefront.

In the new economy, as in the old, there are inequalities and exclusions, as well as opportunities. The Philippines presents an example of both the benefits and the downside of the information society. As Case Study 12.4 shows, the Philippines, providing remote services, has been well placed to benefit from the internet. Similarly, India has seen a booming software market (see Case Study 10.2). Both countries, however, risk losing their highly skilled

Case study 12.4 Two sides of the internet in the Philippines

The Philippines has gained a reputation as a provider of high-quality internet services, such as call centres and other 'back-office' services, but also acquired unwanted publicity in 2000 as the home of the 'lovebug' virus, the world's most infectious computer virus to date.

The Philippines may seem an unlikely location for an internet boom, but its largely English-speaking population and American-style education system, inherited from 50 years of US rule (1898 until the Second World War), have made it a magnet for internet services. America Online, Motorola and Citibank, among many others, have operations there. Staff at call centres in the Philippines earn about $5 a day, compared with rates of $10 an hour in the US. There is also an abundance of skilled programming and web-design talent among its 170,000 computer-related graduates each year. For students, the motivation is strong. Many find better paid jobs abroad, and, with new companies entering the country all the time, there are skilled labour shortages in internet companies.

A Filipino student, Onel A. de Guzman, attends a computing college in Manila, a long way from Massachusetts Institute of Technology (MIT), housed in a former warehouse without flush toilets. Guzman shot to global media attention in 2000, when a virus, transmitted via the email message, 'I love you', was apparently traced to his computer. Quickly spreading to computers around the world, the virus is estimated to have cost $10 billion in lost data and productivity. The Philippines had no law against hacking at the time (it has now passed one) and charges against him for fraud were soon dropped. Guzman said that he may have inadvertently unleashed the programme. Guzman, like many other hackers in this poor country, is skilful at stealing internet access passwords and downloading unlicensed software from the internet without paying for it. Guzman's proposal for his thesis was a method for stealing passwords – the proposal was rejected by his tutors. It was this proposal that, he felt, could have led investigators to his door.

It is estimated that about 77 per cent of the software used in the Philippines is pirated. For people in developing countries, the cost of using the internet is considered unjustifiably expensive and widespread hacking is the inevitable result. The lovebug case highlighted the daunting gap in internet access between rich and poor countries. It also exposed the vulnerability of safety systems. Should Microsoft share the blame? Its email program propagated the virus, made easier by the fact that most of the world's computers run on Microsoft software.

Sources: Arnold, W., 'Computer whizzes at Philippine pay', *New York Times*, 19 May 2000; Arnold, W., 'Virus brings publicity to computer subculture in Philippines', *New York Times*, 15 May 2000; Landler, M., 'A Filipino linked to "love bug" talks about his license to hack', *New York Times*, 21 October 2000.

Case question

What are the attractions of the Philippines as a location for internet companies and how does their presence help the technology gap between rich and poor countries?

workers and for the lives of the bulk of the population in these poor countries, there is little change. While nearly half the population of the US has internet access, the figure is about 0.6 per cent in developing countries, which risk being marginalized by poor access to information. A 'digital divide' may thus be opening up between rich and poor countries (World Bank, 2000c).

There are huge potential benefits from new technologies, but the problems of the global economy seem to persist and even become more threatening. Castells argues that:

> the global economy is at the same time extraordinarily inclusive of what is valued in the networks of business interaction, and highly exclusive of what has little or no interests in a given time and space. (Castells, 2000b, p. 53)

He cites examples of AIDS epidemics, global trade in people, destruction of the world's forests and the expansion of global criminal activity. The technology itself is not to blame, but where are the safeguards that it will be used to serve the values of human well-being for present and future generations?

12.7 Globalization and diversity: the way ahead

Although it is no longer plausible to deny the reality of globalization, the extreme views of the hyperglobalizers, who predicted a withering away of national differences, have not yet come to pass. Increasing integration of economic and financial systems has not as yet brought about convergence. Globalization has enhanced the powers of transnational companies and weakened the abilities of nation-states to set national agendas. At the same time, the Fordist organization has given way to the flexible organization, global in strategic outlook, but adapting to the diversity of different locations, in terms of social and cultural environment, economic systems and systems of innovation. An understanding of the relationship between forces of globalization and local distinctiveness is increasingly seen as essential for companies in international markets.

There are some who argue that, with the demise of nation-states' ability to set moral, legal and economic rules, there needs to be a strengthening of supranational organizations to take on the mantle of governance in the global economy (Drucker, 1997; Giddens and Hutton, 2000). Giddens and Hutton point to the growing role of the EU in taking over the authority formerly the preserve of national governments, as the beginnings of 'cosmopolitan governance with mechanisms for proper democratic accountability and continental citizenship' (Giddens and Hutton, 2000, p. 223). Drucker says, that 'a central challenge ... is the development of international law and supranational organizations that can make and enforce rules for the global economy' (Drucker, 1997). On the other hand, the experience of the IMF and World Bank has been one of finding that a 'one-size-fits-all' approach has proved unsuitable in the divergent economic, social and political settings that exist from country to country. The experience of the most highly developed supranational organization to date, the EU, has been primarily one of struggling both to reconcile divergent national interests and establish structures of legitimacy and accountability, essential for the institutional foundation on which enlargement rests. For international business, the way ahead opens opportunities to grasp the dynamic interaction between forces of globalization, on the one hand, and the needs and expectations of people in diverse national environments, on the other.

12.8 Conclusions

1. The themes of globalization and persisting national diversity have emerged in each of the spheres of the business environment discussed in earlier chapters. These themes represent interactions rather than countervailing forces in the environment.

2. Change in the international environment, through processes of globalization and liberalization, has brought opportunities for economic development, but also exposure to instabilities, as in financial markets.

3. Attention is increasingly focused on the widening gap between rich and poor countries and possible solutions. Heightened awareness of problems of poverty, disease and hunger has led to initiatives from governments in developed countries, as well as initiatives to encourage foreign investment.

4. Social responsibility, including human rights, human development and environmental protection, is now seen as a central objective of transnational companies, responding to a growing awareness of ethical and environmental issues by shareholders and consumers.

5. Responding to the effects of climate change has led to concerted efforts, at international level, to devise a regulatory regime, and companies are well placed to take the lead in reducing greenhouse gas emissions and developing clean technologies.

6. Globalization has perhaps been most pervasive in the information revolution and the rapid spread of the internet. Like the 'old economy', however, the 'new economy' presents risks as well as opportunities in divergent national environments for its successful exploitation.

7. While some would argue that the weakening of nation-states implies that newer global forms of governance are needed, international institutions at present seem not to fulfil that role. For international business, therefore, globalization implies local adaptation and sensitivity to local business environments.

Review questions

1. In which dimensions of the international business environment has globalization penetrated more deeply and in which is national diversity still the norm?
2. What has been the impact of liberalization in national economies on the business environment globally?
3. What factors account for the gaps between rich and poor countries?
4. What is meant by 'social responsibility' in relation to the modern company? In what ways does it represent a departure from stakeholder theories?
5. What are the main issues engaging governments and corporations in relation to protection of the natural environment?
6. What are the pressures on governments to pursue national objectives in environmental protection and how can these be reconciled with global objectives?
7. In what ways has the new information age created a 'digital divide'?

Assignments

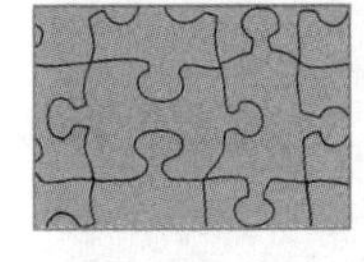

1. Discuss (a) the possibilities for economic development in the poorest countries, and in particular those of sub-Saharan Africa; and (b) the current problems which present obstacles to development.
2. Compare the traditional view of the role of the firm, in relation to its shareholders and society, to the new view envisaged by the broader emphasis on social responsibility.

Further reading

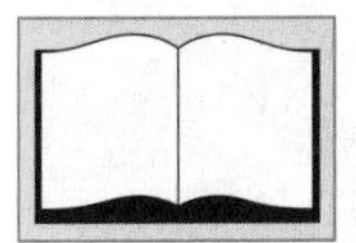

Agittey, G. (2000) *Africa in Chaos* (Basingstoke: Palgrave)

Hutton, W. and Giddens, A. (2000) *On the Edge: Living with Global Capitalism* (London: Jonathan Cape)

Meyer, A. (2000) *Contraction and Convergence: A Global Framework to Cope with Climate Change* (Newton Abbot: Green Books)

Ohmae, K. (2000) *The Invisible Continent: Four Strategic Imperatives of the New Economy* (London: Nicholas Brealey)

Glossary

antitrust laws	laws designed to control monopolies and anti-competitive practices such as price-fixing agreements.
arbitration	means of resolving disputes between parties to a contract, through an independent body agreed by the parties, thereby averting the need for court proceedings.
arm's-length contracting	business dealings between people who interact only for the purpose of doing business; contrasted with relational contracting. Arm's-length contracting is more prevalent in individualist societies.
assimilation of cultures	process by which minority cultures of, for example, immigrants, become integrated into the mainstream culture of a nation.
authoritarianism	rule by a single leader or group of individuals, with unlimited power; contrast with constitutionalism.
balance of payments	credit and debit transactions between a country's residents (including companies) and those of other countries.
bilateral trade agreements	agreements with the status of treaties between two countries, designed to regulate trading relations between them.
biotechnology	the application of scientific and engineering principles to the processing of materials by biological agents to provide goods and services.
bond	a loan document promising to pay a specific sum on a due date.
Bretton Woods agreement	the 1944 agreement between Allied nations in the aftermath of the Second World War, which was intended to bring about exchange rate stability and regulate international finance. It established the International Monetary Fund (IMF) and World Bank.
Buddhism	Asian religion with over 300 million followers worldwide. Emphasizing spiritual attainment rather than worldly gain, it has subdivided into a number of sects.
bureaucracy	organizational form based on hierarchy of status and a multiplicity of formal rules governing operations.

business	economic activity in which goods and services are supplied in exchange for payment, usually money.
business cycle	regular pattern of fluctuations in business activity, divided into phases of prosperity, recession, depression and recovery.
capital account	account on the balance of payments statement which shows the transactions involving the sale and purchase of assets, including investments in shares.
capital flows	the flow of private funds between countries.
capitalism	economic systems based on the private ownership of the means of production, including the individual's ability to sell his or her own labour.
cartel	grouping of producers of a product who, through continuing co-operative agreement, exert control on prices and output. Members of the cartel may be companies or nations.
caste system	social stratification system based on birth; associated with Hinduism.
central bank	bank which is responsible for monetary policy for an economy and for the issuance of notes and coins. It is the banker to the government and the lender-of-last-resort.
centralization	the concentration of power and control among relatively few decision-makers in an organization.
chief executive officer (CEO)	chief officer at the head of a company's organizational structure.
civil law	in any legal system, the law pertaining to relations between private individuals and companies.
civil law system	legal system based on comprehensive legal codes which form the basic law; contrasted with common law systems.
civil society	sphere of activities in society in which citizens are free to pursue personal goals and form associations as they wish; characteristic of pluralist societies.
civil war	armed conflict which takes place between different groups within a state's borders.
class	social grouping based on economic status.
class action	legal action in courts brought by a number of injured parties acting as a group. Class actions are often brought against manufacturers of defective products which have been widely distributed, or against companies that are alleged to have caused widespread harm to the public, as in pollution accidents.

class system system of social stratification based on economic status in society.

coalition government government formed by two or more parties following elections in which no single party wins a majority of seats; likely to occur in multiparty systems and those which have proportional representation.

co-determination a system of relations between business management, trade unions and government, based on co-operation rather than confrontation in labour relations (associated mainly with Germany).

common law legal system based chiefly on the accumulation of case law in decided judgments through a system of binding precedent; contrasted with civil law (codified) systems.

common market grouping of countries which agree to remove trade barriers such as tariffs among members and operate a common trade policy towards non-member countries.

company organization recognized as a legal entity with a separate corporate identity from its members and employees.

comparative advantage the theory (devised by Ricardo) that a country should specialize in producing the products which it can produce more cheaply and efficiently than other countries.

competitive advantage the theory (devised by Porter) that a country's international competitive position is based on four factors: demand conditions; factor conditions; firm strategy and structure; and related and supporting industries.

Confucianism Asian moral philosophy which emphasizes family relationships and duties of loyalty. While not a formal religion, it has had a huge impact on the social and cultural environment in most Asian countries.

constitutionalism source of state legitimacy based on accepted institutional rules, applying to both rulers and ruled; contrasted with, for example, personal or military rule.

convertibility the characteristic of a currency which can be exchanged for other currencies without government restrictions and controls.

corporate governance structures and processes by which a company is controlled at the highest level, in particular the mechanisms for accountability of the board of directors to the shareholders. Corporate governance has come to take on a broader definition, encompassing the interests of stakeholders as well as shareholders.

corruption practices such as payments and favours between businesses, individuals and governments (usually for personal gain), which are outside formal legal channels, and can significantly permeate the business environment in some countries.

criminal law laws which designate offences and set out legal procedure for prosecution by state authorities against those charged with criminal offences.

cultural globalization process of gradual fading of national cultures in the face of global values and symbols, such as global brands, fast food and Western-dominated media.

cultural pluralism the recognition of numerous subcultures within a society; contrasted with the policy of assimilation of immigrants and minority groups into a dominant national culture.

currency flows movements of currency between countries, which influence exchange rates and are an important element of risk for international business.

current account the account on the balance of payments statement that shows the level of trade in merchandise and services.

decentralization in large organizations or countries, processes for transferring decision-making authority to lower levels; associated with empowerment.

demand the aggregate amount of a product that consumers are willing to purchase at particular price.

democracy system of elected government, based on fair and free elections and universal suffrage.

demographic change changes in whole populations brought about by rises and falls in the birth and death rate, as well as migration of people.

demographic crisis problems experienced generally in ageing societies, where there is a growing proportion of elderly people.

deregulation process by which government restrictions and controls are lifted.

developing country a country which is less industrialized and poorer than the advanced industrial economies; also referred to as less-developed countries or Third World countries.

direct taxation — the imposition of taxes directly on income, as in income and corporation tax.

division of labour — organizational principle by which each phase in production is conceived as a specialized task assigned to a particular person. The international division of labour, similarly, assigns particular phases to particular locations.

dumping — the sale of goods abroad at below the price charged for comparable goods in the producing country. Under GATT, importing countries are allowed to impose anti-dumping duties on the exporting country.

e-commerce — business transactions, both business-to-business and business-to-consumers, which are negotiated and agreed on the internet.

economic growth — a country's increase in national income over time, associated with industrialization, increasing investment and technological improvement.

economies of scale — lower costs of production arising from increases in the volume of products produced.

elasticity — the proportionate change in a dependent variable, as in the price elasticity of demand, whereby demand responds to price changes.

embargo — the prohibition imposed by a government on trade with another country by its nationals (as in the embargo imposed by the US on trade with Cuba).

empowerment — management approach which allows employees decision-making authority and responsibility for their own actions.

entrepreneur — person who sets up in business, often referred to as the 'start-up' enterprise, and commits his or her own funds, as well as energy, to the enterprise.

environmental management — assessment of environmental impact and formulation of environmental strategies from the perspective of a company's total operations.

equity — a company's shares (known as 'stock' in the US).

ethnocentrism — view of the world which centres only on one's own culture.

euro — the single currency adopted by the EU under the EMU.

eurobond — a bond denominated in a currency other than that of the country in which it is issued.

eurodollars	US dollars held on deposit in banks outside the US. They need not be European banks.
European Monetary Union (EMU)	The EU programme centred on a single European currency (the euro) and an independent central bank which sets monetary policy. Launched in 1999, there are now 12 states in the 'euro-zone'.
European Union	the regional grouping of European countries which evolved from a common market to the deeper integrative framework of economic union, changing its name from European Community to European Union in 1994.
euro-zone	member states in the EU which have satisfied the Maastricht criteria and joined the EMU. Their number rose to 12 with the admission of Greece in 2001.
exchange controls	restrictions and controls imposed by governments on the movement of currency.
expatriate	in international business, an employee, usually a manager, from the home country of an organization who takes up a post in the company's foreign operations.
export	the sale of goods or services to a buyer in another country.
externalization strategy	the severing of ties with linked suppliers in a supply chain, in favour of more competitive terms from other suppliers in global markets.
factors of production	inputs into the production process, including land, labour, capital and technology.
federal system	system of government in which authority is divided between the centre and regional units (examples are the US and Germany).
first-mover advantages	precept that countries or firms which are first to produce a new product gain an advantage which makes it virtually impossible for others to catch up.
fiscal policy	a government's policy concerning budgetary matters, including taxation and public expenditure.
fixed exchange rate	government policy of fixing the value of a country's currency, by specifying the number of units which can be exchanged for a specific number of units of a foreign currency.
flexible mass production	production model, chiefly associated with Japanese manufacturing companies, which allows for flexibility in production and organization within a hierarchical structure.

floating exchange rate	government policy of allowing the country's currency to be determined by market forces, rather than government control; in contrast to a fixed exchange rate.
Fordism	industrial organization based on large factories producing standardized products for mass consumption, named after the automobile magnate, Henry Ford.
foreign direct investment (FDI)	the establishment by a company of a productive base in another country, usually involving substantial shareholding and managerial control in the foreign operation.
foreign exchange	any financial instrument for making payment in another country's currency.
franchise	form of business organization whereby a trader agrees with a company to carry on business under licence to use the company's brand in a particular area, in exchange for a share of the profits (McDonald's is an example).
free trade area	trade grouping of countries, by which member states agree to eliminate trade barriers such as tariffs on trade among themselves, but operate no uniform trade policy in respect of non-members (NAFTA is an example).
General Agreement on Tariffs and Trade (GATT)	Succession of multilateral agreements on reducing trade barriers, begun in 1947. The most recent 'round', the Uruguay Round, or GATT 1994, has now been subsumed in the World Trade Organization (WTO), from 1995.
globalization	multidimensional processes which are leading to broader and deeper integration between countries and peoples.
global warming	process of climate change by which temperatures are gradually rising and sea levels are rising; generally thought to be caused by the build-up of heat-trapping gases, or 'greenhouse gases'.
gold standard	the setting of exchange rates in terms of the value of gold (in operation from the late nineteenth-century up to the First World War).
government	structures and processes of the state by which laws are made and administered; also refers to the particular officeholders at any given time.
grey market	'unofficial' trade in goods, usually designed to circumvent customs duty or other regulation.

gross domestic product (GDP)	The value of total economic activity in an economy over a particular period.
gross national product (GNP)	GDP plus the income accruing to residents from investments abroad, less income in the domestic economy which accrues to foreigners abroad.
Group of Seven (G7)	Canada, France, Germany, Japan, Italy, the US and the UK. The G7 was formed in 1975, and joined by the European Community in 1977. In 1998, they were joined by Russia, creating the G8.
hedge	in international business transactions, to buy or sell currency in international currency markets for future delivery, as a means of reducing the risk of fluctuations in exchange rates.
hierarchy	vertical differentiation of people in an organization or society generally.
high-context culture	culture in which communication relies heavily on the behavioural dimension, such as 'body language'; contrasted with low-context culture.
Hinduism	Asian religion centred on the Indian subcontinent, polytheistic in nature, and associated closely with a caste system of social stratification.
holding company	company whose main purpose is ownership of other companies, known as subsidiaries.
horizontal integration	mergers or acquisitions between two or more companies in the same industry.
human rights	basic, universal rights enjoyed by all individuals, which are recognized in national and international law.
ideology	all-encompassing system of beliefs and values, or 'world view'.
import	the purchase of goods or services by a buyer in another country.
import quota	a non-tariff barrier to trade which consists of limiting the quantity of an imported product, often requiring a licence specifying the quantity authorized.
import substitution	a policy adopted by many industrializing economies, under which industries produce goods which were formerly imported.
indirect taxation	taxes which are charged other than on income, such as VAT, tariffs and customs duties.
industrial agglomeration	the concentration, or clustering, of several producers in a particular industry in a single location.

industrial society	society based on industrial production and employment, characterized by stratification on the basis of class. Industrial societies are thought of as 'modern', to distinguish them from traditional agricultural societies.
industrialization	process of transition from a mainly agricultural economy to one based on machine production.
inflation	increase in the general level of prices in an economy.
initial public offering (IPO)	offering shares in a public company to the public, which are then traded on a stock exchange.
innovation	creation or improvement of products or processes, including incremental improvements, which bring commercial benefits.
innovation system	structures and institutions which shape a country's innovative capacity, including educational system, level of science and technology and industrial structure.
intellectual property	products of the human mind protected by law, including patents for inventions, copyright for original written, musical or artistic works, and trademarks.
internalization strategy	company strategy which aims to acquire control of raw materials or components, as an alternative to reliance on markets.
international business	business activities, including the buying, selling and production of goods, as well as the provision of services between two or more countries.
international law	body of rules recognized by the international community as governing relations between sovereign states; mainly contained in treaties and international conventions.
International Monetary Fund (IMF)	agency of the UN dating back to the Bretton Woods agreement, which oversees the international financial system.
internationalization	growth in transborder ties, usually through trade; contrast with globalization, characterized by deeper integration through FDI.
intra-firm trade	the sale of goods or services between units of the same parent company operating in different countries.
invention	a new product or process which can be applied industrially. Intellectual property law provides a patent system for recognition and protection of patents.

Islam — major world religion with over a billion followers (known as Muslims). In countries where it is the dominant religion, Islamic law is an important element of the business environment.

joint venture — an agreement between organizations (including government bodies) to produce or sell a product or service. Joint ventures may take many forms, often involving equity holdings, and are typically between a foreign investor and a local partner.

judicial system — system of courts, usually divided between civil courts and criminal courts.

just-in-time — production system which relies on delivery of materials just before they are needed in the production process, thereby reducing the need to hold large stocks of inventory.

kaizen — management philosophy of continuous improvement, involving an entire workforce; developed by the Japanese.

keiretsu — grouping of Japanese companies, usually around a main bank, and characterized by cross-shareholdings.

legislative assembly — elected body of representatives which holds the central law-making function in democratic systems of government.

leveraged buy-out (LBO) — acquisition of a company's equity by a group of persons (often managers of the company) through a loan.

liberalization — policies of deregulation of government controls of the economy, allowing market forces to determine prices.

licensing — usually in relation to intellectual property rights, a firm which owns a patent or trademark may license another firm to produce the product, in return for a royalty fee.

litigation — the practice of using the courts to resolve disputes and settle other claims for compensation, as in negligence and product liability cases.

local content requirements — government rules requiring foreign investors to maintain minimum levels of material and components supplied by local suppliers.

location advantage — aspects of a country's business environment which constitute an attraction for investors, including natural resources and low-cost labour.

low-context culture	culture in which communication is clear and direct, rather than relying on patterns of behaviour; contrasted with high-context culture.
macroeconomics	the study of whole economic systems, in particular, national economies.
management	process of planning, organizing, leading and controlling the work of organization members.
market economy	economy in which ownership of production is in private hands, and allocation of resources is determined by supply and demand.
marketing concept	the philosophy that an organization should try to provide products that satisfy customers' needs through a co-ordinated set of activities that also allow the organization to achieve its goals.
matrix structure	organizational structure incorporating both functional and divisional structures.
melting pot	in relation to societies with large numbers of immigrants, the blend of people from many different cultures to form a single nation. The most notable example is the US.
merger	agreement of two companies to unite to form a new company. An example is the merger of Grand Metropolitan and Guinness to form Diageo.
microeconomics	the study of economic activity at the level of individuals and firms.
migration	movements of people which result in a permanent change of residence.
monetary policy	policies for determining the amount of money in supply, rates of interest and exchange rates.
monopoly	market situation in which a single firm is the sole supplier.
most-favoured nation (MFN)	GATT principle negotiated between countries, by which the most favourable tariff treatment negotiated with one country is extended to similar goods from all countries.
multiculturalism	in societies, the recognition of minority cultures, ethnic groups and languages, with institutional and legal safeguards to prevent discrimination.
multidivisional company	organizational structure with decentralized divisions based on product lines or geographical areas.
multilateral agreement	international agreement between a number of countries, such as the GATT in the area of free trade.

nation	social grouping based on cultural bonds such as language, shared history, shared sense of collective identity and usually a territorial homeland.
nation-state	social, administrative and territorial unit into which the world's peoples are divided.
national culture	distinctive values and patterns of behaviour which distinguish one nation from another, and influence organizational culture and economic and political structures.
national debt	the total debt accumulated by a central government's borrowings over the years.
national security	principle of sovereign states whereby a government protects its inhabitants and territory from armed aggression such as terrorism and invasion.
negligence	in law, the breach of the duty to take reasonable care which causes injury or other harm to another, for which legal redress may be sought in the civil courts. In extreme cases, cases of criminal negligence may give rise to criminal prosecution.
network organization	organization characterized by flexible lines of communication and informal links between different teams and functional groups.
non-governmental organizations (NGOs)	organizations formed by private individuals for particular causes, which aim to influence public policymakers and also offer assistance in specialist fields alongside official agencies. An example is the World Wide Fund for Nature.
non-tariff barrier	tool of government trade policy which acts indirectly to form barriers to trade; includes import quotas, subsidies, and voluntary export restraint (VER).
North American Free Trade Agreement (NAFTA)	free trade grouping consisting of Canada, Mexico and the US.
OLI paradigm	also known as the 'eclectic' paradigm, devised by Dunning, to explain the rationale behind foreign direct investment. It highlights ownership, location and internalization advantages.
oligopoly	market situation in which a few large producers dominate the market.
organization	two or more people who work together in a structured way to achieve a specific goal or set of goals.

Organization for Economic Co-operation and Development (OECD) international organization comprising the major industrialized and industrializing countries. The OECD monitors economic performance and policies among member states.

organizational culture an organization's values, behavioural norms and management style; also known as 'corporate culture'.

parliamentary system system of government in which the voters elect members of parliament, from whom the prime minister and cabinet (the executive) are chosen, usually from the political party with the majority of seats.

partnership two or more people carrying on a business in common, with a view to profit.

patent type of intellectual property by which gives the owner of a new invention or new process exclusive rights for a limited period to exploit the invention commercially, to license others to use it and stop all unauthorized exploitation.

pegged exchange rate linking the value of a currency to the value of another currency.

PEST analysis analytical tool for scanning the business environment, representing political, economic, social and technological environment.

planned economy economic system based on total state ownership of the means of production, in which the state controls prices and output; contrast with the market economy.

pluralism type of society characterized by freedom of association, under which multiple groups and interests, including multiple political parties, can flourish.

politics processes by which a social group allocates the exercise of power and authority for the group as a whole.

polycentrism view of the world which takes in other cultures besides one's own.

portfolio investment investment in a company's shares as an investment only, with a relatively short-term perspective; usually involving a holding of under 10 per cent. Portfolio investment is contrasted with foreign direct investment.

post-Fordism industrial organization in which diversity, flexibility and specialization have replaced the mass production ethos of Fordism.

presidential system system of government in which the head of the executive branch, the president, is elected directly by the voters.

private international law the rules for determining which national law prevails in legal issues between individuals or companies in different countries.

privatization process of transferring assets from state ownership to the private sector; extensively used in the transition economies.

product in marketing, defined broadly to include anything that can be offered to consumers which fulfils a consumer need; includes both goods and services.

product liability legal liability of a producer of a defective product to consumers harmed by the product.

product life cycle theory of the evolution of a product in four stages: introduction, growth, maturity and decline.

proportional representation (PR) system of electoral representation in which seats are allocated in proportion to the votes obtained by each party; seen as more favourable to smaller parties.

protectionism trade policy stance of governments which seeks to promote domestic producers and curtail competing imports.

public law body of law covering relations between citizens and the state.

public sector borrowing requirement (PSBR) with respect to national economies, the extent to which public spending exceeds receipts.

purchasing power parity (PPP) an exchange rate which takes account of the differing purchasing power of different currencies; in particular, a means of measuring the number of units of a foreign currency which would be needed to buy goods or services equivalent to those which the US dollar would buy in the US.

referendum example of direct democracy, in which electors cast a vote on a particular issue, such as joining the EU; may be incorporated in a country's constitution.

regional trade agreement (RTA) agreement between countries in the same broad geographical region to bring down trade barriers among themselves.

regionalism the growth of economic integration within geographic regions through, for example, free trade agreements, common markets, and in the more advanced phases, economic and political union.

relational contracting business dealings in which personal relations between the parties are more important than formal written agreements; contrasted with arm's-length contracting.

research and development (R&D) the systematic search for new knowledge in specific academic disciplines (basic research); and also new knowledge for specific applications (applied research).

royalty payment by an individual or company to the owner of intellectual property (such as a patent or trade mark) for the right to manufacture or sell the product under licence.

rule of law principle of supremacy of the law over both governments and citizens, entailing equality before the law and an independent judiciary.

sanctions actions by governments or by UN authorization, which disrupts free trade to a particular country, in order to attain some other purpose, such as condemnation of that country's political or humanitarian policies. Targeted governments usually contrive ways of getting round sanctions.

segmentation marketing concept used to break down consumer markets, for example, according to social class, education or lifestyle.

separation of powers in systems of government, the separation of legislative, executive and judicial powers in separate authorities, with checks and balances to ensure that no one branch becomes too powerful. The foremost example is the US.

small to medium-size enterprise (SME) classification of businesses which have fewer than 50 employees (small) or 50–249 (medium), although sizes vary from industry to industry and from country to country.

social market model of capitalism capitalist market economy with a strong social justice dimension, including substantial welfare state provisions.

social responsibility emphasis on issues of human rights, human development and environmental protections, especially in relation to management of transnational companies.

society a system of interrelationships which connects individuals together.

sole trader business under the ownership and control of an individual, often extending to family members.

sovereignty	supreme legal authority in the state; also the principle of autonomy and mutual recognition of states in international relations.
stakeholder	anyone who has an interest in a company, even indirectly; includes shareholders, employees, creditors, suppliers and also the investing public generally; usually in the context of stakeholder theory of corporate governance.
state-owned enterprise	an entity owned and controlled by government, such as a nationalized industry; known as a public sector enterprise.
stock exchange	market in which shares in large public companies and other securities are traded. Share prices are an indicator of confidence in companies' performance and in economic activity generally. Major stock exchanges are New York, London and Tokyo.
strategic thinking	bringing together all the information available from those within the organization and converting that knowledge into a vision of the aims that the business should pursue.
strategy	the determination of the basic long-term goals and objectives of an organization, and the adoption of courses of action and the allocation of resources necessary for carrying out these goals.
structure	the design of an organization through which the enterprise is administered.
subcontractor	a legally independent firm which supplies goods or services to another on the basis of market exchange.
subculture	minority culture in a society, often associated with immigrant communities and reinforced by separate language and religion.
subsidiary	a firm which is owned by a parent company.
subsidies	payments by governments from public funds to domestic producers, as part of a strategic trade policy aimed at strengthening local firms' competitive positions.
supply	total availability of a good from all producers in the market in a particular period.
sustainable development	approach to economic development which stresses the environmental impact in the long term.
SWOT analysis	strategic tool used by businesses to assess the organization's strengths, weaknesses, opportunities and threats; combines analysis of both internal and external environments of the business.

takeover — the acquisition of one company by another; usually agreed between the directors of the two companies, but in a 'hostile' takeover the predator company makes an offer directly to the shareholders of the target company to buy them out.

tariffs — taxes imposed by governments on imported goods and services, which act as a barrier to trade.

technology — methodical application of scientific knowledge to practical purposes.

technology transfer — processes of acquiring technology from another country, especially in manufacturing industries. The transfer is commonly through licensing or foreign direct investment.

tort — branch of the law which concerns obligations owed by all organizations and individuals to others within the society.

trade mark — type of intellectual property, which consists of a firm's distinctive logo or symbol, which distinguishes it from other firms. The trade mark may be registered, thus giving the proprietor exclusive use of it and a right to sue in the courts those using it without authority. There is, however, a good deal of illicit use of trade marks, known as 'counterfeiting', particularly in the area of luxury brands.

Trade-Related Aspects of Intellectual Property (TRIPS) — multilateral international agreement on the protection of intellectual property rights.

trade union — organization of workers which aims to achieve higher wages, better working conditions and greater security of employment; usually based on occupations or industries.

transition economy — an economy making the transition from state planning to a market-driven orientation; usually involving privatization of state-owned industries.

transitional democracy — state in which democratic institutions such as free elections are in the early stages, often following a period of authoritarian or military rule. These states are prone to political instability.

transnational corporation (TNC) — firm which has the power to co-ordinate and control operations in more than one country.

treaties — chief instruments of international law.

triad countries — the US, European Union and Japan, each of which is seen as a trade bloc.

unemployed portion of the labour force who are willing to work but are without jobs.

unitary system system of authority within a state, in which all authority radiates out from the centre; contrasted with federalism.

urbanization population movement from rural areas to cities.

vertical integration mergers or acquisitions between firms in successive stages of production or distribution; often referred to as internalization.

voluntary export restraints (VERs) tool of government trade policy by which companies wishing to export into the country are encouraged to limit their exports, or else risk the imposition of quotas or tariffs; used by the US government against Japanese companies wishing to export to the US market.

welfare state the provision of social benefits, such as health service and social security payments, from public funds.

World Bank (International Bank for Reconstruction and Development – IBRD) – Bretton Woods organization set up to fund development projects and broader development programmes; funded by member states.

World Trade Organization (WTO) founded in 1995 as a successor organization to GATT, for the purpose of regulating world trade, including multilateral trade agreements and the settlement of trade disputes between member states.

References

Amin, A. and Thrift, N. (1994) 'Living in the global', in Amin, A. and Thrift, N. (eds) *Globalization, Institutions, and Regional Development in Europe* (Oxford: Oxford University Press) pp. 2–5.

Archibugi, D. and Michie, J. (1997a) 'Technological globalisation and national systems of innovation: an introduction', in Archibugi, D. and Michie, J. (eds) *Technology, Globalisation and Economic Performance* (Cambridge: Cambridge University Press) pp. 1–23.

Archibugi, D. and Michie J. (1997b) 'Globalisation of technology: a new taxonomy', in Archibugi, D. and Michie, J. (eds) *Technology, Globalisation and Economic Performance* (Cambridge: Cambridge University Press) pp. 173–240.

Baily, M. (2000) 'Innovation in the new economy', *OECD Observer*, 11 October.

Bainbridge, D. (1996) *Intellectual Property*, 3rd edn (London: Pitman).

Balassa, B. (1962) *The Theory of Economic Integration* (London: Allen & Unwin).

Barnes, J.E. and Winter, G. (2001) 'Stressed out? Bad knee? Try a sip of these juices', *New York Times*, 27 May.

Barrett, D. (1997) 'Annual statistical table on global mission: 1997', *International Bulletin of Missionary Research*, **21**(1): 24–5.

Bartlett, C.A. and Ghoshal, S. (1990) 'Matrix management: not a structure, a frame of mind', *Harvard Business Review*, **90**(4): 138–45.

Bartlett, C.A. and Ghoshal, S. (1997) 'The transnational organization', in Pugh, D.S. (ed.) *Organization Theory: Selected Readings*, 4th edn (Harmondsworth: Penguin) pp. 64–82.

Bartlett, C.A. and Ghoshal, S. (1998) *Managing Across Borders: A Transnational Solution*, 2nd edn (London: Random House).

Barwise, P. (1997) 'Strategic investment decisions and emergent strategy', in *Mastering Management* (London: Financial Times/Pitman) pp. 562–71.

Bearak, B. (2000) 'In India, the wheels of justice hardly move', *New York Times*, 1 June.

Beeson, M. (2000) 'The political economy of East Asia at a time of crisis', in Stubbs, R. and Underhill, G. (eds) *Political Economy and the Changing Global Order*, 2nd edn (Oxford: Oxford University Press) pp. 352–61.

Beetham, D. (1991) *The Legitimation of Power* (Basingstoke: Macmillan – now Palgrave).

Bell, M. and Pavitt, K. (1997) 'Technological accumulation and industrial growth: constrasts between developed and developing countries', in Archibugi, D. and Michie, J. (eds) *Technology, Globalisation and Economic Performance* (Cambridge: Cambridge University Press) pp. 83–137.

Bhagwati, J. (1998) 'The capital myth', *Foreign Affairs*, 77(3): 7–13.

Birkinshaw, J. (2000) 'The structures behind global companies', in *Mastering Management*, Part 10, *Financial Times*, 4 December.

Bourke, A. (2000) 'Overseas pharmaceutical firms in Ireland – insiders or outsiders?', in *Conference Proceedings of the Third Global Change Conference* (Manchester: Manchester Metropolitan University) pp. 35–48.

Bradshaw, M.J. (1996) 'The prospects for the post-socialist economies', in Daniels, P.W. and Lever, W.F. (eds) *The Global Economy in Transition* (Harlow: Addison Wesley) pp. 263–88.

Brown, G.W. (2000) 'Seeking security in a volatile world' in *Mastering Risk*, Part 4, *Financial Times*, 16 May 2000.

Buckley, P. (1999) 'Foreign direct investment by small and medium-sized enterprises: the theoretical background', in Buckley, P. and Ghauri, P. (eds) *The Internationalization of the Firm*, 2nd edn (London: International Thomson) pp. 99–113.

Cabinet Office (UK) (2000) *Winning the Generation Game* (London: Cabinet Office).

Cantwell, J. (1989) *Technological Innovation and Multinational Corporations* (Oxford: Basil Blackwell).

Castells, M. (2000a) *The Rise of the Network Society*, 2nd edn (Oxford: Blackwell).

Castells, M. (2000b) 'Information technology and global capitalism', in Giddens, A. and Hutton, W. (eds) *On the Edge: Living with Global Capitalism* (London: Jonathan Cape) pp. 52–74.

Chandler, A. (1990) *Strategy and Structure: Chapters in the History of the Industrial Enterprise* (Cambridge, MA: MIT Press).

Coates, D. (1999) 'Why growth rates differ', *New Political Economy*, **4**(1): 77–95.

Coggan, P. (2000), 'The weighting game', *Financial Times*, 8 June.

Cohon, G. (1997) *To Russia with Fries* (Toronto: McClelland & Stewart).

Collier, P. (2000) 'Economic causes of civil conflict and their implications for policy', World Bank research paper. http://www.worldbank.org/research/conflict/papers/civilconflict.htm.

Conference Board (1999) *International Patterns of Institutional Investment* (New York: The Conference Board) cited in *Financial Times*, 6 May.

de Haan, A. (1999) 'Livelihoods and poverty: the role of migration – a critical review of the migration literature', *The Journal of Development Studies*, **36**(2): 1–47.

Denza, E. (1999) 'Two legal orders: divergent or convergent?' *International and Comparative Law Quarterly* (48): 257–84.

Department for Environment, Food & Rural Affairs (DEFRA) (2001) *Climate Change: Draft UK Programme.* http://www.defra.gov.uk/environment.

Diamond, L. (1996) 'Is the third wave over', *Journal of Democracy*, 7(3): 21–39.

Dibb, S., Simkin, L., Pride, W. and Ferrell, O.C. (1997) *Marketing*, 3rd edn (New York: Houghton Mifflin).

Dicken, P. (1998) *Global Shift: Transforming the World Economy*, 3rd edn (London: Paul Chapman).

Dicken, P. and Lloyd, P.E. (1990) *Location in Space: Theoretical Perspectives in Economic Geography*, 3rd edn (New York: Harper & Row).

Dicken, P., Fosgren, M. and Malmberg, A. (1994), 'The local embeddedness of transnational corporations', in Amin, A. and Thrift, N. (eds) *Globalization, Institutions, and Regional Development in Europe* (Oxford: Oxford University Press) pp. 23–45.

Dollar, D. (1999) 'Aid and poverty reduction: what we know and what else we need to know', Paper for World Development Report on Poverty and Development 2000/01 (Washington, DC: Stiglitz Summer Research Workshop on Poverty).

Drucker, P. (1997) 'The global economy and the nation-state' *Foreign Affairs*, **76**(5): 159–72.

DTI (Department of Trade and Industry) (2000) *Small and Medium Enterprise (SME) Statistics for the UK, 1999* (London: Office for National Statistics).

Dunning, J.H. (1993) *Multinational Enterprises and the Global Economy* (Wokingham: Addison Wesley).

Eichengreen, B. (1996) *Globalizing Capital: A History of the International Monetary System* (Princeton: Princeton University Press).

Eurobarometer (1998) *Eurobarometer 48*, at http:europa.eu.int/comm./dg10.

European Bank for Reconstruction and Development (2000) *Transition Report 2000* (London: EBRD).

Fields, J. and Casper, L. (2001) *America's Families and Living Arrangements: March 2000*, Current Population Reports, P20-537 (Washington, DC: US Census Bureau).

Freeman, C. (1997) 'The "national system of innovation" in historical perspective', in Archibugi, D., and Michie, J. (eds) *Technology, Globalisation and Economic Performance* (Cambridge: Cambridge University Press) pp. 24–49.

Freeman, C. and Soete, L. (1997) *The Economics of Industrial Innovation*, 3rd edn (London: Cassell).

Freeman, P. and Robbins, A. (1995) 'The promise of biotechnology for vaccines', in Fransman, M., Junne, G. and Roobeek, A. (eds) *The Biotechnology Revolution* (Oxford: Blackwell) pp. 174–183.

Fukuyama, F. (2000) *The Great Disruption* (London: Profile Books).

Gankema, H., Snuif, H. and Zwart, P. (2000) 'The internationalization process of small and medium-sized enterprises: an evaluation of stage theory', *Journal of Small Business Management*, **38**(4): 15–28.

Gerlach, M. (1991) *Alliance Capitalism: The Social Organization of Japanese Business* (Berkeley: University of California Press).

Giddens, A. (1997) *Sociology*, 3rd edn (Cambridge: Polity Press).

Giddens, A. and Hutton, W. (2000) 'Fighting back', in Giddens, A. and Hutton, W. (eds) *On the Edge: Living with Global Capitalism* (London: Jonathan Cape) pp. 213–23.

Gilpin, R. (2000) *The Challenge of Global Capitalism: The World Economy in the 21st Century* (Princeton: Princeton University Press).

Graham, R. (2001) 'Corsica hope of autonomy rises with historic law', *Financial Times*, 23 May 2001.

Gray, J. (1998) *False Dawn: The Delusions of Global Capitalism* (London: Granta Books).

Griffith-Jones, S. (1999) 'Stabilizing capital flows to developing countries', in Michie, J. and Grieve Smith, J. (eds) *Global Instability: The Political Economy of World Economic Governance* (London: Routledge) pp. 68–96.

Hall, M.R. and Hall, E.T. (1960) 'The silent language of overseas business', *Harvard Business Review*, **38**(3): 87–95.

Hargreaves, D. (1999) 'Pensions will squeeze European budgets' *Financial Times*, 23 November.

Harris, L. (1999) 'Will the real IMF please stand up: what does the Fund do and what should it do?', in Michie, J. and Grieve Smith, J. (eds) *Global Instability: The Political Economy of World Economic Governance* (London: Routledge) pp. 198–211.

Hawthorn, J. (1993) 'Sub-Saharan Africa' in Held, D. (ed.) *Prospects for Democracy* (Cambridge: Polity Press) pp. 330–54.

Held, D., McGrew, A., Goldblatt, D. and Perraton, J. (1999) *Global Transformations: Politics, Economics and Culture* (Cambridge: Polity Press).

Hirst, P. and Thompson, G. (1999) *Globalization in Question*, 2nd edn (Cambridge: Polity Press).

HM Treasury (2000) *Budget: March 2000* (London: HM Treasury). http://www.hm-treasury.gov.uk/budget2000.

Hofstede, G. (1994) *Cultures and Organizations: Software of the Mind* (London: HarperCollins).

Hofstede, G. (1996) 'Images of Europe: past, present and future', in Joynt, P. and Warner, M. (eds), *Managing Across Cultures: Issues and Perspectives* (London: International Thomson Business Press) pp. 147–65.

Home Office (1999) *A Consultation Paper on the Integration of Recognised Refugees in the UK* (London: The Home Office).

Home Office (2000) *Control of Immigration: Statistics, United Kingdom, First Half 2000* (Croydon: Immigration Research and Statistics Service).

Hoon-Halbauer, S.K. (1999) 'Managing relationships within Sino–foreign joint ventures', *Journal of World Business*, **34**(4): 344–72.

Howells, J. and Wood, M. (1993) *The Globalisation of Production and Technology* (London: Belhaven Press).

Hubbard, N. (1999) *Acquisition: Strategy and Implementation* (Basingstoke: Macmillan – now Palgrave).

Huntington, S. (1991) *The Third Wave: Democratization in the Late Twentieth Century* (Norman: University of Oklahoma Press).

ILO (International Labour Organization) (2001a) *World Employment Report 2001*, (Geneva: ILO).

ILO (International Labour Organization) (2001b) *The Elimination of all Forms of Forced or Compulsory Labour* (Geneva: ILO).

Inter-Parliamentary Union (2001) 'Women in national parliaments'. http://www.ipu.org.

Jackson, S. and Schuler, R. (2000) 'Turning knowledge into business', *Mastering Management*, Part 14, *Financial Times*, 15 January 2001.

Johnson, C. (1982) *MITI and the Japanese Miracle* (Stanford: Stanford University Press).

Kahn, J. (2000) 'U.S. offers Africa billions to fight AIDS', *New York Times*, 19 July.

Kapstein, E.B. (1994) *Governing the Global Economy: International Finance and the State* (Cambridge, MA: Harvard University Press).

Keynes, J.M. (1936) *The General Theory of Employment, Interest and Money* (London: Macmillan – now Palgrave).

Kim, S.K. and Kim, S.H. (1999) *Global Corporate Finance: Text and Cases*, 4th edn (Oxford: Blackwell).

Kitson, M. and Michie, J. (eds) (1995) 'Trade and Growth: A Historical Perspective', in Michie, J. and Grieve Smith, J. (eds) *Managing the Global Economy* (Oxford: Oxford University Press) pp. 3–36.

Kotler, P., Armstrong, G., Saunders, J. and Wong, V. (1999) *Principles of Marketing*, 2nd edn (London: Prentice Hall).

Kovacic, W. and Shapiro, C. (2000) 'Antitrust policy: a century of economic and legal thinking', *Journal of Economic Perspectives*, **14**(1): 43–60.

Krugman, P. (1994) *Rethinking International Trade* (Cambridge, MA: MIT Press).

Krugman, P. (1999) *The Return of Depression Economics* (Harmondsworth: Penguin).

Kullberg, J. and Zimmerman, W. (1999) 'Liberal elites, socialist masses, and problems of Russian democracy', *World Politics*, **51**: 323–58.

Labour Party (2001) *Ambitions for Britain: Labour's Manifesto 2001* (London: Labour Party).

Landes, D. (1998) *The Wealth and Poverty of Nations* (London: Little, Brown).

Landwell (2000) *Time for Law and Order*, at http://www.Landwellglobal.com.

Leys, S. (trans. and ed.) (1997) *Analects of Confucius* (New York: W.W. Norton).

Linden, E. (1996) 'The exploding cities of the developing world', *Foreign Affairs*, 75(1): 52–66.

Linz, J. (1993) 'Perils of presidentialism', in Diamond, L. and Plattner, M.F. (eds), *The Global Resurgence of Democracy* (Baltimore: Johns Hopkins University Press) pp. 108–26.

Linz, J. and Stepan, A. (1997), 'Toward consolidated democracies', *Journal of Democracy*, 7(2): 14–33.

London School of Economics (1998) *Social Welfare Systems in East Asia: A Comparative Analysis* (London: LSE Centre for Analysis of Social Exclusion).

Longman, P. and Ahmad, S. (1998) 'The bailout backlash', *U.S. News & World Report*, **124**(4): 37–8.

Lundvall, B.-A. (ed.) (1992) *National Systems of Innovation* (London: Pinter).

Maddison, A. (1991) *Dynamic Forces in Capitalist Development* (Oxford: Oxford University Press).

McGregor, R. (2001) 'Legal evolution with strings attached', *Financial Times*, 2 May.

Miers, D.R. and Page, A.C. (1990) *Legislation*, 2nd edn (London: Sweet & Maxwell).

Mikesell, R.F. (2000), 'Bretton Woods – original intentions and current problems', *Contemporary Economic Policy*, **18**(4): 404–15.

Mintzberg, H. (2000) *The Rise and Fall of Strategic Planning* (London: Pearson).

Moens, G. and Gillies, P. (1998) *International Trade and Business: Law, Policy and Ethics* (Sydney: Cavendish).

Morse, G. (1991) *Partnership Law*, 2nd edn (London: Blackstone Press).

Morse, G. (1995) *Charlesworth & Morse Company Law*, 15th edn (London: Sweet & Maxwell).

Mowery, D.C. and Oxley, J. (1997) 'Inward technology transfer and competitiveness' in Archibugi, D. and Michie, J. (eds) *Technology, Globalisation and Economic Performance* (Cambridge: Cambridge University Press) pp. 138–71.

New York Stock Exchange (2000) *An International Marketplace* (New York: New York Stock Exchange).

OECD (Organization for Economic Co-operation and Development) (1998) 'The retirement decision in OECD countries' (Working Paper AWP 1.4) (Paris: OECD Publications).

OECD (Organization for Economic Co-operation and Development) (1999) 'The core of the matter', *OECD Observer*, 2 October.

OECD (Organization for Economic Co-operation and Development) (2000a) 'Cross-border trade in financial services: economics and regulation', *Financial Market Trends*, 75 (March).

OECD (Organization for Economic Co-operation and Development) (2000b) 'Recent trends in foreign direct investment', *Financial Market Trends*, 76 (June).

OECD (Organization for Economic Co-operation and Development) (2000c) *OECD in Figures* (Paris: OECD).

Ohmae, K. (1995) *The End of the Nation State* (London: HarperCollins).

Ohmae, K. (2000) *The Invisible Continent: Four Strategic Imperatives of the New Economy* (London: Nicholas Brealey).

ONS (Office for National Statistics) (UK) (2000a) *Acquisitions and Mergers Involving UK Companies*, 3rd quarter 2000, 7 November (London: ONS).

ONS (Office for National Statistics) (2000b) *Social Trends 30* (London: Stationery Office).

ONS (Office for National Statistics) (2000c) *Labour Force Survey: Labour Market Trends* (London: Stationery Office).

Parkin, M., Powell, M. and Matthews, K. (1997) *Economics*, 3rd edn (Harlow: Addison Wesley).

Pascale, R. (1984) 'Perspectives on strategy: the real story behind Honda's success' *California Management Review*, **XXVI**(3): 47–72.

Patel, P. and Pavitt, K. (1991) 'Large firms in the production of the world's technology: an important case of "non-globalisation"', *Journal of International Business Studies*, **22**: 1–21.

Patel, P. and Pavitt, K. (1994) 'National innovation systems: why they are important, and how they might be measured and compared', *Economics of Innovation and New Technology*, **3**: 77–95.

Patel, P. and Pavitt, K. (2000) 'National systems of innovation under strain: the internationalisation of corporate R&D', in Barrell, R., Mason, G. and O'Mahony, M. (eds) *Productivity, Innovation and Economic Performance* (Cambridge: Cambridge University Press) pp. 217–35.

Patent Office (UK) (2000) *The Patent Office Annual Report 1999–2000* (Newport, South Wales: Patent Office).

Patten, C. (1998) *East and West* (Basingstoke: Macmillan – now Palgrave).

Paul, A. and Kano, C. (1999) 'Made in Japan', *Fortune*, **140**(11): 190–7.

Paul, R. (2000) 'The increasing maze of international pre-acquisition notification', *International Company and Commercial Law Review*, April. http://www. whitecase.com/.

Pauly, L.W. and Reich, S. (1997) 'National structures and multinational corporate behavior: enduring differences in the age of globalization', *International Organization*, **51**(1): 1–30.

Peel, Q. (2001) 'An upset for enlargement', *Financial Times*, 11 June.

Peiperi, M. (1997) 'Does empowerment deliver the goods?', in *Mastering Management* (London: Financial Times/Pitman) pp. 283–7.

Pettigrew, A.M. (1997) 'Context and action in the transformation of the firm', in Pugh, D.S. (ed.) *Organization Theory: Selected Reading*, 4th edn (Harmondsworth: Penguin) pp. 460–85.

Piercy, N. and Giles, W. (1989) 'Making SWOT analysis work', *Marketing Intelligence and Planning*, 7(5): 5–7.

Pontusson, J. (1977) 'Between neo-liberalism and the German model: Swedish capitalism in transition', in Crouch, C. and Streeck, W. (eds) *Political Economy of Modern Capitalism* (London: Sage) pp. 55–70.

Porter, M. (1998a) *Competitive Strategy: Techniques for Analyzing Industries and Competitors* (with new introduction) (New York: Free Press).

Porter, M. (1998b) *The Competitive Advantage of Nations* (Basingstoke: Macmillan – now Palgrave).

Porter, M. (2000) 'Japan's twin demons', *Financial Times*, 5 July.

Pugh, D.S. (1997) 'Introduction to the Fourth Edition', in Pugh, D.S. (ed.) *Organization Theory: Selected Readings*, 4th edn (Harmondsworth: Penguin) pp. xi–xiii.

Reich, R. (1991) *The Work of Nations: Preparing Ourselves for 21st Century Capitalism* (London: Simon & Schuster).

Rex, J. (1996) *Ethnic Minorities in the Modern Nation State* (Basingstoke: Macmillan – now Palgrave).

Rhodes, R.A.W. (1996) 'The new governance: governing without government', *Political Studies*, XLIV: 654–67.

Ricardo, D. ([1817] 1973) *Principles of Political Economy and Taxation* (London: Dent).

Ridderstråle, J. (2000) 'Business moves beyond bureaucracy', in *Mastering Management*, Part 6, *Financial Times*, 6 November.

Rivlin, R. (2000) 'Old economy, new private optimism', *Financial Times*, 9 June.

Rose, F. (1999) 'Think globally, script locally', *Fortune*, **140**(9): 156–60.

Rozman, G. (1991) 'Comparisons of modern Confucian values in China and Japan' in Rozman, G. (ed) *The East Asian Region: Confucian Heritage and Its Modern Adaptation* (Princeton, NJ: Princeton University Press) pp. 157–203.

Sabel, C.F. (1994) 'Flexible specialisation and the re-emergence of regional economics', in Amin, A. (ed.) *Post-Fordism: A Reader* (Oxford: Basil Blackwell) pp. 101–56.

Sartori, G. (1997) 'Understanding pluralism', *Journal of Democracy*, **8**(4): 58–69.

Schaffer, R., Earle, B., and Agusti, F. (1999) *International Business Law and its Environment*, 4th edn (Cincinnati: West).

Schmitter, P.C. and Karl, T.L. (1993) 'What democracy is ... and is not', in Diamond, L. and Platnerr, M.F. (eds) *The Global Resurgence of Democracy* (Baltimore: Johns Hopkins University Press) pp. 39–52.

Schumpeter, J.A. (1942) *Capitalism, Socialism and Democracy* (New York: Harper & Row).

Sell, S. (2000) 'Big business and the new trade agreements' in Stubbs, R. and Underhill, G. (eds) *Political Economy and the Changing Global Order*, 2nd edn (Oxford: Oxford University Press) pp. 174–83.

Singh, A. (1999) '"Asian capitalism" and the financial crisis', in Michie, J. and Grieve Smith, J. (eds) *Global Instability: The Political Economy of World Economic Governance* (London: Routledge) pp. 9–36.

Smith, A. ([1776]1950) *An Inquiry into the Nature and Causes of the Wealth of Nations* (London: Methuen).

Smith, A.D. (1990) 'Towards a global culture' in Featherstone, M. (ed.) *Global Culture: Nationalism, Globalization, and Modernity* (London: Sage) pp. 171–91.

Smith, A.D. (1991) *National Identity* (London: Penguin).

Stanworth, C. (2000), 'Women and work in the information age', *Gender, Work and Organization*, 7(1): 20–31.

Statham, P. (1999) 'Political mobilisation by minorities in Britain: negative feedback of "race relations"', *Journal of Ethnic and Migration Studies*, **25**(4): 597–626.

Stiglitz, J. (2000) 'The insider', *New Republic*, **222**(16/17): 56–60.

Stoner, J. and Freeman, R. (1992) *Management*, 5th edn (New Jersey: Prentice Hall).

Streeck, W. (1997) 'German capitalism: does it exist? Can it survive?' *New Political Economy*, **2**(2): 237–56.

Stulz, R. (2000) 'Why risk management is not rocket science', *Mastering Risk*, Part 10, p. 6, *Financial Times*, 27 June.

Stutz, F.P. and de Souza, A.R. (1998) *The World Economy: Resources, Location, Trade and Development*, 3rd edn (Upper Saddle, NJ: Prentice Hall).

Terpstra, V. and David, K. (1991) *The Cultural Environment of International Business* (Cincinnati: South-Western Publishing).

Therrien, M. and Famirez, R. (2000) *The Hispanic Population in the United States: March, 2000*, Current Population Reports, P20-535, (Washington, DC: US Census Bureau).

Thomas, J.B., Clark, S.M. and Gioia, D.A. (1993) 'Strategic sensemaking and organizational performance: linkages among scanning, interpretation, action, and outcomes,' *Academy of Management Journal* (April): 239–70.

Tolentino, P.E. (1999) 'Transnational rules for transnational corporations: what next?', in Michie, J. and Grieve Smith, J. (eds) *Global Instability: The Political Economy of World Economic Governance* (London: Routledge) pp. 171–97.

Trompenaars, F. (1994) *Riding the Waves of Culture* (New York: Irwin).

Tyson, L.D. (1992) *Who's Bashing Whom? Trade Conflict in High-Technology Industries* (Washington, DC: Institute for International Economics).

United Nations (1999a) *World Investment Report 1999* (Geneva: United Nations).

United Nations (1999b) *Human Development Report 1999* (Oxford: Oxford University Press).

United Nations (2000) *Human Development Report 2000* (Oxford: Oxford University Press).

United Nations Food and Agriculture Organization (2000) *The State of Food Insecurity in the World*. http://www.fao.org.

United Nations Industrial Development Organization (UNIDO) (2000) *Enhancing Competitiveness of SMEs in the Global Economy: Strategies and Policies*. http:// www.unido.org/doc/ee1214.htmls.

United Nations Office for Drug Control and Crime Prevention (1999) *Global Report on Crime and Justice* (Oxford: Oxford University Press).

United Nations Population Division (1999) *World Urbanization Prospects: the 1999 Revision*. http://www.un.org/esa/population/urbanization.htm.

United Nations Population Division (2000) *Replacement Migration: Is it a Solution to Declining and Ageing Populations*. http://www.un.org./esa/population/migration.htm.

US Patent Office (1999) *USPTO Annual Report 1999*. http://www.uspto.gov/.

Vitols, S. (2000) 'Globalization: a fundamental change to the German model,' in Stubbs, R. and Underhill, G. (eds) *Political Economy and the Changing Global Order*, 2nd edn (Oxford: Oxford University Press) pp. 373–81.

Walby, S. (1999) 'Transformations of the gendered political economy: changes in women's employment in the United Kingdom', *New Political Economy*, **4**(2): 195–213.

Wallace, R. (1997) *International Law*, 3rd edn (London: Sweet & Maxwell).

Ward, S. (2001) 'Pharmaceuticals rights under threat', *Financial Times*, 11 June.

Waters, M. (1995) *Globalization* (London: Routledge).

Weber, M. (1930) *The Protestant Ethic and the Spirit of Capitalism* (New York: Scribner's).

Whitley, R.D. (1995) 'Eastern Asian enterprise structures and the comparative analysis of forms of business organization', in Ghauri, P. and Prasad, S.B. (eds) *International Management: A Reader* (London: Dryden Press) pp. 191–212.

WHO/UNICEF (2000) *The Global Water Supply and Sanitation Assessment 2000*. http://www.wsscc.org/.

WIPO (1999) *International Protection of Industrial Property*. http://www.wipo.int/eng/general/ipip/pct.htm.

Wolin, S. (1993) 'Democracy, difference, and re-cognition', *Political Theory*, **21**(3): 464–83.

World Bank (1999) *Cities Alliance for Cities without Slums*. http://www.worldbank.org/html/fpd/urban/map.html.

World Bank (2000a) *Entering the 21st Century: World Development Report 1999–2000* (Oxford: Oxford University Press).

World Bank (2000b) *Can Africa Claim the 21st Century?* http://www. worldbank.org/afr.

World Bank (2000c) *Global Economic Prospects and the Developing Countries, 2001.* http://www.worldbank.org/prospects/gep2001.

Zimmerer, T. and Scarborough, N. (1998) *Essentials of Entrepreneurship and Small Business Management*, 2nd edn (Englewood Cliffs, NJ: Prentice Hall).

Zweigert, K. and Kötz, H. (1998) *Introduction to Comparative Law*, 3rd edn (Oxford: Clarendon Press).

Index

Entries in **bold** are whole chapters

C

F

G

H

I

M

N

O

P

S

U

V

W

X

Y

Z